THE TUDOR CHRONICLES

THE TUDOR

Susan Doran

CHRONICLES

Quercus

NOTE TO THE READER

The Tudor Chronicles is based heavily on contemporary, or near contemporary, chronicles of the Tudor period. Indeed, it is designed to be read as a chronicle – with one damn event following another – rather than as a history of the Tudor dynasty. The principal aim is to follow events as they unfold, rendered in such a way as to be readily appreciated as a narrative by the non-specialist. Contemporary commentators and participants make their appearance *en route*, in a selection of extracts from documents of the period, while the modern historical voice is perhaps strongest in the extended captions accompanying the many illustrations.

In writing *The Tudor Chronicles*, I have followed certain conventions to help readability. First, I have begun each year on 1 January – which might seem uncontroversial, except that during the Tudor period the new year began on Lady Day, 25 March. (Furthermore, original Tudor chronicles were arranged by the year of each reign, rather than the calendar year.) Second, I have continued to use English dates after 1582, when the calendar on the Continent was reformed by Pope Gregory and the dates of the Catholic countries diverged from those of England by as many as ten days. (On the few occasions when I provide Continental dates, I mark them 'ns': New Style.)

A warning about dates: I have tried to be accurate, but those in the original chronicles are frequently wrong and the secondary sources sometimes disagree. All errors of course are mine; I can only plead that some incorrect or debatable dates might make this work appear more like a genuine Tudor chronicle!

I have generally modernized the spelling of quotations – so for example, 's' usually replaces 'eth' ('shows' for 'sheweth') – but occasionally I have retained original spelling where tone and flavour seem to call for it. Likewise, capitalization has been regularized somewhat to provide consistency, and occasionally punctuation has been modernized where the original might hinder a reader's grasp of the sense. As for names of people, I have given common usage or else followed the spelling that appears in the *Oxford Dictionary of National Biography*; readers should be aware that there was no consistency in the spelling of names during this period.

Author's acknowledgements

This book is very much a team effort. Particular acknowledgement and thanks should be given to a few individuals with whom I have worked closely: Richard Milbank for commissioning and overseeing the book at Quercus; Mark Hawkins-Dady, the project's manager, for editing the text, particularly in suggesting additional material and glosses to make the historical and theological detail comprehensible to a general reader. Elaine Willis for following up my picture requests and offering alternatives when it proved necessary; and Miranda Kaufmann for assisting in the search for, and transcribing of, the featured quotations. Nick Clark and Hugh Adams, the art director and designer respectively, also deserve thanks for their professional and imaginative layouts.

SUSAN DORAN

CONTENTS

INTRODUCTION
The Tudors – what's in a name?

Despite the iconic, even affectionate, status of 'the Tudors' in popular views of English history, calling this chronicle by that name is somewhat anachronistic. The family surname was hardly, if ever, used by the dynasty itself.[1] Before his accession, Henry VII was called 'Richmond', his title at birth; and after the Battle of Bosworth in 1485 he claimed the throne through his mother's Beaufort line and presented himself as the last of the Lancastrian kings. While he made plans to have Henry VI buried in the family tomb in his new chapel at Westminster, his father, Edmund Tudor, and grandfather, Owen Tudor, had their final resting places far away from London, in Wales and Hereford respectively.

In truth, Henry VII had little incentive to draw attention to his Tudor forebears, for – as his enemies were quick to point out – Owen Tudor was of lowly birth and alleged to be a 'bastard'. After Henry VII's death, his son and grandchildren also disregarded the surname, and it did not appear on inscriptions or coins – or in statutes, proclamations and chronicles. Instead, Henry VIII and his three children continued to draw attention to their Beaufort descent by using the portcullis as one of their heraldic badges; but they were equally ready to display their Yorkist lineage, through Elizabeth of York (Henry VII's queen), and to make popular the Tudor rose (though it never actually went by that name). It was only in the mid-18th century that historians consistently adopted the label 'Tudor' for the family that took the throne in 1485 and died out in 1603.

There is, nonetheless, some value in using the family surname. For one thing, it reminds us that Henry VII was a usurper and had to devote most of his reign to throwing off pretenders and rival claimants to the throne. The peaceful accession of his only surviving son was an achievement that was not inevitable and should not be underestimated. Henry VIII also had to endure dynastic insecurities in part because of his Tudor heritage. The turbulent history of Matilda's 'reign' in the 12th century, when the realm was ravaged by civil war, was enough to create unease at the prospect of a woman inheriting the throne. But the danger of a dynastic challenge to Henry's daughter Mary was the more intense because of the weakness of the Tudor title and the presence in England of powerful nobles with Plantagenet blood in their veins. No wonder that the Duke of Buckingham, Henry's nearest male relative in the Lancastrian line, was executed in 1521 for uttering provocative words about his right to the throne. Unfortunately, the remedies Henry VIII later took for resolving the succession problem made matters considerably worse. By bastardizing his daughter Mary, he prevented her early marriage and so limited her chance of ever bearing a child. By bastardizing both his daughters, he made it possible for Lady Jane Grey and Mary Queen of Scots to stake their own claims to the throne. Furthermore, he struck a blow at the principle of hereditary monarchy by using parliamentary statute to authorize the order of succession after his death and by removing his sister's Scottish line from the succession in the terms of his will. (For a dynastic family tree showing details of the Tudor succession, see pages 408 and 409.)

It would be wrong, though, to regard Bosworth as a watershed in English history, even if the traditional periodization has claimed Henry VII's reign as the start of the Early Modern era. Rather, Henry VII continued the work of his Yorkist predecessors in bringing the nobility into line and reforming the finances of the realm. He introduced no new institutions of government, but instead he used the medieval chamber and exchequer to administer his revenues. Many features of late-medieval monarchy and society endured throughout the 16th century: the nobility remained strong in the localities and a partner in government; rebellions still happened; *coups d'état* were attempted; and parliaments could, at times, be difficult.

Nonetheless, some significant turning-points did occur under the Tudors. The break with Rome under Henry VIII was one of the most momentous events in British history, while the imposition of Protestantism on the parishes of England and Wales under Edward VI and Elizabeth I fundamentally changed the religion and culture of the realm. Mary I's reign, too, was not without significance: the loss of Calais – England's last territorial possession on the Continent – finally ended the Hundred Years' War; and the Marian burnings of Protestants dug deep into the collective psyche of the English nation as a result of the popularity of John Foxe's *Acts and Monuments*, usually known as the *Book of Martyrs*. It is a pity Mary should be thought of in this way, as she was a competent ruler who was temporarily successful in returning England to Rome and restoring the practice of Catholicism to the parishes. But bad publicity is the fate of the losers in history, and she lost out because of bodily failure – no children and an early death – and the consequent accession of a Protestant who was to reign for just over 44 years.

'During the Wars of the Roses,' said the playful Sellar and Yeatman in *1066 and All That*, 'the Kings became less and less memorable ... It was therefore decided, since the Stuarts were not ready, to have some Welsh Kings called Tudors ... who, it was hoped, would be more memorable.' And memorable they certainly were: for Bosworth, for Henry VIII's six wives, for the accession of a boy king, for the burnings ordered by a Catholic (married to the King of Spain), and for the reign of the Virgin Queen. There is more to the Tudors than that, of course, and it is to be hoped that *The Tudor Chronicles* provides a more rounded picture of those 118 years.

HENRY VII

HE

Henry Tudor was born on 28 January 1457 in Pembroke Castle, Wales, during the long and turbulent period of English history known as the Wars of the Roses, when the great royal houses of York (its symbol: the white rose) and Lancaster (its symbol: the red rose) vied for power.

He was of royal descent on both sides of his family. His mother, Margaret Beaufort, was a great-grandchild of John of Gaunt, Duke of Lancaster (via a bastard line) and the fourth son of Edward III. On his father's side, his grandmother was Katherine, widow of Henry V and the daughter of Charles V of France.

Nonetheless, Henry had no claim to either the French or English throne. France was governed by Salic Law, preventing succession by a woman or through the female line; and in England a parliamentary statute of 1407 had specifically barred the offspring of John of Gaunt and his mistress, Katherine Swynford, from inheriting the throne – even though their illegitimate children had been legitimated by an earlier statute.

Henry never knew his father, Edmund Tudor, Earl of Richmond, who died of plague nearly three months before his son's birth. During his early years, Henry lived with his mother in Pembroke Castle, but in late 1461 the boy came into the custody of the Yorkist Sir William Herbert. Herbert moved Henry to his ancestral seat of Raglan Castle, officially became Henry's ward (by buying the wardship from the king, to whom it had reverted under feudal law) and left his wife Anne to supervise the child's education. Plans were made to marry Henry to their daughter.

PREVIOUS PAGE: **Henry VII** (see pp. 50–1).

LEFT: **Lady Margaret Beaufort (1443–1509)** was only 13 when she was first widowed and her son Henry Tudor was born. She married twice more: Henry Stafford, second son of Humphrey Stafford, Duke of Buckingham, in January 1458; and Lord Thomas Stanley in 1472. The three rings on her fingers, visible in this portrait, testify to these marriages. While her son was in exile she did her best to preserve his interests, and as a result she was greatly favoured during his reign. At court she wore robes and a coronet matching those of the queen and she came to sign her letters 'Margaret R'. She was also granted a large landed estate for her lifetime. Noted for her piety, particularly as she grew older, she is here shown at prayer before a devotional book in this later (c.1598) panel portrait by Rowland Lockey. The Beaufort portcullis is painted behind her in the cloth-of-gold and in the window, and the Beaufort arms are surmounted by a coronet with a swan and a yale (a mythic beast) as supporters.

ABOVE: **Henry Tudor as a young man** as portrayed by an unknown artist.

Viez touttes ces choses ainsy
aduenues le seizieme Jour du
dit mois le roy eust nouuelles
que marguerite soy disant roy
ne et sa tresmauuaise prentente et vsurpacio

In 1471, however, Henry's life was totally disrupted. At the decisive Battle of Tewkesbury in May of that year, the Yorkist king, Edward IV, finally overcame his Lancastrian rivals. The Lancastrian heir to the throne, Edward Prince of Wales, was killed on the battlefield, and soon afterwards the Lancastrian king, Henry VI, was murdered in the Tower of London. Henry Tudor was now the last of the male Lancastrians left alive and consequently he became the main threat to the Yorkist dynasty. When Edward IV tried to seize the 14-year-old Henry, he escaped abroad – accompanied by his uncle, Jasper Tudor – and made his home at the court of the Duke of Brittany. For the next 14 years Henry remained in exile without lands or prospects, a pawn in international politics and at the mercy of the Breton duke.

The opportunity for a new life came after the death of Edward IV on 9 April 1483. Edward's brother Richard, Duke of Gloucester, usurped the throne that should have passed by descent to Edward's nine-year-old son. After rumours circulated in the autumn that Richard III had murdered the rightful heir and his younger brother in the Tower (forever tainting his reputation), some Yorkists planned a rebellion. The uprising proved abortive, but many of the conspirators and other disaffected Yorkists drifted to Brittany, where they acclaimed Henry as their king. To cement their support, Henry took a solemn oath on Christmas Day 1483 in Rennes Cathedral that he would marry the eldest daughter of Edward IV, Elizabeth of York. In return, the Yorkists in the congregation offered him homage. Henry now made plans to return to England and take the throne.

1485

On 1 August, Henry Tudor and a company of some 2000 soldiers set sail from the Seine estuary for Wales. On the 7th, the small army landed at Milford Haven in Pembrokeshire, from where it advanced, unchallenged by any allies of Richard III, first through North Wales and then towards England. Having marched 115 miles in 8 days, Henry arrived at the English town of

LEFT: **The Battle of Tewkesbury** *on 4 May 1471 saw the defeat of the Lancastrian cause and the ascendancy of the Yorkists. It followed swiftly on the heels of the Battle of Barnet, in Hertfordshire, less than a month earlier (14 April), when Edward and his outnumbered Yorkist force had managed to overcome the Lancastrian army, killing their leaders the Earl of Warwick ('the Kingmaker') and his brother, the Marquess of Montagu. Tewkesbury consolidated that victory.*

As a result Henry Tudor, as the last of the Lancastrian royal line, was forced to flee abroad. He spent the next 14 years in exile. The battle is depicted here in a miniature illustrating the contemporary chronicle History of the Arrival of Edward IV in England and the Final Recovery of His Kingdoms from Henry VI, *written by an anonymous servant of Henry IV. The miniature probably depicts the death of Prince Edward, son of Henry VI.*

Shrewsbury. For the first time on the expedition he encountered resistance: the gates of the town were firmly closed to him. However, soon afterwards the mayor admitted the Tudor army, probably on the instructions of Sir William Stanley, a key figure in the region. Sir William was the younger brother of Henry's stepfather, Lord Thomas Stanley. Henry obviously hoped that both men would join forces with him, but neither of them made any overt commitment to the Lancastrian claimant. Instead they tracked Henry as he marched to the south, each with his own separate retinue, together amounting to about 8000 men.

Meanwhile, Richard III began to make military preparations to defend the throne he had usurped. On 19 August, he moved his headquarters from Nottingham to Leicester and waited there for the powerful men of the realm to arrive with their armies to support him. On 21 August he set up his camp close to Henry's army in the vicinity of Atherstone, ready to fight the next day. That night Richard reportedly had a terrible dream, 'for he thought in his sleep that he saw horrible images as it were of evil spirits haunting evidently about him'.[1] Early the next morning, the two armies met in battle. The Stanleys, however, remained uncommitted and just stood by, watching and waiting for the likely outcome to emerge.

As the battle progressed inconclusively, Richard attempted to win the day by making a mass cavalry charge towards Henry and his bodyguard. He was very nearly successful: Richard and his knights hacked down most of

Battle engaged

And so, when both battle-lines [at Bosworth] had been drawn up and the soldiers caught sight of each other from afar, they put on their helmets and prepared for the fight, awaiting the signal for battle with cocked ears. Between the armies was a marsh which Henry purposely kept on his left, so it would serve to protect his men. When the king saw the enemy pass by the marsh, he commanded his men to attack. They raised a sudden shout and first attacked the enemy with arrows. They, in turn, did nothing to slow the fight, but began to shoot their own arrows. When they drew close to each other, they henceforth did their work with the sword …

While the first lines were thus engaged, Richard was first informed by his scouts that Henry was at a distance, defended by a small bodyguard. Then, as he drew closer, he identified Henry more definitely because of his standards. Enraged, he spurred forward his horse and attacked him from the flank, riding outside the battle-line. Henry perceived Richard coming against him, and, since all his hope was in his arms, he eagerly entered the fray. At their first collision, when some men had been killed and Henry's standard had been overthrown together with his standard-bearer William Brandon, Richard encountered John Cheyney, a very brave man who threw himself in the way, and with great force unhorsed him, cutting his way wherever he went. After Henry had withstood this attack longer than even his own soldiers expected, for they had almost despaired of victory, behold, William Stanley came to their aid with his 3000 men. Then indeed in a trice, the rest of his men took to their heels, and Richard was killed, fighting in the thick of the fray.

[POLYDORE VERGIL, *Anglica Historia*, 1555 EDITION, EDITED ONLINE BY DANA F. SUTTON]

14

Henry's men, including his young standard-bearer, but Henry withstood the shock of the charge and Richard's own men broke up into smaller units. At this crucial moment, Sir William Stanley brought his retinue into the fray on Henry's side. Seeing this, Richard's army scattered in disarray and many took flight. The king, though, refused a chance to escape on horseback and fought 'manfully in the thickest press of his enemies' until he was slain.[2] His coronet was knocked into a bush and retrieved by Lord Thomas Stanley, who placed it on Henry Tudor's head. The soldiers and nobles on the field at once acclaimed their new king.

Although the battle – forever known as Bosworth Field – took place on 22 August, Henry decided to date his reign from the previous day. As a result, all those who fought on Richard's side technically became traitors. However, Henry showed mercy to most of the leading Yorkists. Henry Percy, 4th Earl of Northumberland, who had brought an army to Bosworth to back Richard, was imprisoned for a few months but retained his title and lands. John de la Pole, Earl of Lincoln, who was Richard's nephew through the female line, also escaped attainder (the forfeit of legal rights as a consequence of treason) and did not even spend time in custody. Faring less well, Thomas Howard, Earl of Surrey, lost his titles and land, though he was released from the Tower after three years. The main casualty of Henry's accession was Edward Plantagenet, Earl of Warwick, the son of Edward IV's and Richard III's

RIGHT: **Richard III (1452–85)**, *a younger brother of the Yorkist king Edward IV, usurped the throne in 1483 and was almost certainly responsible for the murder of his royal nephews in the Tower of London. Richard died bravely at the Battle of Bosworth in 1485. Although later labelled a hunchback, a characterization reinforced by Shakespeare, he more probably had a slight unevenness in the shoulders, as mentioned by two chroniclers; but that is not apparent in this likeness, which may be contemporary. Richard is pulling a ring from the fourth finger of his left hand, perhaps signifying his new status as a widower in March 1485.*

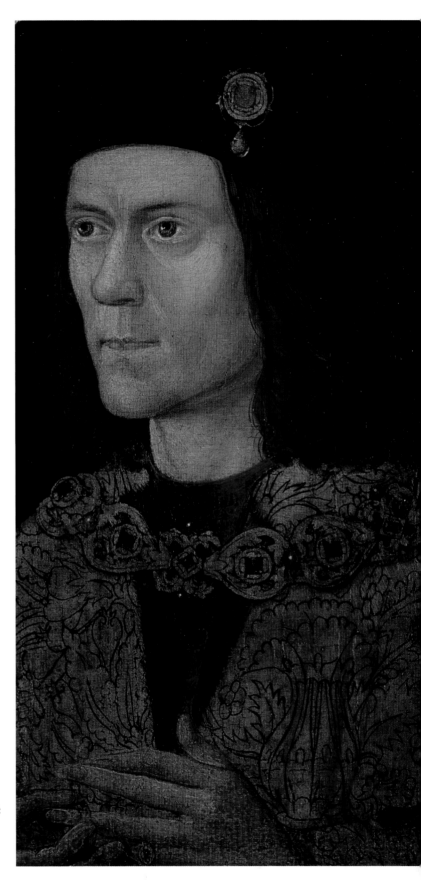

Battle concluded

The story goes that Richard [at Bosworth] could have rescued himself by flight. For those around him, seeing that from the beginning of the battle that their soldiers were fighting slowly and sluggishly, and that others were furtively slinking away from the battlefield, suspected fraud and urged him to flee. And then, when the battle had clearly turned against him, they brought him a swift horse. But he was not unaware that the people loathed him and abandoned all hope of future success, and is said to have replied that on that day he would make an end either of fighting or of his life, such was the man's ferocity and spirit ...

Henry immediately thanked God Almighty with many prayers for the victory he had gained, then, overcome by incredible happiness, he climbed a nearby hill, where, after he had praised his soldiers and ordered the wounded to be tended to, and the dead to be buried, gave his undying thanks to all his nobles and promised he would remember their support.

[POLYDORE VERGIL, *Anglica Historia*, 1555 EDITION, EDITED ONLINE BY DANA F. SUTTON]

deceased brother George, Duke of Clarence. As the son of a brother (not a sister), he was considered a serious danger to the new Tudor dynasty, and he was locked away in the Tower.

Henry rewarded most of his loyal followers well. The two men who benefited the most were his relatives: on 27 October his uncle, Jasper Tudor, was created Duke of Bedford and his stepfather Lord Thomas Stanley was raised to the Earldom of Derby. Lancastrians who had lost land and titles under the Yorkist kings also benefited from the Tudor accession: John de Vere, for example, was restored to his title of 13th Earl of Oxford and appointed lord great chamberlain and lord admiral. Henry granted offices and land to other companions in exile or supporters at Bosworth: most notably, Sir William Stanley was appointed chamberlain of the king's household.

On Sunday 30 October, Henry's coronation took place at Westminster Abbey. At the ceremony Bedford bore the crown and Derby carried the sword of state. The religious ceremony was followed by 'a royal and excellent feast'.[3] A week later Henry announced in his first Parliament that he claimed the English throne by hereditary right and God's judgement in the field of battle. So that there could be no doubt about the legality of his reign, Henry's title was confirmed in law, by statute.

On 10 December the Speaker of the House of Commons urged Henry to act on his promise to marry 'that illustrious Lady Elizabeth, daughter of King Edward IV', and thereby render possible 'the propagation of offspring from the stock of kings'.[4] The same Parliament introduced other important legislation, including a Navigation Act designed to stop 'the decay' of English shipping.

A coronation feast

Upon the 30th day of October [1485], [Henry VII] was solemnly crowned at Westminster, and after that solemnisation within the Monastery was finished, a royal and excellent feast with all circumstances to such a feast appertaining was held within Westminster Hall the same day.

[ROBERT FABIAN, *The Great Chronicle of London*, P. 240]

1486

Henry VII fulfilled the promise he had made at Rennes two years earlier and married Elizabeth of York on 18 January. Two months later, on 10 March, Henry set out on a royal progress to the North of his realm, visiting all the major towns on the route to York.

He spent Easter at Lincoln and entered the city of York on 20 April; he then returned by way of the Midlands, Bristol and the Thames Valley, arriving in Westminster in June. At each town the leading citizens displayed their loyalty to their new monarch, and Henry confirmed their civic privileges and offered redress of their grievances. At famous shrines Henry demonstrated his piety by lighting candles and saying prayers.

While he was on this lengthy royal trip, two Yorkist loyalists, Viscount Francis Lovell and Humphrey Stafford, attempted to stir up rebellion in Yorkshire and Worcestershire, but the few men who responded positively to their call were quickly dealt with. To ensure the future loyalty of local gentlemen from the North and the Midlands, Henry sent many of them down to London and placed them under heavy financial bonds – legally binding agreements that they would maintain their allegiance to the king under penalty of forfeiting a large sum of money, goods or land. Some of these men also lost their local offices to outsiders who were better trusted by the king.

In July, news spread that a Yorkist prince had turned up in Flanders at the court of Margaret of York. Margaret was, by marriage, the Dowager Duchess of Burgundy – the multitude of territories that comprised Franche Comté and the Low Countries – and the sister of Edward IV and Richard III.

17

RIGHT: **The marriage of Henry VII and Elizabeth of York** *was commemorated by this medallion, struck in January 1486. Elizabeth, as the eldest daughter of Edward IV, niece of Richard III and elder sister of the two princes who died in the Tower, had a far better claim than Henry to the throne. Henry waited until after his coronation before marrying the princess in order to make clear that his kingship did not depend on the rights of his wife. He also needed a papal dispensation before the wedding, as Parliament had declared her parents' marriage invalid on the orders of Richard III. The marriage unified the rival houses of York and Lancaster, and their individual emblems of the white and red roses came together in the Tudor rose.*

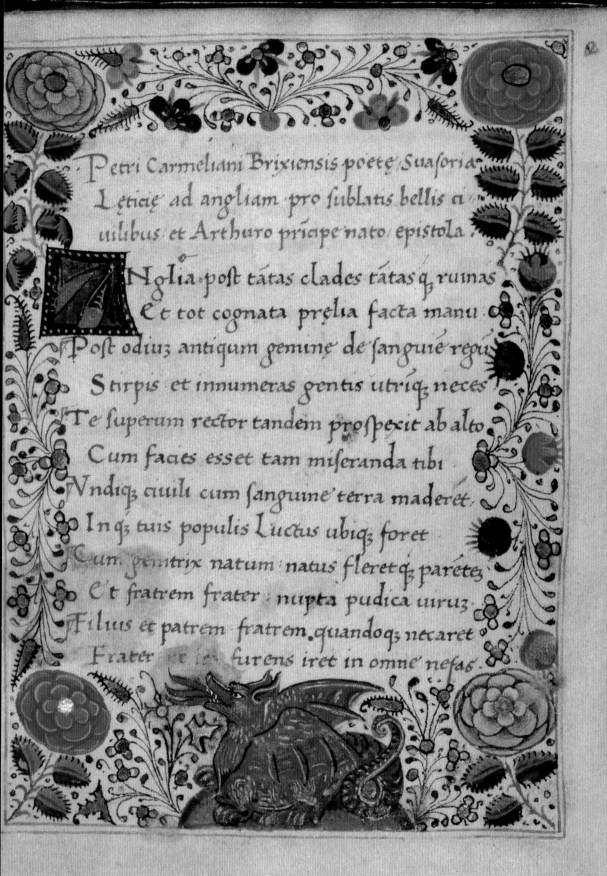

Petri Carmeliani Brixiensis poetę Suasoria
Lęticię ad angliam pro sublatis bellis ci
uilibus et Arthuro pricipe nato epistola.

Nglia post tátas clades tátasq̃ ruinas
Et tot cognata prelia facta manu
Post odiuz antiqum geminę de sanguię regu
Stirpis et innumeras gentis utriq̃ neces
Te superum rector tandem prospexit ab alto
Cum facies esset tam miseranda tibi
Vndiq̃ ciuili cum sanguine terra maderet
Inq̃ tuis populis Luctus ubiq̃ foret
Cum genitrix natum natus fleretq̃ parétez
Et fratrem frater nupta pudica uiruz
Filius et patrem fratrem quandoq̃ necaret
Frater et furens iret in omne nefas

This 'prince' was Lambert Simnel, a youth whose social origins are obscure but whose father was probably a carpenter, organ maker or cobbler. Former Yorkists and the Burgundian duchess coached him to impersonate her (now imprisoned) nephew, Edward, Earl of Warwick. During the autumn, rumours spread in London that this young man, now claiming to be Warwick, had turned up in Ireland.

On 19 September, Queen Elizabeth gave birth to a male heir at St Swithun's Priory near Winchester. Although born a month prematurely, the baby was healthy, and he was baptized five days later in Winchester Cathedral with Elizabeth Woodville (the child's maternal grandmother) standing as godmother and the Earl of Oxford as godfather.

A queen's coronation

[Elizabeth of York] ... *royally apparelled, in a kirtle of white cloth of gold of damask, and a mantle of the same suit, furred with ermine, fastened before her breast with a great lace, curiously wrought of gold and silk, and rich knobs of gold at the end, tasselled; her fair yellow hair hanging down plain behind her back, with a call of pipes over it, and wearing on her head a circle of gold, richly garnished with precious stones ...*

[JOHN LELAND, ON ELIZABETH'S CORONATION, 1487, *Collectanea*, IV, P. 204]

1487

In order to demonstrate that Lambert Simnel was an impostor, Henry paraded the real Earl of Warwick through London on 2 February. Suspecting that Simnel was part of a wider Yorkist conspiracy, he also sent Elizabeth Woodville, whom he had never fully trusted, to live in a convent and imprisoned her son Thomas Grey, 1st Marquess of Dorset, in the Tower. Towards the end of February, Henry's suspicions seemed well-founded when the Yorkist Earl of Lincoln fled Henry's court and joined his aunt, Margaret of York, in Malines, Flanders. Margaret offered the earl some 2000 German mercenaries to use in support of Simnel's pretensions to the throne.

At the start of May, Lincoln, Lovell and the German soldiers arrived in Ireland to meet up with Simnel. Through their influence, he was crowned King Edward VI in Dublin Cathedral on 24 May. A Parliament was called in Dublin in the new king's name, and coins were struck bearing his image. Henry later poked fun at the gullibility of the Irish, claiming that they would crown apes. This was unfair, for Simnel was a comely lad with a certain grace, and the Yorkist cause had deep roots in Ireland where Warwick's father, the Duke of Clarence, had been born and his grandfather had been lord lieutenant.

On 4 June, an army of about 6000 men crossed over from Ireland to Furness in Lancashire and

PREVIOUS PAGE: **Prince Arthur (1486–1502),** *the eldest son of Henry VII and Elizabeth of York, was named after Arthur, the mythical Welsh-descended king of the Britons, whom the Tudors claimed as an ancestor. The prince was baptized in Winchester Cathedral, which some believed was the site of King Arthur's Camelot. This epic poem by the Italian humanist, Petrus Carmelianus, was written to celebrate Arthur's birth and the end of the civil wars. The illustration shows Henry VII's coat of arms framed by two angels; the red and white roses of Lancaster and York respectively decorate the borders. Carmelianus later became Henry VII's Latin secretary and chaplain.*

RIGHT: **Elizabeth of York (1465–1503),** *the wife of Henry VII, died in 1503. Although overshadowed by her mother-in-law, Margaret Beaufort, Elizabeth was described (in the Calendar of State Papers, Venetian) as a 'very handsome woman and in conduct very able'. She carried out the principal duty of a royal consort by bearing Henry eight children, four of whom survived infancy: Arthur, Margaret, Henry and Mary. Here, Elizabeth is shown holding the white rose of York.*

ELIZABETHA · VXOR
HENRICI · VII

The Star Chamber *dealt with cases concerning riots, unlawful assemblies and abuses of the law. It had existed during the 14th century as part of the judicial function of the king's council, but under Henry VII and Henry VIII it became established as a separate court of the king's councillors under the chairmanship of the lord chancellor. The name seems to be derived from the decorative pattern of gold stars on the azure ceiling of the chamber where it met (the camera stellata). It is depicted here in the frontispiece to the 16th-century yearbooks* Anni Regis Henrici septimi.

23

The Battle of Stoke

And upon the 16th day of June [1487] was the field of Stoke, the which was by the force of the Earl of Lincoln, son and heir of the Duke of Suffolk, that late days to fore was fled this land, and so passed to the Duchess of Burgundy, sister unto King Edward the IV, the which duchess as the fame went [as the story goes] aided and excited [incited] the said earl to make war upon England, trusting to have had great aid of some estates of the same, and so being furnished with a small company of Burgundians, having to their captain a fierce and strong soldier named Martin Swart, they to their sorrow landed at [text is blank here] and so held on their journey till they came near unto the aforesaid town or village of Stoke, where they were encountered with the king's host [army], and there fighting a sore and sharp fight for the while that it endured upon the aforesaid 16th day of June. The victory whereof fell unto the king, loved by God.

[ROBERT FABIAN, *The Great Chronicle of London*, PP. 240–1]

then moved rapidly eastwards, crossing the Pennines into Wensleydale before turning southwards. Although the invading force found some recruits among the local gentry, most of the North of England – and especially Yorkshire – remained quiet. When news of their landing reached Henry VII, he was at Coventry. From there he immediately marched to Nottingham, where he awaited troops to take on the rebels. On 16 June, the two forces met at the Battle of Stoke. In a three-hour-long battle Henry's army of some 15,000 men, under the command of Bedford and Oxford, eventually defeated the smaller and less well armed Yorkist army of 8000 men. Lincoln was slain; Lovell escaped into perpetual exile; Simnel was captured. When news of Henry's victory reached London, a *Te Deum* was sung in all the churches.

Soon after the battle, Henry made preparations for his wife's coronation, perhaps in order to win over other disaffected Yorkists. On 24 November Elizabeth of York 'royally apparelled' and with 'her fair yellow hair hanging down plain behind her back'[5] was conveyed from the Tower to Westminster. The next day, equally royally dressed, she was crowned in Westminster Abbey, while Henry looked on from a stage between the pulpit and high altar.

The year also saw an important development in the system of justice. In the Parliament held in November, an important statute was passed that established the 'Star Chamber', a separate court of the king's councillors under the chairmanship of the lord chancellor.

RIGHT: **Lambert Simnel** *was probably not the real name of the pretender who claimed to be the nephew of the Yorkist kings, and who challenged Henry VII unsuccessfully at the Battle of Stoke (1487), the last military engagement of the Wars of the Roses. This report, written by a herald, provides a largely accurate account of the battle and firmly identifies 'the lad' as John ('whose name was indeed John', as mentioned in lines 1–2). Whatever his name, the lad was afterwards imprisoned, pardoned, and ended his days working in the royal kitchens.*

Less fortunate was John de la Pole, Earl of Lincoln, who was killed, along with the German mercenary leader Martin Schwarz, who had brought up to 2000 German pikemen (Landsknechte) to fight against Henry. The rebel dead numbered perhaps as many as 4000.

The lade that hee Rebelle called king Edward whoos Name was
In dede John by a baylont And a gentil esquier of the kinge hows
called Robert Bellingham whiche alsso the same day to the slaunder
of a manly man off Werre called Martyn Swarte And ther was
Slayne therle of Lincoln John and dyvers other gentilmen And
the broune of Lovell put to flyght And ther wer slayne of
Englysshe ovche And lusse ivj And that day the king made
xiij banorett And lij knyghtes Whos Names ensueth

These beo the names of the banorette

Sir Gilbert Talbot

Sir John Chayny] ther iij wer
Sir William Stou] made byfor the
batell

And aft the batell wer made
the same day
Sir John of Arundell
Sir Thoms Cokosay
Sir John ffortescu
Sir Edmu Benyngfeld
Sir James Blount
Sir Richard Crofte
Sir humfrey Stanley
Sir Richard de Laber
Sir John Mortyn
Sir William Trouthbeck

The Names off the knyghtes
made at the same batell

Sir James Audeley
Sir Edward Norres
Sir Robert Clifford
Sir george Opton
Sir Robert Abroughton
Sir John paston
Sir henry Willoughby
Sir Ric Pole
Sir Ric ffitzlowes
Sir Edward Abrough
Sir George Lovell
Sir John Longvile

These noble knyghtes
Wers and liberally payd
the hole fee And thise
that folowen have payd
as yet but parte

1488

On 11 June, the 15-year-old James IV acceded to the throne of Scotland. One of his first acts was to issue a year's safe conduct to Lovell and other Yorkist rebels. James, however, was not militarily prepared for war, so he negotiated a three-year truce with Henry, although he also made overtures to France for a renewal of the traditional Franco-Scottish 'Auld Alliance'.

Meanwhile, in July a French army overran most of the Duchy of Brittany, which had until then been ruled semi-independently by Duke Francis. On 21 August, the duke was forced to make a disadvantageous peace, but he died barely three weeks later, leaving a 12-year-old daughter as his heir. Previously

Henry had given aid to the duke, who had after all offered him hospitality during his years of exile. Now he wanted to help the young duchess, Anne, for otherwise the French would annex the duchy and become unacceptably strong. Henry therefore supplied Anne with loans to raise troops to resist Charles VIII of France but did not send an English army to Brittany, as war would have strained his finances and threatened his security.

In November, Henry called a 'Great Council' at Westminster to consider what was best to do. Possibly following its advice, he decided to negotiate a diplomatic solution by building up an alliance with other rulers who were hostile to France. As a result he sent his secretary, Richard Fox, to Spain to arrange a political alliance and a betrothal between his son and heir, Prince Arthur, and Katherine, the youngest daughter of the monarchs of Spain, Ferdinand of Aragon and Isabella of Castile. Henry also made overtures to Maximilian, the son of the Holy Roman Emperor, who was then acting as regent for his son Philip in the Burgundian lands. Maximilian hoped to marry Anne of Brittany and also wanted to oust France from the duchy.

ABOVE: **Charles VIII (1470–98)** *came to the French throne in 1483 as an unhealthy minor. Later, his army conquered Brittany, and he integrated it into France by marrying its duchess, Anne. In 1494 he invaded Italy to make good his claim to the throne of Naples. Initially successful, he was soon opposed by the League of Venice, which comprised the pope, Spain, the Holy Roman Emperor and the Italian states. Naples was later conquered by Spain. This portrait is attributed to Jean Bourdichon (1457–1521).*

RIGHT: **Isabella of Castile (1451–1504) and Ferdinand of Aragon (1452–1516)** *ruled Spain after their marriage in 1469. For most of Henry VII's reign they were England's allies, a relationship based on the 1489 Treaty of Medina del Campo and the marriage of their youngest daughter Katherine to Arthur, the Prince of Wales. In this group portrait (c.1490) by an anonymous artist, Ferdinand is kneeling on the left and Isabella is on the right. It hangs in Madrid's Prado museum.*

1489

In order to finance an army of 6000 men to aid Anne of Brittany, Henry's Parliament agreed to a novel subsidy for the king's coffers – a ten-per-cent tax on income. Consequently, on 14 February, Henry signed the Treaty of Redon in which he offered the duchess military protection. The next month, he concluded an alliance with Spain at Medina del Campo. Both sides agreed to a betrothal between Arthur and Katherine, and promised that neither realm would assist the rebels of the other.

However the new tax was very unpopular in parts of the North of England. On Wednesday 28 April (the Feast of St Vitalis), the Earl of Northumberland met some of those protesting against it. Following Henry's instructions, he refused to make any concessions. 'When the people heard the royal reply they assaulted the earl as though he were the author of their wrongs and killed him.'[6] Anticipating royal retribution, the ordinary people that were present organized an armed rising. In response Henry mustered an army, and 13 peers and many more gentlemen joined him with their retinues to march against the rebels. Henry evidently feared that the commotion was part of a much wider Yorkist conspiracy, even though 'these rebels have no leader and but little credit'.[7] Henry need not have worried, for 'at his approach the terrified rebels all took to their heels,'[8] and the revolt was over by the time he arrived at York on 23 May. Those ordinary people, the 'commons', who had participated in it 'put halters about their necks, and in their shirts came into a great court of the palace where the king was lodged, and there kneeling cried lamentably for mercy and grace'.[9] About 1500 of them were pardoned and only 6 were executed. Henry left Thomas Howard as his chief lieutenant in the North. Howard had proved his loyalty during this Yorkshire insurrection and was rewarded with office and restoration to the Earldom of Surrey.

'the terrified rebels all took to their heels'

Victory at Dixmude

The Battle of Dixmude was on the 13th day of June [1489], that day being Saturday, and the 4th year of Henry the Seventh, anno 1489, where the English men had great victory, for there was taken and slain a great number, and there was slain the Lord Morley an English man.

[*Chronicle of Calais in the Reigns of Henry VII and Henry VIII*, P. 2]

28

RIGHT: **Maximilian (1459–1519)** *was a member of the Austrian Habsburg family and the widower of Mary, the daughter and heiress of Duke Charles the Bold of Burgundy. After her death in 1482, Maximilian acted as regent for their infant son Philip (later known as Philip the Fair). In 1486 Maximilian was elected and crowned 'King of the Romans' (heir to his father, the Holy Roman Emperor). He allied with Henry VII to stop France from annexing Brittany, but neither of them could prevent Charles VIII's marriage to the Duchess Anne in 1491. In this painting by Bernhard Strigel, which was created in 1516, Maximilian (left) is shown with his family: his elder son Philip, his wife Mary, his grandsons (later to be Charles V and Ferdinand I) and his adopted son Ludwig II of Hungary.*

The future of Brittany preoccupied Henry for the rest of the year. In April, he dispatched the 6000 men promised in the Treaty of Redon. But his ally Maximilian was unable to aid the duchess because of a civil war he was fighting in Flanders. To release Maximilian for the fight in Brittany, Henry sent an expedition of some 1800 English troops under Giles Daubeney, the Lieutenant of Calais, to provide assistance in Flanders. On 13 June, the English attacked the Flemings who were besieging Maximilian's garrison at Dixmude. Wading through ditches in water up to their armpits to defeat the besiegers and capture many of their guns, 'the English men had great victory, for there was taken and slain a great number'.[10] Maximilian, however, did not join the fight in Brittany but instead made peace with France. Despite Breton and English efforts, the French made headway in the duchy during August and managed to retain control of Brest, and in November the duchess made an uneasy peace with France.

The year was personally significant for the English king and his consort, for on 29 November a daughter was born to Elizabeth. She was baptized Margaret.

1490

On 27 February, Henry's heir apparent, Arthur, was given the title of Prince of Wales at Westminster Palace. Meanwhile, Pope Innocent VIII tried to broker a peace between France and England, but, according to Henry, the French 'would never grant any terms save such as were disgraceful to us'.[11] In September, Henry concluded a treaty with Maximilian that set out the terms by which they would both fight the French. In December, Emperor Maximilian underwent a proxy marriage with Anne of Brittany: in a ceremony supposed to signify its consummation, his ambassador, in the presence of witnesses, inserted his bare leg between the sheets of a marriage bed where Anne lay naked. To isolate France further, Henry ratified the earlier treaty negotiated with Ferdinand and Isabella of Spain at Medina del Campo.

1491

Early in this year, Charles VIII of France made preparations to invade and annex Brittany. He provoked another war in Flanders to distract Maximilian and signed an alliance with Scotland. Charles did not expect any Spanish intervention, because Ferdinand and Isabella were preoccupied with a war against the Moors in Granada. Henry was therefore isolated, but he remained determined to continue his protection of Brittany and if necessary go to war. First, he called a great council of his nobles, which met in late June, to discuss the possibility of military action. 'All unanimously concurred in the reasons for war and offered their own best services.'[12] Then, in October, Henry summoned a Parliament to grant two subsidies to fight a war. At its opening, the lord chancellor and Archbishop of Canterbury, John Morton, spoke on the biblical theme of Jeremiah 8:15: 'we expected peace but no good came'. In response, Parliament voted a tax that would be paid in three parts.

31

LEFT: **The education of Prince Arthur** *followed a programme of study then fashionable in Burgundy and devised by Bernard André, the tutor of the prince after 1496. This miniature illustrates a poem written by André that relates to his educational aims. Virtue, it proclaims, is the goal of the prince, far more important than either nobility or wealth. The inset scene shows the poet presenting his manuscript to Arthur, who is also shown at mass in the background.*

André also wrote a number of panegyrics for Henry VII and Henry VIII, between 1485 and his death in 1522, and he compiled the Historia Henrici Septimi *(History of Henry VII), which was edited in the 19th century.*

Henry, however, did not have the resources to send a large army to Brittany, and in the event Charles easily won the duchy. The French took Redon, won Concarneau from the English, and proceeded to besiege Rennes, the only town that was able to offer anything approaching an effective resistance. Holed up in Rennes, Anne refused to take advantage of an offer of safe conduct to leave her duchy. On 15 November she submitted to the French, and the next month she married Charles VIII, 'her principality being accepted as her dowry'. Maximilian, who had now lost his wife, was 'angry beyond words' at this humiliation.[13] Swearing vengeance, he promised to help Henry in military action against France.

On 28 June Queen Elizabeth gave birth to her second son, Henry, at Greenwich: Henry VII now had another male child to bolster a Tudor dynasty. However, a new threat to the succession soon emerged. In mid-November a young man from Tournai, named Pierrechon Werbecque – anglicized as Perkin Warbeck – arrived in Cork, Ireland. Here he played the role of Richard, Duke of York, the younger son of Edward IV, who had been imprisoned by Richard III in the Tower in 1483 and was by now almost certainly dead.

1492

Many in Ireland recognized the pretender Warbeck as 'Richard of York', including Maurice Fitzgerald, 9th Earl of Desmond, who proffered his allegiance. To elicit international support, Warbeck's sponsors sent out letters announcing the safe arrival of 'Prince Richard of York' in Ireland to James IV of Scotland and the Yorkist Margaret of Burgundy. A flotilla of French ships escorted Warbeck to France, where, in the early summer, the French King Charles VIII greeted him 'honourably, as a kinsman and friend'.[14] Knowing of Henry's plans for war, Charles intended to use the pretender as a diplomatic tool.

ABOVE: **Anne of Brittany (1477–1514)** *married Charles VIII of France on 6 December 1491, despite the opposition of Henry VII who had sent troops to Brittany to preserve its independence. On Charles's death Anne married his successor, Louis XII, so that the duchy would remain a possession of the French crown. Anne had no children and the duchy afterwards passed to Louis's cousin, Francis I, who incorporated it permanently into France. The duchess is depicted here on a contemporary bronze medal credited to Nicolas Leclerc and Jean de Saint-Priest.*

RIGHT: **Cork, on Ireland's south coast,** *was the destination of Perkin Warbeck in late 1491. Before then, he had travelled around Europe in a merchant ship. On his arrival in Cork, Warbeck was mistaken for a member of the House of York, and from then on he posed as Richard, the younger son of Edward IV, one of the princes who had been imprisoned in the Tower under Richard III. His story was believed by many of the Irish, and he received support from the Fitzgerald earls of Kildare and Desmond. The city is shown here in a late 16th-century map of Ireland, which first appeared in the 1633 Pacata Hibernia, concerning the Elizabethan troubles in Ireland.*

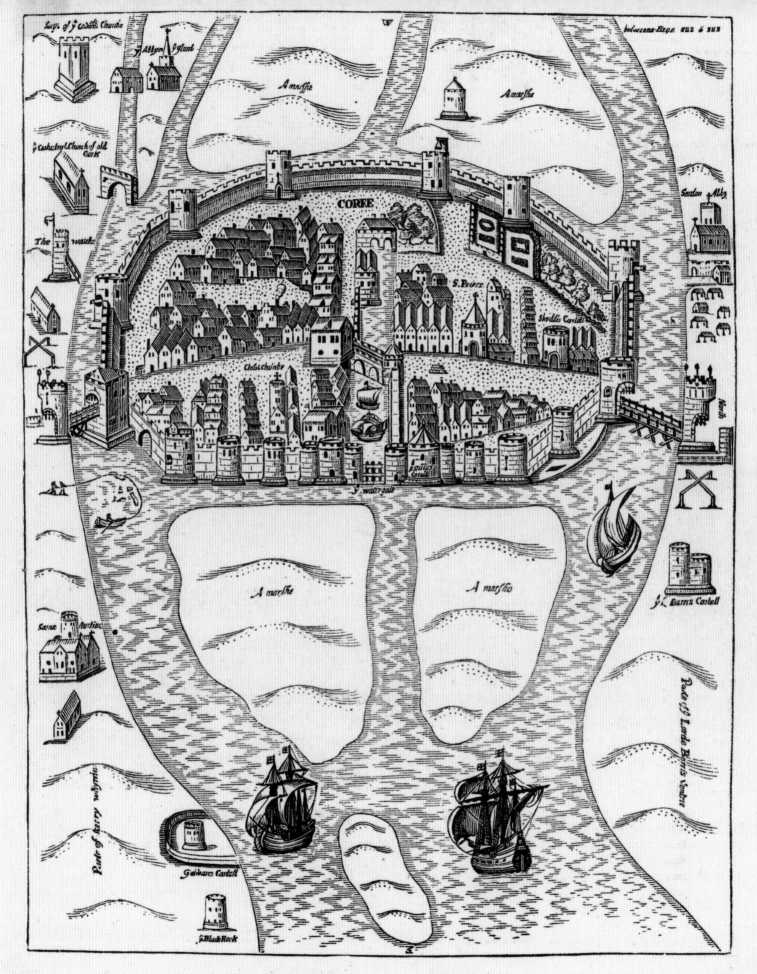

CORK, A.D. 1633.

Stafford, "Pacata Hibernia," 1633.

CRISTO: COLOMBO

In mid-June Henry's navy was engaged in minor skirmishes off the northern French coast, while his admiral, Lord Richard Willoughby de Broke, tried unsuccessfully to land 1500 men near Cherbourg in Normandy. Frustrated by Charles's refusal to abandon Warbeck, Henry decided on all-out war to salvage his honour. In early August he declared war, and over the next few months he mustered the men and munitions needed for an invasion. On 2 October the king landed at Calais, the only surviving English possession on the Continent, with an army numbering some 14,000 men – the largest English force sent overseas during the whole century. On 19 August he marched his army 20 miles towards Boulogne, where he pitched camp and besieged the well-fortified town.

Charles, however, did not want to tie up French troops in a long siege. Having obtained his objectives in Brittany, he planned to pursue his ambitions in Italy. Consequently, on 8 November he sent word 'beseeching the King of England of his peace'.[15] Henry quickly accepted the offer, and the next day the two kings signed a peace treaty at Etaples. By its terms Henry received 'an enormous sum of money to cover his expenditure'[16] on the expedition and reimburse his previous help to Anne of Brittany, as well as a pension of about £5000, paid annually. With this advantageous peace secured, and his honour intact, Henry returned to Calais on 12 November, and from there travelled back to England.

In a supplementary agreement signed on 13 December, Charles promised to renounce all aid to Henry's rebels and traitors. Warned of this development beforehand, Warbeck fled to Margaret of Burgundy's court at Malines. There, the duchess publicly recognized him as her nephew and assigned to him a retinue of 30 men dressed in the Yorkist colours of murrey (a darkish purple) and blue.

Also in this year, the Genoese mariner Christopher Columbus set sail westwards, attempting to locate a sea passage to the Indies.

34

ABOVE: **Christopher Columbus (d.1506)** *sailed across the Atlantic in 1492, hoping to find a route to the (East) Indies. An Italian himself, his patrons were Isabella of Castile and Ferdinand of Aragon. On this voyage he discovered the Bahamas, Cuba, and Santo Domingo. His discoveries opened up the Americas to European explorers and marked the beginning of the Spanish overseas empire. Columbus probably did not sit for any portrait, and this posthumous likeness (by Cristofano dell' Altissimo, c.1525–1605) differs from written descriptions of him.*

RIGHT: **Henry's expedition to France in 1492** *was celebrated in this Latin poem, which was probably intended as a gift for the king. In October 1492, he took a large army to Calais and began to besiege the town of Boulogne. His intention was to display his power to the French king and punish him for protecting the pretender Perkin Warbeck. Charles VIII quickly sued for peace and concluded a treaty that was advantageous to Henry.*

De serenissimi ac Invictissimi Domini dni Henrici anglie
et francie regis septimi hybernieq3 Domini Excell...
in galliam progressu ... Libellus

ELLA CANANT

Alij: Troie Prostrataq3 dicant

Pergama: nec Danaum taceat

sera gesta suorum

Conditor Illiados / et fortia musa Maronis

Prelia Dardanium memoret cum gente Latina:

Cesareos nec non Preclaro carmine honores.

Corduba magniloquo genuit quem carmine vates

Concinat Aeneadum genus alto a sanguine ductum

Nec sera pretereat crudelia facta Neronis

In noua fert alius mutatas corpora formas

Lasciuos alter Veneris describit amores

Et tua magnanimu cur non Henrice Britannu

Certa salus nitidis scribuntur gesta Camenis:

Nunquid adest genus egregia de stirpe creatum?

Nunquid aui: pater ipse tuus diademate magnu

Regali imperium nullo prohibente regebant:

Cy commence vng moult notable et deuot traitie
intitule · Les douze fleurs de tribulation · Prologue

A chiere amie en ihesucrist ses loiaulz
amie en nreseigneur salut et confort En
cellup qui tous les desconfortez reconforte
Sicomme dit la sainte escripture Nulz ne
poeult loialment amer en lamour de charite cest
de ihesucrist se il na iope de tous les biens qui a la
sainte ame poeuent aidier de venir a nreseigneur
Et se il nest doulent de cœur par compassion de
tous les maulz corporelz et espirituelz q̃ la destorbẽt
de paruenir a la iope du ciel Sicõme saint pol le
tesmoingne quant il dit · Gaudere cũ gaudentibz
et flere cum flentibus · Mais ilz sont aulcũes gens

1493

News of 'the resuscitated Duke of York' reached England in January. Believing it unlikely that 'anyone could have fabricated such a fiction as to make a transparent truth gain such currency as truth,'[17] disaffected Yorkists as well as at least two of the king's household servants agreed to give the pretender their support if he made a bid for the throne. As early as 12 January, Lord John Fitzwalter, a steward of the royal household, allegedly promised 50 men-at-arms to fight in the pretender's cause. On 14 March, Sir William Stanley, Henry's step-uncle and the lord chamberlain, became involved in the growing conspiracy and asserted 'that if he were sure that the man was Edward's son he would never take up arms against him'.[18] Some ex-Yorkists went further and began plotting to raise the country in support of the supposed prince or, like Sir Robert Clifford, defected to Margaret's court in Flanders.

Henry took the threat very seriously. He dispatched 200 men to Ireland and ordered the arrest of suspects in the 15 English counties where trouble might brew. He sent out spies to discover the truth about the youth's origins, so that he could expose him as a fraud. Throughout the spring and early summer, East Anglian towns were put on alert and ships patrolled the coast to give warning of an invasion. He also moved, with soldiers and artillery, into Kenilworth Castle in the Midlands.

An impostor's fantasy

I myself [Perkin Warbeck, addressing Isabella of Castile], then nearly nine years of age, was also delivered to a certain lord to be killed, [but] it pleased Divine Clemency, that that lord, having compassion on my innocence, preserved me alive in safety: first, however, causing me to swear on the holy sacrament that to no one should I disclose my name, origin, or family, until a certain number of years had passed. He then sent me therefore abroad, with two persons, who should watch over and take charge of me; and thus I, an orphan, bereaved of my royal father and brother, an exile from my kingdom, and deprived of my country, inheritance and fortune, a fugitive in the midst of extreme perils, led my miserable life, in fear, and weeping, and grief, and for the space of nearly eight years lay hid ... scarcely had I emerged from childhood alone and without means, I remained for a time in the kingdom of Portugal, and thence sailed to Ireland, where being recognised by the illustrious lords, the earls of Desmond and Kildare, my cousins, as also by other noblemen of the island, I was received with great joy and honour.

[LETTER ORIGINALLY IN LATIN, SIGNED 'RICHARD', FROM WARBECK TO ISABELLA, 1493 (BRITISH LIBRARY MS EGERTON 616), AS QUOTED BY I. ARTHURSON IN *The Perkin Warbeck Conspiracy*, PP. 49–50]

LEFT: **Margaret of York (1446–1503), the Dowager Duchess of Burgundy**, *was a sister of Edward IV, Richard III and George, Duke of Clarence. She is depicted here (upper left) at prayer, in this illuminated page from a French moral and religious treatise written by David Oubert in 1475. Margaret's husband, Duke Charles of Burgundy, died in 1477, and she was left childless but with extensive dower lands in Flanders. She then became a firm ally of her stepdaughter's husband, Maximilian. After 1485, according to 16th-century historian Polydore Vergil, she 'cherished such a deep hatred of King Henry that it seemed she would be content with nothing short of his death,' and she did all in her power to succour his enemies. Yorkist exiles were welcomed to her court at Malines; she groomed Lambert Simnel to pose as the Earl of Warwick; and after Simnel's capture at the Battle of Stoke in 1487, she gave strong support to Perkin Warbeck, believing him to be her nephew.*

piese vanbeck nadit de Tournaï suppesé pour Richard
Duc d'porck prmé fils d'Edouard iv Roy d'Angleterre l'an 1492
fut penéu à Londres par la fin de l'an 1499

By the end of June the danger seemed over. No rising took place in England or Ireland. Abroad, Maximilian was distracted by a Turkish attack on his territories in Austria, and Margaret of Burgundy – Warbeck's patron – was unsuccessful in her attempts to raise cash for a mercenary army to invade England. Furthermore, Warbeck's true identity was by now discovered, and Henry was ready to publicize it to the world.

In July an embassy travelled to Flanders to 'publicly assert that the youth was of base birth and had falsely assumed the person and name of Richard Duke of York, who had many years before been murdered with his brother Edward in the Tower of London on the orders of his uncle Richard'.[19] In consideration of this statement, the council of the young Duke of Burgundy, Philip the Fair (who was still a minor under Maximilian's regency), agreed not to assist Warbeck. However, Philip's maternal grandmother, Margaret, was left free to act as she wished in the lands that were part of her dower duchy, and she wished to carry on supporting Warbeck, in whose princely identity she continued to believe. She sent him to Vienna in August to be introduced to Maximilian, who had just been elected Holy Roman Emperor. She also wrote, in Warbeck's support, to Isabella of Castile.

Furious with this further escalation of the Warbeck affair, Henry ordered an embargo on trade between England and the Low Countries. It began on 18 September, when Flemings were expelled from England and their goods seized. The result for England was economic dislocation. On 15 October, a riot erupted in London and foreign merchants were attacked and their goods looted. A later inquiry found 80 men to have been involved, the majority of them servants and apprentices who had been made unemployed by the royal embargo.

ABOVE: **Pierrechon Werbecque, or Perkin Warbeck (c. 1474–1499)**, *was called 'Perkin' by the English instead of the normal English translation, 'Peter', as a mark of contempt. The pretender to the throne created severe problems for Henry from the time he arrived in Ireland until his execution eight years later. Warbeck was helped enormously by the support he received at one time or another from Margaret of York (Dowager Duchess of Burgundy), Charles VIII, Maximilian, and James IV of Scotland. Furthermore, some of Henry's leading courtiers and prominent churchmen were implicated in conspiracies to help the impostor win his 'rightful' throne. Warbeck was eventually executed after the discovery (or fabrication) of his involvement in another plot to depose Henry. This is a French drawing from the 16th century.*

1494

To keep morale high, more splendid celebrations than usual were held at court on Twelfth Night (6 January): after a 'sumptuous and great dinner', the king's players put on 'a goodly interlude' based on St George and the dragon, after which the wine flowed freely and 120 sweet dishes were set before the assembled company.[20] Despite this display of wealth and majesty, all was not well in England. In particular, the economic situation deteriorated further when Philip the Fair's council ordered an embargo on all trade with England and the seizure of English merchants' goods.

In fact, the threat from Warbeck came not from the Low Countries but from Ireland. In the early summer, the Earl of Desmond raised the southwestern province of Munster in support of 'Richard of York'. To meet the crisis Sir Edward Poynings was appointed Ireland's deputy lieutenant, notionally under the three-year-old Prince Henry, who was named lord lieutenant. On 13 October, Poynings arrived at his new post with an army of 653 men, and over the next two months he and Sir James Ormond (the newly appointed constable of Limerick Castle) carried out a devastating scorched-earth policy against actual and potential rebels.

In the meantime, Warbeck accompanied Maximilian on his return to Flanders in August, and then attended the rituals and festivities that marked Philip the Fair's installation as ruler – on reaching his age of majority – of the Burgundian Low Countries. Furious at the honoured status accorded to Warbeck, Henry challenged the youth's pretensions by creating his second son 'Duke of York' in a public and magnificent ceremony on 1 November, All Hallows Day. The young duke had to be carried during the formal procedures, when he was also admitted to the Order of the Bath. Two weeks of festivities followed, including a series of jousts. At around this time, Henry also ordered further arrests of Englishmen thought to be involved in a Warbeck conspiracy.

In December, a Parliament met at Drogheda and passed 49 statutes, including

A Twelfth Night supper

In the time of Christmas before passed, the king kept an honourable household at Westminster, and upon the twelfth day was holding a sumptuous and great dinner in the white Hall ... the mayor with his brethren ... were worshipfully and plenteously served with all manner of dainties ... and after he was desired ... to tarry and see such disports as that night should be showed in Westminster Hall ... which ... at that time was hanged with arras [tapestry], and staged along the hall at the king's cost that the people might well and easily see the said disport ... anon from the kitchen being behind the Common place ... 60 dishes were all served unto the king's mess [table], and forthwith were as many served unto the queen, of the which six score dishes was not one of flesh or of fish, but all confections of sundry fruits and conserves ... and finally as all worldly pleasure has an end, the board was reverently withdrawn, and the king and queen with the other estates ... conveyed into the palace, and the mayor with his company yood [gone] to the Bridge where 2 barges tarried for him, and so came home by the breaking of day, and then the mayor kissed his wife as a double lady.

[ROBERT FABIAN, *The Great Chronicle of London*, PP. 251–2]

a law ('Poynings' Law') that no Irish Parliament could meet without royal permission and that all measures to be submitted to that Parliament had first to be approved by the king.

Just before Christmas, Henry pardoned Sir Robert Clifford, who had joined Warbeck in Flanders early the previous year. Henry wanted to entice him back to England and interrogate him about his associates.

1495

This was another year dominated by the problem of the pretender Warbeck. In early January, Sir Robert Clifford returned to London and turned king's evidence, revealing information about the alleged treasons of Warbeck's co-conspirators. Among those accused were Henry's lord chamberlain, Sir William Stanley, and his steward, Lord Fitzwalter. Show-trials started on 29 January, and their first victims included the Dean of St Paul's, the head of the Blackfriars in England, and Sir Thomas Thwaites, who had been an official in Calais. Twelve men were condemned to death as traitors, but the king commuted the sentence of five of them to imprisonment. Next, Stanley was tried and condemned to death. In this case, however, Henry's mercy extended only to allowing him to be beheaded rather than hanged, drawn and quartered, and Stanley was duly executed on Tower Hill on 16 February. Fitzwalter was put on trial on 23 February, but his life was spared, and he was imprisoned in Guisnes, near Calais, where his brother-in-law held office.

In February, Gerald Fitzgerald, 8th Earl of Kildare, was arrested and transported back to England under suspicion of supporting Warbeck. In reaction to his arrest, the Geraldine clan took to arms, and Kildare's

41

LEFT: **Philip the Fair (1478–1506)** *was the son of Maximilian and Mary of Burgundy. On his mother's death he inherited her title to the Duchy of Burgundy, including the provinces of the Low Countries. He was recognized as an adult ruler in 1495, and two years later he married Joanna, the daughter of Ferdinand and Isabella of Spain. After initially supporting the pretender Warbeck, he made alliances with Henry VII and closed the Low Countries to Henry's rebels and enemies. The painting is a 16th-century Flemish portrait. Around his neck is the badge of the chivalric Order of the Golden Fleece.*

ABOVE: **Luxury goods from Italy and the Low Countries** *were imported into England for wealthy men, especially courtiers. This flask (c.1500) is decorated with the portrait of Henry VII, possibly copied directly from a coin; on its other side is his personal emblem of portcullis and chains. It is made of lattimo (milky) and coloured glass, a type perfected in Venice and especially fashionable in European courts before the end of the 15th century. It may have been created as a special commission or else was one of the gifts for Henry VII brought to London in 1506 on behalf of Guidobaldo da Montefeltro, Duke of Urbino (1482–1508).*

The unfortunate end of Sir William Stanley

Upon the which Monday being the 16th day of February [1495] about 11 of the clock was the said Sir William Stanley led from the Tower Gate unto the scaffold upon the hill between two of the sheriff's officers, and there beheaded. This man was of great strength in Cheshire and Lancashire, and had many mighty landed men at his retinue, so that he might arere [raise] a mighty people in a short season and over that he was of excellent substance in moveable goods beside his land in so much that the common fame was blown of him after his death that the king's officers found of his in his castle of Holt 40,000 mark of ready coin above many rich jewels of gold and silver, and harness [equipment] sufficient for a great host of people the which he all lost with land and fees which extended above £2000 by year ... upon which Sir William's soul and all Christians Jesus have pity and compassion Amen.

[ROBERT FABIAN, *The Great Chronicle of London*, p. 258]

brother seized Carlow Castle. Lord Deputy Poynings besieged the castle during the spring and captured it in July. By this time Desmond was again in revolt and began a siege of Waterford.

In late June, Warbeck himself set out from the Low Countries with 15 small ships supplied by Margaret of Burgundy. He planned to make contact with potential supporters in Norfolk and then march on London. Strong winds, however, diverted his ships to the Kent coast. While Warbeck remained at sea, waiting to see if it was safe to disembark, about 300 of his men landed near Deal on 3 July and set up their banners in nearby villages. Henry's supporters were ready for them and attacked with arrows. Perhaps 150 of Warbeck's men were slaughtered or else they drowned in their attempt to escape.

The 163 who survived were captured, brought to London and hanged 'in sundry places'[21] in the eastern and southern counties, where they were thought to have sympathizers.

Warbeck's flotilla sailed on to Waterford, where on 23 July he met up with Desmond, who was besieging the city. His small force joined the fighting and his ships were used as part of the blockade. In early August Poynings arrived, broke the blockade with his artillery and captured three of Warbeck's ships. Although Desmond eluded capture and refused a pardon, the Irish rebellion was essentially over. Soon after his repulse from Waterford, Warbeck sailed to Scotland where he expected a warm welcome from James IV, who had previously sent him ships and troops. He was not to be disappointed. On 20 November, James received 'Prince Richard' at his palace of Stirling.

Meanwhile, at the English court, the royal couple suffered a personal loss. In October, Elizabeth, the youngest daughter of the king and queen, died aged about four. She was buried in Westminster Abbey.

1496

In the second week of January, James IV of Scotland paid for, and celebrated, the wedding of the pretender Warbeck to a distant cousin, Lady Katherine Gordon. Soon afterwards the king allowed Falkland Palace to be used by Warbeck as his base. Together they planned an invasion of England with the aim of winning the throne for 'Richard IV' and the border town of Berwick for James.

Henry met this danger by building up alliances, fortifying the border and raising an army. He was successful in the first task, when on 24 February he reached an agreement with Philip of Burgundy. The Spanish monarchs Ferdinand and Isabella had informed Philip that Warbeck was an impostor and advised

'with banner displayed, furnished with great people ... for the war'

him against giving assistance. Listening to their counsel, because he was seeking a Spanish marriage alliance, Philip opened up negotiations with Henry, lifted the trade embargo and signed the treaty known as the *Magnus Intercursus*. In accordance with its terms, preferential commercial arrangements were introduced for English merchants in the Low Countries. Just as importantly from Henry's point of view, the treaty stipulated that the Yorkist Margaret of Burgundy would be deprived of her lands if she harboured the pretender again. The Low Countries were now closed to Warbeck.

On 18 July Henry also succeeded in detaching Warbeck from Maximilian when he entered into a 'holy league' against France. The league had actually been formed in March 1495 to stop French incursions into Italy, but only now did Henry join it, albeit with the provision that he would not be expected to fight. In gratitude, Alexander VI's papal nuncio brought to England the papal cap and sword of maintenance – the symbols of Henry's status as protector and defender of the church.

Before Henry could levy troops to defend his northern border, however, James IV and Warbeck mounted their invasion of England, crossing the River Tweed on 21 September 'with banner displayed, furnished with great people and all habiliments for the war'.[22] They expected the northern Yorkists to rally behind 'Richard IV', but no defections took place. James demolished a few isolated towers and briefly bombarded Heton Castle, but he retreated speedily on 25 September. To punish James and protect the border, Henry prepared for war. On 24 October he held a great council (attended by his lords and representatives from every borough), which granted him a loan of £120,000 to fight the Scots.

During the last two months of the year Henry lost both an opponent and an ally. On 24 November, the former rebel Lord John Fitzwalter was finally beheaded after he had made an attempt to escape from his prison in Guisnes. And on 18 December the king's uncle, Jasper Tudor, Duke of Bedford, died without any heirs.

Ireland was quiet during 1496, after the Earl of Desmond had submitted on 12 March. Henry decided that the rebellious Earl of Kildare, who had been cleared of treason, should now rule as his lord deputy, replacing Sir Edward Poynings. The earl arrived on 17 September and did good service in restoring order.

PREVIOUS PAGE: **Alexander VI (1431–1503)** *was pope from 1492 until August 1503. He is shown here in a detail from* The Resurrection *by Pinturicchio (1454–1513), a fresco from 1492–5 located at the Vatican's Appartamento Borgia. In 1495 Alexander helped to form the Holy League to expel the French from Milan. Delighted when Henry joined the league, the pope sent him a sword and cap of maintenance, which were received with due reverence on 30 October 1496.*

RIGHT: **Henry VII** *is depicted as a classical hero in this frontispiece to a volume of Latin poetry presented to the king in 1496. Based on the imagery in Petrarch's* Triumfi *poems, Henry sits on a throne in a niche of a scallop shell, carrying an orb and sceptre and wearing the closed imperial crown.*

THOMAS HOWARD
dux Norff obijt A° dm 1524

1497

In January, Henry requested two subsidies from Parliament to pay for his Scottish war. Parliament complied without complaint, but the taxpayers of Cornwall were resistant. In May, a local blacksmith, Michael Joseph An Gof, organized protesters to march from Bodmin to London. Not only the commons joined the demonstration, but also one nobleman (James Tuchet, 7th Baron Audley) and at least 25 of the West Country gentry. These gentlemen had felt excluded from Henry's patronage, and they probably intended to release the last serious Yorkist claimant, the Earl of Warwick, from the Tower and place him on the throne.

Much of the rebels' ire over taxation was directed at the Archbishop of Canterbury, John Morton. It was said that he told those who entertained him lavishly that they could obviously afford to contribute handsomely to a 'benevolence'; while, at the same time, those who showed frugality, in order to avoid this fate, were told that they must have a great deal stored away from which they could make their contribution.

The marchers progressed to London almost unopposed. On 16 June, the An Gof rebels – by now a crowd of about 16,000 – pitched camp on Blackheath just south of London. On 17 June, the Earl of Oxford, Lord Daubeney and Sir Humphrey Stanley – together commanding forces of about 25,000 men – set upon the rebels. It was a bloody rout, and perhaps 2000 of the rebels were killed in contrast to the small number of casualties on the king's side. Audley, An Gof and other rebel leaders were captured alive and later executed, but the rank and file of the rebels were pardoned. Those who had demonstrated their loyalty to Henry were knighted or promoted.

In early July, Henry began peace talks with the Scottish king but also continued preparations for war. James responded by encouraging Warbeck to leave Scotland. However, not wanting to lose face altogether, James crossed the border and on 1 August began a siege of Norham Castle, which lasted ten days. He only withdrew when the Earl of Surrey attacked Ayton Castle and looked set to move on to Edinburgh. Knowing he could not win a pitched battle, James challenged Surrey to single combat, but 'like a wise man and hardy knight'[23] the earl rejected the offer on the grounds that he was only a lieutenant not a king. Instead, Surrey offered a truce, which James accepted: the seven-year Truce of Ayton was signed in September.

After departing Scotland, Perkin Warbeck crossed to Ireland and made for Cork, but he could find no allies there, and besides he was pursued by the forces of the Earl of Kildare. So he sailed to Cornwall with three small ships and perhaps 120 armed companions. At Bodmin, some 3000

LEFT: **Thomas Howard (1443–1524), Earl of Surrey**, *proved to be a loyal servant of Henry VII after fighting against him at Bosworth. In May 1489 he was restored to his earldom, although most of his lands were withheld, and he was sent north to quell rebellion in Yorkshire. Having shown his value to the new regime, Surrey continued in the North as the king's lieutenant until 1499. In 1497 he repelled a Scottish attack on Norham Castle by* supporters of Perkin Warbeck and shortly afterwards concluded a truce with James IV. Under Henry VIII, Surrey won the great Battle of Flodden (1513) against the Scots and was rewarded with the Dukedom of Norfolk. The portrait is 16th-century.

Cabot, the king's explorer

The Venetian ... who went with a ship from Bristol in quest of new islands is returned, and says that 700 leagues hence he discovered land, the territory of the Grand Cham [Emperor of China]. He ... saw no human beings, but he has brought hither to the king certain snares which had been set to catch game, and a needle for making nets; he also found some felled trees, wherefore he supposed there were inhabitants, and returned to his ship in alarm

... The king has promised that in the spring our countryman shall have ten ships, armed to his order, and at his request has conceded him all the prisoners, except such as are confined for high treason, to man his fleet. The king has also given him money wherewith to amuse himself till then ... his name is John Cabot ... Vast honour is paid him; he dresses in silk, and these English run after him like mad people, so that he can enlist as many of them as he pleases

... The discoverer of these places planted on his new-found land a large cross, with one flag of England and another of St Mark, by reason of his being a Venetian, so that our banner has floated very far afield.

[Lorenzo Pasqualigo to his brothers Alvise and Francesco, London, 23 August 1497, from *Calendar of State Papers*, Venetian, vol. I, no. 752, p. 262]

disgruntled men, 'whereof the most part were naked', joined his cause and marched on Exeter.[24] The rebels, now numbering some 8000 men, assaulted Exeter on 17 September. The city held out well against the rebel force for two days. Unwisely Warbeck then retreated to Taunton, an unwalled city that was impossible to defend. Cut off from an escape route by sea, he fled in disguise into Hampshire where he sought sanctuary at Beaulieu Abbey. The pretender finally surrendered to Lord Daubeney when offered a pardon.

On 5 October, Perkin Warbeck met King Henry at Taunton and publicly admitted that he was an impostor. 'Taking him in his company', Henry returned to London 'in triumphal style'.[25] With Warbeck entirely discredited, Henry could afford to be generous. He treated the young man 'graciously' and allowed him to remain in his court 'at liberty with many other benefits'.[26]

48

RIGHT: **The Italian explorer Giovanni Caboto (c.1450–1498)**, *anglicized as John Cabot, made three important voyages from Bristol in a search for a new route westwards to Cathay (China). On 5 March 1496, Henry gave him and his three sons – Ludovico, Sebastian and Sancio – full authority to sail to all parts, regions and coasts of the eastern, western and northern seas. On his second voyage of 1497, Cabot landed in Newfoundland (or possibly Cape Breton in Nova Scotia), which he claimed for Henry, who rewarded him with an annuity of £20. However, Cabot never returned from his third voyage, which set off in 1498. This scene depicting the Cabots is from a work in the Doge's Palace in Venice.*

1498

During Easter, Henry's court went to Kent, where it heard the news of the French king Charles VIII's death and the accession of Louis XII. In May and June the court went on progress to Oxfordshire, Hertfordshire and Essex. On Sunday 9 June, Perkin Warbeck stole out of Westminster Palace but was recaptured within a week. On his return to the Tower, he was publicly exhibited on scaffolds and stocks, 'mocked by the people and the target of their scurrility'.[27]

This year, John Cabot set out from Bristol on a third voyage in search of lands across the Atlantic. 'In the event he is believed to have found the new lands nowhere but on the very bottom of the ocean, to which he is thought to have descended together with his boat.'[28]

The fate of a pretender

Now [1498] their dying day *began to draw near for Peter [Perkin] Warbeck and Earl Edward of Warwick, since they were sunk by the same storm. For Peter, either because he was irked by being kept in custody, or solicited to a new rebellion by his friends, or again because he was always driven by an urge for self-destruction, decided to attempt an escape ... Therefore he deceived his jailors and fled. But he only managed to put himself into tighter confinement and hastened his execution. For while he hastened towards the coast, but had only gone a short distance, news spread of his escape, and all the roads were blocked by the royal servants who had been his guardians. Terrified by the shouts of his pursuers and forced to turn aside from his intended way, he came to Bethlehem Abbey, a Carthusian monastery, and threw himself on the mercy of the prior of the place, humbly begging him to go to the king and intercede for his life. The prior, taking pity on the man's misfortune, went to the king and told him about Peter, pleading for his life with many entreaties, and this he obtained. And so Peter was fetched back to the court at Westminster and subjected to disgrace. He was placed outside the front door in stocks for an entire day, and was jeered by the common folk, who spared him no insult. On the day he was brought through London for all to see, and subject to the same humiliation for a number of hours in the market place. Finally he was thrown into the Tower.*

[POLYDORE VERGIL, *Anglica Historia*, 1555 EDITION, EDITED ONLINE BY DANA F. SUTTON]

50

RIGHT: **Henry VII in middle age** *remained healthy and active, Polydore Vergil describing him in the 16th century as 'slender, but well built and strong; his height above the average', 'remarkably attractive', and with eyes that were 'small and blue'. However, his teeth were 'few, poor and blackish; his hair was thin and white; his complexion sallow'. This likeness of him is a 16th-century portrait.*

HENRICI · VII

The clergy and the law

For among the English the clergy are held in such respect that a priest condemned of treason, like ordained priests guilty of other crimes, is spared his life, which has come about since by ancient custom bishops do not have the right to try cases for these kinds of wrongdoing, and so they cannot defrock men thus condemned, who are consequently not put to death. What about the fact that those convicted of a capital crime who know how to read are treated the same way, except for traitors? This is because they are deemed to be akin to the clergy, and thus are spared and imprisoned. But, in case they should escape, lest they have any further hope of leading a normal life, the letter M, for murder, is branded on the palm of their right hand beneath the base of the thumb, or else T, for theft. If those thus branded are caught committing the same crime again, they are put to death on the spot. Henry himself was responsible for introducing this custom, in the second year of his reign, and I believe he borrowed it from the French.

[POLYDORE VERGIL, DISCUSSING A PRIEST IMPLICATED IN PLOTS SURROUNDING THE EARL OF WARWICK IN 1498, *Anglica Historia*, 1555 EDITION, EDITED ONLINE BY DANA F. SUTTON]

52

RIGHT: **The Tower of London**, *depicted here c.1500, was frequently used by the Tudors as a jail for political prisoners. This representation is from the frontispiece to a volume of poems presented to Henry VII, and his arms supported by lions can be seen in the border below. Tower Bridge and the gothic St Paul's are in the background. The colonnaded building is probably the customs house. The figure in the White Tower, both writing at a table and looking out from an upper window, is Charles, Duke of Orleans, who was captured at Agincourt in 1415 and was said to have written the poems.*

1499

Two happy family events occurred this year. On 24 February the third son of Henry and Elizabeth was christened Edmund in the friary church at Greenwich. More importantly dynastically, on 19 May a proxy marriage ceremony was enacted between Prince Arthur and Katherine of Aragon at Tickhill Manor, near Bewdley.

On 1 July, Edmund de la Pole, 8th Earl of Suffolk, travelled without licence to St Omer, a town in Picardy ruled by Philip the Fair. His ostensible reason for leaving England was that he feared punishment for killing a man in a London street-fight. However, he also bore resentments against Henry, who had confiscated some of his ancestral estates and reduced him in status from a duke to an earl on his father's death in 1492. His flight caused Henry much anxiety. After all, Suffolk was the younger brother of the Earl of Lincoln who had fallen at Stoke in 1487 and could be another claimant to raise the Yorkist flag against him. Henry, therefore, put pressure on Philip to have Suffolk expelled. Suffolk returned home, but remained at liberty.

In August, news circulated about a Yorkist plan to liberate the Earl of Warwick and Perkin Warbeck from the Tower of London. With this 'evidence' of treason in his hands, Henry ordered the deaths of these two thorns in his side. Warbeck was hanged at Tyburn on 23 November and the unfortunate Warwick was beheaded the next day. 'The entire population mourned the death of the handsome youth', whose only fault was to be born in the Yorkist house.[29]

Es nouuelles dalbion
Il vous en plaist escouter
Mon frere & mon compaignon
Sachiez qua mon retourner
Ay este deca la mer
Recu a ioyeuse chiere

A metropolis described

At present, all the beauty of this island is confined to London; which although sixty miles distant from the sea, possesses all the advantages to be desired in a maritime town ... the Londoners live comfortably ... it abounds with every article of luxury, as well as with the necessaries of life: but the most remarkable thing in London, is the wonderful quantity of wrought silver ... In one single street, named the Strand, leading to St Paul's, there are 52 goldsmith's shops, so rich and full of silver vessels, great and small, that in all the shops in Milan, Rome, Venice, and Florence put together, I do not think there would be found so many of the magnificence that are to be seen in London. And these vessels are all either salt cellars, or drinking cups, or basins to hold water for the hands; for they eat off that fine tin [pewter], which is little inferior to silver. These great riches of London are not occasioned by its inhabitants being noblemen or gentlemen; being all, on the contrary, persons of low degree, and artificers [craftsmen] who have congregated there from all parts of the island, and from Flanders, and from every other place.

[AN ANONYMOUS VENETIAN NOBLEMAN, IN *A Relation of the Island of England about the year* 1500, PP. 41–3]

1500

In May, Henry and Elizabeth visited Calais. On 9 June, he met with Philip the Fair of Burgundy, who came to see him 'to pay his respects'. The two rulers 'had a lengthy exchange of views',[30] and Philip was well entertained with a banquet and dance in which the duke 'danced with the ladies of England'.[31] On 16 June, Henry and Elizabeth returned to England, and just three days later their third son, Edmund, died at Hatfield. He was buried in Westminster Abbey.

On 12 October Cardinal Morton died, 'a man of worthy memory for his many and great acts, and specially for his great wisdom'.[32] Thousands of others died from a 'sweating sickness' that afflicted London from July to November.

ABOVE AND RIGHT: **Hunting and falconry** *were popular sports among the Tudor nobility, as depicted in these woodcut illustrations. The 16th-century* Book of Falconry *shows a falconer with his goshawk, one of the larger birds of prey. The simple hunting scene with dogs is from* A Book of Roxburghe Ballads.

The young Prince Arthur *married Katherine of Aragon at St Paul's on 14 November 1501. Arthur had then passed the minimum male age (by canon law) for 'cohabitation' in marriage, which was 14. Katherine, born also in 1486, was comfortably over the female age for cohabitation, which was only 12. This portrait of Arthur was perhaps painted two years earlier and he looks slender, even frail. He was also rather short; at the age of 15 he stood a foot shorter than his younger brother, Henry. This is the only authenticated portrait of the prince, probably because portrait-painting did not become fashionable until the 1520s. He is holding a white 'gillyflower' (a wild carnation or pink), a symbol of purity and royalty.*

Katherine of Aragon (1485–1536) *was the youngest daughter of the Spanish monarchs Ferdinand and Isabella. Like her first husband, Prince Arthur, she was very well educated. Her skill in Latin and knowledge of classical and vernacular literature brought her the admiration of the Spanish humanist Juan Luis Vives and of Erasmus of Rotterdam, who regarded her as a model of Christian womanhood. Plans began for her marriage to Arthur as early as 1487, but the proxy marriage took place only in May 1499. This portrait of a young woman, thought to be Katherine, is by Michel (or Michiel) Sittow (1469–1525).*

1501

In August, the Earl of Suffolk again left England without royal permission. This time he left with his brother Richard and made for the court of the Holy Roman Emperor, in the hope that Maximilian would support his claim to the English crown. When Henry learned of Suffolk's flight, 'he was greatly disturbed, regretted that he had spared him on the first occasion, and began to fear fresh upheavals'.[33] During October, 61 men from East Anglia who were thought to be Suffolk's friends or followers had to enter into financial bonds to ensure their loyalty to the king.

On 2 October, Katherine of Aragon landed at Plymouth for her marriage to Prince Arthur. From there, her entourage began a slow and ceremonious progress to London, which allowed many people in the South to catch a sight of their future queen. On the afternoon of Friday 12 November, Katherine made a grand entry into London. The city authorities organized elaborate pageants to greet her; and she was welcomed with speeches delivered by actors dressed up to represent saints and the main attributes of chivalric kingship – namely virtue, nobility and policy.

Two days later, Arthur and Katherine, 'both clad in white satin', were married in St Paul's in a ceremony that lasted well over two hours. 'Wonderful it was to behold the riches of apparel of lords and gentlemen of the court that day.'[34] Prince Henry and the Spanish legate led the bride out of the church and escorted her to Baynard's Castle, the historic palace of the house of York, for the lavish wedding feast: it consisted of 12 dishes for the first course, 15 for the second and 18 for the third. After all the celebrations, including a series of jousts, the couple moved to Ludlow on the border with Wales, where Arthur's household was established. The question of whether their marriage was consummated or not would prove vital in years to come.

RIGHT: **Tournaments were frequent and popular** *during Henry VII's reign, and his son Henry was a keen and adventurous jouster until near the end of his life. In this illustration from a Book of Hours (c.1520–30), a game of 'hobby horses' takes place in the foreground, in which pikemen vie with the armoured horsemen, while the action of the 'tilt' is visible in the background.*

A royal marriage

Then upon the Sunday *following being St Erkenwald's Day and the 14th day of November [1501] ... was my lord prince [Arthur] and my aforesaid lady princess [Katherine of Aragon] being both clad in white satin married and solemnised in matrimony by the Archbishop of Canterbury [Henry Deane], having about him 19 bishops and abbots then mitred, and the king and queen with my lady the king's mother [Margaret Beaufort] and many other estates stood in secret wise within the place above named [St Paul's] which through lattice might hear and behold all the circumstance of the said solemnisation which endured well upon 2 hours or more, for over the Sacramental office there were read sundry instruments and other writings ...Wonderful it was to behold the riches of apparel of lords and gentlemen of the court that day and the mighty poysant [heavy] chains of gold ... And when the mass was finished my said lady princess was led by the Duke of York [Henry] upon the right side and a legate of Spain upon that other side, and so conveyed ... into ... the palace.*

[ROBERT FABIAN, *The Great Chronicle of London*, PP. 310–11]

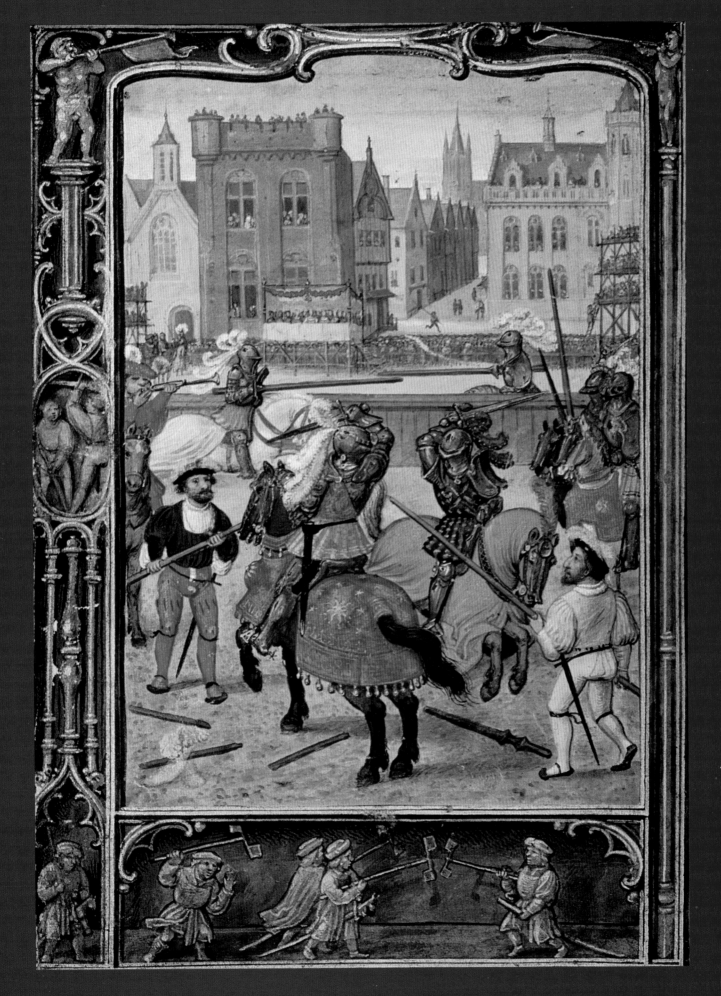

1502

On 24 January 1502, three treaties were signed with James IV of Scotland: a treaty of perpetual peace, a treaty of marriage between the 35-year-old king and Henry's 12-year-old daughter Margaret, and a treaty for preservation of order in the Marches, the Anglo-Scottish border areas. The following day, Margaret was married by proxy to James, and the occasion was celebrated in London with bonfires, free wine and a *Te Deum*.

April, however, brought traumatic news. On 2 April Henry VII's heir apparent, Arthur, died at Ludlow. When Henry was told two days later, 'he sent for the queen, saying that he and his queen would take the painful sorrows together'. She comforted her husband, reminding him of their three surviving children and that 'God is where he was, and we are both young enough' to conceive again. Only after she had returned to her chamber, did she break down so that 'those about her were fain to send for the king to comfort her'.[35] Neither parent attended their son's funeral at Worcester Cathedral, where the Earl of Surrey represented Henry as chief mourner. Soon afterwards Elizabeth did conceive again.

In May, some of the Earl of Suffolk's adherents were arrested. One of them – Sir James Tyrell – was executed and it was claimed that he had confessed to the murder of the two Yorkist princes in the Tower during the reign of Richard III.

Also in this year, a realistic image of the king's visage replaced a more stylized depiction on some of the realm's coins.

LEFT: **The Treaty of Perpetual Peace (1502),** *optimistically entitled, was the document in which the marriage of Princess Margaret (1489–1541) to Scotland's James IV was agreed. The borders of the document, which is held at The National Archives, illustrate the thistle (James's emblem), the Tudor rose, and the marguerete representing Margaret.*

ABOVE: **Innovations in the coinage** *were made during Henry VII's reign. In 1489 the king introduced this new gold coin, the sovereign, which derived its name from the majestic portrait of the monarch enthroned. It was worth 20 shillings, and was effectively the first pound coin.*

A queen's funeral

And upon a Wednesday being the 22nd day of February 1503 the said corpse lying in a char [chariot or cart] and a figure of a queen lying upon the said corpse was conveyed honourably ... through the high streets of the city unto the abbey of Westminster ... and from Whitechapel unto the Temple Bar all the streets were garnished with torches burning ... and upon the other side stood the fellowships in their liveries ... that day burnt at once over 2000 torches ... and at every church ... as the corpse passed, a solemn peal with all the bells was rung, and the curate of that church ready ... to incense the said corpse as it passed by, and thus was this gracious princess with the king's chapel and others ... singing all the way before her conveyed unto Charing Cross where met with her the abbot ... of Westminster, and so with a due solemnity ... brought the corpse unto the minster door, and there laid upon certain lords' shoulders and borne unto the void space between the high altar and the choir where in a vault purposely made for her, since she died, her grace was laid until the new chapel were fully edified and made, upon which soul our lord have mercy and all Christian amen.

[ROBERT FABIAN, *The Great Chronicle of London*, PP. 321–2]

62

RIGHT: **Margaret Tudor and James IV of Scotland** *were married on 8 August 1503. They had five children, only two of whom survived, one of them posthumously. Whether or not they were happy together is unknown, but throughout the marriage James continued to visit his mistress, by whom he had several illegitimate children. The illustration of the couple is from the Seton Armorial, a 1591 bound manuscript containing images of Scottish royalty and coats of arms.*

1503

The year began with yet another grievous family loss for the king. On 2 February, Elizabeth gave birth to a daughter but died nine days later; her baby did not long survive her. Elizabeth's body lay in state for 11 days in the Tower, and was then conveyed for its burial in Westminster Abbey. A funeral procession of 200 mourners accompanied the bier, with an effigy of the queen on top, and passed through the streets of London – lined with torches – to the sounds of the tolling of the church bells and the singing of friars.[36] Henry was ill for several weeks afterwards, and he was thought to be close to death.

The activities abroad of the Earl of Suffolk continued to concern the king. On the first Sunday of Lent (5 March) at Paul's Cross, 'a solemn curse with book, bell and candle' was laid upon Suffolk.[37]

At the Bishop of Salisbury's palace in Fleet Street, Henry, the new Prince of Wales, was betrothed to his brother's widow Katherine of Aragon on 25 June, in order to preserve the alliance with Spain. In the formal agreement drawn up it was settled that the marriage would take place following receipt of the necessary papal dispensation for Henry to marry his sister-in-law, the payment of the second portion of the dowry agreed for the first marriage, and Henry reaching the age of 15 in June 1506.

In early July, Princess Margaret left for Scotland 'where she was joyously and honourably, after their manner, received'.[38] Her marriage to James IV, called for by the treaty of 1502, was solemnized in the chapel of Holyroodhouse on 8 August. Three days previously, on 5 August, King Henry lost his most influential financial administrator, Sir Reginald Bray. He was buried at Windsor.

James the fourt
Began his Rawne.
1489 He maried
Margaret eldest dochter
of Henry the Sebinth:

18

1504

Parliament met in January and passed a new act against 'retaining', the maintenance by nobles of private retinues. The statute closed a loophole in existing legislation by prohibiting retaining for any purpose other than maintaining a lord in his household. This Parliament also passed 51 acts of attainder in an attempt to deal with the Earl of Suffolk and his adherents, as well as legislation to prevent merchant companies fixing prices.

On 9 March, William Warham was enthroned as Archbishop of Canterbury. The following month, on St George's Day (23 April), Henry rode in procession to Windsor with the Knights of the Garter and placed in the chapel a relic of the saint, which was a gift from the Emperor Maximilian. At Westminster Abbey, the king founded a chapel in July.

In October, Edmund Dudley entered the king's service, while Sir Richard Empson became a more influential royal servant. Both men would attract significant unpopularity.

The papal dispensation allowing Prince Henry to marry Katherine of Aragon finally arrived from Rome in November. However, King Henry had reason to question whether this marriage now suited him. On the death of Isabella of Castile on 26 November, a succession dispute had arisen. Although her heir was her eldest daughter Joanna (the wife of Philip the Fair of Burgundy), Isabella had left a will naming her husband Ferdinand as governor of Castile during his lifetime. Spain was now divided between the adherents of Ferdinand and those of Joanna. In these circumstances, an alliance with Ferdinand no longer seemed advantageous.

64

ABOVE: **William Warham (c.1450–1532)** *was appointed lord chancellor on 21 January 1504 and enthroned as Archbishop of Canterbury on 9 March the same year. Before then, he had been employed by Henry VII on a number of diplomatic missions, and he briefly acted as Bishop of London during 1502 and 1503. He became the longest-serving primate of England. This characterful portrait was based on a drawing by Holbein the Younger and painted five years before Warham's death.*

RIGHT: **The indenture for the king's chapel** *in Westminster Abbey (now known as the Henry VII Chapel) marked its founding on 16 July 1504. Regarding himself as heir of the Lancastrian kings, Henry placed his tomb next to Henry V's chantry and planned to transfer to the abbey Henry VI's remains, which were buried at Windsor; this reburial never took place. The cost of the chapel was at least £20,000.*

His indenture

sciptyte made betwene
the moost cristien king
henry the vij by the grace
of god king of Englande
and of ffraunce and lord
of Ireland the xvj day
of July ~ the nynetene
yere of his moost noble
reigne of the oon partie
and the moost Reuerend

ffader in god William Archebusshop of Caunterbury of the seconde
partie and the right Reuerend fader in god Richard Busshop of
wynchestre of þ thirde partie and John Islip Abbot of the monastie
of sainte Peter of Westm and the Prioure and Couuent of
the same place of the fourth partie and the Deane and Chanons
of the king free chapell of oure ladie and sainte Stephen the
furst martir within the king palois of Westm of the vth partie
and the Deane and Chapitre of the Cathedrall churche of sainte
Paule in the Citie of London of the vjth partie and the Mayre
and Comaltie of the Citie of London of the vijth partie Witnessith
that where by indentures made betwene the said king o souuain
lord and the said Abbot Prioure and Couuent for them and
thair Successours being date the date of the date of these present
The Same Abbot Prioure and Couuent haue couenanted
and graunted and bounde them and thair successours to the
said king oure souuain lord his heyes and successours that

1505

Henry VII decided to help Joanna and her husband Philip secure the throne of Castile. In February 1505, he offered them a loan of £138,000 to help pay for their voyage to Spain. Given this new situation, an alliance with Ferdinand was no longer part of Henry's foreign policy agenda. Consequently, on 27 June 1505, Prince Henry formally repudiated his betrothal to Katherine on the grounds that he had not consented to the earlier marriage contract. King Henry then put out feelers for two new marriages: between himself and Maximilian's daughter Margaret, the widowed Duchess of Savoy; and between Prince Henry and Eleanor, the young daughter of Philip and Joanna. However, while planning his marriage, King Henry was also giving thoughts to his death and posthumous reputation: in this year he hired the Italian sculptor Guido Mazzoni to work on his tomb in Westminster Abbey, a project that had begun some four years earlier.

In the sphere of domestic finances, Sir Richard Empson was appointed Chancellor of the Duchy of Lancaster. In this post he set about increasing the king's landed income. He also chaired the council learned in the law (an offshoot of the royal council), where he worked to maximize royal revenues. This he did by such means as exploiting feudal dues such as wardship (the right to take the income from the lands of under-age tenants-in-chief and to arrange or sell their marriages), pursuing old debts and manipulating the penal laws in the king's interests.

'the south-west wind began to blow with such sternness'

1506

In January, a great tempest hit England, inflicting much damage. The same tempest caused Philip and Joanna, who were on their way to Castile, to land at Weymouth on 16 January. Henry saw an opportunity in their misadventure; 'realising that he had been given by divine providence the opportunity of

RIGHT: **Philip the Fair of Burgundy and Joanna of Castile** *had been married in 1496 and together had six children: two boys and four girls. In these panels from a triptych of the Last Judgement, Philip is shown in full armour, with uplifted sword in his right hand, presented as the ultimate earthly judge. On his ermine cape he wears the chain of the Order of the Golden Fleece, and his breast armour is decorated with the Burgundian, Austrian and Spanish coats of arms. His wife, Joanna, bears the same coats of arms on her mantle. The triptych is attributed to the Master of Afflighem Abbey and dated to c.1505.*

laying his hands on' the errant Yorkist the Earl of Suffolk, 'whom he knew to be in Philip's power,'[39] he invited the couple to Windsor 'where they were lodged and feasted with all honour'.[40] On St George's Day, Philip was invested with the Order of the Garter. The tactics worked well. Philip agreed to surrender Suffolk to Henry on condition that the earl's life was spared. On 9 February Henry and Philip even signed an agreement so advantageous to England that it was known in the Low Countries as the *Malus Intercursus* (evil treaty). As one of its terms, the two rulers agreed that neither would harbour the rebels of the other. In March, Suffolk was imprisoned in the Tower and 'exhaustively interrogated'.[41] His evidence, though known to be unreliable, led to the brief imprisonment of George Neville, Baron Bergavenny.

Meanwhile, Ferdinand of Aragon bowed to circumstances and welcomed Philip and Joanna to Castile. However, Philip died suddenly on 25 September, and Ferdinand once again took over the rule of Castile on the questionable grounds that his daughter Joanna had gone mad with grief and was unfit to rule. (She would, though, become known as 'Joanna the Mad'.) Margaret of Savoy was appointed regent in Burgundy, and she rejected the idea of marriage to Henry.

ABOVE: **The 'Book of the Justices of Peace'** *was printed in 1506, and its publication is evidence of the growing importance of JPs in England under Henry VII. They were local gentlemen appointed by the lord chancellor to commissions of the peace. As such they were responsible for justice, operating through the court of quarter sessions. During the Tudor period their functions grew as they were given a range of new duties. For this reason their numbers also grew, and by 1500 there were between 20 and 35 JPs in each county. This is the frontispiece of the book.*

The mirroure of golde for the synfull soule.

The 'Great Tempest'

Also upon the evening of St Mary or the 15th day of January [1506], the south-west wind began to blow with such sternness that it turned over weak houses and trees and reaved [took] off houses the thatch and the tile passingly, the which so continued little or much from the said 15th day unto the 26th day of the said month and over that fell such plenty of rain that thereof ensued mighty and great floods one after another to the great hurt of sundry cattle and specially of sheep in sundry countries near unto the city, during which tempest the weathercock of Paul's was lifted off the socket and blown the length of the churchyard to a house having the sign of the Black Eagle where it fell with such a peise [impact] that it broke down a part of the penthouse of the foresaid tenement.

[ROBERT FABIAN, *The Great Chronicle of London*, P. 330]

LEFT: **The 'Mirror of Gold for the Sinful Soul'**, *whose frontispiece is shown here, was one of several devotional works produced by Margaret Beaufort, Henry VII's mother. Translated from the French, it was printed by Richard Pynson in 1506. Margaret's great-granddaughter Elizabeth Tudor – Queen Elizabeth I – produced another translation of the work while she was a princess.*

1507

Henry VII drew up a new book of rates for the customs in this year. As part of the king's campaign against retaining, and to discourage Yorkist challenges, Baron Bergavenny was indicted for retaining 471 dependants in contravention of the Statute of Liveries. He was fined £100,000 and forbidden to visit Kent, Surrey, Sussex or Hampshire without royal consent. He was probably selected for punishment because of his former friendship with the Yorkist Earl of Suffolk.

In November a marriage treaty was concluded between Charles, the elder son of Joanna and Philip of Burgundy, and Mary, Henry's younger daughter.

1508

In February Henry VII was too ill to leave Richmond Palace for a church service to mark the anniversary of his wife's death. In terms of foreign affairs, Italian politics took a new turn at the end of this year. In December, Pope Julius II formed the League of Cambrai – with Ferdinand of Aragon, Louis XII of France and Maximilian – against the powerful Venetian Republic. The French defeated the Venetians at Agnadello in May, which allowed the pope to seize towns he claimed within the Venetian mainland empire. Henry VII did not intervene or join the league, however, remaining aloof from these events. He saw no advantage in entering the Italian wars.

1509

In early April the ailing king made his will. Late on 21 April he died at Richmond Palace. The rule of the first Tudor monarch came to an end after a 24-year reign, in which, in the view of at least one man, the chronicler Polydore Vergil, this 'champion of justice ... gave the common people a life free from harm'.

'this champion of justice... gave the common people a life free from harm'

LEFT: **George Neville (c.1469–1535), 3rd Lord Bergavenny,** *was the most famous victim of Henry VII's financial rapacity and suspicious nature. In 1507 he was fined an astronomical £70,650 for having 'retained' 471 men and thereby transgressed the 1504 Statute of Liveries. Henry probably picked on Bergavenny because the baron had been a close friend of Edmund de la Pole, the Earl of Suffolk, and seemed to be retaining men with Yorkist connections. The fine was an instrument to guarantee his future loyalty. In the event, he paid very little of it and was pardoned for his offence by Henry VIII on his accession. The pen and chalk drawing is by Holbein the Younger, and is dated to the early 1530s, shortly before Bergavenny's death. At the end of the 1530s, his younger brother, Sir Edward Neville, and sister Jane stood accused of treasonable involvement with Henry VIII's expatriate enemy Cardinal Reginald Pole, and they paid with their lives.*

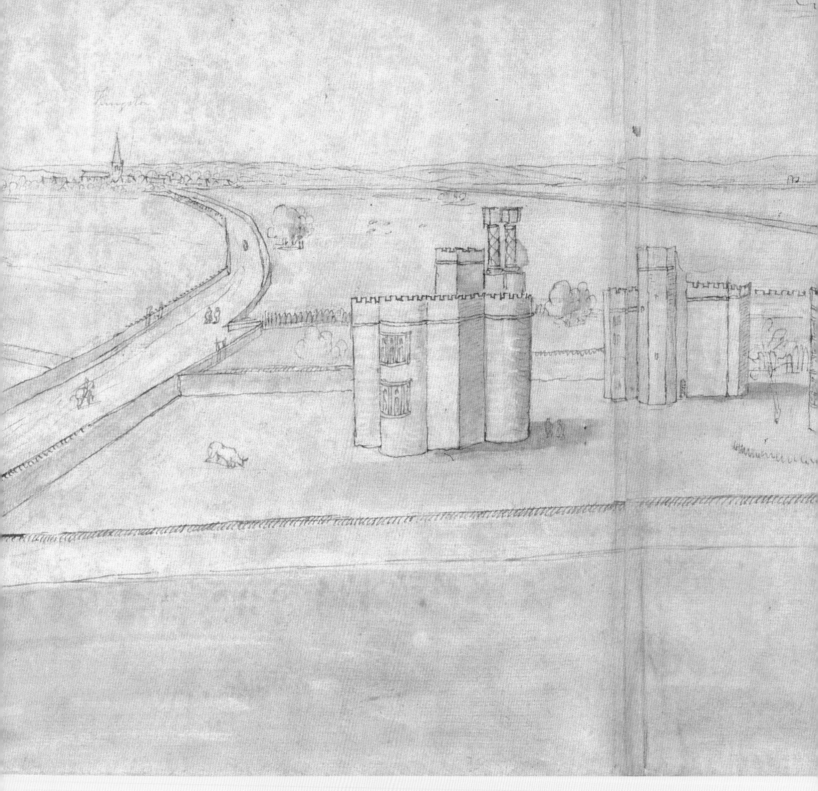

The Palace of Richmond *became Henry VII's favourite residence. Before its erection, the medieval palace at Sheen on the same site was where Henry had usually lived and where his children had had their nursery. But in 1497 a fire badly damaged Sheen and consumed 'many notable and excellent rich jewels and other things of superabundant value', according to The Great Chronicle of London. Henry immediately began a rebuilding programme that lasted over four years, and in the meantime the royal family lived at Eltham. The new palace, renamed Richmond after Henry's earldom, was built in red brick and constructed with courtyards, galleries and gardens in the style of the Burgundian court. This pen and ink drawing, by Anthonis van Wynegaerde (c.1550), presents a view from the other side of the Thames.*

Reflections and relics

... I [Henry VII] am a sinful creature, in sin conceived and in sin have lived, knowing perfectly that of my merits I cannot attain to the life everlasting, but only by the merits of the blessed passion and of thy infinite mercy and grace; nevertheless, my most merciful redeemer, maker and saviour ... We give and bequeath to the altar within ... our said tomb, our great piece of holy cross ... and also the precious relic of one of the legs of Saint George ...

[FROM THE LAST WILL AND TESTAMENT OF HENRY VII]

ABOVE: **Henry's signature** *can be seen at the top right of this first surviving page of his will, dated 31 March 1509. It provides extremely detailed instructions about his wishes, including the imagery on his tomb, the 10,000 masses he required, the alms he wanted distributed, the funeral arrangements and the special bequests. The written will is 37 pages long.*

RIGHT: **Henry VII's deathbed** *on the night of 21 April 1509 is shown in this drawing, surrounded by his courtiers, who are identified by their heraldic shields. It comes from the collection of Sir Thomas Wriothesley (d.1534), Garter King of Arms.*

Henry VII: Conclusion

The 16th-century chronicler Polydore Vergil criticized Henry VII for his severity and rapaciousness, especially in his later years. Was this criticism justified? Henry certainly employed spies and informers, set up show-trials and condemned many men to death for treason on weak evidence. He was also vigorous in raising money by means that some deemed oppressive. He exacted heavy fines from peers, leading gentry and bishops when they had committed technical offences; and he required them to enter into financial bonds to guarantee their loyalty. He encouraged his officials to be ruthless in exploiting his rights as a feudal landlord to the very last penny.

Yet, despite – or more probably because of – this ruthlessness, Henry VII succeeded where his immediate predecessors had not. The first Tudor ruled for 24 years, whereas the previous 24 years had seen 5 kings of England on and off the throne. Henry's son was the first monarch for many years to inherit the throne rather than win it by conquest. This achievement was substantial, for the first Tudor's claim to the throne had been weak, and the king had had to withstand challenges from several pretenders with powerful backers.

The monarchy that his son inherited was also in good shape. Although Henry VII was not liked by most of his nobility, they respected his authority. The royal coffers were full; the machinery of government operated relatively efficiently; the court

Henry VII, a 16th-century verdict

His body was slender but strong and solid, a little above average in height. His appearance was handsome, particularly when his expression was happy in conversation. He had blue eyes, few teeth, and sparse hair. His intellect was great and clever, and he was not averse to learning, his spirit excellent and bold even amidst the greatest perils, and his overall nature was almost divine. He managed his affairs with deliberation and gravity, so that he easily gained a reputation for prudence, since that he was not unaware that many eyes were fixed on the rise and fall of his fortune, and therefore that a sovereign should surpass others in wisdom as well as in power. For who would give a man anything if he knows him to be empty-headed? Furthermore, he was moderate, honest, frugal, affable, and kindly. He hated pride and arrogance so much that he was rough and harsh towards men marked by those vices. No man enjoyed such sway with him that he dared act as he please. What shall we say of the fact that in the end this was not even permitted his mother, an extremely prudent woman? He said this was his practice, so that he would be called a king who chose to rule rather than be ruled. He was a very severe champion of justice, and this one thing did the most to procure him popularity, since he gave the common people a life free from harm at the hands of the powerful and of rogues.

[POLYDORE VERGIL, *Anglica Historia*, 1555 EDITION, EDITED ONLINE BY DANA F. SUTTON]

was magnificent; and the reputation of England stood high among European monarchs.

As for the ordinary people, they unquestionably resented Henry's periods of high taxation, but otherwise life was less hard than it would be in the years to come. Agricultural problems and inflationary trends, resulting from demographic pressures, were only just beginning. The rhythms of life within the parish were undisturbed, in this still unquestionably Catholic kingdom. The cloth trade was booming, bringing employment to towns and the countryside alike. To the next generation, the reign of Henry VII would seem something of a golden age.

ABOVE: **A detail from the illuminated initial** *of the indenture (16 July 1504) for the king's chapel, Westminster Abbey, shows the enthroned Henry VII presenting bound ordinances to a group of kneeling prelates. William Warham, Archbishop of Canterbury, and Bishop Richard Fox of Ely are at the front before the king. Henry provided for prayers to be said daily in the new chapel. However, at the time of his death the monument for his tomb was uncompleted.*

HENRY VIII

Born in 1491, Henry became heir to the throne only in 1502, on the death of his elder brother Arthur. Even before this, though, his education was fitted for a Renaissance prince. Margaret Beaufort, who supervised his studies, provided her grandson with the best tutors of the day, including, for a time, the poet John Skelton.

His educational programme encompassed the classical literature, rhetoric and languages favoured in the 'new learning' of the humanists. As a result, Henry wrote and spoke Latin well. He was also fluent in French and knew some Italian and Spanish. Later in his life he took some lessons in Greek from the humanist scholar Richard Croke. In addition to this training, Henry was steeped in traditional chivalric literature. His library contained copies of Arthurian romances and Burgundian chronicles, such as Jean de Froissart's 'Life of Henry V', and much of his behaviour reflected their values and concepts of honour.

Henry was blessed with several natural talents. He was athletic, jousting with panache and drawing the bow 'with greater strength than any man in England'.[1] He was musical, playing several instruments 'most creditably', 'dancing magnificently', and he composed songs too.[2] He was intelligent and had intellectual pretensions; when king he enjoyed discussions with Sir Thomas More about mathematics, astronomy and theology.

During his father's lifetime, Henry held many titles but no responsibilities. Perhaps fearing that he would follow Arthur and his younger brother Edmund to an early grave, Henry VII was overprotective, limiting his remaining son's independence and freedom of action. While a prince, Henry made little impression on observers but, once king, he grew to be extrovert, charming and good-humoured, at least until he was crossed. Then he became cruel, abusive and unpredictable, and – like his father – he was feared rather than loved.

PREVIOUS PAGE: **Henry VIII** *(see pp. 162–3).*

LEFT: **The young Henry VIII,** *before he grew old and bloated, was considered a good-looking man. His complexion was fair and his hair inclined to ginger. He was tall (about 6 feet 2 inches), and at 21 years old his waist was 32 inches. His face was round and his neck long. When he was 29 years old, the Venetian ambassador described him as 'much handsomer than any other sovereign in Christendom' (Calendar of State Papers, Venetian). This portrait was painted c.1520.*

ABOVE: **John Skelton (c.1460–1529)** *entered Tudor royal service in 1488 and became a tutor to Prince Henry about 1496. In 1503 Skelton left London for Norfolk. Around 1512, he returned to court where he became 'orator regius', a spokesman for the king. In this role he wrote panegyrics and poems celebrating English victories in Scotland and France. Around 1519 he wrote a morality play, 'Magnificence', and soon afterwards penned satirical attacks on Cardinal Wolsey in 'Speke Parott' (1521), 'Colin Clout' (1521–2) and 'Why come ye not to courte?' (1522), which circulated in manuscript. But after 1523 Wolsey became Skelton's patron. The image is from the title-page to a collection of poems,* Against a Comely Coystrowne, *printed c.1527 by John Rastell.*

1509

Henry VII's death was kept secret for two days. On 24 April, his son was proclaimed king and immediately ordered the arrest of his father's two unpopular ministers, Richard Empson and Edmund Dudley. They were blamed for the extortionate money-raising and oppressive law-enforcement policies of Henry VII's last years and, less justifiably, accused of treason.

On Wednesday 9 May, Henry VII's corpse was transported from Richmond to St Paul's, where Margaret Beaufort's chaplain, John Fisher, Bishop of Rochester, delivered the sermon after the mass. Unusually for such an occasion, his words were not just a paean of praise but pointed out faults in the dead king. The next day, a funeral cortège of some six hundred mourners processed towards Westminster Abbey for the burial.

On 11 June, Henry married his brother's widow in the friary church at Greenwich. He claimed – somewhat unconvincingly – that he felt obliged to wed Katherine both by treaty requirements and a deathbed promise to his father. In reality the dynastic union was yet another way Henry could reverse his father's policies. Besides, he wanted a military alliance with Katherine's father, Ferdinand of Aragon, against France. Henry was keen to win honour on the battlefield and reclaim the ancestral lands in France lost by English kings in the mid-15th century.

The wedding ceremony was private. The opportunity for splendid celebrations came on the occasion of the monarchs' joint coronation. On Saturday 23 June, the royal couple left the Tower for Westminster, travelling along streets decked with tapestries and cloths of gold. Henry wore a doublet of crimson velvet trimmed with ermine and a jacket of

Henry and Katherine enthroned

The morrow following being Sunday, and also Midsummer's day [1509], this noble prince with his queen, at time convenient, under their canopies borne by the barons of the five ports [the Cinque Ports] went from the said palace, to Westminster Abbey upon cloth ... the which cloth was cut and spoiled [taken], by the rude and common people, immediately after their repair into the abbey, where, according to the sacred observance, and ancient custom his grace with the queen were anointed and crowned by the Archbishop of Canterbury, with other prelates of the realm there present, and the nobility, with a great multitude of commons of the same. It was demanded of the people whether they would receive, obey, and take the same most noble prince for their king, who with great reverence, love and desire, said and cried, 'yea, yea'. After the which solemnity, and coronation finished, the lords spiritual and temporal did to him homage, and returned to Westminster Hall ... What should I speak or write, of the sumptuous fine and delicate meats, prepared for this high and honourable coronation, provided for as well in the parties beyond the sea, as in many and sundry places, within this realm, where God so abundantly hath sent such plenty ... ?

[Henry VIII (Hall's Chronicle), EDITED BY CHARLES WHIBLEY, VOL. 1, PP. 7–8]

OPPOSITE ABOVE LEFT: **The coronation of Henry and Katherine** *took place a fortnight after their marriage on 11 June 1509. In this title-page from Stephen Hawes's* A Joyful Meditation *(1509), prelates are shown crowning the couple in what was seen as the union of the pomegranate (the emblem of the monarchs of Spain) and the Tudor rose. The pomegranate later became Katherine's personal emblem, ironically symbolizing fertility.*

gold encrusted with precious jewels. Katherine's gown was embroidered white satin; a coronet set with many rich pearls sat on her head; her hair hung down her back 'of a very great length, beautiful and goodly to behold'.[3] He rode on a horse; she was carried in a litter.

The next morning, Henry and Katherine were anointed and crowned at Westminster Abbey. Afterwards, all retired to Westminster Hall for a feast 'more honourable than of the great Caesar'[4] and then to a spectacular tournament, which lasted until nightfall and continued the next day. Among the guests at the coronation was Henry's grandmother, Lady Margaret Beaufort, who died five days afterwards. A few months later, on 1 November, Katherine's pregnancy was announced.

On 18 July, Edmund Dudley was tried and convicted of treason in London. Richard Empson's trial was deferred until October and held in Northampton Castle. Both men were sentenced to death.

Christopher Bainbridge, the Archbishop of York, was appointed Henry's ambassador to Rome on 24 September. His main job was to embolden Pope Julius II to fight against France.

ABOVE RIGHT: **John Fisher (1469?–1535)** *was Bishop of Rochester as well as the first professor of theology at the University of Cambridge, a post founded by Lady Margaret Beaufort. At Cambridge, Fisher encouraged the study of the classics, and he brought the great humanist Erasmus to the university in 1511 to teach Greek and theology. During the annulment crisis, Fisher staunchly defended Katherine's marriage to Henry and valiantly tried to resist the royal supremacy. Made a cardinal in May 1534, Fisher was soon afterwards charged with treason. He was executed on 22 June 1535 and canonized in 1935. This sketch, made at Windsor Castle, is by Holbein the Younger.*

OVERLEAF: **'Pastime with Good Company',** *a song for five voices, is one of the 33 songs usually attributed to Henry VIII and dates from around 1518. Henry was trained as a musician from an early age, played several instruments and sang from sight. He also composed and arranged music, working on masses, motets and part-songs. However, he did not write 'Greensleeves' as is popularly thought. The king was a great patron of music, and by 1547 he employed 58 musicians in his household. This musical notation is from a manuscript in the British Library.*

sett all goodly sport for my cofort who shall me let.

Pastime with good cpany I love & shall do tyl I dye

grutche who lest but none denye so god be plesed thus lene

Wyll I for my pastance hunt syng & dance my hart

is sett all goodly sport for my cofort who shall me lett.

youthe must have su daliance off good or yll su pastance.
Company me thynky then best all thought & fansys to deiest.
ffor idilnes is cheff mastres off vices all then who can say.
but myrth and play is best of all.

Company wt honeste is vertu vices to flie.
Company is good & ill but eny man hath hys fre wyll.
the best ensew the worst eschew my mynde shalbe.
vertu to vse vice to refuse thus shall I vse me.

1510

On 12 January, Henry entered his first joust as king. Though incognito, his identity was revealed during one of the bouts when it was feared, wrongly, that he had been hurt.

Henry's first Parliament met on 21 January. Among the statutes passed were several blaming Dudley and Empson for the injustices of the previous regime. Parliament also abolished the council learned in the law, a specialist branch of the royal council set up by Henry VII.

In the winter and spring of this year, Queen Katherine miscarried twice, the first time possibly in February (though the evidence is confusing) and then again in May.[5]

On 23 March a peace treaty was signed with France (a provisional measure), followed on 24 May by a treaty with Spain.

During May, Henry amused himself 'almost every day of the week with running the ring, and with jousts and tournaments on foot'.[6] 'The king being lusty, young, and courageous, greatly delighted in feats of chivalry, in so much that he made challenge of jousts, against all comers'.[7]

During his summer progress through the Midlands, Henry heard fresh complaints about the injustices of his father's ministers and resolved on their execution. Both Empson and Dudley were beheaded on Tower Hill on 17 August. 'By this action, all the indignation of the people was appeased, and everyone was grateful to the monarch for the punishment of the evil pair.'[8]

Henry at the tilt

From thence, the 8th day of November [1510], his grace [Henry] removed to Richmond, and willed to be declared to all noble men and gentlemen that his grace with two aides, that is to wit Master Charles Brandon and Master [William] Compton, during two days would answer all comers with spear at the tilt one day and at the tourney [tournament] with swords, the other.

And to accomplish this enterprise the 13th day of November, his grace armed at all pieces with his two aides entered the field, their bases and trappers were of cloth of gold, set with red roses, engraved with gold of embroidery: the counter part came in freshly apparelled every man after his device. At these jousts the king broke more staves than any other, and therefore had the prize. At the tourney in likewise, the honour was his.

[*Henry VIII* (*Hall's Chronicle*), EDITED BY CHARLES WHIBLEY, VOL. I, PP. 20–1]

RIGHT: **Desiderius Erasmus (1467?–1536)**, *the internationally celebrated humanist, had a great influence on Tudor scholarship and religious life. He first visited England in 1499, when he met the eight-year-old Prince Henry. After another brief stay in 1506, he returned for five years in 1509. His main English friends were all men of the 'new learning' – Sir Thomas More, John Colet (the Dean of St Paul's) and John Fisher. Erasmus was a great self-publicist, and he commissioned many self-portraits for distribution. His pose here, in Holbein the Younger's contemporary portrait, is the traditional one of the scholarly churchman, while the beret he wears is a symbol of free thought. The text he is working on is his 'Commentary on the Gospel of St Mark'.*

ABOVE: **The tournament of 12 and 13 February 1511** *was held to celebrate the birth in January of the king's shortlived son, Prince Henry. It was the most splendid and expensive of Henry's reign, costing a total of nearly £4400. This picture, from a 60-foot-long vellum roll commissioned by the king, depicts the king as the Challenger breaking his tilting stave on the helmet of one of the 'Answerers'. His charger's protective coat, or bard, is set with the queen's initial 'K'. Queen Katherine herself is depicted to the rear, sitting up in a bed because she has recently given birth. She is attended by ladies in waiting.*

ABOVE RIGHT: **This horse armour for tournaments** *was a gift from Emperor Maximilian I on the occasion of Henry VIII's first marriage. The protective covering, or bard, is embossed with a trailing design of pomegranates – the emblem of Spain – and the fire-steels and 'raguly' crosses of the Burgundian Order of the Golden Fleece. It was manufactured in Flanders by the workshop of Martin van Royne, who later became Henry's royal armourer.*

1511

On 1 January
Queen Katherine
delivered a son. In
celebration 'fires were
made and diverse
vessels with wine set
up'.[9] The prince's
baptism took place on
5 January, and a week
later Henry went on a pilgrimage of thanks to the shrine of the
Virgin at Walsingham. Immediately after Katherine had been
'churched' in February – the ceremony marking a woman's return to
the church after childbirth – a grand tournament was held in her
honour. But, 'after this joy came sorrowful chance', for the baby died
on 22 February. Henry 'made no great mourning outwardly' in order
to comfort his queen, who 'like a natural woman, made much
lamentation'.[10] At the end of September, however, the queen was
again 'thought to be with child'.[11]

In March, in accordance with his treaty with Ferdinand of
Aragon, Henry ordered Lord Thomas Darcy to take 1500 archers to
Spain and help fight the Moors. Darcy's force arrived at Cadiz in mid-
June, but by then Ferdinand had abandoned his crusade. Finding no
use for the English army, the Spanish king ordered it to leave
immediately.

In July Henry sent Sir Edward Poynings with 1000 archers to the
Low Countries to help Margaret of Savoy and Emperor Maximilian
suppress a revolt in Guelderland. Henry's purpose was to win the
emperor as an ally for a future war against France. The expedition
had some success in reducing several towns and castles before the
force returned to England in the autumn.

During this year, Pope Julius quarrelled with Louis XII, and on 4
October he organized a Holy League – comprising Spain, the Empire
and Venice – to combat French ambitions in Italy. Initially, Henry did
not join the league, as many of his clerical councillors opposed a war,
but, after Louis was excommunicated, Henry overcame these
objections. He joined the Holy League on 13 November.

89

1512

At the entertainments on Twelfth Night, 'the king with 11 other were disguised, after the manner of Italy, called a masque, a thing not seen afore in England'.[12]

At the opening of Parliament on 4 February, Archbishop Warham delivered an oration that justified a war against France, and a tax was soon afterwards granted to pay for it. Parliament also passed an act that denied clerics in minor orders the right of 'benefit of clergy' for a trial period. This meant that they would no longer have immunity from the king's courts when accused of serious crimes. (Ecclesiastical courts could not levy the death penalty, so they were perceived as more lenient.)

In May, English troops under Thomas Grey, 2nd Marquess of Dorset, landed at a town on the Spanish-French border with the intent of linking up with Ferdinand's troops and mounting a joint operation in southwestern France. Henry's objective was to re-conquer Guyenne, which Henry VI had lost in 1453. However, the English army – one that comprised 'the hand-picked flower of men in their military prime'[13] – saw no fighting at all, as Ferdinand failed to keep his pledge to assist Dorset's men. Instead, the Spanish king used his English allies as a decoy so that he could grab Navarre. Consequently, 'nothing worth recording was done in these parts by the important English army,'[14] and the soldiers returned home, 'glad that they were departed out of such a country, where they had little health, less pleasure and much loss of time'.[15]

During the summer, the English navy, by contrast, had some success and one disaster. Admiral Sir Edward Howard captured over sixty vessels (or so it was claimed), while patrolling the English Channel. On 10 August, however, catastrophe struck when Howard attacked a French fleet harboured at Brest. During a fierce naval struggle, the magazine of a French ship exploded, and the *Regent* (the largest of the English ships) was caught and destroyed in the flames. Some 600 Englishmen and about 1000 Frenchmen perished. After the ship's loss, Henry ordered the construction of the *Henry Grace a Dieu* as his new flagship.

Henry decided to go in person to fight the French, and in November his Parliament agreed and voted a tax.

'the hand-picked flower of men in their military prime'

Henry by the Groce of God Kings of England &c

ABOVE: **The 1512 Parliament** *called for war against France. In this portion of the Parliament Procession Roll of 1512, Henry is shown holding his sceptre as he processes on his way to the Parliament. In front of him, bearing the symbols of royal dignity, are the son of Edward Stafford, 3rd Duke of Buckingham (holding the sword of state), and the Garter king of arms (holding the cap of maintenance). The whole roll is 18 feet 4 inches (5.6 metres) long. This illustration is from a 17th-century copy at the British Library.*

OVERLEAF: **The 'Henry Grace a Dieu',** *generally known as the* Great Harry, *was built to replace the* Regent, *which had burned in 1512. It was the first four-masted ship in England and the largest to be built by Henry, who had a keen interest in things naval. The king's flagship, it was launched in his presence at Erith in June 1514. It could carry nearly 700 men, with a capacity of 1200 tons. Henry was inordinately proud of this ship, and he showed it off to Charles V when he visited Dover in 1522. The image is from the so-called Anthony Roll, a naval inventory named after the official who compiled it in 1546.*

1513

The year saw the death of Pope Julius II, on 12 February. Two weeks later, Cardinal Giovanni de' Medici was elected by the cardinals as Pope Leo X.

On 25 April, Admiral Howard launched a foolhardy attack on a French fleet anchored off Brest. While attempting to board a French galley, he was forced overboard and drowned. His brother, Sir Thomas Howard, replaced him as admiral, but operations in the Channel had to be suspended because the navy was short of soldiers and supplies.

Leaving behind Katherine as his regent, Henry sailed for Calais on 30 June with an army of around 13,000 men. To prevent a Yorkist coup during his absence from the kingdom (or in the event of his death), Henry ordered the execution of the Earl of Suffolk, who had languished in the Tower since 1506. After enjoying a triumphal entry into Calais, Henry marched his men to the small but well-fortified city of Thérouanne, a French enclave in the Low Countries. Two centuries before, Edward III had captured the city after his great victory at Crécy, and Henry was keen to emulate this feat of arms.

On 10 August, Maximilian arrived at a nearby town, and the two allies quickly arranged a meeting. Despite foul weather, Henry put on a fine display; he and his nobility were 'gorgeously appareled'. By contrast, Maximilian and his retinue all wore black, as they were in mourning for the emperor's deceased wife. On 14 August, the two rulers met again. This time they dined together in Henry's tent, and they displayed 'such cordiality that one might suppose them father and son'.[16]

On 16 August, Henry's army won the so-called 'Battle of the Spurs' against a French force sent to relieve Thérouanne. On 23 August, the besieged city surrendered, and the next day, Henry entered Thérouanne with great pomp – after which the city was looted and destroyed.

While he had been encamped before Thérouanne, Henry received a herald from James IV of Scotland. The messenger delivered an ultimatum that James would invade England if Henry did not withdraw immediately from France. Henry responded defiantly. In late August, James IV crossed into Northumberland. He stormed Norham Castle, razing it to the ground, and 'pushed on a further six miles, laying waste everything with fire and

The English expeditionary force

The army thus lingering [in Biscay, 1513], ever desirous to be at the business that they came for, their victual [food] was much part garlic, and the Englishmen did eat of the garlic with all meats, and drank hot wines in the hot weather, and did eat all the hot fruits that they could get, which caused their blood so to boil in their bellies, that there fell sick three thousand of the flux, and thereof died 18 hundred men ...

[*HENRY VIII* (*Hall's Chronicle*), EDITED BY CHARLES WHIBLEY, VOL. I, P. 46]

94

sword'.[17] Henry's lieutenant, Thomas Howard, Earl of Surrey, quickly mustered troops and confronted the Scots at Branxton Moor (also known as Flodden) late in the afternoon of 9 September. By nightfall the Scots had suffered a devastating defeat. James IV was one of at least 10,000 Scots slain, while the English losses were perhaps half that number.

Henry learned of this great victory while besieging the great city of Tournai, another French enclave in the Low Countries. Mindful of the fate of Thérouanne, the citizens of Tournai capitulated on 23 September without offering much resistance. Two days later, Henry staged a ceremonial entry and accepted the city's keys as King of France. Over the next few weeks, he celebrated his triumph with tournaments and entertainments. On 13 October he departed, leaving behind Sir Edward Poynings as governor with a garrison of 5000 to defend Tournai against recapture, and on 21 October he embarked for his return to England.

The flower of Scotland felled

Thus through the power of God on *Friday, being the 9th day of September, in the Year of our Lord MDXIII [1513] was James the Fourth King of Scots slain at Branstone [Branxton, later called Flodden] chiefly by the power of the Earl of Surrey, lieutenant for King Henry the VIII King of England, which [who] then lay at the siege before Tournai, and with the said king were slain:*

The Archbishop of St Andrews,
    the king's bastard son.
The Bishop of the Isles.
The Abbot of Inchaffray.
The Abbot of Kilwinning.

EARLS:
The Earl of Montrose.
The Earl of Crawford.
The Earl of Argyll.
The Earl of Lennox.
The Earl of Glencairn.
The Earl of Caithness.
The Earl of Cassilis.
The Earl of Bothwell.
The Earl Erroll Constable of Scotland.
The Earl Addill.
The Earl Atholl.
The Earl Morton.

LORDS:
The Lord Lonet.
The Lord Forbos.
The Lord Elphinstone.
The Lord Rothes.
The Lord Inderby.
The Lord Sinclair.
The Lord Maxwell and
    his four brethren.
The Lord Daunley.
The Lord Sempill.
The Lord Borthwick.
The Lord Bogony.
The Lord Arskyll.
The Lord Blakkater.
The Lord Cowyn.

Knights and gentlemen…

[Hall's Chronicle, EDITED BY HENRY ELLIS, P. 563 (MODERNIZED NAMES USED WHERE EQUIVALENTS EXIST)]

95

Within the image: IMPERATOR MAXIMILIAN'

ABOVE: **Henry VIII and Emperor Maximilian I,** *his ally at the time, met near Thérouanne, in the Low Countries, in August 1513. Despite Maximilian's superior status, Henry (on the right) is shown in this Flemish painting as equal in rank and power to the emperor. They are both seen twice: in the fore- and middle-ground. Also in the middle-ground, the Anglo-Burgundian cavalry is depicted beating off the French at the so-called Battle of the Spurs. In the background are the towns of Tournai (left) and Thérouanne, both of which were captured by the English in the war. Henry probably commissioned this painting after his capture of Boulogne in 1544.*

OVERLEAF: **The Battle of the Spurs** *was a trifling victory won by Henry's army in August 1513 at Guinegate, in Flanders. A troop of French cavalrymen, sent to get supplies into the besieged city of Thérouanne, was forced to retreat when confronted by English archers supported by Burgundian artillery. Because the English could see the spurs of the French as they fled in disarray, they dubbed the skirmish the 'Battle of the Spurs'. Very few soldiers were killed, but some 240 French noblemen were captured (including a prince of royal blood) as well as 9 or 10 of their banners and standards. This picture, of the Flemish school, was commissioned by Henry soon afterwards to commemorate his triumph.*

The Bataile of
Spvrs. anno.
1513

1514

Henry rewarded several men, during January of this year, for their role in the victorious campaigns in France and Scotland. Surrey was created 2nd Duke of Norfolk; his son, Thomas, became the new Earl of Surrey; and Henry's favourite, Charles Brandon, was raised to the peerage as Duke of Suffolk, although he had merely captained a ship during 1512. Thomas Wolsey, who had proved remarkably effective in organizing the logistics of the French war, became Bishop of Lincoln.

In February, the king fell ill with measles (or possibly even smallpox), but he soon recovered. In early May, he grew angry when Maximilian tried to postpone a projected marriage between his grandson Charles and Henry's sister Mary. Henry became even angrier when he learned that peace negotiations were in progress between Maximilian and Louis XII. Feeling betrayed and fearing political isolation, Henry decided to listen when Louis sued for peace in June. The two monarchs signed a treaty on 7 August, which allowed Henry to keep Tournai, provided him with a large pension and arranged a marriage between the 18-year-old Mary and the 52-year-old French king (he had recently been widowed). On 18 August, Mary married Louis by proxy.

Henry's other sister, Margaret, the Dowager Queen of Scotland, also remarried in August. Although her late husband had stipulated that she could only govern as regent for their infant son James V for as long as she remained unwed, she took Archibald Douglas, 6th Earl of Angus, as her second husband on 6 August. This marriage upset the Scottish lords, who invited John Stewart, 2nd Duke of Albany (and the heir presumptive), to come over from France and replace her as regent.

On 14 July, Cardinal Christopher Bainbridge, the Archbishop of York, died in Rome. It was generally believed that he had been poisoned by a rival English ambassador, Silvester de Gigli, Bishop of Worcester. However De Gigli escaped arrest, largely because of Wolsey's protection. In September, Wolsey replaced Bainbridge as Archbishop of York: he was now at the head of one of the two provinces into which the English Church was divided.

'the king fell ill with measles (or possibly even smallpox), but he soon recovered'

LEFT: **Louis XII's marriage to Princess Mary**, Henry's younger sister, took place on 9 October 1514. On the afternoon of 6 November, the new Queen of France made a state entry into Paris. Along the processional route, she was greeted by actors in elaborate pageants or tableaux, symbolizing the new Anglo-French union. These pageants were recorded in seven miniatures within a French illuminated manuscript of 1514 (the British Library's Cotton Vespasian B. II, f. 15). In this one, Louis and Mary are shown enthroned, attended by Justice and Truth. Above their figures can be seen a depiction of the Annunciation, to express the hope that, like the Virgin Mary, Queen Mary will soon conceive and provide Louis with a male heir.

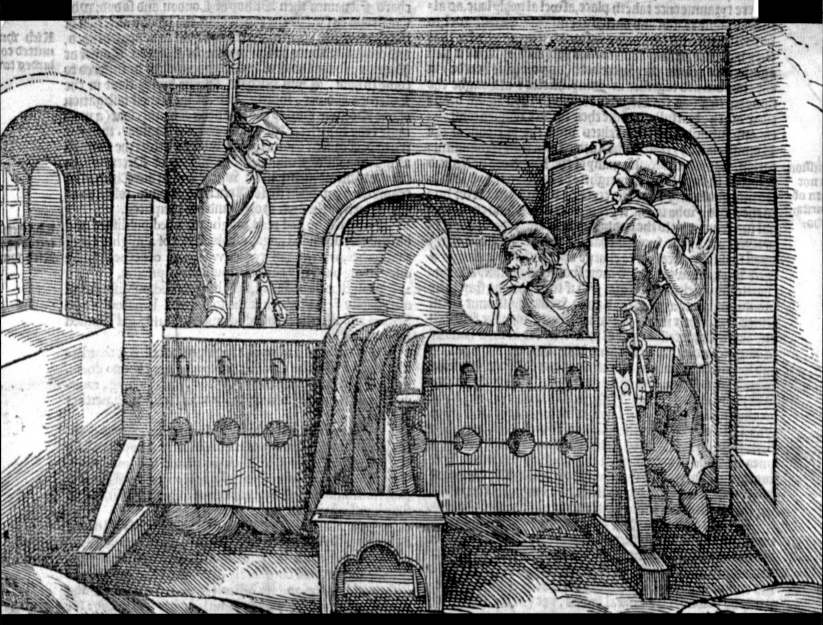

ABOVE: **The Hunne case** *was a 16th-century cause célèbre. In 1511, the London merchant-tailor Richard Hunne quarrelled with his local priest after refusing to pay a fee for the burial of his infant son. The dispute dragged on in the courts for three years until eventually Hunne was arrested on a charge of heresy and imprisoned by the church authorities in the 'Lollards' Tower' (a prison for heretics adjoining St Paul's). There, in December 1514, he was found hanging from a hook in the ceiling of his cell. The Bishop of London announced that Hunne had committed suicide, but few Londoners believed this verdict, and soon*

afterwards a coroner's inquest found his jailers guilty of murder. The Chancellor of the Bishop of London was accused of ordering Hunne's death, but he was never tried. In this woodcut from John Foxe's Acts and Monuments *(also known as the* Book of Martyrs*), published in Elizabeth's reign, the men responsible for Hunne's death are shown leaving his cell after stringing him up to fake a suicide. Foxe saw Hunne as one of the professors of the Gospel who had been martyred by the Roman Catholic clergy, and he treated the case as evidence of the corruption of the pre-Reformation church.*

Mary left for France on 2 October. After a stormy two-day crossing, she met Louis at Abbeville, where their marriage was celebrated on 8 October. Following the ancient custom that France's queens had to be crowned before entering Paris, Mary's coronation took place in the Abbey of St Denis on Sunday 5 November, the day before she made her grand entry into the capital. Her first months as queen were filled with dances, jousts and other entertainments.

On 4 December, the tailor Richard Hunne, who was awaiting trial for heresy, was found hanging in his cell. It was the unfortunate end to three years of spiralling legal battles, and the case became a *cause célèbre*.

1515

Henry's brother-in-law, the childless and frail Louis XII, died on 1 January and was succeeded by his virile 20-year-old cousin Francis I. Henry dispatched the Duke of Suffolk to escort his widowed sister home, but the two married secretly in mid-February while still in Paris.

Henry's own marriage, meanwhile, was still failing to produce a male heir. In January, Katherine gave birth to a premature stillborn son 'to the very great grief of the whole court'.[18]

On 4 February, the Abbot of Winchcombe, Richard Kidderminster, delivered a sermon at Paul's Cross in which he spoke out in favour of clerical immunities from secular jurisdiction. His sermon was timed to coincide with the opening of the Parliament that was due to reconsider the 1512 statute that had limited 'benefit of clergy'. The sermon, coming as it did in the wake of the anti-clerical sentiment inspired by the Hunne case, roused a storm of protest in the House of Commons. At a meeting of the clergy summoned to debate the issue, Dr Henry Standish of the London Franciscans defended the statute, but the bishops, who had a majority in the House of Lords, blocked an extension of the legislation. In November, the Convocation of Canterbury threatened Standish with heresy proceedings for arguing

103

RIGHT: **The royal armouries** were set up at Greenwich in 1515 to produce fine-quality armour for Henry VIII and his court. Eleven 'Almains' (Dutch and German craftsmen) worked there as liveried servants. This armour, made at Greenwich under the master, Martin van Royne, was designed for the king to wear in a foot combat at the Field of Cloth of Gold, held in 1520. It was intended to cover him from head to foot, leaving no opening through which a weapon might penetrate, and would only be worn for a short period. The armour was left undecorated and finished 'rough from the hammer', because the form of armour specified for the event in the tournament was changed two months before the proceedings and an alternative armour had to be hastily prepared.

A dashing English prince

His Majesty is the handsomest potentate I ever set eyes on; above the usual height, with an extremely fine calf to his leg, his complexion very fair and bright, with auburn hair combed straight and short, in the French fashion, and a round face so very beautiful, that it would become a pretty woman, his throat rather long and thick … He speaks French, English, and Latin and a little Italian, plays well on the lute and harpsichord, sings from book at sight, draws the bow with greater strength than any man in England, and jousts marvellously. Believe me, he is in every respect a most accomplished Prince …

[PIERO PASQUALIGO, WRITING ON 30 APRIL 1515, AS TRANSLATED BY RAWDON BROWN IN *Four Years at the Court of Henry VIII*, VOL. I, PP. 86–7]

A rival French prince

His Majesty came into our arbour, and addressing me in French, said: 'Talk with me a while! The King of France is he as tall as I am?' I told him there was but little difference. He continued, 'Is he as stout?' I said he was not; and he then inquired, 'What sort of legs has he?' I replied 'Spare.' Whereupon he opened the front of his doublet, and placing his hand on his thigh, said, 'Look here! And I have also a good calf to my leg.' He then told me he was very fond of this King of France …

[PIERO PASQUALIGO, WRITING ON 3 MAY 1515, AS TRANSLATED BY RAWDON BROWN IN *Four Years at the Court of Henry VIII*, VOL. I, PP. 90–1]

104

against the church's immunities. To protect him, Henry called a meeting at Baynard's Castle. There, he claimed an imperial authority over the church, and Convocation backed down.

On 5 April, Francis renewed the 1514 Franco-English alliance. This, however, did not stop him allowing the Duke of Albany to leave France for Scotland, despite English protests. Two months after his arrival in the north, Albany replaced Margaret as regent and demanded guardianship of the young James V. Fearing for her own safety, the heavily pregnant Margaret fled to England on 30 September, in such haste that she left behind her wardrobe and jewels. A week later, she gave birth to a daughter, whom she named Margaret.

In September, Francis led an army to Italy with the aim of conquering Milan. On the 14th of the month, he won a great victory at Marignano, nine miles from Milan, and entered the city. Envious of this military success, Henry immediately attempted to negotiate a league against the French king.

On 22 December, Archbishop Warham of Canterbury resigned the lord chancellorship, which passed to Thomas Wolsey two days later. A few months earlier, Pope Leo X had created Wolsey a cardinal.

ABOVE: **Hampton Court** *was acquired by Thomas Wolsey in January 1515. He employed leading architects and master craftsmen to work on the building and turned it into a Renaissance palace fit for a king – which, in fact, it later became. In 1525 Wolsey turned the lease of the manor over to Henry, although he contined to live in the palace until 1529. In this later drawing (c.1544) by Anthonis van Wynegaerde, from the* Panorama of London, *the great hall built by Henry is in the centre and the tiltyard enclosed by a wall in the centre foreground.*

1516

'if it was a daughter this time, by the grace of God the sons will follow'

King Henry's father-in-law, Ferdinand of Aragon, died on 23 January and Charles, his 16-year-old grandson, succeeded to the throne of Spain. In foreign affairs, Henry and Wolsey spent much of this year and the next seeking in vain either to build up an anti-French league or to force Francis into making a favourable treaty with England.

On 18 February, Katherine gave birth to a healthy child at Greenwich. To everyone's disappointment the baby was a girl, but Henry put on a brave face, telling the Venetian ambassador: 'We are both young; if it was a daughter this time, by the grace of God the sons will follow.'[19] On 21 February the child was baptized 'Mary' after Henry's sister; a month later, his sister returned the compliment by naming her newborn son 'Henry'.

On 3 May the king's other sister, Margaret, who had come 'poorly out of Scotland', was 'richly received' at the English court with jousts, feasting and celebrations that lasted a month.[20]

1517

A great frost began on 12 January, 'in such wise that no boat might go betwixt London and Westminster'.[21]

Some months later in the capital, during the night of 30 April, serious riots occurred. Apprentices and journeymen went on the rampage and 'maltreated many foreigners', especially French and Flemish artisans.[22] The civic authorities and troops under the command of Shrewsbury and Norfolk restored order. The rioting became known as 'Evil May Day', and fifteen or so of the ringleaders were hanged and quartered. Four hundred others – youths, women and clerics – were arrested and paraded before the king and queen in Westminster Hall on 14 May. As was traditional on such occasions, the prisoners wore only shirts and had halters around their necks, 'as if about to

RIGHT: **Margaret Tudor (1489–1541)**, *Henry's elder sister, was Dowager Queen of Scotland after James IV's death at the Battle of Flodden in 1513. Initially she acted as her young son James's regent, but she lost power after remarrying and was forced to flee to England in 1515. She soon returned to Scotland, but quarrelled with her husband, Archibald Douglas, 6th Earl of Angus: he had not only taken a mistress, but more importantly had* pocketed the rents from her estates. Henry gave her very little support, not allowing her to leave Scotland or to seek a divorce. Eventually, on 11 March 1527, the pope annulled the marriage. This freed Margaret to marry her third husband, Henry Stewart. By the mid-1530s, this marriage had also turned sour. Henry refused to listen to her pleas to return to England, and she died in Scotland.

The sweating sickness

... the king appointed his guests for his pastime this summer [1517], but suddenly there came a plague of sickness, called the sweating sickness, that turned all his purpose. This malady was so cruel that it killed some within three hours, some within two hours, some merry at dinner and dead at supper. Many died in the king's court, the Lord Clinton, the Lord Grey of Wilton, and many knights, gentlemen and officers. For this plague Michaelmas term was adjourned, and because that this malady continued from July to the midst of December, the king kept himself ever with a small company, and kept no solemn Christmas, willing to have no resort for fear of infection: but much lamented the number of his people, for in one town half the people died and in some other town the third part, the sweat was so fervent and infectious.

[*Henry VIII* (*Hall's Chronicle*), EDITED BY CHARLES WHIBLEY, VOL. I, P. 165]

be executed'. Katherine, 'with tears in her eyes and on her bended knees', played out the customary intermediary role of a queen consort and petitioned Henry to exercise the prerogative of mercy.[23] Cardinal Wolsey followed suit, 'some of the chief lords doing the same'. Henry, then ordered the prisoners' release. 'It was a very fine spectacle, and well arranged, and the crowd of people present was innumerable.'[24]

On 16 May, Margaret left for Scotland. Francis had recalled the Duke of Albany to France, and the Scottish lairds had guaranteed Margaret's safety when she returned.

On 7 July, Henry held a great joust in a newly built tiltyard at Greenwich before foreign ambassadors. A hot summer, though, brought a virulent outbreak of sweating sickness (a form of influenza) to London. Its victims died so suddenly that they might be 'merry at dinner and dead at supper'.[25] The court hastily left the city for the country. Cardinal Wolsey, who stayed in London, became seriously ill but survived.

On 31 October, Martin Luther, a theologian at the University of Wittenberg in Saxony, posted his 95 'theses' and called for an academic debate on the legality of papal 'indulgences' granted to individuals for the remission of punishment after death for their sins.

RIGHT: **George Gisze (1497–1562)** *was one of the many foreign merchants operating in London under Henry VIII. He was based in the Steelyard, the centre for those merchants who belonged to the Hanseatic League and who dominated the trade of Northern Europe. Londoners were resentful of their privileges, and this led to the eventual expulsion of the merchants at the end of the 16th century. This life-sized portrait, painted by Holbein the Younger in 1532, depicts the merchant opening a letter* addressed 'to my brother George Gisze in London'. *Among the many objects in the painting are letter-writing equipment, scissors, a clock and a metal box filled with coins.*

O all presen[t]
prinapall [kings]
willethe and
merytes and
theire Succ[essors]
of this Citti[e]
Compenys
may be knou[en]
Willm ffren[ch]
of ffysycion[s]
Requyred a[nd]
and affigne

conuenuente / tokens of honner and wor[...]
by vertu power and auctoritee to myn of[...]
lorde / J haue Seuised ordened and affig[...]
and fforme ffollowenge / that ys to wy[...]
oute of a clowde Argent and Asure. w[...]
arme in ffeffe / charmois / in pont a pow[...]
and to holde vnto the faide Willm ff[...]
the College of ffysicione as aforefayd[...]
company / they then to vse and fmoy to
apall kinge of Armes as abouefayd
the Seale of myn Office and also th[...]
the yere of ower lorde God af CCCC[...]
by the Grace of God kynge of Englan[d]
of England and Jsland Supreme

1518

Growing alarmed at Turkish victories in Eastern Europe and the Mediterranean, Pope Leo preached a crusade in early March. He then dispatched legates to urge rulers to make peace in Europe and unite against the enemy of Christendom. Cardinal Campeggio was sent to England, but Henry would only admit him when Leo agreed to make Cardinal Wolsey a papal legate of equal standing. On 29 July Campeggio made a solemn entry into London, processing past 'the mayor and aldermen with all the crafts of the city standing in Cheapside in their best liveries'. At St Paul's he was greeted by the clergy 'in copes of cloth of gold' and invited to make 'his devotions' at the high altar.[26] However, after this encouraging start to the mission, Campeggio was consistently sidelined by Wolsey.

Wolsey then hijacked the papal initiative for a European peace by concluding, on 2 October, a non-aggression pact that encompassed over twenty European powers. The peace treaty was proclaimed the next day at St Paul's, where Wolsey celebrated a solemn mass with unusual splendour. A 'most sumptuous supper' followed at Wolsey's London residence,[27] and, after the meal had finished, Henry and his younger sister danced incognito before the guests.

On 4 October, English and French representatives signed a bilateral treaty of peace, whereby Henry agreed to restore Tournai to France, while Francis promised to pay Henry a large annual pension and keep the Duke of Albany out of Scotland. To seal the agreement, a marriage was arranged between Henry's infant daughter and the equally youthful *dauphin*. The next day, the two-year-old Mary, 'dressed in a cloth of gold, with a cap of black velvet on her head, adorned with many jewels', was betrothed to the *dauphin* in the queen's great chamber at Greenwich.[28]

During the night of 9–10 November, Queen Katherine gave birth to a stillborn daughter 'to the vexation of everybody. Never had a kingdom so anxiously desired anything as it did a prince.'[29] This pregnancy would be Katherine's last.

'Never had a kingdom so anxiously desired anything as it did a prince'

111

LEFT: **The Royal College of Physicians** *was founded by royal charter on 23 September 1518, with 'a view to the improvement and more orderly exercise of the art of physic, and the repression of irregular, unlearned, and incompetent practitioners of that faculty'. The first president was Thomas Linacre (1460–1524), physician to Henries VII and VIII, and he gave the college use of his own London house just south of St Paul's. In 1546 the college received the grant of arms shown here. Highly decorated, the grant shows a herald pointing to the shield on which is the college's blazon. An arm descends from a cloud to feel the pulse of a patient; the object below is a pomegranate, which is believed to cure agues.*

The cherished Princess Mary

For one day the king showed him [the Venetian ambassador] the Princess [Mary], then two years old, in her nurse's arms. He drew near, knelt, and kissed her hand, for that alone is kissed by any duke or noble of the land, let his degree be what it may; nor does anyone see her without doffing his bonnet, and making obeisance to her. The king then said to him, 'Domine Orator, per Deum immortalem, ista puella nunquam plorat' ['Ambassador, by immortal God, this girl never cries']; and he replied, 'Sacred Majesty, the reason is that her destiny does not move her to tears; she will even become Queen of France'. These words pleased the king vastly.

[SEBASTIAN GIUSTINIAN'S REPORT OF ENGLAND, 10 SEPTEMBER 1519, *Calendar of State Papers, Venetian*, VOL. II, NO. 1287, P. 558]

1519

In January the Holy Roman Emperor, Maximilian, died. His most obvious successor as emperor was his grandson, the 18-year-old Charles, son of Philip the Fair of Burgundy and Joanna, the Spanish *infanta* (and consequently the nephew of Queen Katherine.) Charles was already King of Spain and ruler of the Low Countries. Francis I unsuccessfully stood in the imperial election against him, and Henry also considered entering the race. But Charles was duly elected Holy Roman Emperor, as Charles V, on 28 June.

In contrast to Queen Katherine's lack of fortune in delivering a boy, Elizabeth Blount, the queen's maid of honour, gave birth to a son whose father was the king. Baptized on the first Sunday in June, the child was acknowledged by King Henry and named Henry Fitzroy, the surname being traditional for royal bastards. The king had 'proved' that he could produce a son – though not, so far, with Katherine. A few months later, Elizabeth Blount married Gilbert Tailboys.

ABOVE: **Henry Fitzroy (1519–36)** *was the illegitimate son of Henry and his mistress Elizabeth Blount, and he was, according to Hall's Chronicle, 'well brought up, like a prince's child'. In 1525, worried about the succession, the king seriously considered making the boy his heir. He was given noble titles and sent to York, with a great household, as titular head of the Council of the North. In 1532 he went to France for a year, and after his return he married the Duke of Norfolk's only daughter, a union that was unconsummated because of their youth. He died in July 1536. This miniature was created c.1534 by Lucas Hornebolt.*

RIGHT: **Charles V (1500–58)**, *depicted here c.1530, came to be the richest and most powerful monarch in Christendom by inheriting the Duchy of Burgundy from his father (Philip the Fair), the Kingdom of Spain from his mother (Joanna) and maternal grandfather (Ferdinand), and the Habsburg territories from his paternal grandfather (Maximilian). In 1519, he was also elected Holy Roman Emperor, beating Francis I into second place and intensifying the rivalry between them. It is no wonder that Henry chose to ally with him during the 1520s and 1540s. This 1533 portrait was Titian's first painting of the emperor.*

The Field of the Cloth of Gold

... the kings met in the Val Doré

[in 1520], a little valley between Ardre and Guisnes … The king [of France] was mounted on a beautiful charger, and clothed with a cassock of cloth of gold frieze, a mantle of cloth of gold, richly jewelled, the front and sleeves set with diamonds, rubies, emerald, and large pearls, hanging loose; his barrette [cap] and bonnet of velvet, set with plumes, and resplendent with jewelry … The King of England was dressed in cloth of silver, richly jewelled, with white plumes … the kings descended the valley, gently, with their constables bearing naked swords. On coming near, they gave their horses the spur like two combatants about to engage, but instead of putting their hands to their swords, each put his hand to his bonnet. Then they embraced bareheaded, dismounted and embraced again, and took each other by the arm to a fine pavilion all like cloth of gold, which the King of England had prepared. After a dispute which should go last, the two kings entered together … After some conversation within the pavilion, each king embraced the lords of the other's company, whilst the trumpets and other instruments sounded on each side, so that it seemed like a paradise. At night they took leave of each other.

[Letters and Papers of the Reign of Henry the Eighth, VOL. III, NO. 869, PP. 309–10]

114

1520

On 21 May, Henry and his court left London for meetings with Charles and Francis. He met the emperor at Dover on 26 May and escorted him to Canterbury. In the archbishop's palace, Katherine, 'dressed in a cloth of gold lined with ermine, and beautiful strings of pearls round her neck', greeted and embraced her nephew 'not without tears'.[30] After eating together, the monarchs changed their clothes and returned to the cathedral in a procession of some six hundred lords and ladies for the Whitsunday mass.

On 31 May Henry and Charles parted company, and the English king sailed with some six thousand people to Calais. He met Francis on Thursday 7 June on the feast of Corpus Christi, in the Val Doré, a small valley between Ardres and Guisnes just inside English territory. The two kings rode out to meet as if in combat but instead 'embraced each other two or three times on horseback, bonnet in hand'.[31] They then went into the English pavilion, where they talked in private. Their meeting at the so-called 'Field of (the) Cloth of Gold' concluded with a mass celebrated by Cardinal Wolsey, with parts of the service sung by the French king's chapel choir and other parts sung by the English.

Over the next week they dined, talked and jousted in the friendliest of fashions. Behind their bonhomie, however, lay a deep rivalry that observers could detect in the superb banquets they each held for the other, the lavish entertainments they put on, the magnificence of their attire and the rich gifts they exchanged. Both kings performed equally well in the jousts, taking on all comers while their queens and other ladies looked on. But in an unscheduled incident, Henry challenged Francis to a wrestling match and suffered the humiliation of being thrown to the ground.

On 24 June, the two kings bade each other farewell. Before returning home, Henry and Katherine went to Gravelines to meet Charles V again and his aunt, Margaret of Savoy. This reunion on 10 July 'was very unceremonious and without any pomp'.[32] Four days later Henry and Charles concluded a treaty of friendship.

of the two kings in a tent of cloth of gold. The large building in the foreground is the temporary palace of wood and canvas, painted to look like stone or brick, which the English erected. One eyewitness described it (as recorded in the Calendar of State Papers, Venetian) as 'one of the handsomest and costliest ever witnessed, and so well adorned with carpets, satin and taffetas of various colours to appear a miracle'. White wine and claret flow from the two fountains outside. Top left are the dragon fireworks released by the English on 23 June. They could symbolize the Welsh dragon or the French salamander (Francis's personal emblem). The town of Calais is in the distance on the left.

1521

In late spring, the English church began taking measures to prevent the dissemination of Martin Luther's views. On 12 May, Bishop Fisher of Rochester presided over a burning of Luther's books at Paul's Cross. This spectacle launched the publication of Henry's tract against Luther's heresies.

On 17 May, Edward Stafford, 3rd Duke of Buckingham, was beheaded for treason on Tower Hill. He had probably aroused the king's suspicions when he applied for a licence to raise a retinue of 400 armed men, but he was accused of expressing a wish for the king's death and discussing the possibility of his own succession to the throne.

Meanwhile, armed conflict had reopened abroad between Francis I and Charles V in April. Each monarch blamed the other and appealed to Henry for justice in accordance with the 1518 Treaty of London. On 29 July, Henry commissioned Cardinal Wolsey to mediate between the two kings; but Henry knew that 'if it proved impossible to restrain them', he 'should have to join with one side', and he much preferred to join with the emperor.[33] Consequently, he also instructed Wolsey to conclude two treaties with Charles. The first was for a marriage between the emperor and his daughter Mary (who was then betrothed to the *dauphin* of France). The second was 'for carrying on war against the French king to recover Henry's possessions in France'.[34]

On 2 August, Wolsey arrived in Calais to broker a peace with ambassadors from France and the Empire.

The fate of an overmighty subject

The Duke [of Buckingham] was brought to the bar *[in 1521] sore chafing and sweat marvellously … The Duke of Norfolk as a judge said, 'Sir Edward, you have heard how you be indicted of high treason, you pleaded thereto not guilty, putting yourself to the peers of the realm, the which have found you guilty': then the Duke of Norfolk wept and said, 'You shall be led to the king's prison and there laid on a hurdle [a frame of wood] and so drawn to the place of execution, and there to be hanged, cut down alive, your members to be cut off and cast into the fire, your bowels burnt before you, your head smitten off, and your body quartered and divided at the king's will, and God have mercy on your soul' …*

Alas that ever the grace of truth was withdrawn from so noble a man, that he was not to his king in allegiance as he ought to have been, such is the end of ambition, the end of false prophecies, the end of evil life and evil counsel.

[*Henry VIII (Hall's Chronicle)*, EDITED BY CHARLES WHIBLEY, VOL. I, PP. 225–6]

LEFT: **The 'Assertio septem sacramentorum' of 1521,** *or The Defence of the Seven Sacraments, was Henry's answer to Martin Luther's attack on the seven sacraments and the granting of 'indulgences'. Wolsey encouraged Henry to compose the work, while Sir Thomas More and Bishop Fisher helped him with the theology. This 16th-century scene imagines an audience before the pope, in which Henry bears a roll that is probably the papal bull granting him, in gratitude, the title 'Fidei defensor' (defender of the faith). A cardinal – probably Wolsey – supports Henry, while Charles V is seated opposite him, and they are engaged in what seems to be a theological discussion. Luther was scathing about Henry's defence of the church, declaring that the Assertio proved the old saying that there are no greater fools than kings.*

However, since he immediately 'saw the idea of peace could not prevail against war', Wolsey left a few days later to make an alliance with Charles, mendaciously explaining to the French that he needed a face-to-face meeting with the emperor to obtain the truce. Wolsey entered Bruges on 14 August in grand style, accompanied by a retinue of over 1000 horsemen. Over the next week he held private discussions with Charles and his closest advisers. At last, on 25 August, secret treaties were signed that committed Henry to enter the war against Francis before 1522. In return, Charles pledged to pay Henry nearly £30,000 as compensation for the loss of the French pension once war broke out.

On 28 August, Wolsey was back in Calais, where the French had been kicking their heels and complaining that their treatment 'was dishonourable for the king of France'.[35] Nonetheless, peace discussions continued, albeit unproductively, until December, when Wolsey returned to England. By this time Francis realized that Henry was at best prevaricating and at worst betraying him. In a retaliatory, provocative move, he sent the Duke of Albany to Scotland at the end of the month. One of the duke's first actions in Scotland was to ratify, on 28 December, the 'Auld Alliance' with France against England. Henry, however, had picked the winning side as his ally in the Continental contest. Imperial forces seized Milan in November and Tournai in December.

On 1 December, Pope Leo X died after seven years in office, creating the need for another papal election.

LEFT: **Martin Luther (1483–1546)** *was excommunicated by the pope on 21 January 1521 because of his attacks on the papacy and on the church's doctrines concerning salvation. In April he was given a hearing before the emperor, Charles V, at a diet (assembly) held at the city of Worms. There, Luther refused to recant his views and so the diet passed the Edict of Worms, which declared that he was an outlaw and a heretic. Luther, however, escaped capture and continued to publicize his teachings. Many of his books reached England and were burned by the church authorities in the early 1520s.*

ABOVE: **John Stewart (c.1482–1536), 2nd Duke of Albany,** *was the heir presumptive to the Scottish throne during the minority of James V. Brought up in France, Albany was pro-French and he was used by Francis I to further his interests in Scotland, particularly when Anglo-Scottish relations were troublesome. This black pencil drawing, from the studio of Jean Clouet, was made around 1525–30.*

1522

Cardinal Wolsey won some votes in the papal conclave, but the tiara went to Charles V's tutor Adrian of Utrecht. In the spring, Wolsey occupied himself by ordering a survey of England's financial and military strength in preparation for war against France.

At the end of May, Charles V arrived at Dover on his way to Spain from the Low Countries. Met there by Henry, he inspected the English flagship *Henry Grace a Dieu*. The two monarchs and their large retinues then rode to London, entertained on the way by banquets, pageants, jousts and church services. On the evening of Friday 6 June, they entered London 'in great triumph, not only like brothers of one mind, but in the same attire'.[36] Decorating the streets were tapestries and eight triumphal arches, and 'there were diverse pageants made in diverse places of the city'.[37] Over the next couple of days, the two monarchs discussed their campaign plan for the French war.

On 29 May Henry formally declared war on France. His avowed reasons included the Duke of Albany's return to Scotland, the French invasion of Navarre and Francis's refusal to continue paying Henry his pension. Hostilities began when Lord Admiral Surrey's ships attacked the coast of Brittany and sacked Morlaix, bringing home considerable booty. In August, Surrey led an Anglo-Burgundian force in a pillaging expedition through Picardy in northeastern France. His attempt to take Hesdin failed, however. Even worse, sickness hit his camp in September, causing the foreign soldiers to desert. The English army returned to Calais on 14 October, having achieved very little.

At war against France, Henry expected an invasion from Scotland and ordered his lieutenant-general, George Talbot, 4th Earl of Shrewsbury, to muster an army. The Duke of Albany did indeed assemble a Scottish army in September and marched towards the border. But fearing a repetition of the catastrophe at Flodden in 1513, his men refused to attack Carlisle without French support and forced Albany to sign a truce. In late October, Albany departed for France with the intention of returning with French soldiers.

On Christmas day of this year, the Mediterranean island of Rhodes fell to the Turks; 'much blame [was] put in all princes, because they sent no succour, nor aid to the isle'.[38]

124

RIGHT: **Mary Boleyn (c.1499–1543)**, *painted here by an unknown artist, probably became the king's mistress in 1522, although she was then married to William Carey, a gentleman of the privy chamber. One of Henry's ships even bore the name Mary Boleyn in 1523. It seems likely that the affair ended at some point in 1525. The relationship was kept quiet, but Henry admitted it when he asked the pope in 1528 to grant him a dispensation to marry a woman who was the sister of a former mistress.*

Henry went on to marry Anne, even though she was in the same degree of affinity to him – by virtue of his prior relationship with her sister Mary – as he was to Katherine of Aragon. Indeed, this affinity may have provided the justification for the annulment of Henry's marriage to Anne in 1536.

1523

In April, Henry summoned Parliament to agree funds for an invasion of France. However, some of the Commons – including a newcomer, Thomas Cromwell – expressed doubts about the value of a war, while others raised fears that the country would be denuded of coin if the tax went ahead. When a delegation of MPs offered Wolsey a much smaller grant, he angrily rejected it saying that he 'would rather have his tongue plucked out of his head with a pair of pincers than to move the king to take any less sum'.[39] After some bad-tempered haggling, Parliament voted the largest grant of the reign so far.

In late summer, Henry began his campaign in France. It was timed to coordinate with Charles's military operation in Italy and a rebellion of the Duke of Bourbon in eastern France. Charles Brandon, Duke of Suffolk, and an army of about 11,000 men crossed over to Calais at the end of August with instructions to capture Boulogne. However, on 26 September, Henry – guided by Wolsey – rethought his priorities and ordered the duke to march on Paris. The plan was for a triple onslaught on the capital, with Henry attacking from the north, Bourbon from the south and an Imperial force from the east. Suffolk began well. After receiving Burgundian reinforcements, his army seized the enemy stronghold of Belle Castle (which was razed to the ground), destroyed the well-fortified riverside crossing at Bray and captured Montdidier despite some resistance; other towns also surrendered. Then, in November the weather turned nasty. Heavy rain was succeeded by 'a fervent frost so sore that many a soldier died for cold, some lost fingers, and some toes'.[40] Furthermore, Bourbon's rising petered out, and Francis moved to refortify Paris. In these circumstances Suffolk felt compelled to retreat despite his army being only 50 miles from the city. Nor could he over-winter in France as first hoped. His army was depleted through deaths from plague and by the withdrawal of the Burgundian troops. Suffolk therefore returned home in December. Despite this setback, Henry did not despair but planned a new expedition for the following spring.

In Scotland, the troublesome Duke of Albany landed at Kirkcudbright with several thousand French troops, on 23 September. He mustered a large Scottish army to invade England, but on 23 November the Scots again refused to cross the border.

Also in September, Adrian's brief tenure as pope came to an end with his death. He was succeeded, on 18 November, by Cardinal Giulio de' Medici, who took the title 'Clement VII'.

LEFT: **The 1523 Parliament** *proved to be very resistant to Henry's demands for a huge subsidy (some £800,000) to fight the war against France. In the end, however, it voted over £136,000, a very substantial grant. The opening ceremony is shown here, in the Wriothesley Garter Book. Henry sits enthroned and on his right are the two archbishops, Warham and Wolsey (the latter seen in front of his cardinal's emblem). Behind their bench is Cuthbert Tunstall, Bishop of London, who holds the roll of the opening speech. The royal symbols – the cap of maintenance and the sword of state – are borne by earls standing on the carpet decorated by lilies. The lay lords sit on the king's left with the two dukes (Norfolk and Suffolk) nearest the king and wearing coronets. The spiritual lords are represented by nine bishops in red and seventeen abbots in black. At the top right are the Commons led by their speaker, Sir Thomas More, who played an important role in securing parliamentary consent to the taxes.*

1524

Henry escaped serious personal injury at the tilts on 10 March, when he forgot to close his visor in a joust against the Duke of Suffolk. During the spring, Henry developed second thoughts about a new French campaign. He was irritated with the emperor, Charles, who was proving successful in Italy yet failing to pay Henry the indemnity promised in 1521. Cardinal Wolsey, meanwhile, doubted the wisdom of another expedition because of its cost and logistical difficulties. Both men, consequently, adopted a wait-and-see policy.

On 20 May, the Duke of Albany sailed back to France to negotiate a French marriage for Scotland's James V. In July, the king's mother, Margaret, organized a coup, and in November she ousted the duke from the regency.

This year, Henry ceased sleeping with his 39-year-old wife. Queen Katherine had not conceived for six years. Her age and her history of troubled pregnancies effectively ruled out any prospect that she might produce a male heir.

ABOVE: **This writing box** *made in the mid-1520s may have belonged to the king, but more probably was a gift from him to a courtier or ambassador. The inner lid shows Henry's coat of arms held by putti, with the gods Mars and Venus on either side. St George, the patron saint of England, is depicted to the right of the upper surface of the interior, with the dragon at his feet. The heads in roundels at the front of the box are of Paris (left) and Helen of Troy (right). The box would have stored parchment (or paper) and writing implements, useful for writing letters when its owner was travelling.*

RIGHT: **Thomas Howard (1473–1554), 3rd Duke of Norfolk**, *served Henry well on the Scottish border while he was Earl of Surrey. Soon after he inherited his father's title in 1524, Norfolk tried for political power at court. He resented Wolsey's pre-eminence and disliked his policy of peace with France. Norfolk's fortunes improved once his niece, Anne Boleyn, caught Henry's eye; but he found another adversary in the king's new chief adviser, Thomas Cromwell. As a religious conservative, Norfolk disliked Cromwell's programme of religious reform. In this later portrait, attributed to Holbein the Younger, Norfolk holds the white staff of the lord treasurer and the gold baton of the earl marshal.*

THOMAS · DVKE · OFF · NORFOLK · MARSHALL
AND · TRESVRER · OFF · INGLOND
THE · LXVI · YERE · OF · HIS · AGE

1525

'This season the cardinal being in the king's favour obtained licence to make a college at Oxford and another at Ipswich'.[41] Thus, the building of what would later become Christ Church College, Oxford, began.

At the Battle of Pavia on 24 February, Charles V won an overwhelming victory over the French king, Francis, who was even taken prisoner. Among the dead in the French army was Richard de la Pole, the Yorkist claimant to Henry's throne. The news reached Henry on 9 March while he was in bed and, delighted, he ordered celebratory bonfires to be lit and a *Te Deum* to be sung at St Paul's.

Henry planned to take advantage of his ally's success and embark on another invasion of France. Consequently, on 21 March commissioners were appointed to raise a non-parliamentary grant of money, euphemistically called the 'Amicable Grant'. The sum demanded was very high, amounting to about one-sixth of the annual income of the laity and a third of that of the clergy.

On 26 March, Henry congratulated Charles on his military success and suggested a joint strategy for the future conquest of France. Charles, however, was now ready to make peace with Francis and, worse still for Henry, 'makes it appear that he is dissatisfied with' the English king.[42]

Opposition to the Amicable Grant developed during April. Clerics complained 'sorely' that the required contribution would leave them 'utterly destitute'.[43] The laity was equally resistant. In Cambridgeshire men pleaded extreme poverty; in London the mayor and aldermen protested at the

The Amicable Grant

Now in this time [1525] was that subtle valuation *[the Amicable Grant, a tax levy], laid to their charge, which when they perceived, they murmured much and said, they would pay nothing, except the king's laws, under which they were born, so determined it: But this notwithstanding, commissioners went out to every shire, for the levy of the said money, but for all that could be persuaded, said, lied and flattered, the demand could not be assented to, saying that they that sent forth such commissioners, were subverters of the law, and worthy to be punished as traitors. So that in all the realm were bills set up, in all places: some bills said, that the king had not paid that he borrowed: some said that the subsidy amounted treble, more than he had been bestowed: other said whatsoever was granted, no good came of it: and other said that the cardinal [Wolsey], sent all the money to Rome, thus was the muttering through all the realm, with curses and weepings, that pity it was to behold.*

[*Henry VIII* (*Hall's Chronicle*), EDITED BY CHARLES WHIBLEY, VOL. II, P. 37)

130

RIGHT: **The foundation of Cardinal College, Oxford,** *and the establishment of a school in Ipswich were the cornerstones of Cardinal Wolsey's educational patronage. It was agreed that he would dissolve the Priory of Saint Frideswide in Oxford and use its resources for these projects. Henry's letter patent of 5 May 1526, illustrated here, confirmed all the possessions granted to Cardinal College. Henry is shown within the initial 'H' on an* architectural throne within a shell niche. It is thought that the Flemish miniaturist Lucas Hornebolt (or Horenbout) was responsible for the portrait. After the fall of Wolsey in 1530, Henry stripped the college of its endowment, but in 1546 it was re-endowed as Christ Church, the name it carries today as part of the University of Oxford.*

z Domini
conceptum
perpositam
Archiepus
terras atqᵹ
maximo n
z xpiane i
egregia cuis
X gratia n
firmaru ho
mioz mhsif saaens
cuisdem regni aut
z non residen uer a
heirs vel successoz
successoz mioz uxᵹ
z assessionibᵹ z qual
X malefcoᵹibᵹ quos
aᵹuuerís terris teu
officiui illus pertm
qs uxm Decanus

mioz non ingrediatur sina maiua tras teu feos seu possessiones psiit as
torestᵹ ip heir z m essiᵹ et

'men that had no work, began to rage'

rates demanded; in Suffolk insurrection was threatened as 'men that had no work, began to rage, and assemble themselves in companies'.[44] In the prosperous wool towns of Lavenham, Sudbury and Hadleigh, 'there rebelled four thousand men'.[45] In the face of such overt hostility, Henry abandoned both the Amicable Grant and his projected invasion of France.

During May, Charles V jilted Henry's nine-year-old daughter, Princess Mary, and jettisoned the English alliance. Shortly afterwards, Henry treated his illegitimate son Henry Fitzroy as a potential heir to the throne. On 7 June, the six-year-old boy was installed as a Knight of the Garter; on the 18th he was created Duke of Richmond and Somerset (denoting his Tudor and Beaufort ancestry respectively), with pre-eminence over all other dukes. Fitzroy was also made Lieutenant-General of the North, a position traditionally given to a junior prince of the royal family. Even so, Princess Mary was not neglected: she was sent with a magnificent household to Ludlow as the nominal administrator of Wales.

On 30 August, Henry and French ambassadors signed five treaties, collectively known as the Treaty of the More, named after the Hertfordshire royal house where it was concluded. Peace between England and France was proclaimed on 6 September. Henry then wrote to Pope Clement to enlist his support for the release of Francis.

Plague returned to England during the year and 'in this winter was great death in London'.[46]

Plague in London

In this winter was great death in London, wherefore the term was adjourned, and the king for to eschew the plague, kept his Christmas at Eltham with a small number, for no man might come thither, but such as were appointed by name: this Christmas in the king's house was called the still Christmas. But the cardinal [Wolsey] in this season, lay at the manor of Richmond, and there kept open household, to lords, ladies, and all other that would come, with plays and disguising in most royal manner: which sore grieved the people, and in especial the king's servants, to see him keep an open court, and the king a secret court.

[*Henry VIII* (*Hall's Chronicle*), EDITED BY CHARLES WHIBLEY, VOL. II, P. 56]

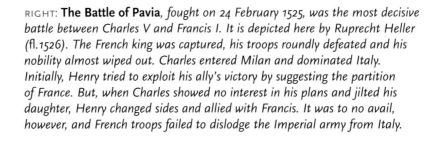

RIGHT: **The Battle of Pavia**, *fought on 24 February 1525, was the most decisive battle between Charles V and Francis I. It is depicted here by Ruprecht Heller (fl.1526). The French king was captured, his troops roundly defeated and his nobility almost wiped out. Charles entered Milan and dominated Italy. Initially, Henry tried to exploit his ally's victory by suggesting the partition of France. But, when Charles showed no interest in his plans and jilted his daughter, Henry changed sides and allied with Francis. It was to no avail, however, and French troops failed to dislodge the Imperial army from Italy.*

1526

In January, Charles V set Francis free, after the French king promised to keep the peace and agreed to leave his sons in Spain as hostages. However, Francis had no intention of abiding by a treaty made under duress.

Also in January, Wolsey issued ordinances at Eltham 'for the establishment of good order and reformation of sundry errors and misuses' in the king's household.[47] To save money, the number of gentlemen in Henry's privy chamber was halved. Those dismissed were men whom Wolsey identified as potential rivals.

The publication abroad of William Tyndale's English translation of the Bible this year created alarm among senior English clerics. Wolsey instigated the arrests of suspected heretics and searches for heretical books. On 11 February the humanist reformer Robert Barnes and some German merchants recanted their unorthodox opinions at Paul's Cross. Wolsey then presided over a book-burning and read out a proclamation listing heavy penalties for possessing heretical books. Bishop Fisher gave the sermon. Later, on 27 October, Bishop Tunstal of London preached a sermon at St Paul's against Tyndale's New Testament, claiming to have found no fewer than 2000 errors in it. Copies of the book were then burned.

Henry's pursuit of Anne Boleyn, the younger daughter of Sir Thomas Boleyn, in the traditional displays of 'courtly love', was made public in the Shrove Tuesday jousts. Henry appeared in the guise of a tortured lover, with the legend 'Declare I dare not'. Henry had, in earlier years, been the lover of Anne's elder sister, Mary, who was not known to have borne him any child.

On 22 May a league against the emperor was formed at Cognac, signed by France, the papacy, Venice, Florence and Milan. Henry did not join, but he did agree to be its official 'protector'. On 8 August Henry and French representatives signed the Treaty of Hampton Court, whereby each side promised not to make a separate peace with Charles. Meanwhile, the Turks under Suleiman the Magnificent marched through the Balkans: on 29 August King Louis of Hungary was defeated by the Turks at the Battle of Mohacs. Despite papal pleas that Christian princes

ABOVE: **This miniature of Katherine of Aragon** *was given to Francis I in 1526, when Henry and Francis were exchanging such images of their families as a sign of their amity. It was painted by the Flemish artist Lucas Hornebolt, who is (together with his father, Gerard) credited with bringing the art of miniature-painting to England. By then, though, Katherine was no longer Henry's bedfellow and the king was in the midst of his courtly pursuit of Anne Boleyn.*

RIGHT: **William Tyndale's New Testament,** *translated into English from the Greek, was printed in the German city of Worms in 1526 and smuggled into England, where it was denounced as heretical. It was written in an accessible English style and printed in a pocket-sized edition. The page depicted here is from the Gospel of St John. Tyndale's later translations of the Pentateuch and Jonah were the first English translations from the Hebrew. In 1536, Tyndale was captured in the Low Countries and burned at the stake in Antwerp.*

The Gospell off Sancte Jhon.

The fyrst Chapter.

IN the begynnynge was that worde/ād that worde was with god: and god was thatt worde. The same was in the begynnynge wyth god. All thyngf were made by it/ and with out it/ was made noo thige/that made was. In it was lyfe/ And lyfe was the light of mē/ And the light shyneth i darcknes/ād darcknes cōprehēded it not.

There was a mā sent from god/ whose name was Jhon. The same cā as a witnes/ to beare witnes of the light/that all men through hī myght beleve. He was nott that light: but to beare witnes of the light. That was a true light/ whi ch lighteneth all men that come ito the worlde. He was in the worlde/ ād the worlde by hī was made: and the worlde knewe hym not.

He cā ito his awne/ād his receaved hī not. vns to as meny as receaved hī / gave he power to be the sōnes of god: i that they beleved ō his name: which were borne not of bloude nor of the will of the flesshe / nor yet of the will of men: but of god.

And that worde was made flesshe/and dwelt amonge vs/and we sawe the glory off yt / as the glory off the only begotten sonne off the father/

Henry's love letter

Debating with myself the contents of your letter, *I have put myself in great distress, not knowing how to interpret them, whether to my disadvantage, as in some places is shown, or to my advantage, as in others I understand them; praying you with all my heart that you will expressly certify me of your whole mind concerning the love between us two. For of necessity I must ensure me of this answer having been now above one whole year struck with the dart of love, not being assured either of failure or of finding place in your heart and grounded affection. Which last point has kept me for some little time from calling you my mistress, since if you do not love me in a way which is beyond common affection that name in no wise belongs to you, for it denotes a singular love, far removed from the common ... If it shall please you to do me the office of a true, loyal mistress and friend and give yourself up, body and soul, to me who will be and have been your loyal servant (if by your severity you do not forbid me), I promise you that not only shall the name be given you, but that also I will take you for my only mistress, rejecting from thought and affection all others save yourself, to serve you only.*

[A LETTER FROM KING HENRY TO ANNE BOLEYN, AS QUOTED BY ERIC IVES, *Anne Boleyn*, PP. 103–4; THE ORIGINAL IS IN THE VATICAN LIBRARY]

combine to drive the Turks out, European rulers – including Henry – were too preoccupied with their own quarrels to defend Eastern Europe. At home, 'all this summer the king took his pastime in hunting.'[48]

Bad weather struck England in the latter part of the year. During the autumn and winter, so much rain fell that 'there ensued great floods which destroyed corn fields and pastures, and drowned many sheep and beasts'.[49]

1527

In February, a French embassy arrived in England to negotiate a treaty of 'eternal peace'. The ambassadors were treated to tournaments, orations, masques and banquets, and on 30 April the Treaty of Westminster was signed.

This was the year in which Henry began to move towards the annulment of his marriage to Katherine as a solution to dynastic and personal problems. On 17 May, Cardinal Wolsey – exercising his authority as papal legate – opened a secret court in his palace at York Place to examine whether Henry was cohabiting unlawfully with Katherine. A papal dispensation had been obtained to allow Henry and Katherine to marry in 1509, despite the impediment derived from Katherine's shortlived (and, it was assumed, consummated) marriage to Prince Arthur. However, Henry now claimed that his marriage was invalid, because it contravened the injunction in scripture (Leviticus 18:16) that prohibited sex between a man and his brother's wife. During the court's proceedings, Wolsey presented an impressive argument against the sufficiency of the papal dispensation and then referred the matter to a tribunal of theologians and lawyers.

RIGHT: **Henry's Book of Hours** *contained a declaration of love for Anne Boleyn, who steadfastly refused to become his mistress. On the page showing the man of sorrows, Henry wrote a lament in French: 'If you remember me according to my love in our prayers I shall scarcely be forgotten since I am your Henry Rex forever.' She replied in English on the page showing the Annunciation: 'By daily proof you shall me find / to be to you both loving and kind.'*

There, Bishop Fisher gave his unwelcome opinion that the original dispensation was legal but that it was up to the present pope to make a judgement.

Wolsey informed Henry on 2 June that the case needed to be heard in Rome. But, on that same date, news reached England that Imperial troops had run amok in early May and sacked Rome, causing Pope Clement to take refuge in the Castel St Angelo before fleeing to Orvieto. Not only was the pope now preoccupied with more important matters than Henry's annulment, but also he would now do nothing to offend Katherine's nephew, Charles V. Nevertheless, on 22 June Henry told Katherine that he no longer considered her his lawful wife. She countered by saying her marriage to Arthur had never been consummated and so her marriage to Henry was valid.

In mid-June, 'sweating sickness' hit London again. To compound these woes, the epidemic was followed by harvest failure.

On the afternoon of 11 July, Wolsey crossed the Channel at the head of a magnificent embassy for a conference with Francis at Amiens. He decided not to raise Henry's 'private matters' (the

ABOVE: **The Treaty of Amiens** between Henry and Francis I was ratified in August 1527 and brought to England in October. This treaty pledged perpetual peace between the two monarchs. Here, a portrait of Francis occupies the top left-hand corner and his fleur-de-lys shield is centred in the bottom border. The gold leaf and rich illuminations signified the importance attached to the treaty by both sides.

RIGHT: **Cardinal Thomas Wolsey (c.1472–1530)** was Henry's most trusted minister until his fall in 1529–30. He was the son of an Ipswich butcher and grazier, and his administrative and diplomatic ability led to swift advancement in church and state, including the acquisition of rich benefices and the office of lord chancellor. He was made a cardinal in 1515 – and he is depicted here in the appropriate dress – and temporarily a papal legate, legatus a latere, in 1518. Then in January 1524, he became legatus a latere for life, a position that gave him legal supremacy over the English Church. He was an able administrator who initiated reforms in the judicial courts, the royal household and the church. He also established commissions to investigate illegal enclosures (both the enclosure of common land and the conversion of arable land into pasture). Wolsey was reported as being 'very handsome, learned, extremely eloquent, of vast ability and indefatigable' (Calendar of State Papers, Venetian).

CARDINAL WOOLSEY

ABOVE: **Pope Clement VII (1478–1534)** *was caught between a desire to appease the English king and a fear of offending the emperor during the early negotiations surrounding Henry's 'great matter': the annulment. Consequently, the pope promised Henry much but delivered nothing. In 1529, however, events in Italy convinced Clement that he had more to fear from Charles V than Henry, and he threw in his lot with the emperor. This was a serious miscalculation, which resulted in Henry's break with Rome. The painting is a close copy of Sebastiano del Piombo's portrait of 1531–2.*

annulment) at the meeting despite finding 'much affection in the French king'.[50] On 18 August a fresh set of treaties was signed, in which it was agreed that Henry's daughter should marry Francis's second son, the Duke of Orleans.

In November, Henry dispatched his own special envoy, the experienced diplomat William Knight, to the pope. On 23 December, Clement handed over a dispensation that would allow Henry to marry again, but the text did not contain a clause stating that Henry's marriage to Katherine had been invalid. This meant that Henry only had permission to enter into a bigamous union and any offspring from it would be illegitimate. Knight also obtained a commission for Wolsey to hear the case against Katherine, but the terms allowed her to appeal to Rome. His mission therefore was a total failure.

1528

On 22 January Henry declared war on Charles V and imposed a ban on all commerce between their realms. Unpopular with merchants and clothiers, the embargo provoked a wave of unrest in March, and Cardinal Wolsey was compelled to seek peace by early April.

With regard to the annulment issue, in February Wolsey sent two trusted members of his household, Edward Fox and Stephen Gardiner, to the pope with instructions to bring back a 'decretal commission'. This legal document would empower two papal legates (preferably Wolsey and Cardinal Campeggio) to determine Henry's case in England without any appeal to Rome. The two envoys were also told to scotch rumours that Henry loved another woman and to explain that the king was acting solely out of conscience.

After protracted and sometimes bitter negotiations, the envoys received a commission on 13 April, empowering Wolsey and Campeggio to decide the case in England. However, the commission was insufficient since it did not specifically prohibit a right of appeal to the papal court, the curia. Katherine would certainly appeal, and the pope would be forced to give a judgement in her nephew Charles's interests unless Italy could be cleared of Imperial troops. Further pressure was put on the pope. At last, on 8 June, Pope Clement caved in and issued a secret decretal commission to Campeggio and

Sweating sickness returns

In the very end of May [1528] began in the city of London the sickness called the sweating sickness, and afterward went all the realm almost of the which many died within 5 or 6 hours. By reason of this sickness the term was adjourned and the circuits of Assize also. The king was sore troubled with this plague for divers died in court… so that the king for a space removed almost every day, till at the last he came to Titynhangar a place of the Abbot of St Albans and there he with a few determined to bide the chance that God would send him, which place was so purged daily with fires and other preservatives that neither he nor the queen nor none of their company was infected with that disease, such was the pleasure of God. In this great plague died Sir William Compton knight and William Carey esquire which were of the king's privy chamber, and whom the king highly favoured and many other worshipful men and women in England.

[*Henry VIII* (*Hall's Chronicle*), EDITED BY CHARLES WHIBLEY, VOL. II, P. 137]

Wolsey. But no sooner had Campeggio left for England than Clement changed his mind and ordered the cardinal to make no judgement and instead to prevaricate.

From June and throughout the summer, sweating sickness again hit the realm. Among the many people who died in this outbreak were courtiers such as Sir William Compton and William Carey, the husband of Mary Boleyn.

In early October, Campeggio arrived in England. In his first interview with the king, he found Henry was so convinced that his marriage was invalid that 'an angel descending from Heaven would be unable to convince him otherwise'.[51] Katherine was equally obdurate. Although Henry had guaranteed that their daughter would remain as heir presumptive, she insisted on putting her case before a legatine court and refused to enter a nunnery as Campeggio recommended. She also assured the cardinal that her marriage with Prince Arthur had not been consummated.

Because of popular support for Katherine, Henry called a meeting of courtiers and prominent Londoners to Bridewell on 8 November. There he explained his 'scruples of conscience' and professed his admiration for Katherine, futilely attempting to show that it was not personal preferences that led him to press for an annulment. Throughout this period, Henry 'kept a good countenance toward the queen with as much love, honour and gentleness, as could be showed to such a princess, but he abstained from her bed'.[52] That Christmas he spent with Anne Boleyn at Greenwich.

1529

Katherine, the tenacious queen

... two legates came to the queen at ... Bridewell *... When she heard the cause of their coming, no marvel though she were astonished for it touched her very near. And when she had paused a while she answered: 'Alas my lords it is now a question whether I be the king's lawful wife or no? When I have been married to him almost 20 years and in the mean season [time] never question was made before? Divers prelates yet being alive and lords also and privy councillors with the king at that time, then adjudged our marriage lawful and honest, and now to say it is detestable and abominable, I think it great marvel: and in especial when I consider ... that ... our fathers ... forsaw what might follow of our marriage, and in especial the king my father, sent to the Court of Rome, and there after long suit, with great cost and charge, obtained a licence and dispensation, that I being the one brother's wife, and peradventure [possibly] carnally known, might without scruple of conscience, marry with the other brother lawfully, which licence under lead I have yet to show, which things make me to say, and surely believe, that our marriage was both lawful, good, and godly.*

[*Henry VIII* (*Hall's Chronicle*), EDITED BY CHARLES WHIBLEY, VOL. II, PP. 147–8]

In February, Henry granted Wolsey the wealthy see of Winchester, which was vacant. The same month, rumours of Clement's death reached England and Henry hoped to have Wolsey elected as pope, but Clement inconveniently lived on and proved as unhelpful as ever, still failing to provide Henry with assurances that the outcome of the marital case would be determined in England.

On 31 May, the legatine court finally opened in the Parliament chamber at Blackfriars. On 18 June Katherine appeared before the court, denied its competence to hear the case and formally registered her appeal to Rome. Notwithstanding her protest, the legates continued to hear arguments presented by both sides. On 21 June Katherine again appeared, and on this occasion she knelt before the king protesting that she had been a good and obedient wife to him. She then withdrew, in spite of a command that she continue to attend. On 25 June she was declared contumacious, in contempt of court on account of her absence. Towards the end of July, Campeggio adjourned the case until October; but Pope Clement summoned the case to Rome.

RIGHT: **Thomas Wolsey's fall from power** *in October 1529 was the result of his failure to obtain the annulment of Henry's first marriage. This letter was written just after his dismissal from office and it is signed, plaintively, 'your grace's most prostrate poor chaplain, creature and beadsman'. Here, Wolsey pleads for the king's 'grace, mercy, remission and pardon', explaining that the remembrance of his 'folly and the sharp sword' of the king's displeasure have penetrated his heart. Wolsey was pardoned in early 1530, but his intrigues with the Imperial ambassador led to his arrest in November 1530. He died on his way* down to London. Wolsey had aroused opposition during his career. A rich pluralist (who sired two children), he had come, in the eyes of some, to personify the corruptions within the church. His pre-eminence and low birth had also made him deeply unpopular with many of the nobility.

Moste gracyous and mercyfull Soueraygn lorde, thow that I yo[r]
poore herny and wrecchyd prest do dayly p[ur]sue try and calle upon
yo[r] Royal maieste for grace mercy remyssyon and pardon, yet
m moste humble wyse I beseche yo[r] hyghnes nat to thyncke that
yt proceidyth of any mystruste that I haue in yo[r] mercyfull
goodnes nor that I wolde membyr or moleste yo[r] maieste by
any indysscret or importune Suyt, but the same onely commyth
of an Inwarde and ardent desyre that I haue cotynmally to
declare vnto yo[r] hyghnes how that next vnto god I desyre not
couet any thyng in thys worlde but the atteynyng of yo[r]
gracyous fauor and forgeuenes of my tresspace. And for thys
cause I can nat desyst nor forbere but to be a cotynuall and
moste lowly Suppbyant to yo[r] benygne grace, for Suerly moste
gracyous kyng the remembrance of my folly w[ith] the Sharpe
Sworde of yo[r] hyghnes dyspleasure hath so penetrat my
hert that I can nat but lamentally try and most remrsly
pray and say, Suffocat, nunc cotume pyssime rex manu tuam
ob amorem illius Stelle omq vbera preciosa contra venerem
delictoy nostroy qu dulcoter Suyt I xp[s] Jesus who Inuytyth
yo[r] hyghnes to mercy and forgeuenes sayng dimittite et dimitte
vobis et beati misericordes qm ipi misericordiam cosequentur
wych that I may Shortly atteyne at yo[r] gracys hand. And
yo[r] hyghnes the Semblable at gode w[ith] the increasse of yo[r]
moste Royall astat in thys worlde And eternal ioy and glory
in an other I shall cotynualy pray to almyghty god as yo[r]
moste prostrat poore chapleyn creature and bedsman

By then, international events had turned against Henry and Wolsey. On 21 June Imperial forces had defeated the French in Italy, at the Battle of Landriano, and in July Imperial troops entered the Papal States. The pope hurriedly concluded a treaty with Charles, and on 3 August Francis followed suit. There was now no possibility of the pope agreeing to Henry's annulment. As Wolsey had failed to deliver the king's desired outcome in this most important of matters, the cardinal's fall into disfavour now seemed likely.

Henry went on summer progress during August. Plans were made to consult theologians and canon lawyers in European universities, and even rabbis, for their opinions on the validity of the annulment.

On 9 October, Wolsey was indicted in the Court of King's Bench for exercising the office of papal legate illegally, contrary to the 14th-century statute of *praemunire*, which limited foreign jurisdiction in England. On 18 October, Wolsey was ordered to surrender the great seal, by which the lord chancellor exercised the king's authority. He was also dismissed from the king's council. On 25 October, the seal was delivered to Sir Thomas More in the king's privy chamber, and the following day More took his oath as the new lord chancellor.

On 3 November Parliament opened. The House of Commons immediately brought forward grievances against the clergy relating to mortuary fees, probate fees, pluralism and non-residence. Bills reforming these matters passed both houses. Forty-four complaints against Wolsey were also presented.

Katherine's popular support

The pleading was in open court, *before whom the king did not spare to justify his intention. If the matter was to be decided by women, he would lose the battle; for they did not fail to encourage the queen at her entrance and departure by their cries, telling her to care for nothing, and other such words; while she recommended herself to their good prayers, and used other Spanish tricks.*

[FRENCH AMBASSADOR JEAN DU BELLAY TO FRANCIS I, 22 JUNE 1529, FROM *Letters and Papers of the Reign of Henry the Eighth,* VOL. IV PART III, NO. 5702, P. 2526]

LEFT: **Sir Thomas More (1478–1535)** *replaced Wolsey as lord chancellor in October 1529. 'Everyone rejoices at his promotion, for besides the esteem in which he is generally held for his uprightness of character, he is considered the most learned man in the kingdom', according to the* Calendar of State Papers, Venetian. *More's reputation was based on his humanist scholarship and the political satire* Utopia, *published abroad in 1516. During his chancellorship More introduced legal reforms and campaigned actively against heresy. He privately opposed Henry's annulment, but continued in public office until Henry imposed his supremacy on the Convocation of Canterbury on 15 May 1532. The next day, More resigned. In 1534, he refused to swear oaths endorsing the statutes passed against papal jurisdiction, and he was executed on 6 July 1535 after a trial heavily weighted against him. Five hundred years later the pope canonized him. In this painting, following one by Holbein the Younger, he is shown wearing the collar of the royal servant. The 'SS' design was the livery of the Lancastrians, and the clasp is made up of the Beaufort portcullis, from which hangs the Tudor rose.*

Wolsey in adversity

Sir William [Gascoigne, *Wolsey's treasurer*] said unto my lord [Wolsey] 'Sir, I am sorry for your grace, for I understand ye shall go straightway to the Tower.' 'Is this the good comfort and counsel,' quoth my lord, 'that ye can give your master in adversity? It hath been always your natural inclination to be very light of credit [gullible] and much more lighter in reporting of false news. I would ye should know, Sir William and all other such blasphemers, that it is nothing more false than that. For I never (thanks be to God) deserved by no ways to come there under any arrest, although it has pleased the king to take my house ready furnished for his pleasure at this time. I would all the world knew, and so I confess, to have nothing, either riches, honour, or dignity, that hath not grown of him and by him; therefore it is my duty to surrender the same to him again as his very own with all my heart, or else I were an unkind servant.'…

… Then [1529] was there brought a bill of articles into the Parliament House to have my lord condemned of treason; against which bill Master Cromwell inveighed so discreetly, with such witty persuasions and deep reasons, that the same bill could take there no effect. Then were all his enemies compelled to indict him in a praemunire, and all was done only to the intent to entitle the king to all his goods and possessions, the which he had gathered together and purchased for his colleges in Oxford and Ipswich, and for the maintenance of the same, which was then a-building in most sumptuous wise. Wherein when he was demanded by the judges, which were sent him purposely to examine him, what answer he would make to the same, he said: 'The king's highness knoweth right well whether I have offended his majesty and his laws or no …'

[GEORGE CAVENDISH, 'LIFE OF THOMAS WOLSEY', IN *Two Early Tudor Lives*, PP. 103 AND 116–7]

1530

On 7 March, Pope Clement called Henry to Rome for a hearing of the matrimonial case and forbade him to marry Anne Boleyn on pain of excommunication. In response, Henry demanded an immediate papal annulment.

Early in April, Wolsey left London for his diocese at York. Henry's new advisers were members of the Boleyn family and ex-members of Wolsey's household – Edward Fox, Stephen Gardiner and Thomas Cromwell.

During the summer, Henry received favourable decisions on the annulment from seven European universities, and these were printed in the *Censurae academiarum* (*Determinations of the Universities*). English theologians, meanwhile, compiled a manuscript, termed the *Collectanea satis copiosa* ('Sufficiently abundant collections'), which contained arguments that the king exercised supreme jurisdiction within England and could not be summoned to Rome.

In the early autumn, 15 of the higher clergy (most of them supporters of Katherine) were accused of offences against the statute of *praemunire* on the grounds that they had cooperated with Wolsey while he was papal legate. However, as soon as Henry received notification that the pope still insisted on his presence at Rome, he decided to call off the attack on individuals and instead to charge the whole clergy.

On 4 November, Wolsey was arrested on a charge of high treason, immediately after Henry learned of

RIGHT: **Anne Boleyn (c.1507–36)** *was as determined to marry Henry VIII as he was to marry her. She captivated Henry not by her beauty, but by her elegant style, lively personality and refusal to become his mistress. The* Calendar of State Papers, Venetian *contains the description that 'Madam Anne is not one of the handsomest women in the world; she is of middling stature, swarthy complexion, long neck, wide mouth, bosom not much raised.' Her only notable feature was her eyes, 'which are black and beautiful', as indeed is evident in this English portrait from 1534.*

ANNA · BOLINA ⋯⋯⋯⋯⋯⋯⋯⋯⋯⋯ ANG · REGINA

his secret communications with the emperor. He was, however, spared the ignominy of a trial, for on 29 November he died at Leicester Abbey *en route* to London. The cause was dysentery, though 'some reckon he killed himself with purgations'.[53]

Despite his campaign for an annulment, Henry kept Christmas at Greenwich with Katherine, still England's queen.

1531

'he unwittingly passed on poisoned soup to his servants'

Parliament opened on 6 January. One statute it enacted made boiling alive the punishment for murder by poison. The only victim of this act was a cook wrongly blamed for attempting to poison Bishop Fisher of Rochester. In February the bishop escaped an assassination attempt when he unwittingly passed on poisoned soup to his servants and members of the poor, two of whom died. Another notable measure passed in this session was a Poor Law that ordered the whipping of vagabonds and unlicensed beggars.

In Convocation Henry accused all the English clergy of transgressing the statute of *praemunire* by accepting Wolsey's authority as a papal legate, and he demanded a fine of about £100,000 in return for a general pardon. The dispute between the king and Convocation soon widened, and it culminated on 7 February with Henry's demand that the clergy recognize him as their supreme head. After some resistance led by Fisher, the clergy succumbed, merely adding the proviso 'as far as the law of Christ allows'. A general pardon followed.

Despite the quarrel with Rome, the fight against heresy continued. On 16 August the preacher Thomas Bilney was burned at Norwich. He had been arrested after preaching against images and distributing Tyndale's forbidden Bible.

A month earlier, on 11 July, Henry had set off on his royal progress without Queen Katherine. They never saw each other again. 'All men said there was no mirth in that Christmas because the queen and the ladies were absent.'[54]

148

RIGHT: **The 'Determinations of the Universities' (1531)** *was an English translation of the* Censurae academiarum *published the previous year. It presented the favourable judgements reached by seven foreign universities on the issues that lay behind the king's annulment: first that a Christian was prohibited from marrying his brother's widow; and second that the pope had no authority to issue dispensations to allow such marriages. The book's publication was thus part of the government's propaganda campaign to win support for Henry's annulment.*

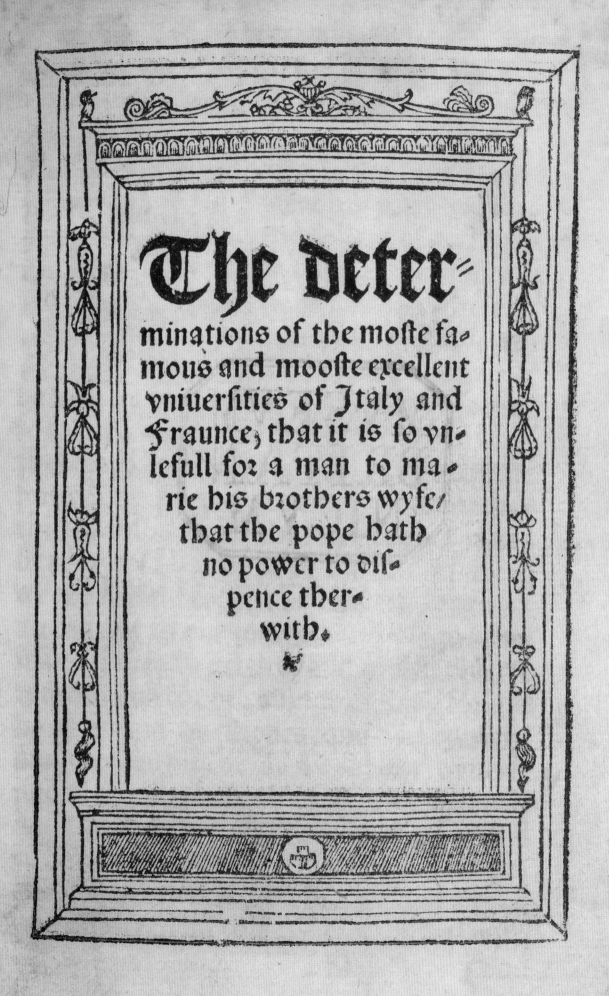

The deter=
minations of the moste fa=
mous and mooste excellent
vniuersities of Jtaly and
Fraunce, that it is so vn=
lefull for a man to ma=
rie his brothers wyfe,
that the pope hath
no power to dis=
pence ther=
with.

Thomas Cromwell (c.1485–1540) *became Henry's most influential minister during the 1530s. He sat on the council from 1531 and received his first major office, the mastership of the king's jewels, in 1532. He acted as secretary while Stephen Gardiner was absent abroad during 1533, and he was formally granted the position in April 1534. A strong advocate of the royal supremacy, he was appointed Henry's vicar-general of the church in January 1535. Because of his advocacy of religious change and sponsorship of reformers, Cromwell was deeply unpopular with conservatives like Gardiner and the Duke of Norfolk. They rejoiced in – and helped bring about – his downfall in 1540. Cromwell is shown here wearing the Order of the Garter, in a painting after Holbein the Younger.*

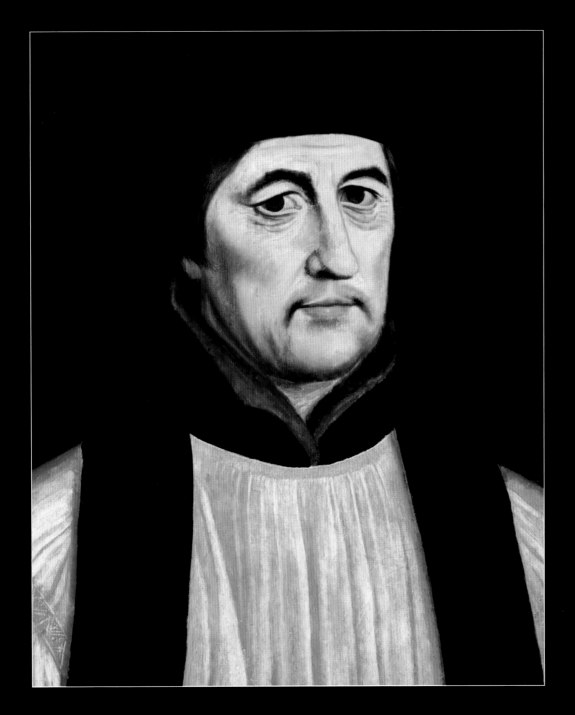

Bishop Stephen Gardiner of Winchester (1495?–1555) *led the clerical opposition to Henry's attempts to have himself declared supreme head of the church in the Convocation of April 1532. This probably cost him promotion to Canterbury on Archbishop Warham's death later in the year. After the Act of Supremacy was passed in Parliament, Gardiner accepted – indeed openly defended – the royal supremacy, but he was never again fully trusted by the king. Gardiner spent most of Edward VI's reign in prison for opposing the Protestant reforms, but he re-emerged under Mary to help bring about the Catholic restoration. He is shown here in an English painting of the 16th century.*

1532

In the parliamentary session that opened on 15 January, Henry introduced a bill to abolish annates, a payment sent to Rome. Opposition to the bill was so strong, however, that he had to go three times to Parliament in mid-March to push the measure through. Even then, the bill was amended so that annates were withheld only for a limited period.

The House of Commons, meanwhile, debated its own complaints against the clergy. On 18 March the speaker presented a petition entitled 'The Commons' Supplication against the Ordinaries' to the king for remedy. It contained a list of perceived clerical abuses, and referred to the king as the only sovereign of the clergy. Henry passed this petition on to Convocation, where it was discussed during April. The task of responding fell to Stephen Gardiner, the new Bishop of Winchester, who denied that convocation needed royal assent for its decisions. Henry was predictably furious, and on 10 May he put three explicit demands before his clergy. Together they amounted to a recognition that all ecclesiastical legislation had to be subject to his approval. Convocation submitted and surrendered its legislative independence to the crown on 15 May. The next day Sir Thomas More resigned as lord chancellor, to be later replaced by Thomas Audley. On 22 August, Archbishop Warham – who disliked both the annulment and Henry's bludgeoning of the church – died, leaving a vacancy at Canterbury.

Henry was now ready to present Anne Boleyn as his future consort. On 1 September she was created Marchioness of Pembroke, and on 11 October she accompanied him to Calais for a meeting with the French king. Francis had expressed support for the annulment and promised to supply cavalry and ships in the event of an Imperial invasion of England.

Leaving Anne at Calais, Henry spent four days with Francis at Boulogne. On 25 October he returned to Calais, accompanied by Francis and a large French retinue. After a splendid dinner (in which 170 different dishes were served, cooked alternately in the French and English styles), Anne made her appearance leading a masque of six ladies. She claimed Francis as her dancing partner, and they later spent much of the evening in intimate conversation. After this recognition of Anne's status, there was no further reason for Henry and Anne to remain in Calais, but they were delayed there by heavy storms until 12 November. It is likely that during this time they consummated their relationship, confident that Francis would use his influence to secure a papal annulment or defend them against a papal excommunication.

'Henry was now ready to present Anne Boleyn as his future consort'

ABOVE: **A letter patent** *creating Anne Boleyn Marchioness of Pembroke in her own right was issued on 1 September 1532 at Windsor Castle. Dressed in ermine-trimmed crimson velvet and bedecked with jewels, Anne received the mantle and coronet from King Henry. She now had precedence over all the other ladies at court and was of a sufficiently high status to be presented to the French king as Henry's future wife. Her falcon badge can be seen in this illuminated initial letter from the letter patent.*

1533

By January, Anne was known to be pregnant. The child (believed to be a boy) had to be born in wedlock if he were to succeed his father on the throne; consequently Anne's marriage to Henry could no longer be delayed – even if it meant schism.

On 25 January, Henry and Anne married secretly. The break with Rome was next on their agenda. In Parliament, Henry introduced a bill of appeals that proclaimed his status as 'supreme head' and declared that a foreign court had no jurisdiction in England. An English ecclesiastical court now had the authority to render a final decision about Henry's marriage. The verdict was bound to be favourable, since on 30 March Thomas Cranmer – a committed supporter of the annulment – was consecrated as the new Archbishop of Canterbury.

On 5 April, Convocation agreed that Henry's marriage was invalid. The only voice of dissent came from Bishop Fisher, who was arrested the next day. On 9 April, Henry ordered Katherine to cease using her title as queen, and on Easter Saturday (the 12th) Anne 'was proclaimed queen at Greenwich'.[55]

On 10 May, the stage-managed inquiry into the validity of Henry's marriage to Katherine began at Dunstable Priory. On 23 May Cranmer judged it invalid, and five days later he declared the marriage to Anne – now made public – lawful.

Over Whit weekend, Henry flaunted Anne before his subjects at her coronation. On Saturday 31 May, huge crowds gathered to watch the procession from the Tower to Whitehall Palace and gaze upon their new queen, resplendent in white and nearly six-months pregnant. A few notables – like Sir Thomas More – stayed away, but thousands turned up even if, as was reported, they neither raised their caps nor cheered when Anne's litter passed by. The next morning, Anne was crowned. The religious ceremony was followed by a grand banquet, and jousts were held over the next two days in the new tiltyard erected at Whitehall.

'their new queen, resplendent in white and nearly six-months pregnant'

LEFT: **Nikolaus Kratzer (c.1487–c.1550)** *was Henry VIII's astronomer royal from at least 1519 until 1545 and a tutor to Thomas More's daughters. A friend of Hans Holbein the Younger, Kratzer had this portrait painted by the artist in 1528. He is shown in the process of making a ten-sided sundial. Parts of the incomplete dial lie alongside a ruler and a woodcutting knife on the left of the table. Other instruments on display include an auger, scissors, a divider and a hammer.*

'The Ambassadors', *painted in 1533, is one of the most famous paintings by Hans Holbein the Younger (1497/8–1543). It is a double portrait of Jean de Dinteville (dressed fashionably on the left) and Georges de Selve, Bishop of Lavour, both of them diplomats who arrived separately in England as ambassadors in 1533. The painting also exudes symbolic meanings. On the two shelves of the table are objects associated with the four mathematical sciences within a humanist curriculum: astronomy, arithmetic, geometry and music. While alluding to the men's interest in this 'new learning', many of these items also symbolize discord: the dividers among the geometrical instruments, the lute with a broken string, the arithmetic book open on a page beginning with the word 'divide', and even the misalignment of the instruments for use in the northern hemisphere. The hymn-book is Lutheran and draws attention to the confessional divisions in Europe. Allusions to mortality can be seen in the skull on the floor and the memento mori attached to Dinteville's hat. This overall pessimistic emphasis on chaos and death is countered by the references to Christ's redemptive power in the half-hidden crucifix (upper left) and in the date on the sundial: 11 April, which was Good Friday in 1533.*

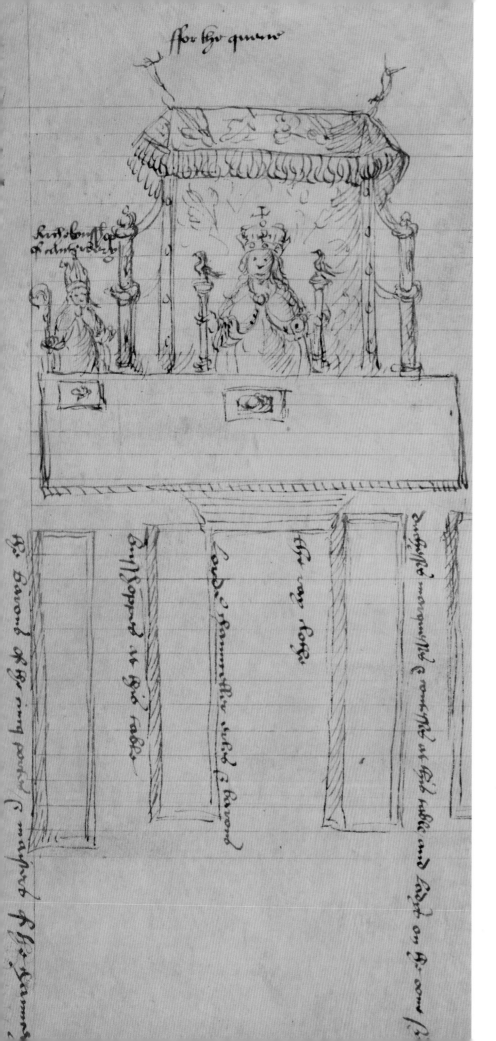

On 11 July Pope Clement nullified the Dunstable proceedings and ordered Henry to abandon Anne. He also drew up a bull of excommunication, but its operation was suspended in the hope that Henry would obey his directive.

Anne was in Greenwich when she gave birth on 7 September – to a daughter. At the christening on 10 September, Katherine's supporters were forced to participate prominently, alongside the Boleyns. The baby was named Elizabeth after her two grandmothers. As was customary at the birth of a girl, the planned jousts were cancelled, but bonfires were lit the following day and 'at every fire a vessel of wine for people to drink'.[56]

Thomas Cromwell, now Henry's leading minister, took the lead in stamping out all voices of opposition to the annulment and the new marriage. He first turned against Elizabeth Barton, a Benedictine nun, whose prophecies against the annulment were gaining credence. Consequently, in November, Cromwell ordered her arrest on a charge of treason. On 23 November she and six of her followers – two monks, two observant friars and two laymen – were forced to stand on a scaffold at Paul's Cross while a preacher denounced her as fraudulent.

LEFT: **A contemporary plan** *for Queen Anne's coronation in Westminster Hall, 1 June 1533, shows the queen seated under a canopy, bearing a sceptre in each hand. To her right is the Archbishop of Canterbury. Below her is a seating plan for the nobility, bishops and royal officers who attended.*

1534

Parliament now passed a wave of legislation designed to settle the succession and remove the remnants of papal jurisdiction from England. In February, Katherine's title was changed to 'Dowager Princess of Wales'. On 23 March, Parliament passed an Act of Succession that declared the validity of Henry's marriage to Anne and the right of their children to succeed to the throne. All Henry's subjects were required to swear an oath subscribing to the statute on pain of life imprisonment. In March, Parliament approved an act that terminated all papal taxes.

During the spring, a more rigorous crackdown on dissidents began as the oath of succession was applied. Sir Thomas More was ordered to take it on 12 April: he was imprisoned in the Tower five days later when he refused. Bishop Fisher suffered the same fate. On 20 April the oath was administered to prominent Londoners outside the clergy. They all complied, but probably they were terrified into submission, for the oath was demanded on the day that Elizabeth Barton and her six followers were executed. No doubt many citizens could see the victims' body parts affixed to the gates of the city and London Bridge. In May, Katherine and the Princess Mary were also required to swear the oath. They refused, but escaped imprisonment. Instead, Katherine was banished to Kimbolton Castle near Huntingdon and denied all contact with her daughter.

Some time during July or August, Anne suffered a miscarriage.[57] The summer also saw unrest in Ireland, when Thomas Fitzgerald, who was Lord Offaly and the only son of the 9th Earl of Kildare, led a rebellion. His reason was dissatisfaction with Cromwell's plans for governmental changes, which included the dismissal of Kildare as Ireland's lord deputy. Henry sent troops to Ireland with instructions to restore order.

On 11 August the friars observant, a reformed branch of the Franciscan order, were evicted from their houses because two leading friars had reprimanded the king for his treatment of Katherine and the church.

Principle and treason

Master Rich [afterwards Lord Rich], *then newly made the King's Solicitor ... [was] sent to Sir Thomas More into the Tower to fetch away his books from him… and… pretending friendly talk with him… said…:*

'Forasmuch as it is well known, Master More, that you are a man both wise and well-learned, as well in the laws of the realm as otherwise, I pray you therefore, sir, let me be so bold as of good will to put unto you this case. Admit there were sir,' quoth he, 'an Act of Parliament that all the realm should take me for king. Would not you, Master More, take me for king?'

'Yes sir,' quoth Sir Thomas More, 'that would I.'

'I put the case further,' quoth Master Rich, 'that there were an Act of Parliament that all the realm should take me for pope. Would not you, then, Master More, take me for pope?'

'For answer, sir,' quoth Sir Thomas More, 'to your first case. The Parliament may well, Master Rich, meddle with the state of temporal princes. But to make answer to your other case, I will put you this case: Suppose the Parliament would make a law that God should not be God. Would you then, master Rich, say that God were not God?'

'No sir,' quoth he, 'that would I not, since no Parliament may make any such law.'

'No more' said Sir Thomas More, as Master Rich reported of him, 'could the Parliament make the king supreme head of the church.'

Upon whose only report was Sir Thomas More indicted of treason upon the statute whereby it was made treason to deny the king to be the supreme head of the church.

[WILLIAM ROPER, 'LIFE OF SIR THOMAS MORE', IN *Two Early Tudor Lives*, PP. 244–5]

Item quedam billa formam cuiusdam actus in se continens exhibita est prefato domino Regi in parliamento pro eo cuius bille tenor sequitur in hec verba

8

Albeit the kynges majestie justly and rightfully is and oweth to be the supreme heed of the churche of England and so is recognysed by the clergy of this realme in theyr convocacions yet neverthelesse for corroboracion and confirmacion therof and for increase of vertu in Christis religion within this realme of England and to represse and extirpe all errours heresies and other enormyties and abuses heretofore used in the same be it enacted by auctorite of this present parliament that the kyng our soveraign lorde his heires and successours kynges of this realme shalbe taken accepted and reputed the onely supreme heed in erthe of the churche of England called Anglicana ecclesia and shall have and enjoy annexed and unyted to the ymperiall crowne of this realme as well the title and style therof as all honours dignities preheminences jurisdictions privileges auctorites ymmunities profites and comodites to the said dignite of supreme heed of the same churche belonging and apperteynyng And that our said soveraign lorde his heires and successours kynges of this realme shall have full power and auctorite from tyme to tyme to visite represse redresse reforme order correcte restrayne and amende all suche errours heresies abuses offences contemptes and enormyties what so ever they be whiche by any maner spirituall auctorite or jurisdiction ought or maie lawfully be reformed repressed ordered redressed corrected restrayned or amended moste to the pleasure of almightie god the increase of vertu in Christis religion and for the conservacion of the peace unyte and tranquillite of this realme any usage custome forreyne lawes forreyne auctorite prescripcion or any other thinge or thinges to the contrarie therof not withstandinge. Cui quidem bille lecte et ad plenum intellecte per dictum dominum Regem ex assensu et auctoritate parliamenti pro eo talis est responsum

Le Roy le voult

Item quedam alia billa formam cuiusdam actus in se continens exhibita est prefato domino Regi in parliamento pro eo cuius bille tenor sequitur in hec verba

9

Where at the last session of this present parliament in the acte then made for the establishment of the succession of the heires of the kynges highnes in the imperiall crowne of this realme it is conteyned amonges other thinges that all and singuler the kynges subiectes as well the nobles spirituall and temporall as other shulde make and take a corporall othe than so ever hit shulde please the kynges majestie or his heires to appoint that they shulde truely firmely and constantly without fraude or gyle observe fulfille mayntayne defende and kepe to theyr cunnyng witt and uttermoste of theyr power the hole effectes and contentes of the said acte as in the same acte amonge other thinges more playnly appereth And at the daye of the last prorogacion of this present parliament as well the nobles spirituall as temporall as other the comons of this present parliament then assembled in the highe house of the parliament moste lovyngly accepted and toke suche othe as then was devysed in writinge for mayntenance and defence of the said acte and mente and intendyd at that tyme that eny other the kynges subiecte shulde be bounde to accepte and take the same upon the payne conteyned in the said acte the tenor of whiche othe hereafter ensueth: ye shall swere to beare faith truthe and obedyence alonely to the kynges majestye and to his heires of his body of his most dere and entierly belovyd laufull wyfe Quene Anne begotten and to be begotten And further to the heires of our said soveraign lorde accordyng to the lymytacion in the statute made for surete of his succession in the crowne of this realme mencioned and conteyned and not to any other within this realme nor forreyn auctorite or potentate And in case any othe be made or hathe be made by you to any persone or persones that then ye to repute the same as vayne and adnychillate And that to your cunnyng witte and uttermoste of your power without gyle fraude or other undue meane you shall observe kepe mayntayne and defende the said acte of succession and all the hole effectes and contentes therof and all other actes and statutes made in confirmacion or for execucion of the same or of any thinge therin conteyned And this ye shall do agenst all maner of persones of what estate dignite degree or condicion so ever they be And in no wyse do or attempte nor to your power suffre to be done or attempted directly or indirectly any thinge or thinges prively or appertly to the let hinderance damage or derogacion therof or of any parte of the same by any maner of meanes or for any maner of pretence So helpe you god all sayntes and the holye evangelystes.

And for asmoche as yt is convenyent for the sure mayntenance and defence of the same acte that the said othe shulde not onely be auctorysed by auctorite of parliament but also be putteprisee and expressed by the hole assent of this present parliament that it was mente and entended by the kynges majestie the lordes and comons of the parliament at the said daye of the said last prorogacion that every subiect shulde be bounden to take the same othe accordyng to the tenor and effect therof upon the peynes and penalities conteyned in the said acte Therfore be hyt enacted by auctorite of this present parliament that the said othe above rehersyd shalbe interprete expounded reputed accepted and adiuged the very othe that the kynges highnesse the lordes spirituall and temporall and the comons of this present parliament mente and entended that every subiecte of this realme shulde be obliged and bounden to take and accepte for mayntenance and defence of the same acte upon the peynes conteyned in the said acte And that every of the kynges subiectes upon the said peynes shalbe obliged to accepte and take the said othe.

And be yt further enacted by auctorite aforesaid that the commissioners that hereafter shalbe appoynted to receyve suche othe of the kynges subiectes or two of theym at the leste shall have power and auctorite to certifie in to the kynges benche by writinge under theyr sealles every refusell that hereafter shalbe made afore theym of the same othe by any person or persons cunnyng afore theym to take the same othe And that every suche certificat to be made by suche commissioners as is aforesaid shalbe taken as stronge and as available in the lawe as an endictment of xii men lawfully founden of the said refusell So that the person and persons agenste whome any suche certificat shalbe made shalbe compelled to answere thereunto as if they were endicted And that suche processe iudgement execucion and every other thinge shalbe hadde used and mynystred of and upon every suche certificat agenste the offendours as yf they had ben lawfully endicted of suche offences by the due course and order of the commen lawes of this realme. Cui quidem bille lecte et ad plenum intellecte per dictum dominum Regem ex assensu et auctoritate parliamenti pro eo talis est responsum

Le Roy le voult

Item quedam alia billa formam cuiusdam actus in se continens exhibita est prefato domino Regi in parliamento pro eo cuius bille tenor sequitur in hec verba For asmoche as it is of very dutie suche to be the naturall inclinacion of all good people lyke...

The death of Pope Clement VII took place on 25 September. Three weeks later, on 13 October, Alexander Farnese was elected Pope Paul III.

In November, Parliament introduced two important pieces of legislation: an Act of Supremacy, which recognized the king as supreme head of the church, and a Treasons Act, which made it punishable by death to 'maliciously wish, will, or desire, by words or writing' harm to Henry, Anne or their heirs.[58] Even before the acts became law, commissioners demanded from senior clerics an oath accepting the royal supremacy over the church. The penalty for non-adherence was death.

The Act of Supremacy

Be it enacted by authority *of this present Parliament that the king our sovereign lord his heirs and successors kings of the realm shall be taken accepted and reputed the only supreme head in earth of the Church of England called Anglicana Ecclesia and shall have & enjoy annexed and united to the imperial crown of this realm as well the title and style thereof, as all honours, dignities, pre-eminences, jurisdictions, privileges, authorities, immunities, profits and commodities to the said dignity of supreme head of the same church belonging and appertaining: And that our said sovereign lord his heirs and successors kings of the realm shall have full power and authority from time to time to visit repress redress reform order correct restrain and amend all such errors heresies abuses offences contempts and enormities whatsoever they be, which by any manner spiritual authority or jurisdiction ought or may lawfully be reformed repressed ordered redressed corrected restrained or amended, most to the pleasure of Almighty God the increase of virtue in Christ's Religion and for ... the peace unity and tranquility of this Realm*

[FROM THE ACT OF SUPREMACY, *Statutes of the Realm*, VOL. III, P. 492]

LEFT: **The Act of Supremacy** *declared that 'the king's majesty justly and rightly is and ought to be the supreme head of the Church of England'. The legislation of the previous year had already eroded papal power in England, and this act confirmed Henry's new title and position. However, the statute was worded to make it clear that Parliament was recognizing Henry's existing authority over the church rather than allowing him new powers.*

ABOVE: **Henry VIII is shown in this psalter** *of 1540–2 playing a harp, as did the biblical psalmist King David. After assuming the royal supremacy, Henry commonly modeled himself on the Old Testament king who was God's elect. Psalm 52 is illustrated here. The king's jester, Will Somers, is also depicted, because the psalm contains the verse 'The fool says in his heart "There is no God."' Annotations in the king's own hand in the margins comment on matters of religion and politics.*

MARCI 16
TE IN MVDVM VNIVERSV ET SEVDICATE
CELIVM OMNI CREATVRE

1535

In January, Thomas Cromwell was appointed vicar-general over the church. He now ordered a census of ecclesiastical wealth for tax purposes and prepared a visitation to assess the condition of the realm's monasteries.

During April, Cromwell rounded up those who refused to take the oath of supremacy. John Houghton, Prior of the London Charterhouse, and Dr Richard Reynolds of Syon Abbey, Middlesex (a Bridgettine house for nuns and priests), together with two other Carthusian priors, were put on trial and sentenced to death. The Vicar of Isleworth was tried separately. On 4 May, the five men were dragged on hurdles from the Tower to Tyburn, where they were hanged, drawn and quartered. In late May, three more monks from the London Charterhouse were imprisoned in the Tower, where they were chained standing and offered only meat to eat (meat being forbidden by their rule). Eight days after their trial on 11 June, they were executed at Tyburn.

On 22 June, the realm's most outspoken critic of the annulment, Bishop Fisher, was beheaded on Tower Hill for refusing to swear the oath of supremacy. On 6 July, Sir Thomas More was beheaded for the same offence.

From July to October, Henry and Anne were on progress in the West Country and southern counties. Henry spent most of his days hunting. During the trip Anne displayed her personal commitment to religious reform when she ordered an investigation into the relic of Christ's blood at Hailes Abbey. She also became pregnant again.

After the census of ecclesiastical property was completed, Cromwell started work on the visitation of the monasteries. In July, he appointed six canon lawyers (both clerics and laymen) as visitors to inquire into the monasteries' spiritual health and to investigate the need for reform. The real purpose of the visitation, however, was to collect enough incriminating evidence to justify a partial suppression of the monasteries. Henry could then confiscate their resources and remedy his financial problems. During the summer, the religious houses in the West of England were visited. In the autumn it was the turn of the houses in the East and Southeast.

The Irish rebel, Thomas Fitzgerald, called 'Silken Thomas', surrendered on 24 August. Despite being promised a pardon, he was imprisoned in the Tower, where he remained until his execution along with his five uncles on 3 February 1537. Seventy other rebel leaders were also executed.

LEFT: **Henry VIII, as depicted here in 1535**, *has filled out and grown his beard, in imitation of his principal Continental rival, Francis I. He displays his evangelical credentials as he holds a scroll inscribed 'Go ye into all the world, and preach the Gospel to every creature' (Mark 16:15). The painting is attributed to Joos van Cleve (c.1485–1540/1).*

OVERLEAF: **The 'Valor ecclesiasticus'**, *drawn up in 1535, contained valuations of all ecclesiastical property in England and Wales; in scope it was comparable to the 11th-century Domesday Book. The census, held now at The National Archives, was initiated because new legislation had made the church liable to pay one-tenth of its net income as taxation to the crown, and Henry naturally needed to know how much he was owed. The extent of wealth it exposed may have tempted him into dissolving the smaller monasteries and confiscating their assets. At any rate, 399 religious houses in England and Wales were suppressed the following March. The image of Henry on this illuminated page, which begins the returns for Derbyshire, reinforces his authority: he is very much the dominant presence among his officials.*

smglozum Comiozum Manecrozum

Aliarum possessionum et xedditum ac

um spialium quam tempozalium omnut

...batne Pziozatibz Collectis Hospitalib

...ntitas liberis Capellis et aliis pzom

...ubustingz situat in et per totum Con

...pertmen pzout inferius continetur

1536

Katherine of Aragon died on 7 January, at Kimbolton House, possibly as a result of coronary thrombosis. She was buried quietly at Peterborough Abbey. During her final illness she remained forbidden from personal contact with her daughter Mary.

On 24 January, Henry fell heavily in the tiltyard at Greenwich and lay unconscious for about two hours. The shock caused Anne to miscarry five days later, reportedly a male foetus. In late January, rumours circulated at court that Henry was attracted to Jane Seymour, one of Queen Anne's ladies in waiting. These rumours gained credibility when (on 18 April) Henry moved her brother, Edward Seymour, into rooms at Greenwich, where the king could meet Jane undetected.

In March, Parliament debated the fate of the religious houses and passed a law dissolving the smaller monasteries (defined as those with a gross income of less than £200 per annum).

On 30 April a royal musician, Mark Smeaton, was arrested. Under interrogation (and possibly torture) he confessed to adultery with Queen Anne. Henry learned this news while attending the May Day tournament at Greenwich with Anne. Leaving hurriedly, he took with him Henry Norris, the groom of the stool who was in charge of the royal privy purse, and Norris too was then accused of the same offence. On 2 May, Anne was arrested with her brother, George Boleyn, Viscount Rochford. They were charged with incest and plotting to

166

RIGHT: **The London Carthusian monks** *were among the victims of the 1534 Acts of Supremacy and Treasons. In May 1535 six of the Carthusians were hanged, drawn (disembowelled) and quartered (hacked into pieces) at Tyburn. Contravening all precedents, they still wore their habits on the scaffold, having not been degraded from holy orders. Two years later, ten Carthusians were chained to the wall in London's Marshalsea prison and starved to death for refusing to take the oath of supremacy. Woodcuts, such as this one, showing the sufferings and martyrdom of the Carthusians, were printed and circulated during Mary I's reign.*

PIO AC CATHOLICO LECTORI S.

Cardinalis   Compost.

ra sesquimillesimum tricesimo quinto, Henricus Angliæ Rex, eius nominis octauus, cum sese sacrilego quodam ausu, contempta Romanæ Se.
um Regnum declararet, inauditam quandam ac plus quam horrendam crudelitatem exercuit in hos. xviij. Carthusianos, qui se indeuictos sanctæ Ro
ei assertores præbuere, ac nullo vel carceris vel carnisicinæ metu adigi potuere, ut illius impiæ ac nefariæ a sancta Sede apostolica defectioni consenti
is ac sacrosanctæ passionis imaginem præfixa tibi ostendit tabula. Anno itaq; domini M. CCCCCXXXV. passi fuerunt pro defensione liber-
e assertione decem & octo Carthusiani, omnes professi domus Londoniarum; non uno tempore, sed diuersis diebus et annis, diuersoq; genere mortis.
nt super crates vimineas, et sic ab equis tracti per ciuitatem Londoniensem usq; ad locum institiæ, qui distabat a carcere tribus miliaribus, per loca in-
quidem ex his fuere tres Priores, passi anno. 1535. quarta Maij, quorum ista sunt nomina. Joannes Houghton, Prior domus Londoniarum, Robertus
s Vuebster, Prior domus visitationis beatæ Mariæ. Post hos eodem anno, die.19. Iunij alij tres. Humfridus Mydelmore Vicarius, Vuilhelmus exMeu
monachus. Qui tres per.14. dies continuos steterent in foetidissimo carcere eruti, iniectis ad colla, brachia, & rum circulis ferreis, et cathenis astricti et li-
solutione pro quacunq; necessitate fienda. Et nouissime anno. xlij die Nouembris quarta, Vuilhelmus Hoorne laicus, qui per annos quatuor stetit
e tracti essent, suspensi fuerunt, sed mox præcisis funibus priusquam spiritum exalarent demissi & denudati, quibus spiritum paululum recipienti
a euulsa viscera et igni iniecta. Hinc capitibus amputatis, eorum corpora in quatuor sunt partes secta et confestim illæ partes caldarijs iniectæ et paulu-
iensis suspensæ. Una uero pars Prioris domus Londoniarum ad portam monasterij sui scilicet Carthusianorum. Anno autem.1537. quinto idus
aluter ch sacerdotes, suspensi et relicti in patibulis. Eodem etiam anno.37. quarto Calendas Iunij, incarcerati fuerunt alij decem numero, scilicet Richar-
dotes, Joannes Dany diaconus, Vuilhelmus Grencuuode, Thomas Schrynen, Robertus Salt; Vualterus Peersoon, Thomas Redijng, & Vuilhelm'
miseria suffocati, excepto Vuilhelmo Hoorne præscripto, qui passus est ea quæ sex primi, ut superius est expressum. Ecce frater in Christo charissime, hæc
istum Iesum indeuictam fidem, & fidem suam erga sanctam Romanam ecclesiam & sedem apostolicam obedientiam, suo pretioso sanguine, tanquam ado
Tyrannis consignare non dubitarunt. Hæc illa est gloriosa martyrij corona quæ diuino amore penitus abreptis contingit athletis, in hos intuere, horu

murder the king. That week, four other courtiers were arrested for adultery with the queen. Two were released, but Francis Weston and William Brereton were tried with Norris on 12 May and convicted. The Imperial ambassador, no friend to Anne, thought they 'were sentenced on mere presumption or on very slight grounds, without legal proof or valid confession'.[59]

On 15 May, Anne and Rochford were tried in the Tower before a crowd of some 2000 people. Anne made 'wise

Dissolving the lesser monasteries

Forasmuch as manifest sin, *vicious, carnal and abominable living is daily used and committed among the little and small abbeys, priories and other religious houses of monks, canons, and nuns, where the congregation of such religious persons is under the number of twelve persons, whereby the governors of such religious houses, and their convent, spoil, destroy, consume, and utterly waste, as well their churches, monasteries, priories, principal houses, farms, granges, lands tenements, and hereditaments, as the ornaments of their churches, and their goods and chattels, to the great infamy of the king's highness and the realm, if redress should not be had thereof. And albeit that many continual visitations hath been heretofore had, by the space of two hundred years and more, for an honest and charitable reformation of such unthrifty, carnal, and abominable living, yet nevertheless little or none amendment is hitherto had… that a great multitude of the religious persons in such small houses do rather choose to rove abroad in apostasy, than to conform themselves to the observation of good religion; so that without such small houses be utterly suppressed, and the religious persons therein committed to great and honourable monasteries of religion in this realm, where they may be compelled to live religiously for the reformation of their lives, there cannot else be no reformation in this behalf.*

[From the Act of Suppression 1536, *Statutes of the Realm,* vol. III, p. 575]

and discreet answers to all things laid against her',[60] but she and her brother were nonetheless found guilty. In a limited act of mercy, Henry commuted their sentence to decapitation instead of burning (the punishment for incest). He also arranged for a skilled French executioner to use a sword rather than an axe on Anne. On 17 May, Anne's marriage to Henry was declared invalid, and her alleged lovers were beheaded. Two days later, Anne herself was executed.

The next morning, Henry was secretly betrothed to Jane Seymour. Their private wedding took place on 30 May at Whitehall, and on 4 June (Whitsunday) Jane was proclaimed queen. Three days later she went by barge from Greenwich to Westminster to the sounds of guns fired from ships on the Thames.

The Parliament that opened on 8 June excluded Anne's daughter, Elizabeth, from the succession. This parliamentary session was also notable for passing a statute that absorbed Wales into England. The principality and Marcher lordships were now to be organized in counties administered by justices of the peace and subject to English law.

On 22 June, under severe pressure, Princess Mary formally accepted the royal supremacy and the invalidity of her parents' marriage. Henry now forgave Mary her earlier disobedience and restored her to favour.

In July, after acrimonious debate, convocation issued Ten Articles of Religion. They were reformist but not Lutheran in character, as they did not embrace the theology of 'justification by faith alone'. This doctrine asserted that individual salvation resulted from faith alone and could not be earned by acts of piety. In August, Cromwell issued injunctions to enforce the Ten Articles and implement additional reforms in the parishes. These injunctions called for the placing of a Bible in every church, attacked 'superstitious' images and the cult of the saints, and abrogated certain holy days.

LEFT: **This design**, *executed by Holbein the Younger, was for a gold cup enriched with pearls and gems that was presumably intended as a gift from Henry to his new bride, Jane Seymour. Henry and Jane's wedding was held on 30 May 1536, a fortnight after the execution of Queen Anne. Jane's motto, 'bound to obey and serve', is repeated on the lid and foot of the cup. Its submissive tone was fairly typical for queen consorts, but it also reflects Jane's amenable personality and helps explain her attractiveness to Henry. The initials 'H' and 'J' are repeated at intervals and tied by a lover's knot.*

The death of Anne

... at eight of the clock in the morning [19 May 1536], Anne Boleyn, Queen, was brought to execution on the green within the Tower of London, by the great White Tower, the Lord Chancellor of England, the Duke of Richmond, Duke of Suffolk, with the most of the king's council, as earls, lords and nobles of this realm, being present at the same; also the Mayor of London, with the aldermen and sheriffs, and certain of the best crafts of London, being there present also. On a scaffold made there for the said execution the said Queen Anne said thus: 'Masters, I here humbly submit me to the law as the law has judged me, and as for mine offences, I here accuse no man, God knoweth them; I remit them to God, beseeching him to have mercy on my soul, and I beseech Jesu, save my sovereign and master the king, the most godly, noble and gentle prince that is, and long to reign over you'; which words were spoken with a goodly smiling countenance; and this done, she kneeled down on her knees and said 'To Jesus Christ I commend my soul'; and suddenly the hangman smote off her head at a stroke with a sword.

[*Wriothesley Chronicle*, EDITED BY W.D. HAMILTON, PP. 41–2]

The 'Oath of the Honourable Men'

Ye shall not enter into this our *Pilgrimage of Grace for the commonwealth, but only for the love that ye do bear unto almighty God, his faith, and to holy church militant [and for] the maintenance thereof, to the preservation of the king's person [and] his issue, to the purifying of the nobility, and to expulse all villain blood and evil councillors against the commonwealth from his grace and his privy council of the same. And that ye shall not enter into our said Pilgrimage for no particular profit to yourself, nor to do any displeasure to any private person, but by the counsel of the commonwealth, nor slay nor murder for no envy, but in your hearts put away fear and dread, and take afore you the Cross of Christ, and in your hearts his faith, the restitution of the church, the suppression of these heretics and their opinions, by the holy contents of this book.*

[THE OATH WRITTEN BY ROBERT ASKE AND SWORN BY THE PILGRIMS, 1536, FROM A TRANSCRIPT REPRODUCED IN R.W. HOYLE'S *Pilgrimage of Grace*, PP. 457–8]

During September, clerics in the North of England preached against government policy. On 1 October the Vicar of Louth, in Lincolnshire, delivered a Sunday sermon urging his parishioners to resist royal commissioners who, he (wrongly) claimed, intended to confiscate all the ornaments in their parish churches. Within days, organized protests spread throughout the county, and articles of grievance were drawn up. This movement collapsed after the king declared the participants to be traitors.

The momentum of protest then moved to Yorkshire. A local lawyer, Robert Aske, mustered about 10,000 men and led an army into York. The participants called their insurrection the 'Pilgrimage of Grace'. From York the pilgrims marched towards Pontefract Castle, which Lord Thomas Darcy (who had grown weary of the 'king's proceedings') obligingly surrendered after a short siege on 20 October before joining the leadership of the Pilgrimage. By this time, the rebel force contained about 30,000 men from six northern counties and was advancing south.

An underpowered royal army under the Duke of Norfolk and the Earl of Shrewsbury confronted the rebels at Doncaster. Neither side relished a fight. The royal army was heavily outnumbered, while Aske's men wanted their grievances redressed rather than civil war. Talks therefore began on 26 October, and a truce was agreed. On 3 December the pilgrims drew up articles listing specific grievances and goals. While most called for a reversal of Henry's religious and political innovations, some related to local economic problems. Norfolk accepted the articles and promised a general pardon. Aske went to Henry's court, expecting to advise the king on the future government of the North.

RIGHT: **Queen Jane (*c.* 1509–37), Henry's third wife**, *is shown here in Holbein the Younger's portrait (1536) wearing the gabled hood that was fashionable in the first half of the 16th century; under it was a caul covering her hair. Her tight-fitting bodice edged with jewels was also the height of fashion. A jewel, formed of the letters 'HIS' (the Greek name for Christ) with a cross and three pendant pearls, is pinned to the bodice and displays conventional piety. Unlike her predecessors, Jane was not crowned queen. Her coronation was indefinitely postponed because of an* outbreak of plague at Westminster in the autumn. Her death on 24 October 1537, after delivering a son, was blamed on her attendants' giving her unsuitable food and allowing her to catch cold. However, she probably developed puerperal fever or suffered a haemorrhage caused by the retention of parts of the placenta in her uterus. She was 28 years old.

1537

During January and February, further unrest disturbed the North. Incited by a Yorkshire gentleman, Sir Francis Bigod, some former 'pilgrims' made rash assaults on Hull and Scarborough, and soon afterwards a mob recklessly tried to take Carlisle Castle. Reprisals swiftly followed: 74 people were hanged at Carlisle, 47 in Lincolnshire, and many more in Yorkshire. Now in a stronger position, Henry felt able to go back on earlier promises. Lord Darcy was beheaded at Tower Hill on 30 June and Aske hanged at York on 12 July. Further popular unrest in the shape of corn riots took place in Somerset during April. Thirteen men and one woman were hanged and quartered for their participation.

In February of this year, Thomas Cromwell summoned a meeting of theologians to draft a new statement of doctrine, which he hoped would be more radical than the Ten Articles. The assembly produced the *Institution of a Christian Man*, known popularly as the 'Bishops' Book'. It was published in October, but without the king's approval.

A solemn procession passed through London on 11 October to pray for Queen Jane, who was experiencing a long and difficult labour. At about two o'clock the next morning she delivered a healthy child – a royal son – who was baptized Edward. The celebrations were tremendous: free wine, bonfires, gun salvoes from the Tower, and a *Te Deum* in the churches. But on 24 October Jane died, and on 12 November her corpse was transported from Hampton Court to St George's Chapel, Windsor, for burial. The court kept a period of

Enter a prince, exit a queen

In October on St Edward's Eve *[1537] was born at Hampton Court the noble Imp Prince Edward, whose godfathers at the christening were the Archbishop of Canterbury, and the Duke of Norfolk and his godmother the Lady Mary the king's daughter, and at the bishoping [confirmation] was godfather the Duke of Suffolk. At the birth of this noble prince was great fires made through the whole realm and great joy made with thanksgiving to almighty God, which had sent so noble a prince to succeed in the crown of this realm: But lord what lamentation shortly after was made for the death of his noble and gracious mother Queen Jane, which departed out of this life the 14th day of October, next following: and of none in the realm was it more heavier taken than of the king's Majesty himself, whose death caused the king immediately to remove unto Westminster, where he mourned and kept himself close and secret a great while.*

[*Henry VIII (Hall's Chronicle)*, EDITED BY CHARLES WHIBLEY, VOL. II, PP. 279–80]

LEFT: **The Pilgrimage of Grace** *took as its banner the five wounds of Christ to symbolize the northern rebels' commitment to the devotional practices of Catholicism. In pre-Reformation England, the five wounds had been a popular cult devoted to charitable acts as well as to masses and prayer. On this embroidered badge, belonging to one Thomas Constable of Everingham, Christ's hands and feet complete with nails occupy the corners, while the fifth wound is represented by a bleeding heart-shaped wafer over the chalice at the mass.*

OVERLEAF: **Prince Edward's baptism** *took place on 15 October 1537 in Henry's newly redecorated chapel at Hampton Court. Three to four hundred courtiers and clerics took part in the torchlit procession at midnight from the queen's bedchamber to the chapel and back. Both of Henry's daughters participated: Mary was the godmother and Elizabeth (carried by Jane's elder brother, Edward Seymour, the Earl of Hertford) bore the holy oil, the 'chrism'. This contemporary drawing of the event was probably by a herald.*

mourning that lasted until Christmas, and the widowed Henry wore black until the following Candlemas (2 February).

On 16 November, the prior of the Cluniac house at Lewes on England's south coast surrendered the monastery's lands to the king. This marked the beginning of a campaign to cajole or coerce the heads of the larger monasteries into dissolving their institutions.

The Irish Parliament closed on 20 December. It had been sitting since May 1536, and during that time it had introduced legislation that severed Ireland's connection with Rome.

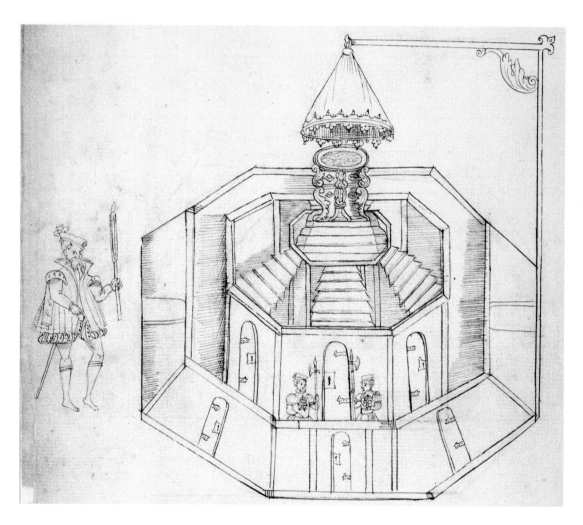

174

RIGHT: **The Whitehall mural**, *showing Henry VII, Elizabeth of York, Henry VIII and Jane Seymour, was painted by Holbein the Younger in 1537, but it was destroyed when Whitehall Palace burned down in 1698. This small copy, made for Charles II, is the only record of the original, which was probably situated behind the throne in the privy chamber. (However, a preparatory cartoon does exist, which shows that in the original the figures were life-size.)*

Henry and Jane are shown standing in front of Henry's parents. The Latin verses in the centre call both kings heroes, but debate whether the achievements of father or son are the greater. Henry VII brought peace after the Wars of the Roses; Henry VIII drove out the pope and brought in religious reform. As Henry VIII visually dominates the picture, the answer seems evident.

SI IVVAT HEROVM CLARAS VIDISSE FIGVRAS,
SPECTA HAS MAIORES NVLLA TABELLA TVLIT.
CERTAMEN MAGNVM LIS QVÆSTIO MAGNA PATERN�E
FILIVS AN VINCAT VICIT VTERQVE QVIDEM.
ISTE SVOS HOSTES PATRIÆQVE INCENDIA SÆPE
SVSTVLIT, ET PACEM CIVIBVS VSQVE DEDIT.

FILIVS AD MAIORA QVIDEM PROGNATVS AB ARIS
SVBMOVET INDIGNOS SVBSTITVITQVE PROBOS,
CERTÆ VIRTVTI PAPARVM AVDACIA CESSIT
HENRICO OCTAVO SCEPTRA GERENTE MANV.
REDDITA RELIGIO EST ISTO REGNANTE, DEIQVE
DOGMATA CÆPERVNT ESSE IN HONORE SVO.

PROTOTYPVM ISTEC MAGNI VDINIS 1550 OPERE SECTORIS
FECIT HOLBENIVS IVBENTE HENRICO VIII.
ECTYPVM A REMIGIO VAN LEEMPVT BREVIORI TABELLA
DESCRIBI VOLVIT CAROLVS II. M. B. F. ET H. R.
A DNI MDCLXVII

Dissolving the larger monasteries

Where divers and sundry abbots, priors, abbesses, prioresses, and other ecclesiastical governors and governesses of divers monasteries, abbacies, priories, nunneries, colleges, hospitals, houses of friars, and other religious and ecclesiastical houses and places within this our sovereign lord the king's realm of England and Wales, of their own free and voluntary minds, good wills and assents, without constraint, coaction, or compulsion of any manner of person or persons, since the fourth day of Feb, the 27th year of the reign of our now most dread sovereign lord, by the due order and course of the common law of this his realm of England … have severally given, granted, and by the same their writings severally confirmed all their said monasteries, abbacies, priories, nunneries, colleges, hospitals, houses or friars, and other religious and ecclesiastical houses and places … renounced, left, and forsaken … Be it therefore enacted by the king our sovereign lord, and the Lords spiritual and temporal, and the Commons, in this present Parliament assembled, and by authority of the same, that the king our sovereign lord shall have, hold, possess, and enjoy to him, his heirs and successors for ever, all and singular such late monasteries, abbacies, priories, nunneries, colleges, hospitals, houses of friars, and other religious and ecclesiastical houses and places … not only all the said late monasteries … but also other … which hereafter shall happen to be dissolved, suppressed, renounced, relinquished, forfeited, given up, or by any other means come unto the king's highness … All monastic lands shall be within the survey of the court of augmentation except such as come by attainder.

[FROM THE ACT FOR THE DISSOLUTION OF THE GREATER MONASTERIES (1539), *Statutes of the Realm*, VOL. III, P. 753]

1538

In January, Thomas Cromwell ordered the destruction of shrines and relics. On 24 February, a sermon was preached at Paul's Cross against idolatry and feigned miracles. At its end, the preacher dramatically broke the rood – the crucifix – of Boxley Abbey, long revered for its miraculous qualities. Over the next months, relics and images were conveyed to London, publicly exposed as objects of superstition and burned so that 'the people should use no more idolatry unto them'.[61] While Henry approved this attack on 'superstition' and idolatry, he listed some 250 emendations to the Bishops' Book. For him it was too 'Lutheran'.

In May, Pope Paul III summoned a general council of the church, and in June he negotiated a ten-year truce between King Francis and Emperor Charles. As a result, Henry feared a crusade would be launched against him.

On 22 May, a friar, John Forrest, was burned as a heretic and traitor before a crowd of about 10,000. He was, though, the only papist to die at the stake during Henry's reign.

On 29 August, Sir Geoffrey Pole was arrested on suspicion of communicating with his brother, the dissident Reginald Pole, who was living in exile. Cardinal Reginald Pole was the king's second cousin, but the split from Rome and the executions of Fisher and More had thoroughly alienated him from Henry. In October, Geoffrey implicated his elder brother (Henry, Baron Montague) and cousin (Henry Courtenay, the Marquess of Exeter) in treason.

Early in September, Cromwell completed a new set of injunctions. They declared open war on pilgrimages, 'feigned relics' and idolatrous images and ordered that an English Bible be placed in every church. 'Also this year diverse

RIGHT: **The cult of St Thomas Becket** *came under attack in 1538. In September, royal commissioners destroyed his shrine at Canterbury, burned the martyr's bones and removed the stained glass windows narrating the saint's story from the cathedral so that, in the words of the Wriothesley Chronicle, 'there shall be no more mention of him never'. Attempts were made to efface the memory of the saint elsewhere, and in this copy of William Caxton's* Golden Legend, *c.1487, his martyrdom has been half-heartedly crossed out. Henry's particular animus against St Thomas arose because he had asserted the immunities of the church and defended the legal privileges of 'benefit of clergy'.*

Aynt Thomas the martir was sone to gylbert lequet a Burgeys of the cyte of london / And was born in the place

Bytwene them / be promyced to wedde her / yf she wold become Crysten / And told to her the place of hys dwellynge in england / And after By the puruesaunce of god the said aylbert escaped /

religious houses of great possessions were suppressed.'[62] During the autumn, however, Henry clamped down on religious radicals in an attempt to underline the doctrinal conservatism of his church. On 1 October, he ordered a heresy commission to act against those who denied Christ's corporeal presence in the mass. On 16 November, he presided in person over the show-trial of John Lambert, who was charged with this offence. Dressed in white for purity, Henry delivered a defence of the Catholic doctrine on the mass and, the same day, issued a proclamation condemning 'sacramentarians' and disallowing clerical marriage. On 22 November, Lambert was burned at Smithfield.

On 4 November, the nobles tainted with treason, Montague and Exeter, were arrested, and on 9 December they were beheaded. Lady Margaret Pole, Countess of Salisbury (Reginald's elderly mother), was taken into custody, interrogated and left in the Tower.

In December, Paul III finally pronounced the long-deferred bull of excommunication against Henry and instructed Cardinal Pole to persuade Francis and Charles V to enter into a league for a holy war against England.

1539

The international situation worsened for Henry when, on 12 January, the French king and the Holy Roman Emperor signed the Peace of Toledo and agreed to make no alliance with another power without mutual consent. The danger of a Franco-Imperial invasion was now acute. The next month, on 14 February, Sir Nicholas Carew, Henry's 'master of the horse', was convicted of treasonable plotting with the Marquess of Exeter and Lord Montague, and he was beheaded on 8 March.

Also in March, mindful of the foreign threat, Henry began attending to the defences of the realm: he ordered the improvement of fortifications along the sea coast and the mustering of men. A great muster of 15,000 uniformed and armed men took place at Mile End, London, on 8 May.

In April, the first edition of the English Great Bible was printed, its frontispiece graphically embodying Henry's supremacy over the church.

On 19 May, Parliament passed a statute that confirmed the king's right to all the monasteries not

Abolishing 'Diversity of Opinions'

The king's most royal majesty *most prudently pondering and considering that by occasion of variable and sundry opinions and judgments of the said articles, great discord and variance had arisen as well among the clergy of this his realm, as amongst a great number of vulgar [ordinary] people his loving subjects ... commanded ... a great and long deliberate and advised disputation and consultation ... it was ... finally resolved ... First, that in the most blessed Sacrament of the Altar ... is present really, under the form of bread and wine, the natural body and blood of our Saviour Jesus Christ ...*

Secondly, that communion in both kinds is not necessary ...

Thirdly that priests after the order of priesthood received as afore may not marry by the law of God;

Fourthly that vows of chastity or widowhood by man or woman made to God advisedly ought to be observed by the law of God ...

Fifthly that it is meet and necessary that private masses be continued and admitted in this the king's English Church and Congregation...

Sixthly that auricular confession is expedient and necessary to be retained and continued used and frequented in the Church of God.

[FROM THE ACT ABOLISHING DIVERSITY IN OPINIONS (THE SIX ARTICLES), *Statutes of the Realm*, VOL. III, PP. 739–40]

178

RIGHT: **The Great Bible of 1539** *was the first officially authorized Bible in English. The work of 'diverse excellent learned men', it was based largely on the 1537 translation by Miles Coverdale. Thomas Cromwell was instrumental in commissioning the work, and he contributed 600 marks to finance it. In the frontispiece, the new order is on display, with Henry as supreme head of the English Church, distributing the word of God to the clergy on the left and the laity on the right. At the bottom, ordinary men and women are crying out 'Long live the king.' Archbishop Cranmer (on the left) and Thomas Cromwell (on the right) are shown just above their coats of arms in the middle section, though in a subsequent printing Cromwell's image was replaced with that of an older man after Cromwell's downfall in 1540.*

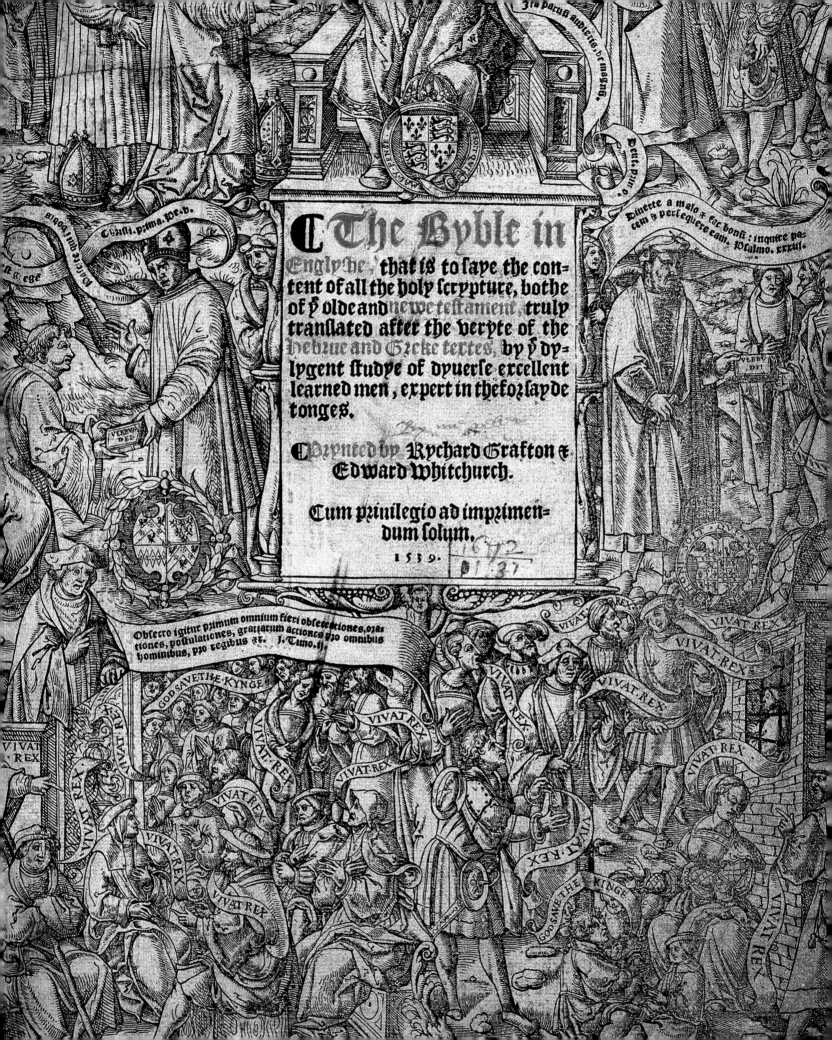

covered by the 1536 dissolutions. About 150 of the greater monasteries had already surrendered their property; the remainder followed suit over the next year. Parliament also passed a statute known as the Act of Six Articles. This measure was a setback for reformers, as it defined many of their beliefs as heresy, including their denial of the corporeal presence in the mass and their rejection of clerical celibacy. Two reforming bishops, Hugh Latimer and Nicholas Shaxton, resigned their sees in July. Archbishop Cranmer chose to stay in post, but sent his German wife abroad.

Irish matters reared their head in August, when Ulster chieftains invaded the English Pale – the English-controlled area around Dublin. Ireland's lord deputy, Lord Leonard Grey, inflicted a devastating defeat on them at Bellahoe on the borders of Meath and Monaghan.

To end his dangerous diplomatic isolation, Henry considered a new marriage. Earlier that year he had dispatched his court artist, Hans Holbein the Younger, to Cleves to paint Anne, the sister of Duke William of Cleves. The duke had a close relationship with the German Lutheran princes hostile to the emperor. On 4 October Henry agreed to marry Anne, and on 27 December she arrived near Deal, in Kent, for the wedding.

In November, the abbots of Glastonbury, Reading and Colchester were hanged, drawn and quartered for treason because they would not surrender their religious houses to the king.

The king's household was augmented in December by the appointment of 50 gentlemen pensioners 'to wait on the king's highness'.

1540

Impatient to see his new bride, Henry arrived incognito at Rochester, Kent, on 1 January, but rather than impress her this action seemed to perplex and wrongfoot her. He left her the following day to continue her journey to London alone. They met next at Blackheath, where Henry, looking regal and relaxed, greeted Anne 'with most lovely countenance and princely behaviour' and escorted her to Greenwich.[63] The wedding took place in the queen's closet on 6 January. Because the day was Epiphany, the customary entertainment was curtailed, but on 4 February they travelled in state to Westminster by barge. By then, however, Henry desperately wanted an annulment of this, his fourth marriage, as he was unable to consummate it.

Henry continued to strike out against the perceived enemies of his idiosyncratic brand of reform, both papists and Protestants. On 23 March, the last surviving monastery – Waltham Abbey – surrendered. Also in March, three notorious reformist 'evangelicals' – Robert Barnes, William Jerome and

Thomas Garrett – were thrown in the Tower of London after preaching the heretical message of justification by faith alone. On 30 July they were burned at Smithfield, alongside three men loyal to Rome, who were hanged, drawn and quartered.

In April, Thomas Cromwell resigned his duties as secretary to his protégés Ralph Sadler and Thomas Wriothesley. On 18 April, Henry granted Cromwell the Earldom of Essex and the senior court office of lord great chamberlain. But then, on 10 June, Cromwell was arrested in the council chamber and charged with treason, heresy, felony, extortion and corruption. In truth, he had simply lost the trust of the king because of his tardiness in arranging an annulment of the Cleves marriage. He was condemned by an act of attainder, without trial, on 29 June.

On 9 July, Archbishop Cranmer annulled the royal marriage on the grounds that Anne had entered a previous contract of marriage and that her marriage to Henry was unconsummated. Three weeks later, Henry married Katherine Howard (niece of the powerful and conservative Duke of Norfolk) quietly at Oatlands Palace in Surrey. That same day, 28 July, Cromwell suffered a particularly gruesome execution on Tower Hill.

The summer that year was hot and dry. The drought caused death in cattle from lack of water and sickness in humans from dysentery, agues and pestilence. Henry and his court left London for the country.

The fall of Cromwell

The 19th day of July [1540], *Thomas Lord Cromwell, late made Earl of Essex … being in the council chamber, was suddenly apprehended, and committed to the Tower of London, the which many lamented, but more rejoiced, and specially such as either had been religious men, or favoured religious persons, for they banqueted, and triumphed together that night, many wishing that that day had been seven years before, and some fearing lest he should escape, although he were imprisoned, could not be merry. Other who knew nothing but truth by him, both lamented him and heartily prayed for him … he was attainted [subjected to a bill of attainder] by Parliament … And the 28th day of July was brought to the scaffold on Tower Hill … And then made he his prayer, which was long, but not so long, as both godly and learned, and after committed his soul, into the hands of God, and so patiently suffered the stroke of the axe, by a ragged and butcherly miser, which very ungoodly performed the office.*

[*Henry VIII* (*Hall's Chronicle*), EDITED BY CHARLES WHIBLEY, VOL. II, PP. 306–7]

OVERLEAF LEFT: **Anne of Cleves (1515–57)**, *Henry's fourth wife, was married to the king for only six months during 1540. She spoke no English and knew little of men, while Henry found her unattractive and was unable to consummate their marriage. Yet the 'Flanders mare' of popular repute was certainly not ugly – as the portrait by Holbein the Younger attests – and at least one chronicler, Edward Hall, noted her 'beauty and good visage'. Anne obligingly consented to an annulment without rancour, stayed in England, and was granted two houses and a pension of £4000 a year.*

OVERLEAF RIGHT: **Katherine Howard (1518/24?–42)** *was a cousin of Anne Boleyn and a niece of the Duke of Norfolk. In late 1539 she entered the privy chamber of Anne of Cleves, who was about to become Henry's fourth wife. Sexually alluring, Katherine soon caught Henry's attention, and they married on 28 July 1540, shortly after his divorce from Anne. Before her marriage, Katherine had already had a sexual relationship with Francis Dereham; after it, she rashly began another one, with the courtier Thomas Culpeper.*

Anne of Cleves (1515–57)

Katherine Howard (1518/24?–42)

1541

Queen Katherine accompanied Henry down the Thames from Westminster to Greenwich on 19 March, her first passage through London.

The peace of the kingdom was interrupted during the spring by a rising, which broke out in Yorkshire. However, it was easily quelled and its leaders were hanged. Two perceived enemies of the state also met their ends: Lady Margaret Pole was beheaded on 27 May, and a month later, on 28 June, Lord Leonard Grey was executed for treasonable conduct while he was Ireland's lord deputy. Earlier in June, on the 18th, the Irish Parliament had changed Henry's title from 'Lord' to 'King of Ireland'. Gaelic chiefs were now subjects, from whom Henry demanded obedience.

On 30 June, Henry and Katherine left on the king's first northern progress. His company numbered as many as five thousand and included war horses and artillery. By 16 September they had reached York. Henry hoped James V would meet him there, but by the end of the month the Scottish king had not arrived. The court left Hull for the south on 6 October and arrived at Hampton Court a few weeks later.

In the international sphere, Francis and Charles were again on the brink of war by July, and both monarchs made overtures for an alliance with Henry.

While attending the All Souls' Day mass (2 November), Henry received a letter from Archbishop Cranmer telling him that the queen had taken two lovers before her marriage. Henry was stunned and disbelieving. On 6 November, he left

Henry, 'King of England and Ireland'

Some days ago the king ordered the estates *of that portion of Ireland which is now [1541] under his rule to be convoked, for the purpose of communicating to them, among other things, that he wishes and intends to set up under the name of 'Kingdom of Ireland' that part of the country where his lordship and rule are at present obeyed, and consequently to call and entitle himself King of Ireland; in expectation of which new title all business has been for some days suspended in Chancery, as well as in the Exchequer Court, in order that all of a sudden, and conjointly as it were, the king's name may appear decorated with his new title of 'King of England and Ireland' in all letters patent, provisions, &c., emanating from those two offices, and that by that means the news may be spread and circulated in every quarter.*

[IMPERIAL AMBASSADOR EUSTACE CHAPUYS TO THE EMPEROR, FROM *State Papers, Spanish*, VOL. VI, NO. 173, P. 342]

RIGHT: **This letter by Queen Katherine,** *who was executed in February 1542 after she was found guilty of adultery, was written to her lover Thomas Culpeper and used as evidence against her. In it, she enquires after his health as she has heard he was sick. She writes of her pain to be apart from him and her wish that he could be with her, noting 'it makes my heart to die to think what fortune I have that I cannot be always in your company'. The letter ends 'Yours as long as life endures'. It was not to endure long.*

Katherine at Hampton Court, and two days later she admitted her guilt to Cranmer. Worse news followed, when one of Katherine's ex-lovers – Francis Dereham – accused Thomas Culpeper, a member of the privy chamber, of committing adultery with the queen. Both men were convicted of treason on 1 December and executed on the 10th: Culpeper was beheaded (unusually at Tyburn rather than the Tower), while Dereham was hanged, disembowelled, beheaded and quartered. Katherine's other relatives and associates were rounded up, accused of concealing what they knew, but all except Jane, Viscountess Rochford (the widow of George Boleyn, Anne's brother), were eventually pardoned and released. Katherine was removed to the former convent at Syon, Middlesex.

On Christmas Eve a fire broke out at the London house of Sir John Williams, master of the king's jewels. In the evacuation many of the royal jewels stored there were stolen.

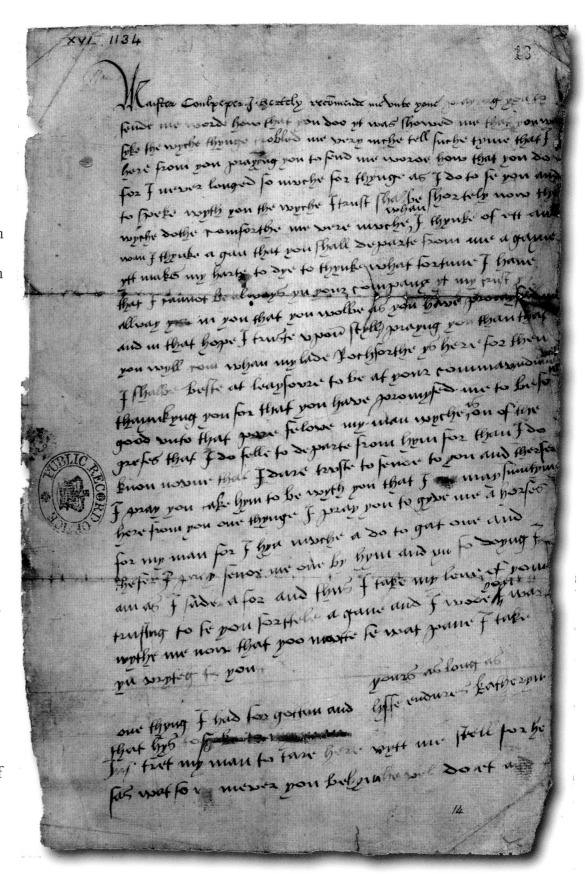

GNO APPELLATVM NONCIVTZ

inam simile.

Nonsuch Palace in Surrey *was one of the many great palaces built by Henry VIII. The construction began in 1538 on a site that needed to be first cleared of its village, church and manor house. The structure, with its great towers, was almost complete by 1541, and a considerable part of the expensive decoration was finished by Henry's death. The palace was intended to rival Francis's new residence at Fontainebleau, and the walls were covered with stucco figures made in a similar mannerist style.*

Nonsuch was demolished in 1682–3, when Charles II's mistress broke up and sold off the property to cover her gambling debts. This pen and watercolour drawing by Joris Hoefnagel shows it around 1582, and the scene in the foreground depicts Queen Elizabeth's procession approaching the house.

1542

On 10 February, Queen Katherine entered the Tower. Three days later, she and Lady Rochford were executed.

The summer of this year was very wet, causing floods. Nevertheless, in September Henry prepared a great army of men to invade Scotland. He was irritated with the Francophile policies of James V and determined to secure his northern border before embarking on a war against France. On 21 October, the king's lieutenant-general, the Duke of Norfolk, entered Scotland, burning and wasting all the borderlands without meeting any serious resistance. He withdrew after four days when the soldiers' beer ran out.

On 24 November, James V led a retaliatory Scottish army of about 17,000 across the border with the intention of capturing Carlisle. They were ambushed by 3000 English soldiers in the swamps of Solway Moss, and they hastily fled. Only 20 Scots fell in the encounter (though several drowned while in flight), but at least 1000 were taken prisoner, while 3000 of their horses, 30 standards and 20 guns were captured in the débâcle. Three weeks later, on 14 December, James died, leaving his one-week-old daughter, Mary, as queen.

About 21 of the most prominent Scottish captives were brought down to the Tower of London. On 19 December they were paraded through London on their way to make submission to the king at Westminster, and on 27 December they joined the court, where they were royally entertained. There, they swore allegiance to Henry and promised to arrange a marriage between his heir Edward and the new Queen of Scotland. The situation with France, meanwhile, remained tense: 'In this year there was neither perfect peace, nor open war between England and France.'[64]

Also in this year, Parliament created six new dioceses endowed from the spoils of the monasteries. It also passed an act making witchcraft a felony, though it was soon repealed.

LEFT: **This 'Protestant Allegory' by Girolamo da Treviso** hung at Hampton Court towards the end of Henry VIII's reign. The four evangelists are shown stoning the pope, who lies sprawling on the ground, flanked by two female allegorical figures, Avarice and Hypocrisy. The city in the distance could be Jerusalem, as above it is a burning candle symbolizing the true light of the Gospel. This candle contrasts with another in the immediate foreground, which has been extinguished by a cooking pan and represents the false doctrine of Rome. Treviso served Henry from 1538 until 1544, mainly as an engineer.

ABOVE: **Henry Howard (c.1517–47), Earl of Surrey, and Thomas Wyatt (1503–42)** are credited with bringing the sonnet form of poetry from Italy to England. The sonnet ('little song') is a lyric of 14 lines, whose original metre and rhyming scheme were adapted in England to the iambic pentameter – the familiar rhyme scheme later used by Shakespeare. Most of Surrey and Wyatt's verse circulated in manuscript at court, and it was not until 1557 that their sonnets appeared in print for the first time. This epitaph on Wyatt, written by Surrey, is dated about 1545. Its full title (modernized) is 'An Excellent Epitaph of Sir Thomas Wyatt with Two Other Compendious Ditties, Wherein Are Touched and Set Forth the State of Man's Life'.

1543

The winter and spring saw shortages of fuel, salty fish and meat. As a result, London civic officials agreed to eat only one course at their Easter feast, with no more than seven dishes for the mayor and six for the aldermen.

On 11 February, an Anglo-Imperial treaty was signed. Henry and Charles pledged to attack France jointly within the next two years. Later, in June, Henry declared war on France and sent an army over to Calais.

On 24 March, religious conservatives put together heresy accusations against Cranmer. Henry probably saw them during April, but the archbishop won back the king's confidence in May by acquiescing in a retreat from further religious reform. He accepted the conservative revisions made in Convocation to the Bishops' Book, now called the King's Book, and made no protest against a parliamentary statute that restricted the reading of the Bible to men over the rank of yeomen and to gentlewomen. In a quite separate problem for Cranmer, on 18 December the archiepiscopal palace at Canterbury was almost destroyed by a fire that also killed one of Cranmer's brothers-in-law.

On 1 July, Henry and Scottish commissioners signed the Treaties of Greenwich, which approved the terms for the marriage between Prince Edward and Mary, Queen of Scots. But on 11 December the Scottish Parliament formally repudiated the treaties and instead reaffirmed the 'Auld Alliance' with France.

LEFT: **Katherine Parr (1512–48)** *married Henry in the queen's closet at Hampton Court, on 12 July 1543. Eighteen people, including the king's daughters, attended. Already twice widowed, Katherine came to Henry's attention while serving in Mary's household. The new queen was attractive, vivacious and serious-minded, taking a keen interest in theological debates and favouring religious reform. Consequently, religious conservatives tried to have her convicted of heresy; she was saved only when she submitted before Henry and promised to follow his guidance on all matters. Katherine became the first English queen to have her works published when, on 29 May 1545, her* Prayers, or Meditations *was issued under her own name. This portrait, attributed to Master John, is dated to c.1545.*

The king defends his archbishop

KING.   *Know you not*
How your state stands i'th' world, with the whole world?
Your enemies are many, and not small; their practices
Must bear the same proportion, and not ever
The justice and the truth o'th' question carries
The due o'th' verdict with it; at [with] what ease
Might corrupt minds procure knaves as corrupt
To swear against you? Such things have been done.
You are potently oppos'd, and with a malice
Of as great size. Ween you of [Do you expect] better luck,
I mean in perjured witness, than your Master [Christ],
Whose minister you are, whiles here he lived
Upon this naughty Earth? Go to, go to,
You take [regard] a precipice for [as] no leap of danger,
And woo your own destruction.

CRANMER.   *God, and Your Majesty*
Protect mine innocence, or I fall into
The trap is laid for me.

KING.   *Be of good cheer,*
They shall no more prevail, than we give way too.
Keep comfort to you, and this morning see
You do appear before them. If they shall chance
In charging you with matters, to commit you,
The best persuasions to the contrary
Fail not to use, and with what vehemency
Th' occasion shall instruct you. If entreaties
Will render you no remedy, this ring
Deliver them, and your appeal to us…

[HENRY VIII ASSURES ARCHBISHOP CRANMER OF HIS SUPPORT AGAINST OPPONENTS IN THE COUNCIL, IN SHAKESPEARE'S *The Life of King Henry VIII*, ACT 5, SCENE 1]

Henry, war hero

The 18th day [1544], the king's highness *having the sword borne naked before him by the Lord Marquess Dorset, like a noble and valiant conqueror rode into Boulogne, and the trumpeters standing on the walls of the town, sounded their trumpets, at the time of his entering, to the great comfort of all the king's true subjects, the same beholding. And in the entering there met him the Duke of Suffolk, and delivered unto him the keys of the town, so he rode toward his lodging, which was prepared for him on the south side of the town. And within two days after, the king rode about all the town, within the walls, and then commanded that Our Lady Church of Boulogne should be defaced and plucked down, where he appointed a mount [fortification] to be made, for the great force and strength of the town.*

When the king had set all things there in such order, as to his wisdom was thought best, he returned into England, to the great rejoicing of all his loving subjects.

[*Henry VIII* (*Hall's Chronicle*), EDITED BY CHARLES WHIBLEY, VOL. II, P. 350]

During this year Henry VIII married for the sixth time. His new bride, 20 years his junior, was the recently widowed Lady Latimer, Katherine Parr. They wed on 12 July.

This year, the Mayor of London took action against vice. He punished many harlots from the city's brothels by ducking them in the Thames on a 'cucking-stool'.

1544

Before going on a military campaign in France, and potentially risking his life, Henry made new arrangements for the succession that set aside the conventional rules of primogeniture. In March, Parliament passed a statute that restored his daughters Mary and Elizabeth to a place in the succession, after Prince Edward, although neither of them was legitimized. The act – Henry's third Act of Succession – also

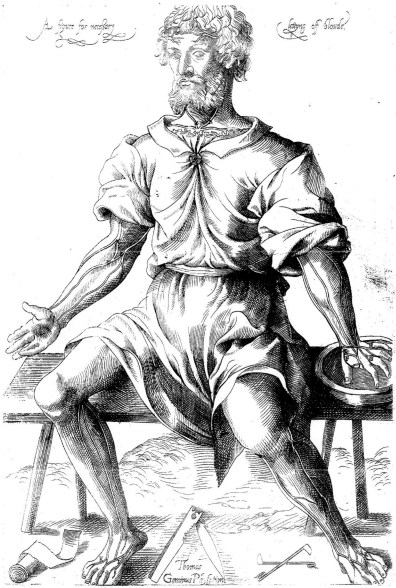

A table instructiue whan and how a man may conueniently let bloude of all the necessary veynes of mans body beyng profitable for all Chirurgeons and Barbers.

A figure for necessary letting of bloude

Thomas Geminus Phesicion

LEFT: **London prostitutes** *were based in the 'stews' – brothels – in Southwark, on the south bank of the Thames. This 16th-century English woodcut depicts a whorehouse, the women's trade made evident by their bare-breasted appearance. Punishments enacted against prostitutes included the cucking-stool or 'stool of repentance'. Periodically, when concerns were raised about disease, the stews were closed down.*

ABOVE: **The letting of blood** *was a common medical remedy in Tudor England. In the medical orthodoxy of the day, drawing on the Hippocratic theory of the body's four 'humours', the practice was intended to purge excessive humours. It was often applied to correct conditions that could be traced to a particular humour in the blood. There existed a complex set of rules about the most propitious times for bloodletting: the best time was when the sun, moon or Lord of the Ascendant occupied the zodiacal sign controlling the disease in question. This broadsheet is the work of the engraver and instrument-maker Thomas Geminus (d.1562), who is better known for producing an English edition of copper engravings based on Vesalius's Compendium of Anatomy.*

laid down that the king's will would determine the future line of succession if all his children were to die childless.

On 3 May, Sir Thomas Wriothesley was appointed lord chancellor. Also in early May, Edward Seymour, Earl of Hertford, led 15,000 men into Scotland on an expedition to burn Edinburgh and ravage the Eastern Lowlands as a reprisal for the Scottish repudiation of the Treaties of Greenwich. On 22 May (Ascension Day), bonfires were lit in London to celebrate the 'victory' in Scotland, but the Scots still refused to agree to the marriage between their infant queen and Henry's son.

At the same time, Henry prepared two large armies for France: one under the Duke of Norfolk and Lord John Russell, the other under the Duke of Suffolk. Altogether, at least 38,000 soldiers crossed the Channel. However, instead of planning a march to Paris as Charles V wanted, Henry ordered Norfolk and Russell to besiege Montreuil and directed Suffolk to set up camp before Boulogne. In June, the king ordered that the litany be sung in English in every parish church to pray for his success in France.

On 14 July, Henry arrived at Calais and joined Suffolk's army before Boulogne. On the 19th, the siege of Boulogne began. The English navy successfully blockaded the town, while the English army bombarded it. On 11 September, the castle was blown up; on the 14th the town capitulated; and on the 18th Henry rode into the town in triumph, 'having the sword borne

'Henry rode into the town in triumph ... to the sound of trumpeters'

naked before him' to the sound of trumpeters standing on the town walls.[65] (Norfolk, however, had to abandon the siege of Montreuil.) Despite the victory, the campaign had exposed the extent of Henry's by-now poor health and the problems that his considerable weight caused him, given that he was dependent on the mechanism of a crane to mount his horse.

Henry arrived home on 30 September. By this time Charles V had made a separate peace with Francis, and Henry was left to fight on against France alone. In order to pay for his French and Scottish wars, Henry took the measure of debasing the coinage. When plate and bullion were melted down and minted into coins, the standard of fineness of gold and silver in them was reduced. The crown gained a sum of around £363,000 from this practice.

ABOVE: **'The Family of Henry VIII'** *was probably painted to commemorate the 1544 statute that restored the bastardized Mary and Elizabeth to a place in the succession. Mary is shown on the left wing and Elizabeth on the right. An enthroned Henry sits alongside his heir Edward and Edward's mother Jane, by now, of course, several years dead. Through the open doorway can be glimpsed the garden at Whitehall, with the king's beasts carved on columns. The royal servants shown include Henry's jester, Will Somers, who is wearing the livery of the royal household.*

1545

Henry demanded a 'benevolence' on 6 January to help cover the costs of his war. One London alderman who refused to pay was ordered to serve in the king's army against the Scots (where he was captured). On 5 February, the Earl of Hertford defeated the French, who had attempted to recapture Boulogne. But during his absence from the northern border, the Scots routed a small English army at Ancrum on 27 February. This encouraged further resistance in Scotland. During September, Hertford's army renewed the scorched-earth policy and destroyed the great abbeys in the Tweed valley.

For those of his subjects who could read, Henry authorized, in June, the use of a new primer – a prayer-book for private use – in English and Latin. It was printed together with an English litany.

The end of the Mary Rose

But one day above all other [in 1545], *the whole navy of the Englishmen made out, and purposed to set on the Frenchmen: but in their setting forward a goodly ship of England called the* Mary Rose, *was by too much folly, drowned in the midst of the haven, for she was laden with much ordnance, and the ports left open, which were very low, and the great ordnance, unbreached, so that when the ship should turn, the water entered, and suddenly she sank. In her was Sir George Carew knight, captain of the said ship, and four hundred men, and much ordnance.*

[*Henry VIII* (*Hall's Chronicle*), EDITED BY CHARLES WHIBLEY, VOL. II, PP. 351–2]

During June, parts of northeastern England were hit by bad weather. Tempests did great damage in Derbyshire, Cheshire and Lancashire; 'also there fell hailstones as big as a man's fist'.[66] Because of subsequent harvest failures, corn had to be imported from Danzig and Bremen.

The summer saw the engagement of the French and English navies. On 19 July, a French fleet of 235 ships sailed towards the Isle of Wight and Portsmouth. An English fleet of a similar size, commanded by the lord high admiral, John Dudley, Viscount Lisle, sailed out to meet it. As four French

ABOVE AND RIGHT: **The ship 'Mary Rose'** *sank while executing a sharp turn on 19 July 1545. The vessel was raised by archaeologists in the 1980s. Many objects were preserved inside the hull, including instruments used by the barber surgeon and his assistant, including (as can be seen here) a bleeding bowl with a urethral syringe (above right). Cannon balls and other artifacts were recovered, including the carved handle (bottom right).*

ships moved to exchange shots with the
English flagship, *Henry Grace a Dieu*, the
second ship of the line, the *Mary Rose*,
turned sharply, capsized and sank rapidly.
Over 400 people drowned, including the vice-
admiral, Sir George Carew. Soon afterwards the
French fleet attacked and burned the
Sussex coast near Brighton, but
was forced to retreat. The French
had hoped to capture an English
town that could then be exchanged
for Boulogne.

On 22 August, the king's brother-in-law and close
friend Charles Brandon, Duke of Suffolk, died, 'whose death all
true Englishmen may lament'.[67] Henry paid for the burial at Windsor.

Because of Henry's growing infirmity, Sir Anthony Denny and
Sir John Gates were licensed on 20 September to affix the sign
manual (the royal stamp of signature) on all his documents.

To meet the escalating cost of the wars, the November
Parliament agreed to the dissolution of chantries, colleges and
hospitals. In his closing address to Parliament on Christmas Eve, Henry
lauded his 'middle way' policy in religion; he criticized the clergy who
were 'too stiff in their old Mumpsimus' and others (reformers) who were
'too busy and curious in their new Sumpsimus'.[68]

197

1546

To improve the morals of the nation's capital, on 3 April Henry issued a proclamation closing the bankside 'stews' frequented by the prostitutes of Southwark.

In a number of sermons in March and April, a London preacher, Dr Edward Crome, expounded heretical opinions on the mass, denied the existence of purgatory and asserted a belief in justification by faith alone. For this flouting of the law, he was called before the king's council and threatened with heresy proceedings. Over the next months, his associates were arrested.

At Paul's Cross on 27 June, Crome recanted his heretical views, and Nicholas Shaxton followed suit shortly afterwards. However, Anne Askew, a Lincolnshire gentlewoman who had friends at court, refused to recant, and on 28 June she was convicted of heresy for denying the corporeal presence in the mass. On 16 July, Shaxton presided at the burning of Anne Askew and other Protestants. Soon afterwards, Queen Katherine came under suspicion of heresy, and she only escaped prosecution when she promised Henry she would submit to his opinion on all matters.

Peace came at last, in June, when England and France concluded the Peace of Ardres (or Camp). Under its terms Henry

The order and manner of the burning of *Anne Askew*,
Iohn Lacels, *Iohn Adams*, *Nicolas Belenian*, with certaine of
the Counsell sitting in Smithfield.

ABOVE: **The burning of Anne Askew (c.1521–46)** *took place on 16 July 1546. The execution is shown here in a woodcut from John Foxe's* Acts and Monuments *(Book of Martyrs), published in Elizabeth's reign. Anne was a Protestant gentlewoman with powerful friends at court. In May 1546 she was arrested for heresy and tortured on the rack in the hope that she would incriminate Queen Katherine as well as the wives of influential courtiers and councillors. She was burned in Smithfield, alongside John Lascels (or Lacels), John Hadlam (or Adams), a tailor, and John Hemley. Nicholas Shaxton, who had recently recanted his own Protestant heresies, delivered the sermon from the pulpit within the arena. The privy councillors looked on from a stand.*

ABOVE: **Henry Howard (1517?–47), Earl of Surrey** *and the eldest son of Thomas Howard, 3rd Duke of Norfolk, was beheaded on 19 January 1547. It was the last execution of Henry VIII's reign. Surrey had been found guilty of treason after he had talked of his father's right to be regent on Henry's death and had drawn attention to his direct descent from Edward the Confessor by quartering the royal arms into his heraldic bearings. This painting formed part of the charge against him and also displays his extravagant clothing and Italianate tastes. The portrait is dated to around 1546, but the artist is unknown.*

The king's will

Remembering the great benefits given to him by Almighty God, and trusting that every Christian that dies in steadfast faith and endeavours, if he has leisure, to do such good deeds and charitable works as Scripture commands, is ordained, by Christ's Passion, to eternal life, Henry VIII makes such a will as he trusts will be acceptable to God, Christ and the whole company of Heaven and satisfactory to all godly brethren in earth … For himself he would be content that the body should be buried in any place accustomed for Christian folks, but for the reputation of the dignity to which he has been called, he directs that it should be laid in the choir of his college of Windsor, midway between the stalls and the high altar, in a tomb now almost finished in which he will also have the bones of his wife, Queen Jane. And there an altar shall be furnished for the saying of daily masses while the world shall endure.

[EXTRACT FROM HENRY'S LAST WILL AND TESTAMENT, FROM *Letters and Papers of the Reign of Henry the Eighth*, NO. 634, P. 320]

RIGHT: **Henry's last will**, *dated 30 December 1546, laid down the arrangements for government under his son, still a minor, as well as the line of succession if Elizabeth were to die without heirs. On his death the country was to be ruled by a council of 16 men, who should decide matters by majority vote. The succession laid down that – assuming all Henry's children died childless – the throne would pass through the line of his younger sister Mary (and not the Scottish line of his elder sister Margaret). As the will was signed by the application of a dry stamp (observable at the top), its validity came to be contested.*

agreed to sell the captured Boulogne to France after eight years. By now the king's thoughts were turning to the practicalities for managing the kingdom after his death.

In November, Henry quarrelled with Stephen Gardiner, Bishop of Winchester, ostensibly over the bishop's refusal to exchange certain lands. After this, Henry removed Gardiner's name from the list of councillors he had previously selected to govern the realm during his son's minority. On 12 December, the aged Duke of Norfolk and his son Henry Howard, the Earl of Surrey, were arrested on a charge of treason. The earl had augmented his coat of arms with that of Edward the Confessor. Aware that his health was failing, King Henry wanted to remove a powerful nobleman who (on account of his royal lineage) might make a bid for the regency during the minority rule of his son. Henry preferred to see a council governing the realm until Edward reached maturity, and he made provisions for this in his will.

Queen Katherine spent Christmas at Greenwich, while Henry stayed in London. On 30 December, he approved a revision of his will.

1547

The Earl of Surrey was beheaded on 19 January. His father's date of execution was the 28th, but he was saved by the death of King Henry himself in the early hours of that morning. At the king's deathbed were his secretary, Sir William Paget, and Edward Seymour, the Earl of Hertford, who took charge of his will and made plans to exercise power during the minority of his son: King Edward.

In the name of god and of the glorious and blessed
virgin our Lady Sainct Mary and of all the holy
company of heaven We Henry by the grace
of god king of England France and Ireland
defender of the faith and in earth ymmediately
under god the Supreme hed of the church of
England and Ireland of that name theight
calling to our remembrance the great gifts and
benefitts of Almighty god given unto us in this
transitory lyfe given unto him our most lowly
and humble thanke knowledging our self insufficient
in any part to deserve or recompense the same
But fear that we have not worthely received
the same And considering further also to our self
that we be as all mankind is mortall and born
in sinne beleeving neverthelesse and hoping that every
christian creature lyving here in this transitory and
wretched woorld under god dying in stedfast
and perfaict faith endevoring and exercising himself
to observe in his lyf tyme if he have leasur such
good deedes and charitable workes scripture commaundeth
and as may be to the honour and please of god

Henry VIII: Conclusion

Henry VIII's reign began well. He won great praise for reversing many of his father's policies, for executing the deeply unpopular officials Dudley and Empson, and for reopening the traditional war against France: 'Our king is not after gold, or gems, or precious metals,' wrote Lord Mountjoy to Erasmus, 'but virtue, glory, immortality'.[69] Henry's early successes against Scotland and France seemed to fulfil these expectations: once again England seemed a military power to be reckoned with. During the long periods of peace, Henry's magnificence, as displayed in his tournaments, summit meetings, and the furnishings of his 55 royal palaces, made him seem the equal of the pre-eminent rulers in Europe.

Increasingly, however, England could not bear the cost of Henry's expenditure. For a short time the sales of monastic lands and the melting down of church plate helped to fill the gap in financing his conspicuous consumption and his later wars. During the mid-1540s, however, Henry had to resort to financial expedients such as high taxation, foreign loans and the debasement of the currency, which seriously harmed the economy of England, not least by exacerbating the existing inflationary trend. The trophy that was the city of Boulogne was an extravagant white elephant of no strategic value and too expensive to defend. Ministers privately discussed its return even during Henry's lifetime.

Furthermore, Henry's rule became increasingly brutal and tyrannical. His anxiety about the succession led to many deaths; his determination to impose the royal supremacy over the church, while also retaining traditional beliefs, resulted in still more. Nonetheless, there was no reign of terror under Henry: those executed for political or religious offences ran into the hundreds rather than the thousands. While a number of the condemned were innocents (notably Sir Thomas More, Lady Margaret Pole and Anne Boleyn) and some paid the ultimate price for perceived failure despite years of service (notably Thomas Wolsey and Thomas Cromwell), many others were undeniably guilty of treason, such as the 287 people who participated in rebellion.

Much changed in England and Wales as a result of Henry VIII's rule. The realm now lay outside the administrative and spiritual jurisdiction of Rome; monasteries no longer existed, their libraries dispersed and most of their buildings demolished; shrines attracting pilgrimages were no more; Wales was integrated into the administrative system of England; Ireland was now styled a 'kingdom' and governed more directly from London. Henry VIII, for better or worse, left an indelible mark on British history.

ABOVE: **Henry VIII looked portly and bad-tempered** *in his last years – and every inch a tyrant – in this engraving by Cornelis Matsys (c.1510–57), who worked in Antwerp. The depiction is a long way from images of Henry's majestic virility produced by Holbein the Younger earlier in the reign.*

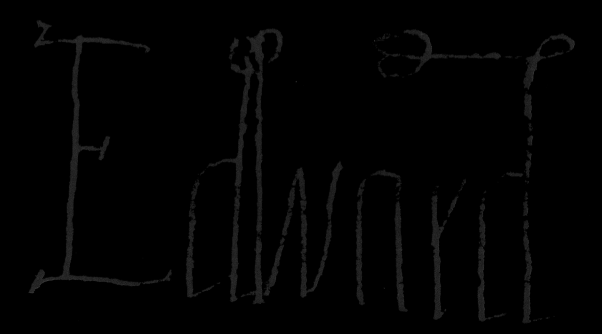

EDWARD VI

PARVVLE PATRISSA, PATRIÆ VIRTVTIS ET HÆRES
ESTO, NIHIL MAIVS MAXIMVS ORBIS HABET.
GNATVM VIX POSSVNT COELVM ET NATVRA DEDISSE,
HVIVS QVEM PATRIS, VICTVS HONORET HONOS.
ÆQVATO TANTVM, TANTI TV FACTA PARENTIS,

Henry VIII's long-awaited male heir, Edward, was born in Hampton Court Palace on 12 October 1537, the eve of the feast day of King St Edward the Confessor. He was a healthy infant, until the autumn of 1541 when he developed malaria. But he recovered well and until his last few months enjoyed an active life, hunting, riding and jousting. He enjoyed splendour, as did his father, whether revels at court or costly jewels.

Until he was six, Edward 'was brought up ... among the women',[1] who included his nurse, governess and two sisters. The only important male influence (apart fom his father) was Dr Richard Cox, who had been the headmaster of Eton and was appointed Edward's tutor when the prince was about three. This regime ended around July 1544, when Henry disbanded Edward's nursery, named new male household officers, and appointed Dr John Cheke, the first Regius Professor of Greek at Cambridge University, to work with Cox as royal tutor. Assisting Cheke were Roger Ascham and Anthony Cooke. All these men were Cambridge-educated humanists, the intellectual stars of their day. Under their tutelage Edward acquired a classical education: by the age of eight he could write letters in Latin and knew by heart four books of the 4th-century Roman writer Cato. He began studying Greek in 1549, and later read the historian-biographers Herodotus, Thucydides and Plutarch, along with the works of the writer-orator Pliny the Younger and Aristotle's *Politics*. Modern languages were not neglected: Edward spoke French and possibly learned Italian and Spanish. Following the humanist curriculum, the prince was also taught mathematics, geometry, astronomy and music.

Edward's tutors were all inclined towards Protestantism and favoured religious reform. Not surprisingly, under their influence Edward grew up to be strongly anti-papal and suspicious of superstition. By the end of his short life he had become a staunch believer in predestination, the Calvinist doctrine that God pre-ordained some souls for salvation (the elect) while condemning others (the reprobate) to eternal damnation.

Too young to rule, Edward was dependent first on his maternal uncle, Lord Protector Somerset, and then on John Dudley, Earl of Warwick (and later Duke of Northumberland), who was president of his council. As the reign progressed, however, Edward took on some political responsibilities in preparation for when he would come of age.

PREVIOUS PAGE: **Edward, Prince of Wales**, *wore the insignia that went with the title, although he was never formally invested with it. In this majestic 1546 portrait by William Scrots, the three ostrich plumes with a crown hang from a jewelled chain wound twice around his shoulders. Through the window can be seen a deer park with Hunsdon House, Hertfordshire, in the distance: Edward stayed there briefly in 1546.*

LEFT: **The young Prince Edward** *was about 14 months old when Holbein the Younger painted him in this earliest surviving portrait. He looks a bonny child, and indeed he was healthy until shortly before his death. He is holding a toy rattle as if it were the sceptre of an adult monarch. The Latin verses are in praise of Henry VIII: they call upon the child to emulate his father, for surpassing him would prove impossible.*

1547

The announcement of Henry's death on 28 January was postponed for three days. During this intervening period, Hertford and Sir William Paget worked together to organize a bloodless political coup. On 31 January, when Edward was proclaimed king, they secured the council's agreement that Hertford should be appointed 'lord protector' of the realm during Edward's minority. On 17 February, new titles of nobility were distributed: Edward Seymour, the Earl of Hertford, became Duke of Somerset; Henry's lord chancellor, Baron Wriothesley, was created Earl of Southampton; and John Dudley, Viscount Lisle, was raised as Earl of Warwick.

On 14 February, Henry VIII was buried alongside Queen Jane at Windsor. As was customary, his children did not attend the requiem mass. A week later, Edward's coronation took place and was followed by several days of jousts. Some time in the spring, the dowager queen, Katherine (Parr), secretly married Thomas Seymour, Baron Sudeley, younger brother of the new lord protector, an action which greatly annoyed Somerset.

The Earl of Southampton was dismissed as lord chancellor on 6 March and temporarily removed from the council. Although he had been accused of malpractice, his loss of influence arose from his unwillingness to agree to Somerset assuming regal powers.

Outside the realm, on 31 March, Francis I of France died and was succeeded by Henry II. In April, Emperor Charles V defeated the German Lutheran princes of the Schmalkaldic League at the Battle of Mühlberg, in Saxony. Many German Protestants afterwards took refuge in England.

The breaking of images

The sixteenth day of November [1547] the King's Majesty's visitors began that night to take down the rood with all the images in Paul's Church, which were clean taken away, and by negligence of the labourers certain persons were hurt and one slain in the falling down of the great cross in the rood loft, which the popish priests said was the will of God for the pulling down of the said idols. Likewise all images in every parish church in London were pulled down and broken by the commandment of the said visitors.

[CHARLES WRIOTHESLEY (HERALD), *A Chronicle of England during the Reigns of the Tudors*, VOL. II, P. 1]

RIGHT: **Edward Seymour (1500–52), Earl of Hertford and later Duke of Somerset,** *was the elder brother of Henry's Queen Jane and therefore uncle of Edward VI. On Henry's death, he overturned the legal arrangements made by the late king for the government of the realm during Edward's minority, and assumed the positions of lord protector and governor of the king's person. The council agreed to this change, but expected Somerset to rule with its advice; however, over the next two years the duke became increasingly autocratic. He also introduced destabilizing policies: an expensive war in Scotland, an investigation into illegal enclosures, and religious reform. The result was serious unrest in 1549 and the near-bankruptcy of the crown. The council closed ranks and dismissed him from office in October 1549. Although he returned to the council, he was later beheaded for treason. The painter of this portrait has not been identified.*

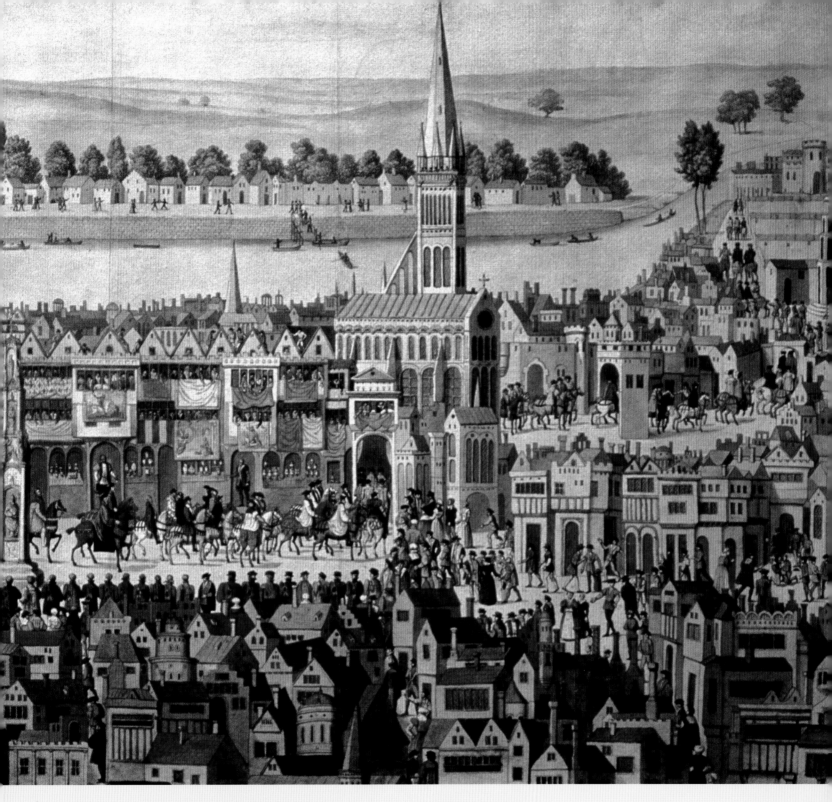

Edward VI's coronation procession *took place on 19 February 1547. The nine-year-old king rode on horseback for five hours from the Tower of London to Westminster Palace, during which time he was greeted with pageants celebrating his royal pedigree, education and religion. The pageants were based on those written in 1432 for another boy-king, Henry VI, but they were adapted to include praise of the royal supremacy and religious reform. This drawing is a 1785 copy of a mural originally at Cowdrey House in Sussex. In it, Edward can be seen under a fringed canopy, flanked by Lord Protector Somerset and Sir Anthony Browne, the master of the horse and owner of Cowdrey, who commissioned the original mural. The group have left the City and are approaching Westminster along the Strand.*

On 31 July, Somerset ordered a royal visitation of the church with responsibility to implement religious reform. A new government campaign of image-breaking began in August and continued through the autumn. In many places, churches were whitewashed and the Ten Commandments were written on their walls. Sometimes this was done at night to avoid violence. The regime was clearly moving in a Protestant direction. On 5 September, Bishop Stephen Gardiner of Winchester was imprisoned in London's Fleet Prison for criticizing Archbishop Cranmer's *Book of Homilies*, which incorporated Protestant doctrines.

North of the border, on 10 September, a large English army under Somerset, with naval support, defeated a huge Scottish force at the Battle of Pinkie (or Pinkie Cleugh), near Musselburgh, east of Edinburgh. After this victory, Somerset began installing English garrisons in Scottish castles in the Lowlands. He hoped to control the country and force the Scots to abide by the Treaties of Greenwich, and so agree to the marriage between Edward and their infant queen, Mary.

During December, Parliament repealed several pieces of Henry VIII's legislation: the 1534 Treasons Act, the 1539 Act of Six Articles (for 'abolishing diversity in opinions') and the 1539 Proclamations Act. Two important religious statutes were also passed: one permitting communion in both kinds (wine as well as bread for the laity), the other dissolving chantries, those endowed chapels where masses were said for the dead. This Parliament also introduced the harshest poor law of the century: all 'idle' vagrants were ordered to be branded with the letter 'V' and adjudged slaves of a master for two years. Other beggars were to be sent to their home parish where they would be provided with work. However, earlier in the year, in June (St Michael's Day), London had introduced the first compulsory poor rate to provide some relief for the city's poor.

1548

Religious reform continued apace during the first part of the year. On 27 January, Cranmer ordered that candles, palms and ashes should cease to be used during Lent. He also banned traditional Easter practices, such as creeping to the cross on Good Friday, and inserted some long English passages into the Latin mass to be used on Easter Sunday (1 April). In Cornwall, there was unrest at these changes, and during Easter week William Body, a layman acting as Archdeacon of Cornwall, was murdered in Helston. On 30 June, Stephen Gardiner was imprisoned in the Tower of London because of his opposition to religious reformation.

The government took measures against illegal enclosures of land in June and established a royal commission in the Midlands, Berkshire and Buckinghamshire to investigate abuses. John Hales, a sympathetic reformer, sat as its chairman.

¶ A Proclamacion, set furthe by the Kynges Maiestie, With thassent and consent of his moste dere Uncle Edwarde Duke of Somerset, Gouernor of his moste royall persone, and of his dominions and Subiectes Protector, and others of his highnes priuie counsaill, against enclosures, lettyng of houses to decaie, and vnlawfull conuertyng of arable ground to pastures, the first daie of June in the second yere of his maiesties moste gracious reigne.

Orasmuche as the kynges Maiestie, the Lorde Protectors grace, and the rest of his priuie Counsaill, hath been aduertised and put in remembraunce, aswell by diuerse supplicacions, and pitifull complaintes, of his Maiesties poore subiectes, as also by other, wise and discrete men, hauyng care to the good ordre of the realme, that of late by the inclosyng of landes and arable groundes, in diuerse and sundery places of this realme, many haue been driuen to extreme pouertie, and compelled t[o]

seke them liuynges in other countreis, with greate mi[serie ...] tyme past. x.xx.yea, in some place.C.or CC.christian [...] to the bryngyng furthe and norishyng of youthe, and [...] sties realmes with faithfull subiectes, who might ser[...] to the defence of this realme, now there is nothyng ke[...] heretofore was tilled and occupied with so many men[...] in worke and labor, but also Capōs, Hennes, Chikon[...] kettes, is now gotten by insaciable grediness of myn[...] dwelled vpon with one poore Shephard: So that th[...] solacion, houses decayed, parishes diminished, the fo[...] by the gredy couetousnes of some men, eaten vp and [...] houses by Shepe and Bullockes. And that althoug[...] tes and lamentacions, hath been heretofore made, an[...] iesties father and grandfather, the kynges of moste f[...] Henry the. viii. with the consent and assent of the l[...] mentes assembled, diuerse and sundery lawes and act[...] ces, in their seuerall tymes hath been made for the re[...] men, doth not cease daily to encroche hereupon, and m[...] bryngyng arable groundes into pastures, and lettyn[...] doune, decaie, and bee waste: Wherefore, his highne[...] dre zeale to his moste louyng subiectes, and specially[...]

uaill for their liuyng, and not to liue an Idle and lopteryng life : and of a moste necessarie regarde, to the suertie and defence of his realme, whiche muste bee defended against the enemie, with force of menne, and the multitude of true Subiectes, not with flockes of Shepe, and droues of Beastes: And further is aduertised, that by the vngodly and vncharitable meanes aforesaied, thesaied Shepe and Oxen, beyng brought into a fewe mennes handes, a greate multitude of them beyng together, and so made greate droues and flockes, aswell by naturall reason, as also as it maie be iustlie thought, by the due ponishement of God, for suche vncharitablenes: greate Rottes and Murrins, bothe of Shepe and Bullockes, hath lately been sent of God, and seen in this realme, the whiche should not by all teason so sone fall, if thesame wer disparsed into diuerse mennes handes, and thesaid catell also, by all likelihode of truthe should be more chepe, beyng in many mennes handes, then as thei be now in fewe, who maie hold them dere, and tary their auauntage of the Market: And therefore , by thaduise of his moste entierly beloued vncle, the Duke of Somerset, Gouernor of his persone, and Protector of all his real[...]

mes, Dominions, and Subiectes, and the rest of his Maiesties priuie counsaill, hath waied moste depely all thesaied thynges: And vpon the foresaied consideracions, and of a Princely desire and zeale, to se that Godly lawes, made with great trauaill, and approued by experience, and by the wise heddes, in the tyme of thesaied moste prudent Princes, should not be made in vain, but put in vre and execution, hath appoynted, accordyng to thesaid Actes and Proclamaciōs, a view and enquirie to be made, of all suche as contrary to thesaied Actes and Godly ordinaunces, hath made Enclosures and Pastures , of that whiche was arable ground, or let any House, Tenement, or Mese decaye, and fall doune, or otherwise committed or doen any thyng to the contrary: of the good and wholsome articles, conteined in the saied Actes: And therfore willeth and commaundeth, all his louyng subiectes, who knoweth any such defaultes and offences, contrary to the wealthe and proffite of this realme of Englande , and thesaied Godly lawes and Actes of Parliament, doen and committed by any persone, whosoeuer he or thei bee, to insinuate and geue informacion of the offence, to the kynges Maiesties Commissioners, who be appoynted to here thesame, so truly and faithfully, that neither for fauour nor feare, thei omitte to tell the truthe of any, nor for displeasure name any man, who is not giltie thereof: That a conuenient and spedie reformacion, might bee made herein, to the honor of God, and the kynges Maiestie, and the wealth and benefite of the whole realme.

God saue the Kyng.

Excusum Londini, in ædibus Richardi Graftoni
Regij Impressoris.

Cum priuilegio ad imprimendum solum.

ABOVE AND LEFT: **A proclamation of June 1548** *announced a government inquiry into illegal enclosures, the unlawful conversion of arable into pastoral land and the neglect of houses. The Duke of Somerset and many in his entourage blamed the enclosure of common land on landowners' personal greed, and they regarded their attack on the practice as part of a programme for widespread moral regeneration and religious reform.*

THOMAS CRANMER, BIS
MARTIR

On 22 July, the commission sent an interim report to Protector Somerset, but impatience at the slowness of government action provoked enclosure riots in Buckinghamshire during August. These events took place in a summer that 'was a great drought for lack of rain, and in July the plague reigned sore in London'.[2]

Also in June, a French expeditionary force arrived in Scotland. The English effort to coerce the Scots into a royal marriage – the 'rough wooing' – failed when, on 7 August, the five-year-old Scottish Queen Mary sailed for France to marry the *dauphin*.

On 5 September, Baron Sudeley's wife, Katherine, the dowager queen, died of puerperal fever after childbirth. The widower soon afterwards made plans to marry Princess Elizabeth, who had lived in Katherine's household until May. Any marriage, though, would require the consent of the council.

A proclamation of September banned all sermons until the 'king's further pleasure'.[3]

On 21 or 22 November, a barrel of gunpowder accidentally caught alight at the Tower of London, resulting in damage to the Tower and the death of a prisoner.

1549

In January of this year, Parliament took further steps away from Henry's religious orthodoxy by sanctioning clerical marriage and agreeing to an Act of Uniformity that enforced a Book of Common Prayer written in English rather than Latin. On 5 March, Parliament also passed an Act of Attainder against the protector's brother, Baron Sudeley, who had been arrested on a charge of treason. He was beheaded a fortnight later.

As a result of the lord protector's moves towards reformation of the church, two Protestant theologians from Strasbourg – Martin Bucer and Paul Fagius – arrived in England on 23 April. In July, they took up posts at the University of Cambridge.

In May, riots against enclosures occurred in many of England's southern counties. They were quickly pacified or suppressed 'by good policy of the council and other noblemen of the country'.[4] However, the year witnessed two rebellions

'by good policy of the council and other noblemen of the country'

LEFT: **Archbishop Thomas Cranmer (1489–1556)** *kept his Protestant beliefs quiet under Henry VIII, and he came out of the closet only during Edward's reign. In his coronation sermon of February 1547, the archbishop called Edward VI a second Josiah (Josiah was the young Old Testament king who banished idolatry from Israel). Over the next years, Cranmer introduced reforms in theology, the liturgy and religious practice. As seen here, he also changed his appearance, growing a beard like an Old Testament prophet or a Continental clerical reformer. The portrait, by an unknown artist, hangs in Lambeth Palace.*

of note. On 6 June, demonstrators protested at Bodmin, in Cornwall, against the new Book of Common Prayer due to be used on Whit Sunday (9 June); on Whit Monday, villagers in Sampford Courtenay in Devon compelled their priest to abandon the new liturgy. Then, thousands of protestors from both counties marched to Exeter under the banner of the 'Five Wounds of Christ'. Attempts to suppress the rising by negotiation failed, and on 2 July the rebels began to besiege Exeter.

On 8 July, Robert Kett, a Norfolk tanner and minor landholder, turned a demonstration against enclosure at Wymondham into a protest march on the regional capital, Norwich. The protestors – who came to number about 20,000 – encamped outside the city, mainly on Mousehold Heath. After rejecting a royal pardon, they attacked and occupied Norwich on 22 July. During this month, disturbances arose in another 15 counties, when the ordinary people 'pulled down parks and grounds that was enclosed of divers lords and gentlemen'.[5] In late July, government troops successfully broke up the camps of protestors in Suffolk but failed to retake Norwich.

In the Southwest, Lord John Russell and Lord William Grey of Wilton fought against the rebels at Clyst St Mary between 3 and 5 August. The rebel army was routed, and two days later the siege of Exeter was lifted. Some Cornishmen regrouped at Sampford Courtenay, where they were defeated on 17 August.

In East Anglia, on 25 August, an army of over 9000 men under Warwick stormed and entered Norwich. Kett retreated to Dussindale, where two days later about 3000 of his men were slaughtered. Captured the next day, Kett was hanged from Norwich Castle in December.

From outside the realm, news arrived in late August that the French had taken forts held by the English close to Boulogne. And in the North, Protector Somerset was forced to withdraw soldiers from Haddington Castle, the main English garrison in Scotland.

The council versus the lord protector

Because the trouble between us and the Duke of Somerset may have been diversely reported to you, we should explain how the matter is now come to some extremity. We have long perceived his pride and ambition and have failed to stay him within reasonable limits, but he has laboured to bring the king and country to confusion, continually declaring he meant never to account to any superior. He would reject or pass over in silence the council's advice. We resolved to treat the matter with him. But a few of us had not dined together more than twice when he took the Tower and raised the country about Hampton Court ...

[THE COUNCIL WRITING TO PRINCESS MARY, 9 OCTOBER 1549, AS PARAPHRASED IN *Calendar of State Papers Domestic, Edward VI*, NO. 403, P. 146]

RIGHT: **Thomas Seymour (c.1509–49), Baron Sudeley and lord admiral**, *was the ambitious younger brother of Protector Somerset and thus also an uncle to Edward. About four months after Henry VIII's death, he married the dowager queen, Katherine, to gain precedence at court. He also attempted to obtain direct access to the king by using a private key to enter the privy chamber. On one occasion, however, he found the door bolted on Somerset's orders and he became so angry that he lost control and shot dead Edward's dog. After Katherine's death in September 1548, Sudeley secretly showed interest in marrying the* 14-year-old Elizabeth and possibly also plotted a coup. On 17 January 1549 he was arrested. The warrant for his execution was signed by the king on 18 March 1549 and counter-signed by Somerset, Cranmer and other members of the council. Two days later Sudeley was beheaded. Some questioned the justice of the act, because Sudeley had not been put on trial. Inscribed in the background of the painting is a poem extolling the baron's virtues.

'such division through all London that some kept holy day and some none'

In September, the Bishop of London, Edmund Bonner, who had spoken against the new religious legislation in Parliament, was imprisoned. On 1 October he was removed from his see after being tried by Cranmer in an ecclesiastical court.

On the same day, the deeply unpopular Somerset heard rumours of a plot to unseat him from power. He moved King Edward from Hampton Court to the better-defended Windsor Castle, but surrendered on 10 October in the face of opposition from the council and was sent to the Tower soon afterwards. The protectorate came to an end on 13 October when the office was abolished, and the council took over the work of government.

Parliament sat from 4 November until the following 1 February. It passed a law against unlawful assemblies and another permitting the removal of superstitious images.

1550

During January and February, the Earl of Warwick triumphed over his rivals in the council, who had been the principal plotters against Somerset: the earls of Arundel and Southampton were banned from court. Warwick became lord president of the council, a position that gave him charge of its business and membership; and his son, son-in-law and friends entered the privy chamber and thereby controlled access to the king.

In February, the Protestant Nicholas Ridley replaced Bonner as Bishop of London. Bonner remained in prison.

In late March, peace was made between England and France. By the Treaty of Boulogne, England immediately surrendered the French town to Henry II on payment of 400,000 crowns. England also withdrew from Scotland, leaving the French politically dominant there. Despite this humiliation, the realm celebrated with 'great bonfires with great cheer'.[6]

The Duke of Somerset was readmitted to the council on 10 April, and a marriage was arranged between his daughter, Anne, and one of Warwick's sons. April also saw a drive against 'bawdry, whoredom and scolding'[7] in London.

On 2 May, Joan Bucher (Joan of Kent) was burned in Smithfield 'for great heresies',[8] including the denial of the humanity of Christ. In July, John Hooper – who had recently returned from Zurich where he had been influenced by the reformer Heinrich Bullinger – was nominated to the see of Gloucester. However, when he refused to wear the prescribed vestments, an acrimonious dispute developed among the bishops over the issue.

Also in July, Sir John Gates arrived in Essex, at the command of the council, to prevent any escape to the Continent of the Catholic Princess Mary, the king's elder half-sister, as there were reports that Imperial ships were waiting off the coast for that purpose. However, Mary decided not to flee.

On Assumption Day (15 August), there was 'such division through all London that some kept holy day and some none',[9] and in November bishops were ordered to replace altars with communion tables.

The coinage of the country was debased in December in order to raise revenue, and 'corn waxed very dear'.[10]

ABOVE: **Hugh Latimer (c.1485–1555)** *had been Bishop of Worcester until 1539 and was a prominent Protestant zealot who had been imprisoned twice for his views under Henry VIII. He became a regular preacher at court during Edward's reign. In this Elizabethan woodcut (from John Foxe's* Acts and Monuments, *or* Book of Martyrs), *Latimer is shown delivering his 1549 sermon for Lent before the king from a pulpit that had been built in the privy-garden at Whitehall during the last decade of Henry VIII's reign. In April 1550, Edward ordered that preaching at court should take place weekly, rather than just at Lent or on special occasions.*

220

John Dudley (c.1504–53), *Duke of Northumberland, was created Viscount Lisle in 1541 and Earl of Warwick in 1547, before gaining the dukedom in 1551. Under Henry VIII and during the protectorate he enjoyed a successful military career, and after the fall of Somerset he outmanoeuvred opponents to wield power as lord president of the council. In this position, he pursued a policy of peace abroad and reform and retrenchment at home. With the king's approval, Northumberland tried to divert the succession by excluding Henry VIII's two daughters and placing his daughter-in-law, Lady Jane (Grey), on the throne.*

INVIDIA TORQVET AVTOREM.

221

Henry FitzAlan (1512–80), 12th Earl of Arundel, *served four of the five Tudor monarchs, as a soldier, diplomat and courtier. In July 1546, he was appointed lord chamberlain and sat on the privy council. Conservative in religion, he was ousted from office by John Dudley, Earl of Warwick, in January 1550. This painting of 1550 portrays Arundel posing as a Roman emperor. Its inscription, 'Let envy turn upon its author', may be a warning directed towards Warwick. In November 1551, Arundel was implicated in Somerset's plotting and so spent a year in the Tower. On his release he was outwardly prepared to accept Queen Jane, but he was one of the first to defect to Mary.*

1551

In February, the imprisoned Stephen Gardiner was deprived of his bishopric of Winchester. Other Henrician (or Catholic) bishops lost their sees in August and October, and committed Protestants filled the vacancies. On 8 March, Hooper was consecrated as Bishop of Gloucester, as he had eventually agreed to wear the traditional vestments. However, he was not required to swear by the saints in his oath, because Edward had crossed out the offending phrase.

In February, an elite band of 850 mounted 'gendarmes' was established. Although tiny, this was England's first standing army. However, it had to be disbanded in Michaelmas 1552 as an economy measure.

Princess Mary came to London in March, having been summoned by Edward, who was demanding her household's conformity to the new Prayer Book. Her 130 attendants rode to court, ostentatiously carrying rosaries and other symbols of

Catholicism to demonstrate their opposition to the government's religious policies.

On 25 May, a 'great earthquake'[11] hit London and its outskirts, while in June there was 'great tempest of weather'.[12] July saw an outbreak of the 'sweating sickness', which caused many deaths, especially of young men. To avoid the illness, the court moved to Hampton Court Palace. At the same time, economic conditions deteriorated. On 9 July, a further debasement of the currency was proclaimed, 'and the victuals as dear after as it was before and worser, that the people cried out of it in every place'.[13] Unemployment also rose, when England began to experience a downturn in the cloth trade after the boom of the previous two years. The recession would last until 1554.

A treaty was signed at Angers on 19 July which arranged a marriage between King Edward and Elizabeth, the daughter of Henry II of France. As another sign of Anglo-French friendship, Edward was invested with the French chivalric Order of St Michael.

In August, the council finally ordered Princess Mary to obey the law and to cease hearing the Latin mass. Two members of her household were arrested, and over the next year Mary was placed under great pressure to conform, but she held firm.

On 11 October, Edward made several new creations and promotions. They included the elevation of the effective head of government, the Earl of Warwick, to the Dukedom of Northumberland. A few days later, the duke moved against his political rivals. After dining with the king on 16 October, Somerset was arrested on a charge of high treason and sent to the Tower. Over the next few days, about a dozen of his friends were rounded up and imprisoned, including Sir William Paget. It is probable that Somerset was plotting to oust Northumberland from the council, but the duke struck first. On 1 December, Somerset was put on trial at Westminster Hall before 28 of his peers. He was found 'not guilty' on two charges of treason, but guilty of felony for gathering armed men at his residence, a crime that carried the death penalty.

LEFT: **Furniture in the mid-Tudor period** *was fairly simple and predominantly made of oak, although leather seats and backs made an appearance around the middle of the century. The upright armchair would have been made more comfortable with cushions. The cushion cover is richly embroidered with silk and metal thread in long-armed cross and tent stitches. The coat of arms is of Stanley and Windsor. Both items are from London's Victoria and Albert Museum.*

ABOVE: **Communion cups during Edward's reign** *had to be capacious so that lay parishioners could take wine at communion (as well as bread), as was now ordered by statute. Royal visitors confiscated the ornamental chalices previously used in the Catholic mass and thereby forced church wardens to acquire new plain cups. Some were adapted from ordinary domestic goblets, but others were specially made, such as this silver-gilt communion cup from 1549, which has a cover bearing the royal arms.*

Mary's Continental defender

The emperor [Charles V] continued, 'Ought it not to suffice you that ye spill your own souls, but that ye have a mind to force others to lose theirs too? My cousin, the princess, is evil handled among you; her servants plucked from her, and she still cried upon to leave mass, to forsake her religion, in which her mother, her grandmother, and all our family have lived and died.' [Dr Wooton, English ambassador] Said to His Majesty that when he left England she was honourably entertained in her own house, with such about her as she herself best liked, and thought she must be so still, since not hearing to the contrary he was driven to think there is no change. 'Yes, by St Mary, saith he, of late they handle her evil, and therefore say you hardly to them, I will not suffer her to be evil handled by them. I will not suffer it. Is it not enough that mine aunt, her mother [Katherine of Aragon], was evil entreated by the king that dead is, but my cousin must be worse ordered by councillors now? I had rather she died a thousand deaths, than that she should forsake her faith and mine. The King's Majesty is too young to skill of such matters.' Professing that it became him [Wooton] not to dispute with His Majesty, yet was forced somewhat to answer him, said he knew the King's Majesty was young in years, but yet, the Lord be praised for his gifts poured upon him, as able to give an account of his faith as is any prince in Christendom being of thrice his years; and as for the Lady Mary, though she had a king to her father, hath a king to her brother, and is akin to the emperor; yet in England there is but one king, and the king hath but one law to rule all his subjects by. The Lady Mary being no king, must content herself to be a subject ...

[Dr Wooton, English ambassador to the emperor at Augsburg, writing to the council, 30 June 1551, as summarized in *Calendar of State Papers Foreign, Edward VI*, no. 393, p. 137]

1552

On 13 January, seven women were whipped in London for vagabondage. A more severe punishment, however, befell Somerset who, on 22 January, was beheaded for his crime. His execution was unpopular and so, to avoid disturbances, it was held earlier than expected. On 26 February some of Somerset's adherents – Sir Michael Stanhope, Sir Thomas Arundel, Sir Ralph Vane and Sir Miles Partridge – were also executed, by hanging or beheading. However, four months later, in June, some of his allies were released from the Tower, including Sir William Paget.

Parliament sat from 23 January to 15 April. The session passed statutes legitimizing the children of married clergy and authorizing the use of a revised English Prayer Book that destroyed the last vestiges of the Catholic mass. The new Prayer Book was not published until October because of last-minute disagreements about kneeling at communion, nor was it used until November. Parliament also ordered the collection of parish alms.

On 2 April, Edward became sick with measles and smallpox. He recovered quickly, but his immune system may have been damaged, for soon afterwards the young king developed consumption. In December he again fell sick, this time with a bad cold.

In this year, a house for orphans and a house for the sick were built in London.

LEFT: **The whipping of beggars and vagrants,** *as depicted in this mid-16th century woodcut, was common in Tudor England. Poor Laws tried to make a distinction between the deserving poor, who were offered relief or licences to beg, and 'sturdy beggars', deemed capable of productive work, who were whipped, returned to their home parishes or placed in houses of correction.*

Death of the Duke of Somerset

He [the Duke of Somerset] was beheaded *soon after eight o'clock in the morning, being brought to his execution the sooner to prevent the concourse of the people, who would be forward to see the last end of one so well beloved by them. It was the greatest company as have been seen. The king's guard being there with their arms, there were a thousand more with halberds of the privilege of the Tower, from Ratcliff, Limehouse, Whitechapel, St Katherine, and Stratford Bow, as Hoxton, Shoreditch.*

And there the two sheriffs being there present seeing the execution of my lord. And his head to be off. And after shortly his body was put into a coffin and carried into the Tower and there buried in the church of the north side of the choir of St Peter. The which I beseech God have mercy on his soul. Amen.

And there was a sudden rumbling a little before he died as it had been guns shooting and great horses coming, that a thousand fell to the ground for fear. For they that were at the one side thought no other but that one was killing other. That they fell down to the ground, one upon another with their halberds. They thought no other but that they should flee. Some fell into the ditch of the Tower and other places, and a hundred into the Tower ditch, and some ran away.

[Henry Machyn, *A London Provisioner's Chronicle* (diary), entry for January–June 1552, online edition by Richard W. Bailey, Marilyn Miller and Colette Moore]

225

Englands Fa

Cap. Davis

Sr. Walter Rawleigh.

ous Discoverers

Sr. Hugh Willoughby.

Cap. Smith.

Sir Hugh Willoughby (d.1554?) *left England with the pilot Richard Chancellor on 23 June 1553 to find a northeast passage to the lucrative spice markets of Asia. The voyage was financed by London merchants and courtiers. As they rounded the north of Norway and Sweden, their three ships were scattered by a storm and Willoughby lost his way. He eventually froze to death, when trapped in ice on the Arzina River in Russia. Chancellor, however, successfully piloted his ship to Archangel on the White*

Sea coast and visited Ivan IV's court in Moscow. There he received assurances that commerce between the two realms would be welcomed in Russia. After his return to England in late 1554, a Muscovy Company was established. Mary issued it with a charter in 1555 and it carried on a regular and direct trade with Russia via the northern route to the White Sea. This print, celebrating 'England's Famous Discoverers' of the 16th and early 17th centuries, depicts Willoughby centre-right of the royal arms

1553

On 6 February, Mary rode to court to see Edward who was still ill. By March, some observers believed that he was dying. It was possibly about this time that he drafted his 'device for the succession', which proposed arrangements that ran counter to Henry VIII's 1544 Act of Succession. On 11 April, he left London by barge for Greenwich.

In April, Archbishop Cranmer proposed a reform of canon law, but Northumberland sabotaged it in the House of Lords. The same month, Edward handed over his palace of Bridewell, in Fleet Street, to be a workhouse 'for the poor and idle persons' of London.[14]

On 10 May, three ships departed from Tilbury to find a northeast passage to the lucrative spice markets of Asia, but they had to put into Harwich. They left England again on 23 June.

In May, Archbishop Cranmer prepared a new catechism and primer for publication that laid down the doctrines of the church. Cranmer also produced 42 articles of faith, which were given royal assent on 2 June, though they were never published. About this time, Edward ordered visitors to confiscate church ornaments, including vestments, jewels and plate.

On 21 May, one of the Duke of Northumberland's sons, Guildford Dudley, wed the king's cousin, the 15-year-old Lady Jane Grey. In early June, King Edward collapsed and, knowing death was now close, he altered his 'device' so that Jane could inherit the throne herself. On 12 June, he ordered his justices to draw up letters patent to this effect. Despite their reluctance they finally complied, and Edward signed the letters on 17 June. Four days later they were signed by over 100 people: councillors, household officers, London civic dignitaries and peers.

In early July, the council summoned Mary – who was at Hunsdon in Hertfordshire – to her dying brother's bedside. Once she was in London, she could be imprisoned and would consequently be unable to challenge Jane's succession to the throne. However, an unknown informant warned Mary of the plot, and to avoid capture she fled the next day towards her estates in Norfolk.

On Thursday 6 July, King Edward, the third Tudor monarch, died 'towards night' at Greenwich. There were now two prominent claimants to the throne: the Catholic Mary Tudor, heir by law, according to Henry VIII's last Succession Act, and Lady Jane Grey, heir according to the wishes of Edward VI and recognized by Northumberland and the council.

228

RIGHT: **The 'devise for the succession'** *was drawn up by Edward in his own hand in 1553, and it is now conserved at London's Inner Temple. Originally he and Northumberland optimistically planned to name the sons of Lady Jane Grey as heirs, but there was no time for Jane to conceive. Hence, amendments were introduced to the device. As seen here, the words 'L. Jane's heires masles' [heirs males] were altered to read 'L. Jane and her heires masles'. Edward's half-sisters – Mary and Elizabeth – were excluded from the succession on the grounds that they were illegitimate, of half-blood to the king, and likely to marry foreigners.*

My deuise for the succession.

1. For lakke of issu of my body. To the L Fran=
ceses heires masles, To the L Janes heires masles, To the L Katerins heires
masles, To the L Maries heires masles, To
the heires masles of the daughters wich she
she shal haue hereafter. Then to the L Mar
gets heires masles. For lakke of such issu,
To theires masles of the L Janes daughters
To theires masles of the L Katerins daughters
and so furth til yow come to the L mar-
gets heires masles.

2. If after my death theire masle be entred into
18 yere old, then he to haue the hole rule
and gouernance therof.

3. But if he be under 18, then his mother to
be gouernes til he entre 18 yere old. But to doe nothing w'out th'auise of 6
parcel of a counsel to be pointed by my
last will to the nomore of 20.

4. If the mother die befor theire entre into 18
the realme to be gouerned by the coun.
Prouided that after he be 14 yere al
great matters of importaunce be opened
to him.

5. If i died w'out issu, and ther were none
heire masle, then the L Fraunces to be regent
for lakke of her the L eldest daughters
and for lakke of them the L Marget to be

Edward VI: Conclusion

Edward died before he could show his mettle as king, but his actions and behaviour suggest that in character he resembled his father: authoritarian, strong-willed and unsentimental. However, unlike his father he was an enthusiastic Protestant, and his reign was to prove the peak of religious reform in England. Indeed, Elizabethan zealots were to represent him to their own queen as the model of godly rule that she should follow.

England did not fare well, though, during the early years of Edward's minority, suffering as it did from political instability at the centre, disturbances in the localities, a crippling war in Scotland, and inflation and financial dislocation owing to successive debasements of the currency. Once the Earl of Warwick took control, matters improved, although not immediately or dramatically. Peace with France helped enormously, as did the greater financial responsibility shown by the government. However, for a time political instability persisted as conspiracies and purges continued at the centre, culminating in the Duke of Somerset's execution and the arrest of his friends in October 1551. In the localities, moreover, the dreadful harvests of 1550 and 1551 caused inflation to soar, with the price of flour doubling in London. For good reason, the government feared unrest, and it took measures to prevent a repeat of the 1549 disturbances: some councillors, for example, were licensed to retain 50 or 100 horsemen that could be used to suppress risings if necessary. Parliament also approved the principle that lord lieutenants should be appointed to suppress commotions, rebellions or unlawful assemblies.

Warwick's regime was generally unpopular. So, in search of allies amongst the 'evangelicals' on the council – men like Archbishop Cranmer – Warwick decided to follow Somerset's path of religious reform. As a result, a consistent feature of the Edwardian years was the destruction of the traditional fabric of life in the localities. Parishioners were no longer able to perform the seasonal rituals of the English church or enjoy semi-secular customs, such as Plough Monday gatherings or Corpus Christi plays. Churches were denuded of their images, wall-paintings, altars, bells and decorations. Communities lost their chantries and colleges. For the evangelical minority, the reign was an exciting moment of moral regeneration; for the silent majority, it was a time of despair.

ABOVE: **'King Edward VI and the Pope'** *by an unknown artist, c.1570, is a propaganda painting that sums up the Elizabethan view of the reign of Edward VI. Henry VIII on his deathbed hands power over to his son, who continues the work of overthrowing popery. Lord Protector Somerset stands beside the king. Protestant members of the council – including* Warwick/Northumberland, John Russell (Earl of Bedford) and Archbishop Cranmer – face outwards, while the Catholics watch the Reformation with horror. Outside the window, soldiers can be seen destroying statues of saints and pulling down an image of the virgin. The blank white spaces may have been intended for anti-Catholic inscriptions.

MARY I

Marye

DIE · · · 1 5 4 4

ARI · DOUGHTER · TO ·
MOST · VERTVOVS · PRINCE ·
HENRI · THE · EIGHT ·

GE · OF · XXVIII · YERES

Born in February 1516, Mary was the only child of Henry VIII and Katherine of Aragon. Thanks to Katherine's influence, the princess was exposed to the humanist 'new learning' in preparation for a public life as a queen or queen-consort. Her education was not as rigorous as that of her half-sister Elizabeth, but Mary nonetheless studied Latin and possibly some Greek, spoke Spanish and French fluently, and understood Italian. She was musical, as were her father and siblings, taking 'pleasure in playing on the lute and spinet'.[1] She also shared their taste in fine clothes and rich jewels.

In 1525, the nine-year-old Mary was sent with her own household to Ludlow as the nominal Princess of Wales. During her 19-month stay in the Welsh Marches she travelled extensively, making ceremonial entries into various castles and towns. In April 1527 she returned to court in order to meet French ambassadors who were negotiating a marriage for her and one of Francis I's sons. A betrothal was contracted but put on hold owing to the questions that suddenly arose over the validity of her parents' marriage. During the next six years Mary continued her studies at court, seemingly undisturbed by the annulment proceedings.

All changed after Henry's marriage to Anne Boleyn and the birth of Elizabeth. Because Mary refused to recognize her father's second marriage, she lost her title of princess, her jewels and her independent household. She was sent to Hatfield, in Hertfordshire, to act as lady-in-waiting to her infant half-sister and was denied communication with her mother, even when Katherine was dying. Anne's own death released Mary from this humiliating, and potentially dangerous, situation. However, her expected restoration to favour with her father did not come until – through the intercession of Henry's third wife, Jane – she accepted the royal supremacy. Thereafter she spent time at court and later grew particularly close to her last stepmother, Katherine Parr, who was just six years her senior.

On her father's death, Mary became a wealthy landowner in her own right. Horrified by the Protestantism of Edward's regime, she stayed away from court on her estates in Hertfordshire and East Anglia, where she encouraged her household to become a local Catholic centre. In 1549 and 1550, the

PREVIOUS PAGE: **Princess Mary was 28** *when this painting was commissioned in 1544, from the artist 'Master John'. She had just been restored to the succession, although still branded illegitimate. Dressed as a princess, she wears a French gown with oversleeves folded back to reveal a rich facing of crimson velvet. The bodice is made of brocade, decorated in a stylized pomegranate pattern. Mary was not at all dowdy, as she is sometimes mistakenly portrayed; rather, she delighted 'in arraying herself elegantly and magnificently' (Calendar of State Papers, Venetian).*

LEFT: **Mary had a fine collection of jewels.** *Some were inherited from her father and brother, others were gifts from her husband. In this painting by Hans Eworth (fl.1520–74) of Mary as queen, she displays her religious faith by, among other things, the jewelled cross hanging from her jewelled choker.*

'all the
people
were sore
annoyed
with his
words'

government tried without success to force her to use the new Protestant Prayer Book and cease hearing the Catholic mass. In March 1551, Edward himself entered the fray and ordered his half-sister to court, where he intended to berate her for her disobedience. On this occasion, Mary showed her defiance by entering London accompanied by 130 supporters, each one holding a rosary. Throughout that year, Mary maintained her resistance even when members of her household were arrested. At last, Edward and the council backed down. Fearing the intervention of her cousin, Emperor Charles V, if Mary were arrested, the council decided to turn a blind eye to her religious activities.

Mary was 37 when she became queen. Well-educated, strong-minded, independent and experienced in running a household, there was no reason to suppose that she would not make a fine monarch, even though she faced the challenge of being the first reigning queen in the country's history.

1553

Edward's death was kept secret for four days to enable preparations to be made for the accession of Lady Jane Grey, daughter-in-law of the Duke of Northumberland. On 9 July, Bishop Ridley preached that Mary and Elizabeth were both bastards: 'all the people were sore annoyed with his words, so uncharitably spoken by him in so open an audience'.[2] Then, on 10 July, the king's death was proclaimed, and Lady Jane Grey travelled by barge to the Tower of London, where she was 'received as queen'.[3] The same afternoon, she was proclaimed queen at Cheapside.

Meanwhile, Mary – based in East Anglia – quickly mobilized support for her claim to the throne. She was joined by nobles, gentlemen and 'innumerable companies of the common people'.[4] Two days later, the Duke of Northumberland left London with an army to meet Mary's force. While he was absent, Northumberland's fellow councillors defected to Mary's cause, and on 19 July they proclaimed her as queen. Realizing his cause was lost, Northumberland surrendered in Cambridge on the 23rd. Mary had succeeded, and there had been no bloodshed.

Dressed magnificently in purple velvet and satin, Mary entered London with her retinue on 3 August to 'the inestimable joys and rejoicing of the people'.[5] When she arrived at the Tower, she released political prisoners, notably the 80-year-old Duke of Norfolk, Bishop Gardiner of Winchester and Edward Courtenay (the only surviving son of Henry, Marquess of Exeter). Gardiner and Norfolk were both sworn in as members of the queen's council, and Gardiner was appointed Mary's lord chancellor. Courtenay was elevated to become the Earl of Devon.

On 8 August, the late King Edward was buried in Westminster Abbey, according to Protestant rites.[6] Two days later, Mary held an obsequy for him, and the day after she heard a requiem mass for him in the chapel of the Tower.

Mary issued a proclamation on 18 August, in which she urged her subjects to follow her religion and avoid religious controversy. Although she pardoned many of those implicated in Jane's attempted coup, others were imprisoned, while Northumberland was

A 'queen' of nine days

Today I [Baptista Spinola] saw Lady Jane Grey *walking in a grand procession to the Tower. She is now called queen, but is not popular, for the hearts of the people are with Mary, the Spanish queen's daughter. This Jane is very short and thin, but prettily shaped and graceful. She has small features and a well-made nose, the mouth flexible and the lips red. The eyebrows are arched and darker than her hair, which is nearly red. Her eyes are sparkling and reddish brown in colour. I stood so near her grace that I noticed her colour was good but freckled. When she smiled she showed her teeth, which are white and sharp. In all a gracious and animated figure. She wore a dress of green velvet stamped with gold, with large sleeves. Her headdress was a white coif with many jewels ... The new queen was mounted on very high chopines [platform overshoes] to make her look much taller, which were concealed by her robes, as she is very small and short.*

[EYEWITNESS REPORT BY BAPTISTA SPINOLA, A GENOESE MERCHANT IN LONDON, 10 JULY 1553]

LEFT: **Lady Jane Grey (1537?–54)** *was the elder daughter of Frances Brandon and Henry Grey, Duke of Suffolk. On her mother's side, she was the granddaughter of Mary Tudor (the younger sister of Henry VIII) and Charles Brandon, Duke of Suffolk. Henry's will had settled the succession on Frances and her heirs if his own three children died childless; but Edward VI made Jane his direct heir and disinherited his two half-sisters. He knew Jane to be a committed Protestant. Furthermore, as she was already married to an Englishman – the Duke of Northumberland's son, Guildford – Edward had no reason to fear that she might marry a Catholic or foreigner. The 15-year-old Jane 'reigned' for only nine days. No likeness of Jane has been definitively identified, but this miniature, formerly attributed to Lucas Hornebolt but now ascribed to Levina Teerlinc (d.1576), may well be of her.*

beheaded alongside two other prominent conspirators on 22 August. On the scaffold he recanted his heretical views. The leading Edwardian Protestants Nicholas Ridley, Bishop of London, and the court preacher Hugh Latimer were arrested in mid-September. Archbishop Cranmer was initially left in position, but he was arrested at the end of the month.

On 30 September, Mary went on her coronation procession through London. She wore a blue velvet gown decorated with ermine, and on her head was 'a caul of cloth of tinsel beset with pearl and stone' and a 'round circlet of gold' studded with precious stones.[7] Elaborate pageants greeted her, some of them praising her as the representative of true religion. The next day she was accompanied by a procession of clerics into Westminster Abbey, where she was crowned and anointed with newly consecrated oil sent from abroad. In order to focus on the religious significance of the ceremony, there were no coronation tournaments.

Mary's first Parliament assembled on 5 October. It asserted Mary's legitimacy and repealed Henry VIII's treason legislation along with nine Edwardian religious statutes. Although England was still in schism, the mass was now legal again and it was no longer treasonable to deny the royal supremacy over the church. The Parliament also declared legitimate the marriage of Mary's mother to Henry, thus removing any lingering question about Mary's right to rule.

On 27 October, Mary informed her council that she intended to marry Emperor Charles V's son and heir, Prince Philip of Spain. However, on 16 November, Parliament petitioned Mary to marry an Englishman. In the eyes of some, the Earl of Devon was the most suitable candidate.

Mary's providential triumph

Great was the triumph here at London; *for my time I never saw the like, and by the report of others the like was never seen. The number of caps that were thrown up at the proclamation were not to be told. The Earl of Pembroke threw away his cap full of angelletes [gold coins]. I saw myself money was thrown out at windows for joy. The bonfires were without number, and what with shouting and crying of the people, and ringing of the bells, there could no one hear almost what another said, besides banqueting and singing in the street for joy.*

[MARY'S ENTRY INTO LONDON IN AUGUST 1553, FROM THE ANONYMOUS CONTEMPORARY *Chronicle of Queen Jane*, PP. 11–12]

LEFT: **The accession of Mary** *was treated as a providential event, since a Catholic queen had triumphed over the heretical Duke of Northumberland. In 1553, all expected Mary to restore the mass and repeal the religious legislation of Edward VI's reign; initially however, there was uncertainty about whether or not she would rescind the royal supremacy and end the schism with Rome. In this illuminated capital, Mary is placed on the throne by angels while Northumberland is visible in retreat, on the right. The new queen is dressed in her coronation robes and her hair is flowing loose under an imperial crown. This is the first portrait of Mary to appear in the Plea Rolls, a document that records details of legal suits or actions in a court of law, now housed in The National Archives.*

The execution of Lady Jane

By this time was there a scaffold made upon the green over against the White Tower, for the said Lady Jane to die upon ... (she) being nothing at all abashed ... neither with the sight of the dead carcass of her husband [Lord Guildford Dudley] ... she said ...: 'Good people, I am come hither to die, and by a law I am condemned to the same. The fact, indeed, against the queen's highness was unlawful, and the consenting thereunto by me: but touching the procurement and desire thereof by me or on my [be]half, I do wash my hands thereof in innocence, before God, and the face of you, good Christian people, this day', and therewith she wrung her hands, in which she had her book ... Then she said the psalm of Miserere mei Deus, in English, in most devout manner, to the end ...

Then the hangman [sic] kneeled down, and asked her forgiveness, whom she forgave most willingly. Then he willed her to stand upon the straw: which doing, she saw the block. Then she said, 'I pray you dispatch me quickly.' ... She tied the kercher [handkerchief] about her eyes; then feeling for the block said, 'What shall I do? Where is it?' One of the standers-by guiding her thereunto, she laid her head down upon the block, and stretched forth her body and said: 'Lord, into thy hands I commend my spirit!' And so she ended.

[FROM THE ANONYMOUS CONTEMPORARY *Chronicle of Queen Jane*, PP. 55–9]

1554

On 2 January, Charles V's ambassadors arrived to negotiate the marriage for his son. As they rode through London, 'the people nothing rejoicing, held down their heads sorrowfully'.[8] The terms of the matrimonial treaty were publicized on 14 January, but although the articles protected England's interests by, among other things, excluding Philip from exercising political power, discontent remained strong. In late January, a three-pronged rebellion against the marriage was attempted, led by Sir Peter Carew in Devon, Sir James Croft and Henry Grey, Duke of Suffolk, in the Midlands, and Sir Thomas Wyatt in Kent. However, only Wyatt's rebellion got off the ground. The Kentishmen's march on London looked threatening, especially after a force of London militia sent against it actually deserted to the rebels. However, Mary rallied support with an effective and rousing speech at the Guildhall on 1 February, the city gates were closed, Wyatt's supporters began to fade away, and he surrendered, his rebellion coming to nothing.

On 12 February, Princess Elizabeth was ordered down to London under suspicion of involvement with Wyatt. The same day, Lady Jane and her husband, Lord Guildford Dudley, were beheaded at the Tower. On 22 February, Mary formally pardoned 400 rebels, but others were imprisoned (notably Sir Nicholas Throckmorton) or executed. Before noon on 18 March, Palm Sunday, Elizabeth was conveyed to the Tower. She remained there until mid-May, when she was placed under house arrest in Woodstock. Edward Courtenay, the Earl of Devon, who had also had contact with some of the rebels and had been questioned by Lord Chancellor Gardiner, remained under a cloud of suspicion. To everyone's surprise, Throckmorton was acquitted of treason by a London jury on 17 April, but the jurymen were taken into custody and had to pay a heavy fine before release. Throckmorton remained in jail until January 1555.

Between 14 and 20 April, the Protestants Cranmer, Ridley and Latimer debated theology with Catholic university divines in a rigged disputation at Oxford. The aim was to discredit Protestant opinions and secure high-profile recantations.

On 20 July, Prince Philip landed at Southampton and, five days later, married Mary in Winchester Cathedral. Afterwards, there was 'such triumphing, banqueting, singing, masking, and dancing as was never in England heretofore'.[9] On 3 August, the court started out for London, where the royal couple made a great entry on Saturday 18 August. The city 'was beautified

Mary described

She is of low stature, with a red and white complexion, and very thin; her eyes are white and large, and her hair reddish; her face is round, with a nose rather low and wide; and were not her age on the decline she might be called handsome, rather than the contrary. She is not of a strong constitution, and of late she suffers from headache and serious affection of the heart, so that she is often obliged to take medicine, and also to be blooded. She is of very spare diet, and never eats until 1 or 2 p.m., although she rises at daybreak, when, after saying her prayers and hearing mass in private, she transacts business incessantly, until after midnight, when she retires to rest ... she seems to delight above all in arraying herself elegantly and magnificently ... She also makes great use of jewels ... in which ... she delights greatly, and although she has a great plenty of them left her by her predeccesors, yet were she better supplied with money than she is, she would doubtless buy many more.

[VENETIAN AMBASSADOR GIACOMO SORANZO'S REPORT TO THE SENATE, 18 AUGUST 1554, *Calendar of State Papers Venetian*, VOL V, NO. 934, PP. 532–3]

ABOVE: **Sir Thomas Wyatt the Younger (c.1521–54)** *plotted rebellion in order to prevent the marriage of Queen Mary to Philip of Spain. On 25 January 1554, he raised his standard and began a march from Kent to London with about 3000 men. On 1 February, Mary delivered a speech at the Guildhall to stiffen the citizens' resolve against the rebels, and on 7 February the rebels found the city barred to them. Wyatt was tortured in an attempt to make him implicate Elizabeth, but he exonerated her in his speech on the scaffold on 11 April. This profile portrait, by an unknown artist, is from 1550.*

OVERLEAF: **Lady Jane Grey's book of devotions** *is thought to be the one she read on her journey to the scaffold and held during her final speech. It may have originally belonged to the Duke of Somerset. Jane wrote farewell messages in the lower margins. Shown here is one to John Bridges, the Lieutenant of the Tower: 'Forasmuch as you have desired so simple a woman to write in so worthy a book (good) master lieutenant therefore I shall as a friend desire you and as a Christian require you to call upon god to incline your heart to his laws to quicken you in his way and not to take the word of truth utterly out of your mouth.' The book is held at the British Library.*

The songe of dus
tern & Ambrose.

Praise the
O god we knowlege
the to be the lorde.

All therthe mought the wor
ship the, whiche arte the father
everlasting

To the crie further all aun
gelle, the heavene, and all y^e
powers therin

To the thue crieth Cheru
byn and Seraphyn continually.

Forasmuche as you have desired so symple
a woman to writte in so worthye a booke
and of soch faithfulnes therfore I shall

Holy arte thow Holy arte
thow Holy arte thow ▆▆▆▆

Thow arte the lorde god of
hostes.

Heauen and earthe are fulfil
led w^t the glorie of y^i magestye

The glorious company of y^e
apostelles praise the

The godly felowshipe of the
prophetes worship the ▆▆▆

The faire felowshipe of mar
tyrs praise the.

The holy congregacon of ~

as a frende desyre you and as a christian warne
you to call vppon god to enclyne your harte to
his lawes to quicken you in his waye and no

with sumptuous pageants and hanged with costly silks and cloth of gold'.[10] One of the pageants caused trouble, however, as it displayed a figure of Henry VIII holding a book on which was written *Verbum Dei*, 'Word of God'. Because this implied approval of Henry's religious policies, Gardiner called in the painter and berated him 'with vile words calling him traitor'.[11] Later, the book was painted over to show gloves instead.

On 12 November, the king and queen attended the opening of Parliament. Philip rode on horseback and Mary travelled on his right in an open chariot, because she was believed to be pregnant. Cardinal Reginald Pole addressed Parliament on 28 November. Just a week earlier, on the 20th, he had returned to his homeland as the papal legate after a 20-year exile, during which time he had been an enemy of the state under the threat of attainder. On St Andrew's Day, 30 November, he reconciled the realm to Rome. Parliament then revived three heresy acts and repealed 18 acts relating to the church passed under Henry. Lay owners of ex-monastic lands – beneficiaries of Henry's dissolution of the religious houses – were, however, permitted to retain possession of their property.

During this year, Protestant bishops were deprived and replaced by Catholics. The new bishops then evicted married priests from their livings. Many Protestants went abroad.

1555

On 24 January, there was 'great running at the tilt at Westminster with spears both Englishmen and Spaniards'.[12] Great jousts also were held on Lady Day (25 March).

John Hooper and John Rogers (who was the vicar of St Sepulchre in London and Prebendary of St Pancras in St Paul's Cathedral) became on 29 January the first Protestants to be condemned to death by the heresy acts. They had been in prison for a year, refusing to recant their views. Rogers was burned at Smithfield on 4 February; Hooper's burning followed five days later, at Gloucester, where he had once been bishop. Over the next three and a half years, nearly 300 people would be burned for heresy. At first prominent Protestant clerics and preachers were targeted, but later ordinary men and women came to be included among the victims.

In March 1555 Pope Julius III died. His successor, Marcellus, soon fell ill and lasted a mere three weeks. In England, attempts were made to re-establish monastic life when, on 7 April, 25 Observant friars 'were put in at Greenwich again'.[13] The religious changes were, however, not

LEFT: **The marriage of Queen Mary and Philip** *took place on St James's Day, 1554. It was a reasonably successful union – except for their failure to have a child. Mary was older than her husband and he took mistresses when abroad, but no strong disagreements arose between them. Philip was initially unpopular, but little overt hostility towards the marriage was shown in England after Wyatt's rebellion until English involvement in Philip's Continental war and the fall of Calais. This painting records the alliance and is very similar to a number of shilling and half-shilling coins that Mary introduced in 1554. The painting (1555) also incorporates the crown from the front of the coin and the royal coats of arms of England and Spain from its back. Around the arms is the motto of the Order of the Garter, 'Evil be to him who evil thinks'. Philip was awarded the Garter at Windsor in August 1554, on his way to London.*

The burning of John Hooper

The third fire was kindled within a while after, which was more extreme than the other two [which blew out after burning his hair and 'nether parts']: and then the bladders of gunpowder broke, which did him small good, they were so placed, and the wind had such power. In the which fire he prayed with somewhat a loud voice: 'Lord Jesus have mercy upon me! Lord Jesus have mercy upon me! Lord Jesus receive my spirit!'

And these were the last words he was heard to utter. But when he was black in the mouth, and his tongue swollen, that he could no[t] speak, yet his lips went till they were shrunk to the gums: and he knocked his breast with his hands, until one of his arms fell off, and then knocked still with the other, what time the fat, water, and blood dropped out at his fingers ends, until by renewing of the fire, his strength was gone ... So immediately bowing forwards, he yielded up his spirit.

[JOHN FOXE, *Acts and Monuments* (*Book of Martyrs*), MODERNIZED FROM THE 1583 EDITION ONLINE]

The burning of Ridley and Latimer

Then brought they a faggot kindled with fire, and laid the same down at Dr Ridley's feet. To whom Master Latimer spoke in this manner: 'Be of good comfort Master Ridley, and play the man; we shall this day light such a candle by God's grace in England, as (I trust) shall never be put out ... he [Latimer] soon died (as it appeared) with very little pain or none ... But Mr Ridley, by reason of the evil making of the fire unto him ... burned clean all his nether parts before it touched the upper ... In which pains he laboured, till one of the standers by with his bill pulled off the faggots above ... And when the flame touched the gunpowder, he was seen stir no more ...

[JOHN FOXE, *Acts and Monuments* (*Book of Martyrs*), MODERNIZED FROM THE 1583 EDITION ONLINE]

Lord receiue my spirite.

ABOVE: **The burning of John Rogers,** *the first Protestant martyr of Mary's reign, took place on 4 February 1555. The authorities had assumed that threats of burning would persuade Protestant heretics to recant and receive a pardon. Some of Edward's bishops did, while others reached a later accommodation. But many refused to recant, and so the executions took their course. The story of these deaths was memorialized under Elizabeth in John Foxe's* Acts and Monuments, *also known as the* Book of Martyrs. *This woodcut from it shows a large crowd watching the scene at Smithfield at the climax, when Rogers washed his hands in the flames. Around him, men and women throw up their hands in what can only be read as gestures of acclamation. The horseman is probably Sir Richard Southwell, a privy councillor, who examined Rogers and attended the burning.*

Ill.me Prınceps. Quoniam exploratum habemus, nihil nobis fœliciter posse contingere, quod non statim futurum sit ual,
de oratum vᵉ Excell.ᵉ, vᵒqᵉ Illust. Reipᵉ, itaqᵉ, cum D E V S, hoc tempore, singulari sua benignitate, Optatiß. nobis
Filium concesserit, nihil prius facere potuimus, qᵌ vt hic lætus nuncius, nris potius literis, qᵌ aliorum sermonibus, ad vos
perferretur. Id quod nos facimus, ut vos vocemus, non solum ad nostri gaudij participationem, verum etiam ad piarum
precum communionem, quas D E O, vna nobiscum, pro hoc beneficio, tam optato nobis, tam expectato nris omnibus Amicis,
libenter (non dubitamus) facietis. D E V S V. E. diu seruet incolumem. Ex Regia nra, Hamptonia.

M.̊ D.̊ L.̊ V.̊

Maria

No 377.

ABOVE: **A letter signed in advance** by Queen Mary to the Doge of Venice
in 1555 informs him that she has given birth to a son. This was one of
several letters written in the hand of Mary's Latin secretary, Roger
Ascham (who had served Edward VI in the same capacity), announcing
the birth of a royal son – the word could be altered if a girl were born.
The exact date is left blank and would have been inserted, had Mary
indeed delivered a child. Of course, Mary was not actually pregnant
although she displayed many of the symptoms. The letter is held at The
National Archives.

welcome everywhere. On Easter day, 14 April, a priest at St Margaret's Church in Westminster was 'broken on the head and on the arm with a wood knife' while administering wafers in the mass, his assailant objecting to the Catholic mass as an act of idolatry.[14]

In early April, Queen Mary withdrew for her confinement, and on 30 April 'tidings came to London' that she 'was delivered of a prince. And so there was great ringing through London and divers places'.[15] The rumour, however, was untrue, and by late July everyone realized that the queen was not pregnant after all. Mary's symptoms may have been the result of a phantom pregnancy or an illness such as cancer of the womb.

In May, Philip, Mary and Cardinal Pole sponsored a peace conference between Spain, England and France at La Marque, but it ended unsuccessfully on 9 June. Meanwhile an anti-Habsburg Neapolitan cardinal was elected Pope Paul IV on 23 May. Soon afterwards he signed a secret treaty with France and encouraged France's ruler, Henry II, to resume war against Spain.

The country was beset with very poor weather in the summer, resulting in crop failures and a bad harvest. Concerned by the poor state of the royal finances, during September the privy council suggested measures of retrenchment to deal with crown debts, which included reducing the cost of maintaining Calais.

By now, Philip had left England. On 26 August, he and Mary rode from Whitehall to the Tower, 'where they took boat to Greenwich',[16] before Philip departed for the Spanish Low Countries.

On 12 September, Archbishop Cranmer's trial opened in Oxford. Ridley and Latimer were tried for heresy shortly afterwards, and on 16 October both men were burned together outside Balliol College, Oxford, while Cranmer was forced to watch from his prison.

In October, Charles V began to withdraw from his various responsibilities as emperor. On 25 October, Philip became ruler of the Low Countries, replacing the regent, Mary of Hungary; and Charles's brother, Ferdinand, was chosen to be the new emperor. Although Philip had initially left much of his household in England, he withdrew it by December, suggesting he would not be returning soon.

The imprisoned Cranmer was formally removed from the see of Canterbury on 4 December. On 2 December, Pole had opened a legatine synod at Westminster. Decrees were issued enforcing clerical

A false pregnancy

Sire: Everything in this kingdom depends on the queen's safe deliverance. Her doctors and ladies have proved to be out in their calculations by about two months, and it now appears that she will not be delivered before eight or ten days from now ... It is almost incredible how the delay in the queen's deliverance encourages the heretics to slander and put about false rumours; some say that she is not with child at all, but that a suppositious child is going to be presented as hers, and that if a suitable one had been found this would already have been done. The expressions worn on people's faces are strange; folk have a more masked appearance than I have ever seen in the past.

[IMPERIAL AMBASSADOR SIMON RENARD TO CHARLES V, TWICKENHAM, 24 JUNE 1555, FROM *Calendar of State Papers, Spanish*, VOL. XIII, NO. 216, PP. 224–5]

A voyage to Guinea

They brought from thence *[Guinea]* at the last voyage four hundred pound weight and odd of gold, of two and twenty carats and one grain in fineness: also six and thirty butts of grains *[pepper]*, & about two hundred and fifty elephant's teeth *[ivory tusks]* of all quantities ... some of them were as big as a man's thigh above the knee. *[There]* was brought the head of an elephant, of such huge bigness ... this head divers have seen in the house of the worthy merchant Sir Andrew Judde, where also I *[Captain John Lok]* saw it, and beheld it, not only with my bodily eyes, but much more with the eyes of my mind and spirit, considering by the work, the cunning and wisdom of the workmaster: without which consideration, the sight of such strange and wonderful things may seem rather curiosities, than profitable contemplations.

[ACCOUNT OF CAPTAIN JOHN LOK'S 1554 VOYAGE TO GUINEA, IN RICHARD HAKLUYT'S 1602 COMPILATION *The Principal Navigations*, VOL. VI, PP. 163–4]

residence, encouraging preaching and establishing seminaries in the dioceses for boys intending to enter the clergy.

At about midnight on 12–13 November, Lord Chancellor Gardiner died. Dirges were heard in parish churches until his burial at his see of Winchester in February.

1556

Archbishop Nicholas Heath of York replaced Gardiner as lord chancellor on 1 January. About a fortnight later, Philip became King of Spain, now a reigning monarch in his own right. One of his first actions was to make a short-lived truce with France in the Treaty of Vaucelles, in February. Meanwhile, Mary, mindful of the attitude of Parliament and popular opinion, continued to resist Philip's desire for an English coronation.

On 7 March, a comet 'did shoot out fire, to great wonder and marvel to the people, and continued certain nights'.[17] Two weeks later, on Saturday 21 March, Cranmer was burned at Oxford. After the deaths of Latimer and Ridley, he had signed several recantations, including one made after he learned that Mary would not spare his life. On the day of his burning, however, he renounced them all, and on the stake he put his right hand first in the fire as a sign of his repentance. The next day, Cardinal Pole was consecrated as the new Archbishop of Canterbury.

RIGHT: **Philip II of Spain (1527–98)** *was the son of Charles V (King of Spain and Holy Roman Emperor) and Isabella, the sister of the King of Portugal. A widower by the age of 20, he took Queen Mary as his second wife in July 1554, following the negotiations conducted by Charles, designed to secure his succession in the Low Countries after his father's abdication or death. Before the wedding, Philip protested against the terms of the marriage treaty, as it restricted his rights and power in England. Nonetheless, he adhered to it fully afterwards. On Mary's death, Philip proposed marriage to Queen Elizabeth in an attempt to keep England Catholic and pro-Habsburg. However, even before she had formally rejected his suit, Philip became betrothed to the daughter of Henry II of France.*

Also during March, the council uncovered a conspiracy against Philip and Mary. Protestant exiles based in France, led by Henry Dudley and Christopher Ashton, were plotting to invade southern England, put Elizabeth on the throne and marry her to the Earl of Devon, who was now abroad and probably aware of the plot. Their colleague in England, Sir Anthony Kingston, apparently intended to remove £50,000 from the exchequer to pay for the enterprise, a plan which nearly succeeded. As the plot unravelled, Dudley and Ashton escaped back to France, but others were arrested. Eight were executed and Kingston died on his way to stand trial. In May, Elizabeth was interrogated at Hatfield House, Hertfordshire, and her governess Katherine Astley was taken to the Tower. The Earl of Devon soon ceased to figure in the plans of dissidents, for he died in September.

This year's harvest was again very poor, after a wet winter. It was the third bad harvest in succession, and produced more corn riots. The realm suffered further, when a series of epidemics began to afflict the people. Alarmed by the Dudley plot, Mary appealed to her cousin Charles V to persuade Philip to return to England: 'Consider the miserable plight into which this country has now fallen.'[18]

In September, Pope Paul was at war against the Habsburgs, and the Duke of Alva invaded the Papal States under King Philip's direction. France was quickly drawn into the conflict on the papal side. Although Mary was not obliged by her matrimonial contract to follow her husband into war, England was bound by the Anglo-Imperial treaty of 1543 to enter the war should Henry II invade the Low Countries.

Princess Elizabeth made her presence felt in the capital, when she rode into London on 28 November 'with a great company of velvet coats and chains'.[19] She remained there for only five days. Why she was summoned, and why she departed so soon, were not recorded.

On 29 November, Doctor Feckenham, the Dean of St Paul's, was consecrated as the new Abbot of Westminster with some 15 monks under his charge. He immediately began to restore the shrine of St Edward the Confessor in its accustomed place.

'Consider the miserable plight into which this country has now fallen.'

LEFT: **Exercising the royal touch** or 'king's evil' to cure scrofula – tuberculosis of the lymph nodes at the side of the neck – was revived by Mary after Edward VI had dismissed the practice as superstitious. It was thought that the holy oil with which the monarch was anointed gave her the miraculous power to cure the disease. Here Mary is shown seated while a young patient kneels and is touched by her. Elizabeth continued to exercise the royal touch, as it displayed the power of the monarchy. Mary also enthusiastically revived the blessing of 'cramp rings', to aid victims of epilepsy and 'palsy', but Elizabeth did not choose to continue that particular practice, regarding it as superstitious.

SI SIC POLE TV
AE POTVISSET
MENTIS IMAGO
PINGI
NIL OCVLI
PVLCRIVS ASPI
CERENT

1557

On 20 January, the gentlemen pensioners, 'in bright harness and many Barbary horses', mustered before the queen at Greenwich. 'And there came a tumbler played many pretty feats before the queen and my lord cardinal that Her Grace did laugh heartily'.[20]

In an act of purification and symbolic rejection of heresy, on 26 January commissioners exhumed and burned the bones of the two esteemed reformers Martin Bucer (d.1551) and Paul Fagius (d.1549), who had been buried in Cambridge.

Also in January, the council resolved to reform the navy.

On 27 February, an ambassador arrived from Russia. He was warmly greeted by merchants from the newly established Muscovy Company and was entertained by the city's mayor and aldermen. Another arrival in England, on 20 March, was King Philip. He received a 32-gun salute, and in London bells were rung and a *Te Deum* was sung in the churches. On 23 March, Philip rode through the city with Mary. The king now put pressure on Mary to declare war against France.

The former Bridgettine Convent of Syon at Isleworth, Middlesex, was re-established on 1 March. About 21 sisters and 3 brothers of the original community, dispersed at the dissolution, returned.

On 25 April, Thomas Stafford, grandson of the 3rd Duke of Buckingham and a political exile at the French court, captured the poorly protected Scarborough Castle in Yorkshire, aided by a small

A 'very grave' queen

When younger she [Mary] was considered, not merely tolerably handsome, but of beauty exceeding mediocrity. At present, with the exception of some wrinkles, caused more by anxieties than by age, which makes her appear some years older, her aspect, for the rest, is very grave. Her eyes are so piercing that they inspire not only respect, but fear, in those on whom she fixes them, although she is very shortsighted, being unable to read or do anything else unless she has her sight quite close to what she wishes to peruse or to see distinctly. Her voice is rough and loud, almost like a man's, so that when she speaks she is always heard a long way off. In short, she is a seemly woman, and never to be loathed for ugliness, even at her present age, without considering her degree of queen.

[VENETIAN AMBASSADOR GIOVANNI MICHIELI, 11 MAY 1557, *Calendar of State Papers, Venetian*, VOL. VI, II, NO. 884, P. 1054]

LEFT: **Cardinal Reginald Pole (1500–58),** *the grandson of the Yorkist Duke of Clarence, had fled England when Henry broke from Rome to become a dissident in exile, and was made a cardinal on 22 December 1536. As a humanist scholar, he represented the cutting edge of Catholic reform and spirituality while living in Italy during the 1540s. He returned to England in November 1554. On 30 November he absolved the realm from the sins of heresy and schism and reconciled it to Rome. He did much to further Catholic renewal under Mary, encouraging preaching* and resistance to heresy, but he was hampered by obstacles placed in his way by Pope Paul, who was highly suspicious of Pole's humanism (and politically hostile to King Philip and the Habsburgs). Pole thus lost his position as papal legate in 1556, but evaded a summons to Rome (where he would probably have been tried for heresy). The key figure in the English Catholic restoration, alongside Mary, he died only a few hours after his queen. The portrait is a contemporary Italian one, which now hangs in Lambeth Palace.

contingent of French soldiers. He announced himself Duke of Buckingham and declared his intent to protect the realm from foreign (Spanish) interference. The local population ignored his call for a rising, however, and three days later the castle was re-taken by Henry Neville, 5th Earl of Westmorland. Stafford was beheaded for treason at Tyburn on 28 May, and quartered the next day.

Mary proclaimed war against Henry II on 7 June. The French king had carried out numerous acts of hostility (including Stafford's raid) against her realm. Philip and Mary set off for Dover on 3 July, and on 6 July Philip sailed for the Low Countries; he would not return to England again. Shortly afterwards Mary sent over 7000 men under William Herbert, Earl of Pembroke, to fight against France.

On 14 June, Pope Paul IV recalled Cardinal Pole to Rome on suspicion of heresy, and six days later he nominated the elderly and infirm William Peto as the new English legate. Paul was using the power of his papal office as a weapon in his political war against Spain. Mary, however, refused to permit Pole's departure or to accept Peto as legate.

In June, the Irish Parliament passed legislation authorizing the establishment of an English plantation of settlers in Leix and Offaly. In England, 'this summer reigned ... diverse strange and new sicknesses'.[21]

French forces suffered defeat at the Battle of St Quentin on 18 August. Although no English soldiers had actually participated in the victory, *Te Deums* were sung, and that night there were 'bonfires and drinking in every street in London'.[22] On 27 August, the Spanish – with English help – captured the town of St Quentin itself: six days later church bells were once again rung and bonfires lit in celebration. On 19 September, 'came a commandment down to all parishes in London that they should go on procession at Paul's and *Te Deum laudamus* sung in all churches' for the winning of Péronne in France.[23] On 6 October, further celebrations were ordered for the end of the war between the pope and the emperor. As the campaigning season was over, Pembroke's army returned to England.

In December, five months after they had last been together, the 41-year-old Mary told Philip that she was pregnant. Also that month, the council began to receive intelligence that a French attack on Calais might be imminent.

1558

On 1 January, a French army led by Francis, Duke of Guise, besieged Calais. A hasty relief expedition was organized, under the Earl of Rutland, but the town capitulated on 7 January, 'the which was the heaviest tidings to London and to England that ever was heard of'.[24] Efforts to reverse the situation later in the month failed, and the country feared a French invasion in the summer. Parliament opened on 20 January. In response to the dire foreign situation, it granted the queen a subsidy and passed two statutes reforming the militia.

On 9 February, 'a commandment came that all bishops, priests, and clerks should go [in] a procession about London, and my lord mayor and the alderman and all the crafts in London in their livery to pray to God, and all the children of all schools and of the hospitals in order about London – called the general procession'.[25]

Princess Elizabeth rode into London on 25 February 'with a great company of lords and noblemen and noblewomen'.[26] She saw her half-sister three days later. During March, Mary drafted her will, stating that she believed herself to be 'with child' and leaving her throne to the issue of her body. By then, though, it was clear that Mary could not be pregnant. King Philip counselled Mary against using Parliament to overturn the 1544 Succession Act, which named Elizabeth as next in line to the throne. He also revived a plan to marry Elizabeth to his ally, the Duke of Savoy. During April Elizabeth rejected a direct proposal of marriage from Eric, the King-Elect of Sweden, a Lutheran. In June, Philip's ambassador, the Count of Feria, held an interview with Elizabeth to sound out her religious and political views.

On 24 April, Mary Queen of Scots married the *dauphin* of France. The war with France continued during the summer months without any further decisive actions. During July, Lord Admiral Edward Fiennes de Clinton attempted to conquer the French coastal town of Brest with 7000 men, but the men met unexpected resistance and soon ran out of supplies; Clinton also unsuccessfully attempted a landing in Normandy. However, the English fleet had greater success in controlling the Channel. In September, negotiations began for peace between England, Spain and France. Charles V, Philip's father, died this month at his retreat in the monastery of San Jerónimo de Yuste.

The autumn saw a widespread scarcity of food, accompanied by severe sickness and a devastating influenza epidemic. The queen herself fell ill in October. Later that month, she amended her will to indicate that the succession should go to the next lawful heir, thereby accepting that she was unlikely to produce children: by the terms of the 1544 statute and her father's will, that meant Elizabeth. The Count of Feria, dispatched by Philip back to England, felt there was little hope of the queen's recovery, because 'so rapidly does her condition deteriorate from one day to the next'.[27] He quickly made contact with Elizabeth to assure her of Philip's friendship. Mary died peacefully early in the morning of 17 November. Her cousin, archbishop and friend, Cardinal Pole, died later that day. King Philip recorded his 'regret' at his wife's passing.

Scotia

Anglia

Ibernia

Britania

Normandia

Calcuma

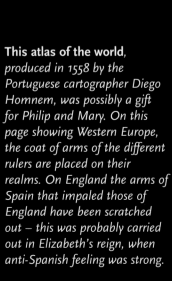

This atlas of the world,
produced in 1558 by the Portuguese cartographer Diego Homnem, was possibly a gift for Philip and Mary. On this page showing Western Europe, the coat of arms of the different rulers are placed on their realms. On England the arms of Spain that impaled those of England have been scratched out – this was probably carried out in Elizabeth's reign, when anti-Spanish feeling was strong.

Mary I: Conclusion

Unlike her half-brother Edward, Mary was neither trained to be a monarch nor exposed gradually to the business of government. Nonetheless, her education equipped her well for carrying out a public role as England's first reigning queen. Furthermore, during her father's rule she had observed and learned the exercise of queenship from her step-mother Katherine Parr; and during Edward's reign, she gained direct experience in running a household and in building up a local affinity of supporters.

Mary's reign is, though, remembered mainly for the burnings of Protestants – a policy to which the queen, later called 'Bloody Mary', remained committed, though many tried to dissuade her from it – and the loss of Calais. According to the Elizabethan martyrologist John Foxe, Mary claimed that 'when I am dead and opened you shall find Calais lying in my heart'. Her unpopular marriage to Philip and her phantom pregnancies have also tarnished her reputation, while the string of terrible harvests and devastating epidemics of the mid-1550s convinced many 16th-century commentators that God was definitely not on her side.

Yet Mary was in many ways a strong and successful ruler. She displayed courage and determination during both the accession crisis of July 1553 and Wyatt's rebellion of early 1554, when her advisers recommended flight. Her government was stable: the purges and coups of the Edwardian years were not repeated, and disagreements between councillors were contained. Much-needed reforms were initiated, not least a revision of the customs' duties in a new 1558 book of rates and the stabilization of the currency.

The policy closest to Mary's heart – reunion with Rome and the restoration of Catholic worship – was implemented effectively. Although condemned by ardent Protestants, it was popular with many, perhaps most, of her subjects. Admittedly, the laity did not endow new monasteries and nor did parish churches return to their former glory. However, priests were able to perform Catholic rituals, as altars, roods and images were put back in place, and ordinary people could once again participate in the traditional festivities of the Catholic year. The burnings proved a brutal but effective deterrent, just as they had on the Continent, and former Protestants increasingly conformed. Had Mary lasted another ten years, England would undoubtedly have been fully re-Catholicized.

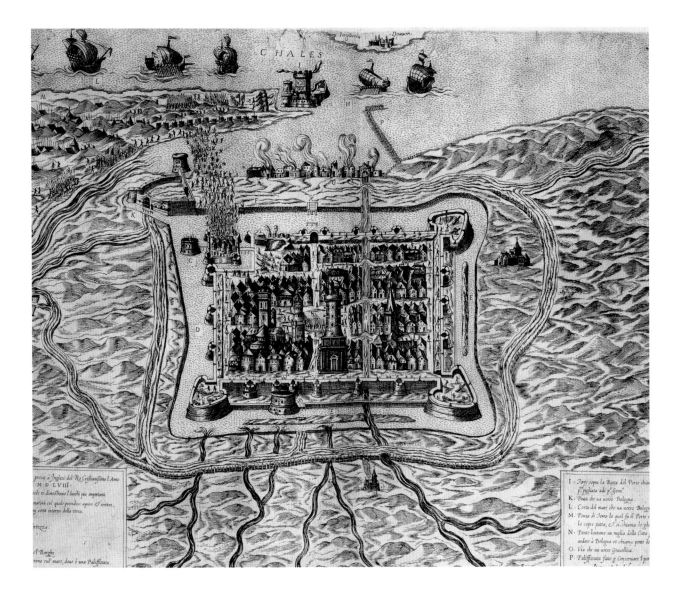

ABOVE: **The fall of Calais**, *England's historic toehold on the Continental mainland, was the most enduring result of Mary's reign, and it was considered a disaster at the time. The Duke of Guise mounted a surprise mid-winter attack on the English territory on 31 December 1557. Aided by the freezing weather, his army crossed the surrounding marshes and the town was taken a week later. At the Treaty of Cateau-Cambrésis (April 1559) the new queen, Elizabeth, had to accept that Calais would remain part of France for eight years, after which the French king would pay her an indemnity or return it. When the time was up, however, the French refused to pay because Elizabeth had given assistance to the Calvinist faction during the first of the civil-religious wars that wracked the country in the later 1500s. This Italian etching (1602) recreates Calais at the time of its defeat.*

Elizabeth I

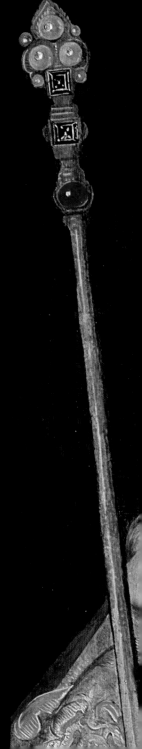

The birth of Elizabeth on 7 September 1533 was a bitter disappointment to Henry VIII and Anne Boleyn, who had desperately wanted a son. Nonetheless, until she was two and a half years old the baby enjoyed the title 'princess' and lived in her own household, where she had precedence over her half-sister Mary. In 1536, however, Elizabeth's bastardization and demotion followed Anne's execution. The next year, Elizabeth joined the household of her newborn half-brother Edward, where she remained, except for short visits to court, until Henry died. In 1544, she and Mary were restored to the succession although the taint of bastardy was not removed.

Throughout this time Elizabeth received an excellent education. Under the tutelage of first Katherine Astley (sometimes called Ashley; *née* Champernowne) and then the Cambridge scholars William Grindal and Roger Ascham, she became a fine linguist, speaking and writing Latin, Greek, Italian and French. She also learned music and grew up to be an accomplished keyboard and lute player.

After her father's death, the 13-year-old Elizabeth went to live with her stepmother, the dowager queen, Katherine (Parr). Within months, Katherine remarried, and her new husband was the ambitious and attractive Lord Thomas Seymour of Sudeley. He shamelessly flirted with his young charge Elizabeth, so that she began to 'blush when he were spoken of'.[1] Perhaps because of her growing attachment to him and his irresponsible attentions towards her, Elizabeth left her stepmother's household in May 1548. Later that year she moved to Hatfield in Hertfordshire, one of the manors she was allocated as her inheritance from Henry. Katherine, meanwhile, died after childbirth.

The arrest of Sudeley on 17 February 1549 exposed Elizabeth to sudden danger. Lord Protector Somerset, Sudeley's elder brother, had learned of his plan to marry the princess and believed that Elizabeth too was implicated in treason. Her servants, including Katherine Astley, were sent to the Tower, where they admitted Sudeley's inappropriate behaviour and discussions of marriage. Elizabeth was interviewed at Hatfield but gave nothing away. Unable to prove her guilt, the lord protector left her alone

PREVIOUS PAGE: **Queen Elizabeth I**, *as painted in coronation regalia (see pp. 268–9).*

LEFT: **The young Elizabeth** *is portrayed here as pious, learned and royal. One of the two books that are visible is open, and the princess has her finger marking a place in the other, all suggesting her active scholarly pursuits. Her dress is of rich materials, and she wears pearls on her French hood, in rows around her neck, and alternating with gems in the square edging of her neckline and matching girdle. Jewels also clasp her sleeves, while rings draw attention to the long slender fingers, of which she was so proud and said to make 'a display'. The inscription calls her the daughter of the king, so the painting was completed before January 1547; it has been attributed to William Scrots, c.1546.*

and in disgrace; but after his fall she was received for short stays at Edward's court and partially repaired relations with her brother.

After Mary's accession, Elizabeth was in even greater danger. She was known to be a Protestant and faced strong pressure from Mary to attend mass. Uncomfortable at court, she left for one of her Hertfordshire manors in December 1553 but was hauled back to London for interrogation after Sir Thomas Wyatt's rebellion in 1554. Wyatt had planned to marry Elizabeth to Edward Courtenay, newly made Earl of Devon (and the last of the Yorkist line), and put them both on the throne as Protestant rulers, and there was some evidence that Elizabeth knew of the conspiracy. Again, Elizabeth held up well to questioning, but she was, nevertheless, sent to the Tower, where she remained until 19 May. She was then removed to Woodstock in Oxfordshire and kept under close surveillance for just under a year. While there, she attended Catholic services but demanded an English Bible.

In October 1555, Elizabeth was allowed to return to Hatfield with her old servants. However, in March 1556, she again came under suspicion when a new plot against Mary was revealed. This time, King Philip saved Elizabeth from serious investigation (and possible execution). His protection arose from his concern that Elizabeth's death would leave Mary Queen of Scots (soon to marry the French *dauphin*) as heir to the English throne. As far as he was concerned, a heretic on the throne of England would be preferable to a French puppet, especially if Elizabeth could be made to marry a Catholic pro-Habsburg nobleman or prince. But for the remainder of Mary's reign, Elizabeth resisted marriage to one of Philip's allies; she had no intention of limiting her options, tying herself to Spain, or handing over power to a husband. Instead she bided her time. She kept clear of conspiracy, avoided flaunting her Protestant views and built up political and military support in case she had to fight for her throne. In the event, Mary overcame her animosities to Elizabeth sufficiently not to interfere with the line of succession as laid down by Henry VIII, and Elizabeth's path to the throne was clear in November 1558.

1558

Immediately after her accession, Elizabeth appointed her old friend Sir William Cecil as her principal secretary and Lord Robert Dudley as master of the horse. On 23 November, she left Hatfield for London, escorted by over 1000 lords, ladies and gentlemen. Five days later, she rode through the city 'apparelled in purple velvet, with a scarf about her neck'.[2]

A requiem mass was held for Mary on 13 December, the day before her burial in Westminster Abbey. However, on Christmas Day Elizabeth walked out of mass after the reading of the gospel because the

RIGHT: **Sir William Cecil (1520–98)**, *later Lord Burghley, was Elizabeth's leading councillor throughout her reign. Under Edward VI he had been a principal secretary, but under Mary he had semi-retired from public life. Although, like Elizabeth, he outwardly conformed and attended the mass, he did so reluctantly as he was a committed Protestant. Naming Cecil as her secretary on 17 November 1558 was Elizabeth's first public act as queen. Although she nicknamed him 'her spirit', they often differed over policy. Elizabeth was less tolerant of Protestant nonconformity and more willing to reach an accommodation with Mary Queen of Scots than was Cecil. Here he is depicted later in life, riding on a mule through the grounds of his house, Theobalds, in Hertfordshire, and holding a carnation and a sprig of honeysuckle in his right hand. Behind him, on a tree, hangs his coat of arms within the Garter and below it is his motto,* Cor unum, via una *('One heart, one way').*

officiant, Bishop Owen Oglethorpe of Carlisle refused to obey her order that he should not elevate the host (the consecration of the wafer and wine by the priest, a rite that implied the Catholic doctrine of transubstantiation rejected by Protestants). On 31 December, Elizabeth issued a proclamation ordering the litany, epistle and gospel to be read in English just as they had been under her father, and she intimated that further religious changes would soon be authorized by Parliament.

During December, Henry II of France tried unsuccessfully to persuade the pope to recognize Mary Queen of Scots – Elizabeth's cousin and now the French king's daughter-in-law – as the Queen of England.

The queen's secretary

I [Elizabeth] give you [Sir William Cecil] this charge, that you shall be of my privy council and content yourself to take pains for me and my realm. This judgement I have of you, that you will not be corrupted by any manner of gift, and that you will be faithful to the state, and that without respect of my private will, you will give me that counsel that you think best, and if you shall know anything necessary to be declared to me of secrecy, you shall show it to myself only. And assure yourself I will not fail to keep taciturnity therein, and therefore herewith I charge you.

[ELIZABETH'S WORDS TO SIR WILLIAM CECIL, 20 NOVEMBER 1558, FROM A COPY AT THE NATIONAL ARCHIVES: SP12/1 NO. 7]

1559

On 12 January, Elizabeth travelled by barge from Whitehall to the Tower of London. On the afternoon of Saturday 14 January, her coronation procession rode through the city to Westminster, greeted by pageants that praised her dynasty and the Protestant religion. The next day, Bishop Oglethorpe crowned Elizabeth 'with all accustomed ceremonies' at Westminster Abbey.[3] After the ceremony, she carried the sceptre and orb to Westminster Hall 'with a most smiling countenance for every one, giving them all a thousand greetings'.[4] When the banquet was over, there followed two days of tournaments.

Elizabeth's first Parliament assembled on 25 January. At its opening, a former Protestant exile of Mary's reign, Dr Richard Cox, delivered a 90-minute sermon on the need for religious reform. During the parliamentary session, a Bill of

RIGHT: **The 'Accession Portrait' of Elizabeth** *portrays her in coronation robes and exudes majesty. Her hair is loose as was traditional for queens at their coronation, and on her head is a gold imperial crown, set with precious jewels. Many versions of this striking portrait exist; this one dates from the beginning of the 17th century and may have been commissioned either to celebrate an anniversary of the queen's accession day or in connection with her funeral.*

Supremacy passed both Houses with amendments, but a Bill of Uniformity was lost in the House of Lords, where the bishops commanded a majority. Over the Easter recess, a public disputation on theology took place at Westminster, after which two of the participating bishops were detained in the Tower for behaving 'indiscreetly'.[5] This left the lay lords who were prepared to follow royal policy with a small majority in the Upper House. On 3 April, the government introduced new bills of Supremacy and Uniformity into Parliament, both of which received the royal assent on 8 May.

On 7 April, Elizabeth announced the agreement of the Peace of Cateau-Cambrésis, which ended her sister's war against France and Scotland. Despite signing the treaty, Mary Queen of Scots continued to bear the heraldic arms of England and thus implicitly claimed its throne.

After supper on 25 March, thousands watched as Elizabeth was 'rowed up and down [the] Thames' alongside 100 boats, 'with trumpets and drummers and flutes and guns and squibs hurling on high'.[6] On St George's Day, four new Knights of the Garter were elected, including Lord Robert Dudley and Thomas Howard, 4th Duke of Norfolk.

LEFT: **King Eric XIV of Sweden (1533–77)** *was one of the numerous European princes who bombarded Elizabeth with matrimonial proposals during the early years of her reign. She rejected offers from Eric, Philip II, two Austrian archdukes and many minor dukes. Eric had the greatest staying power, and in 1561 he set off for England to woo the queen. However, he had to give up the attempt when his ships were beaten back by storms. This portrait was painted in 1561 by Steven van der Meulen, who was sent to Sweden for the purpose.*

The dismantling of Mary's church proceeded apace. Edmund Grindal replaced Edmund Bonner as Bishop of London on 29 May. On 21 June, five more bishops were similarly deprived for refusing to take the oath of supremacy, and Protestants took over their sees. In July, royal commissioners were appointed 'to ride about the realm for th'establishing of true religion'.[7] During the course of their travels they destroyed roods, images and altars. The monastic houses reopened by Mary were once again suppressed.

On 10 July, Henry II of France died after a jousting accident, and Francis II, the young husband of Mary Queen of Scots, became king. Fears deepened in England that the French monarchs would actively claim Elizabeth's throne.

While on her summer progress, Elizabeth was sumptuously entertained for five days by the Earl of Arundel at Nonsuch Palace. But during her absence, a Protestant removed a silver cross and two candlesticks from the royal chapel because he found such 'popish' ornaments offensive.

In early October, Duke John of Finland came to court with a matrimonial proposal for Elizabeth from his brother, King Eric of Sweden. Another ambassador had already arrived to seek her hand for a son of the Holy Roman Emperor.

On 17 December, Matthew Parker was consecrated as the new Archbishop of Canterbury, a position that had been vacant since the death of Cardinal Reginald Pole in November 1558.

In December, Elizabeth decided to aid the Scottish Protestant lords who had taken up arms against their French Catholic regent, Mary of Guise. Elizabeth was responding to the danger that military reinforcements were due to arrive from France to crush the rebellion. This army, it was suspected, would be used to invade England on behalf of Mary Queen of Scots once the Scottish lords had been defeated. After sending a fleet to Leith to block the arrival of a French convoy, Elizabeth agreed, albeit reluctantly, to send the Duke of Norfolk north 'for the preparation of the army to be sent into Scotland'.[8]

The queen, her lord and the lord's wife

During the last few days Lord Robert [Dudley] has come so much into favour that he does whatever he likes with affairs and it is even said that Her Majesty visits him in his chamber day and night. People talk of this so freely that they go so far as to say that his wife has a malady in one of her breasts and the queen is only waiting for her to die to marry Lord Robert. I can assure Your Majesty [Philip II of Spain] that matters have reached such a pass that I have been brought to consider whether it would not be well to approach Lord Robert on Your Majesty's behalf, promising him your help and favour and coming to terms with him.

[SPANISH AMBASSADOR DE FERIA TO KING PHILIP, 18 APRIL 1559, *Calendar of State Papers, Spanish*, VOL. 1, *Elizabeth 1558–1567*, NO. 27, PP. 57–8]

'The dismantling of Mary's church proceeded apace'

271

1560

On 27 February, Elizabeth took the Scottish Protestants under her protection when the Duke of Norfolk signed the Treaty of Berwick. At the end of March, 10,000 soldiers under William, Lord Grey of Wilton, crossed the border, and on 6 April they laid siege to Leith, where a French garrison was based. The fighting was hard, and on 8 May the English 'were repulsed with a shower of bullets, that overwhelmed them from above, and there were many slain, yet more wounded'.[9] Peace negotiations soon began, however, and the Treaty of Edinburgh was signed on 6 July. Following its terms, England and France both withdrew from Scotland. Mary Queen of Scots, however, refused to ratify the treaty, as it denied her right to bear the arms of England and consequently compromised her right to the succession after Elizabeth's death. But the English government feared that Mary's refusal meant that she would continue to claim the English throne while Elizabeth was still alive.

ABOVE: **The royal Maundy ceremony** *was performed by the queen every year on the Thursday before Easter. This miniature of 1560, painted on vellum by Levina Teerlinc, shows Elizabeth in the left foreground, wearing a purple-blue long-trained gown and long white apron, about to ritually wash the feet of the poor in imitation of Jesus. Poor women are shown seated in two rows running from the front to the back, their number being the same as Elizabeth's age in years. Also depicted are choirboys, gentlemen of the Chapel Royal (in copes), courtiers, and gentlemen pensioners holding the pole-axes that signified their role.*

The painter was one of the daughters of the Bruges illuminator Simon Bening (or Benninck) (1483?–1561). Levina was trained in her father's workshop. She came to England, entering Henry VIII's service around 1545, but few miniatures thought to be by her now exist, and none are signed.

On 8 September, Lord Dudley's wife, Amy, broke her neck after falling down some stairs. Although there was some talk of murder or suicide, a coroner's jury decided it was death by misadventure. Now a widower, Dudley was 'in great hope to marry the queen, for she maketh such appearance of good will to him'.[10] Elizabeth, however, could not afford the scandal and damage to her reputation that such a marriage would bring.

In September, Elizabeth ordered that her Protestant subjects should cease defacing ancient monuments and tombs as part of their iconoclastic fervour.

France lost its second king in as many years, when, on 5 December, Francis II died. His ten-year-old brother, Charles IX, became King of France, with their mother, Catherine de' Medici, as his regent.

In December, attempts to restore the coinage began. Since 1545, silver shillings and testons (sixpenny pieces) had been mixed with alloy as a way of earning crown revenue, and though the Duke of Northumberland had begun to restore their full value, there remained many debased coins in circulation. The process of restoration lasted until October 1561 and involved devaluing the currency as well as calling in debased coins and exchanging them for new, finer ones. In the short term, the reform caused uncertainty, but ultimately it produced sound money that helped the economy.

Lord Robert Dudley, widower

Cousin Blount, immediately upon your departure *from me there came to me Bowes, by whom I do understand that my wife [Lady Amy Dudley] is dead as he says by a fall from a pair of stairs. Little other understanding can I have of him. The greatness and the suddenness of the misfortune doth so perplex me until I do hear from you how the matter stands, or how this evil should light upon me, considering what the malicious world will bruit [report], as I can take no rest. And because I have no way to purge myself of malicious talk that I know the wicked world will use, but one, which is the very plain truth to be known ...*

[LORD ROBERT DUDLEY, WRITING TO THOMAS BLOUNT, 9 SEPTEMBER 1560, AS QUOTED BY S. ADAMS IN *Leicester and the Court*, P. 136]

Murder or mishap?

... it was found by this inquest *that she [Lady Amy Dudley] was cause of her own death, falling down a pair of stairs, which by report was but eight steps. But the people say she was killed by reason he forsook her company without cause ... Many times before it was bruited [rumoured] by the Lord Robert his men [Lord Robert's men] that she was dead. And P. [a witness] used to say that when the Lord Robert went to his wife he went all in black, and how he was commanded to say that he did nothing with her, when he came to her, as seldom he did. This [Sir Richard] Verney [another witness] and diverse others his servants used before her death, to wish her death, which made the people to suspect the worse. And her death he mourned, leaving the court, lay at C. (Kew) whither the lords resorted to him to comfort him. Himself all his friends, many of the lords and gentlemen, and his family be all in black, and weep dolorously, great hypocrisy used.*

[REPORT OF THE INQUEST INTO LADY DUDLEY'S DEATH IN 'A "JOURNAL" OF MATTERS OF STATE ... UNTIL THE YERE 1562', IN *Religion, Politics and Society in Sixteenth-Century England*, EDITED BY I. ARCHER et al., P. 66]

273

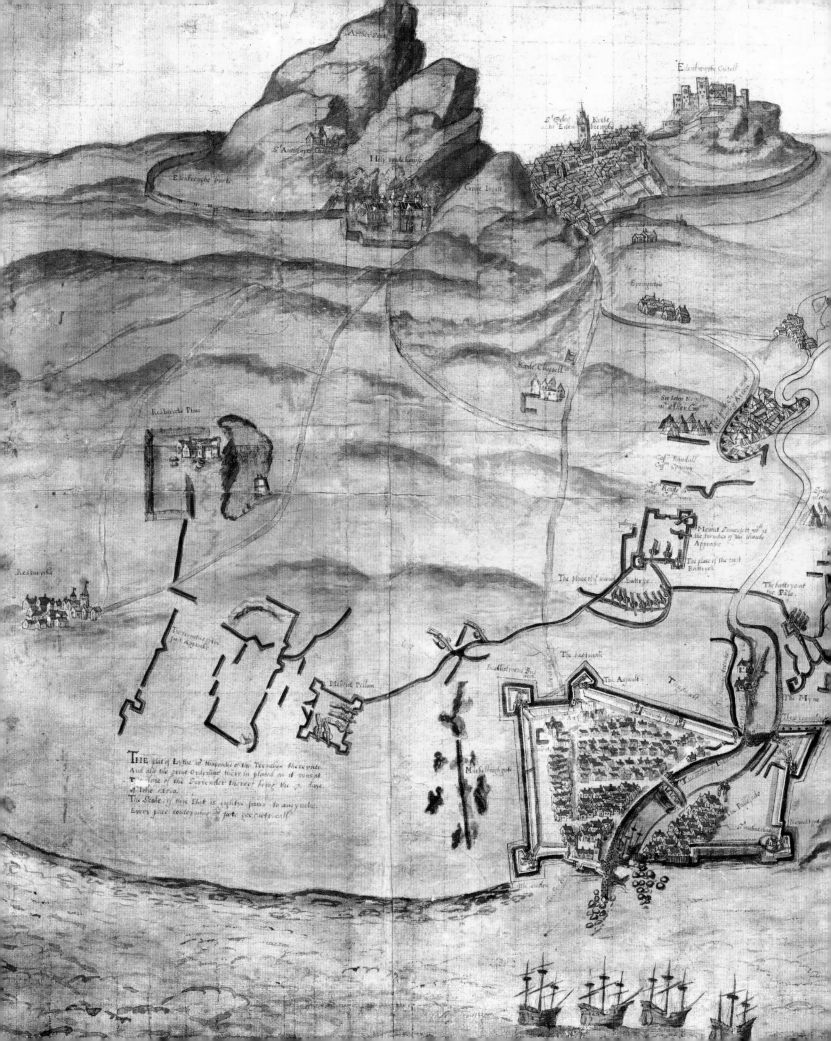

Arthur Seate

Edenbroughe Castell

St Antonyes Chapell

St Gyles the Esten Kyrke of Edenbrughe

Edenbrughe Parke

Holy Rude howse

Canon Jeate

Eromonton

Reskawyke Place

Roode Chappell

Sr John Nevell wt other Gentlemen

Capt Randall Capt Conway

Capt Reade other Capytaines

Mewnt Somersett wch is the trenches of the seconde Approche

polpoge

The place of the last Battrye

Reskawyke

The place of the second Battrye

The battrye at the Pile

The trenchet of the first Approche

Mr Pellam

The trenches

The Assault

Musselborow Bay

Tyllstiock

The Myre

The chentrett

THE plat of Lythe wt thapproche of the Trenches thervnto.
And also the great Ordenance there in placed as it was at
the daye of the Surrender thereof being the 7 daye
of Iulie 1560.
The Scale of this Plat is eightie faces to any inche.
Every face conteyninge 36 foote orthwtcall

Musselborow gate

Sr Michaell ......

The westgate

The English siege of Leith *took place during Elizabeth's*   275
Scottish campaign in the spring of 1560. Although the
siege was militarily unsuccessful, the French garrison in
Leith surrendered to the English on 7 July, the day after
peace was agreed. This contemporary map provides the
only extant portrayal of the French defences as well as
an authentic picture of mid-16th century Edinburgh.
The roofs of buildings are red, blue or brown according
to whether they were made of tile, lead/slate or thatch.
The blue shading represents high ground. The orientation
of the map is south–north, from the top of the map to
the bottom.

1561

On 4 June, the steeple of St Paul's was struck by lightning, and its roof was consumed in the fire. Catholics believed this was a sign of God's displeasure at the Protestant reforms.

In June, Elizabeth allowed ships to be used for trade with Guinea in Africa, an area claimed by the Portuguese king. When his ambassador protested, Elizabeth told him later that her merchants could trade in the realm of any friendly ruler just as their merchants could trade in hers.

In early July, Elizabeth denied the widowed Mary Queen of Scots a passport to travel through England on her return to Scotland unless the Treaty of Edinburgh was first ratified. Immediately afterwards, Elizabeth began her progress to East Anglia. While there, she issued orders on 9 August that no wives of bishops or university fellows 'should dwell in the colleges or cathedral churches'.[11] When Mary made her way to Scotland on 18 August, she sent an embassy to Elizabeth to demand recognition of her right to the English succession. To Mary's disappointment, Elizabeth refused to acknowledge her as heir.

Also in August, Katherine Grey (the younger sister of the late Lady Jane Grey) exposed a scandal when she admitted she was pregnant by Edward, Earl of Hertford and the son of the late Protector Somerset. The couple were sent to the Tower, where their son was born on 24 September.

A proclamation in October ordered the Ten Commandments to be displayed behind the communion table in churches. On 28 October, two candlesticks were again removed from the Chapel Royal, but 'the cross remained on the common [communion] table' to the dismay of many Protestants.[12]

This year, corn prices rose as a result of a poor harvest during the summer.

ABOVE: **Lady Katherine Grey (1540?–68)**, *the younger sister of Lady Jane, was imprisoned in the Tower when she was found to be pregnant in August 1561. She protested that she was married to the child's father – Edward Seymour, the Earl of Hertford – but under pressure from Elizabeth an ecclesiastical commission found that no marriage had occurred and their son was thus a bastard. Hertford, also imprisoned in the Tower, visited Katherine secretly, and in February 1563 she gave birth to a second son. In August 1563, she was transferred to the country, where she died on 22 January 1568. This miniature by Levina Teerlinc shows her holding her child and wearing a miniature of her husband.*

RIGHT: **An Irish chieftain** *is seated at a feast and entertained by a bard and a harper, in this etching. This is not an entirely accurate picture of native Irish customs and clothes, but it represents the hostile stereotype of a barbarous people presented in Elizabethan England. The picture is one of a dozen included in John Derricke's* Image of Irelande, *an extended narrative poem published in 1581, which detailed Henry Sidney's military triumphs against the native Irish.*

1562

On 6 January, the Ulster chieftain Shane O'Neill was received at court. He surprised everyone by wearing traditional costume – a yellow undershirt (as if 'steeped in urine'[13]) with wide sleeves, a short tunic, and a rough hairy cloak. He submitted himself before the queen and afterwards 'was sent home with honour'.[14]

During the summer, performers acted a play, *The Tragedy of Gorboduc*, before Elizabeth on 18 August. Written by Thomas Sackville and Thomas Norton, it depicted in blank verse the tumults that followed an uncertain succession.

An outbreak of monstrous births

This year in England [1562] were many monstrous births. *In March a mare brought forth a foal with one body and two heads, and as it were a long tail growing out between the two heads. Also a sow farrowed a pig with four legs like to the arms of a manchild with arms and fingers, etc. In April a sow farrowed a pig with two bodies, eight feet, and but one head; many calves and lambs were monstrous, some with collars of skin growing about their necks, like to the double ruffs of shirts and neckerchiefs then used. The four and twentieth of May, a manchild was born at Chichester in Sussex, the head, arms and legs whereof were like to an anatomy, the breast and belly monstrous big, from the navel as it were a long string hanging; about the neck a great collar of flesh and skin growing like the ruff of a shirt or neckerchief, coming up above the ears pleated and folded, etc.*

[RAPHAEL HOLINSHED, *Holinshed's Chronicles of England, Scotland and Ireland*, 1807 EDITION, VOL. IV, P. 204]

277

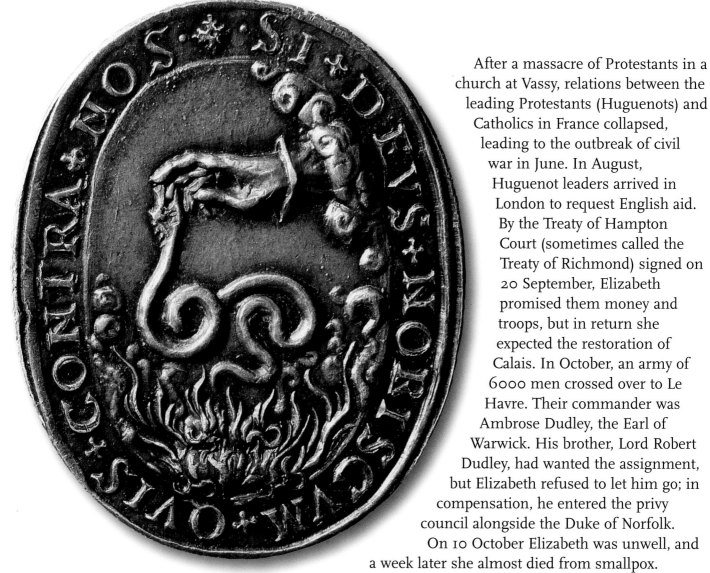

After a massacre of Protestants in a church at Vassy, relations between the leading Protestants (Huguenots) and Catholics in France collapsed, leading to the outbreak of civil war in June. In August, Huguenot leaders arrived in London to request English aid. By the Treaty of Hampton Court (sometimes called the Treaty of Richmond) signed on 20 September, Elizabeth promised them money and troops, but in return she expected the restoration of Calais. In October, an army of 6000 men crossed over to Le Havre. Their commander was Ambrose Dudley, the Earl of Warwick. His brother, Lord Robert Dudley, had wanted the assignment, but Elizabeth refused to let him go; in compensation, he entered the privy council alongside the Duke of Norfolk.

On 10 October Elizabeth was unwell, and a week later she almost died from smallpox. Thinking herself about to die, she protested that 'although she loved, and always had loved Lord Robert dearly, as God was her witness, nothing improper had ever passed between them'.[15] During the crisis her councillors could not agree on the succession.

In December, bad news arrived from France: Francis, Duke of Guise, had defeated the Huguenots at the Battle of Dreux and captured their leader, the Prince of Condé.

In this year, the sea captain John Hawkins began his slaving expeditions in Africa. Also, during this year there was an unusual number of reported 'monstrous' births.

278

ABOVE: **A silver medallion** was produced in 1562 in thanksgiving for the queen's recovery from smallpox. The hand is shown coming through the clouds and holding a snake over a fire – a probable allusion to the biblical account of St Paul being bitten by a snake yet left unharmed through the intervention of God (from Acts 28:1–6). The Latin inscription reads si Deus nobiscum, quis contra nos ('if God is with us, who shall be against us').

RIGHT: **Blacksmithery** was one of the trades regulated by the 1563 Statute of Artificers. In this picture, a smith is magnetizing an iron rod by pounding it with his hammer so that it will work as a compass needle, pointing north ('septentrio') and south ('auster', the south wind). The illustration is from William Gilbert's De magnete, published in 1600.

1563

Alarmed by Elizabeth's near fatal attack of smallpox, Parliament in January petitioned her to marry or name a successor. Elizabeth consented to consider the petition and hinted that she was already taking action to marry. This Parliament also passed several important statutes: an act excluding Catholics from sitting in the Commons; a new act against witchcraft; another Poor Law; and the Act of Artificers, which made a seven-year apprenticeship essential for certain named trades and set upper wage limits for skilled workers.

In February, Convocation agreed upon the 39 Articles of Faith as the doctrinal foundation of the English Church. Attempts to introduce moderate changes to church ceremonial were, however, rejected because of opposition from Elizabeth.

Loe here the pearle,
  whom God and man doth loue:
Loe here on earth,
  the onely starre of light:
Loe here the Queene,
  whom no mishap can moue:
To chaunge her mynde,
  from vertues chief delight:

Loe here the heart,
  that so hath honord God:
That for her loue,
  we feele not of his rod:
Pray for her health,
  such as good subiectes bee:
(Oh Princely Dame,)
  there is none like to thee.

In March, the French Huguenot and Catholic factions made peace at the Treaty of Amboise, and soon afterwards a united French force began to besiege the English garrison based in Le Havre, the town which Elizabeth was hoping to exchange for Calais. Hard-pressed by the French, the garrison suffered a further blow in July when bubonic plague broke out among the troops. At the end of the month Warwick, who had been badly wounded in the leg, was forced to surrender to the French so that he could evacuate those of his men who were still alive.

Warwick's soldiers brought the plague home with them. Over the next nine months, about 20,000 people died in London alone. 'The poor citizens of London were this year plagued with a three fold plague: pestilence, scarcity of money, and dearth of victuals.'[16] There were further consequences of the disease. It gave the government of the Low Countries an excuse to impose an embargo on trade with England in November. Actually, the Catholic regime in Brussels was more concerned about heresy than plague, and one of its objectives was to put pressure on English merchants who were held responsible for the growth of Protestantism in their territories. The policy proved ineffective. Calvinism continued to make inroads in the towns of the Low Countries, while English merchants soon found an alternative mart at Emden.

Uncommon natural events also shook the kingdom. In September, an earthquake hit many parts of England, especially Lincolnshire and Northamptonshire. During the first 12 days of December terrible storms took place; 'the like had not been seen nor heard by any man living'.[17]

On the Continent, the papal Council of Trent finally closed on 4 December. It had been first convened in 1545 in response to the Protestant challenge, and in its various sessions had successfully defined Catholic doctrine and initiated reform.

'The poor citizens of London were this year plagued with a three fold plague: pestilence, scarcity of money, and dearth of victuals'

LEFT: **Elizabeth I in her regalia** appears here in a broadsheet above verses beginning 'Loe here the pearl, / whom God and man doth love / Loe here on earth, / the only star of light' and exhorting readers to 'pray for her health' as all good subjects do. This print was manufactured in 1563. It was designed to be bought and pinned up in houses of the middling sort. The wood engraver was Gyles Godet.

1564

New Year's Eve was particularly cold; the Thames froze over, and Londoners skated and played football on the ice.

In early March, Elizabeth suggested that Mary Queen of Scots should marry Lord Robert Dudley. By this means, Elizabeth hoped that Mary could become her ally rather than a competitor for her throne. Initially offended, Mary considered accepting the proposal if, in return, she would be named as Elizabeth's heir.

Peace was concluded between England and France. After the failure of the previous year's expedition Elizabeth had to accept the permanent loss of Calais.

During her summer progress, Elizabeth visited the University of Cambridge, where 'she personally visited all the colleges, and in a Latin oration, gave them great thanks' for their love and loyalty.[18]

On 29 September, Lord Robert's status was raised when he was created Earl of Leicester and Baron of Denbigh. His elevation to the peerage now qualified him to marry Mary Queen of Scots. This was not the only royal union being considered this year, as negotiations also began for a marriage between Elizabeth and Archduke Charles of Austria, who was the brother of the new Holy Roman Emperor, Maximilian II.

In London, on 20 November, three houses were 'sore shaken and the maid died',[19] because of the 'negligence of a maiden with a candle, in an hundred pound weight of gunpowder'.

LEFT: **Robert Dudley (1532/3–88), Earl of Leicester,** *was the fifth son of John Dudley, Duke of Northumberland. After his wife Amy died in September 1560, there were rumours that he would marry Elizabeth – causing consternation in some, such as William Cecil who, in 1566, recorded objections, describing the earl as 'infamed by the death of his wife', 'far in debt' and 'like to prove unloving or jealous of the queen's majesty'. However, Elizabeth resisted the temptation and Dudley had to be content with the earldom, bestowed in 1564, and his position as a leading figure in her household and government. The portrait is by Steven van der Meulen.*

ABOVE: **A cope** *was traditionally part of the vestments worn by the clergy at the communion service. Protestants, however, strongly condemned their use as 'popish', and many ministers refused to wear them. This resulted in a crisis in early 1565, when Elizabeth ordered strict adherence to her Prayer Book and injunctions. Eventually she was forced to retreat, and the cope was restricted to cathedrals and collegiate churches; elsewhere, officiating ministers needed only to wear a surplice. This cope was made for Cardinal Morton (1420–1500). His punning device is below the hood: a 'mort' (falcon) stands on a 'tun' (barrel).*

1565

From 1 January, trade was renewed with the Low Countries. The embargo had been lifted because of the economic damage it was doing to the Low Countries.

On 25 January, Elizabeth ordered Archbishop Parker to impose conformity in clerical dress and religious ceremonies on church ministers. Many Protestants were refusing to wear clerical outdoor dress and the cope at communion as well as omitting to use 'popish' rites prescribed in the Prayer Book. This provoked a conflict between hardline Protestants on the one side and the archbishop backed by the queen on the other.

In March, Elizabeth told Mary Queen of Scots that her marriage to the Earl of Leicester would not result in her formal recognition as Elizabeth's heir, should Elizabeth die childless. As a result, on 29 July, Mary rejected Leicester and instead married her cousin Henry Stuart (or Stewart), Lord Darnley. Elizabeth was furious. Since Mary and Darnley shared a grandmother in Margaret Tudor, the elder sister of Henry VIII, Elizabeth believed that this union was designed to strengthen the Stuart claim to the English throne.

Elizabeth continued to discuss the possibility of her own marriage to Archduke Charles of Austria, but difficulties soon arose because he wished to hear the mass and would not attend Protestant services in England.

In August, Elizabeth imprisoned her cousin, Lady Mary Grey, for marrying Thomas Keyes, a lowly officer at court, without royal permission. Although the marriage posed no threat to the queen, it was an inappropriate match for a member of the royal family. Apart from the social disparity involved, the couple were regarded as physically incompatible and therefore a subject for scorn: Mary was a dwarf and her husband the tallest man at court. The couple never saw each other again.

On 13 October, the Earl of Leicester's brother-in-law, Sir Henry Sidney, was appointed Lord Deputy of Ireland. In Rome, the reforming pope, Pius IV, died on 9 December. He was to be succeeded by Pius V, who wanted a stronger stance to be taken towards the Protestant regime in England.

'Elizabeth imprisoned her cousin, Lady Mary Grey, for marrying Thomas Keyes'

284

RIGHT: **Mary Queen of Scots (1542–87) and Henry Stewart (1545–67), Lord Darnley,** *were married in July 1565, much to Elizabeth's ire. The match strengthened Mary's claim to the English throne, as both husband and wife were great grandchildren of Henry VII. As a punishment, Elizabeth had Darnley's mother put in the Tower and dispossessed his father of lands in England. The marriage produced a son, but in personal terms it had already turned sour. The couple are depicted here in a simple pen and ink drawing from the period. Darnley is identified as Duke of Albany, the Scottish title Mary conferred on him a week before the marriage. Mary's dress reveals the lion of Scotland.*

Henrie Stewart Duke of
Albanye and Marie
Quem of Scotland
1566

Clarkenwell:

Snythe
Fyeld

S. Gyles in
the fyelde

Holborne

Charin
crosse

Suffolke P.   Durisme P. Savoye   Somerset Place   Arundell P.

Beere howse

The Corte   The Temple   Whyt freers

                                             Brydwell   Blak freers   Benard Ca

Peter bredge

Lamberth Marsh

                                             Papys Garden

Wastar

Stelar Chamber

y Quenes
Bredge

The slaugh
ter house

Lamberth

286

Hæc eß Regia illa totius Angliæ ciuitas LONDINVM, ad flu-
uium Thamesim sita. Cæsari, vt plures exiß timāt, Trinobantum
nuncupata, multarum gentium comertio nobilitata, exculta domib. ornata tē
plis, excelsa arcibus, claris ingenijs, viris omnium artium doctrinarumq, gene
re præstantibus, percelebris. Demiq, omnium rerum copia, atque opium excellētia
mirabilis. Inuehit in eam totius orbis opes ipse Thamasis, onerarijs nauibus per
sexaginta millia passuum, ad vrbem præalto alueo nauigabilis.

The Spitel fields

The Spvel fields

V Goounefounders P.

Patern Gate

THE · TOWRE

Beere howse

Towles

Beere howse

S. Mary Ouerie

S. Mary Spittel

Whitester P.

Cum Privilegio.

287

STILLIARDS) Hansa, Gothica dicFio, conuentum, vel congregationem sonans, multarum ciuitatum est confoederata Societas, tum ob præstita Regibus, ac Ducib. benefi-
cia: tum ob securam terra, mariq̄, mercaturæ tractationem, tum deniq̄, ad tran-
quillam Rerumpub. pacem, & ad modesam adolescentum institutionem conseruan-
dam, instituta: plurimor Regum, ac Principum, maximè Angliæ, Galliæ, Daniæ, ac
Magnæ Moscouiæ, nec non Flandriæ, ac Brabantiæ Du cum priuilegijs, ac immuni-
tatib. exornata sunt. Habet ea quatuor Emporia, Cuntores quidam vocarit, in quibus
ciuitatum negotiatores resident, suosque mercatus exercent. Hor. alterum hìc Londini, domestica oeconomia nitet, habens domum Gildeballā Teutonicā quā vulgo Stiliard, nūcupat

1566

As a French gesture of friendship towards England, the Duke of Norfolk and the Earl of Leicester were installed as Knights of the Order of St Michael on 24 January.

The dispute over clerical garments continued, and 37 London clerics who refused to wear the prescribed dress were suspended from their benefices in March. However, by the end of the year all but eight ministers, three lecturers, and three or four curates had conformed.

In May, work began on erecting a bourse (trading centre) in London, and on 7 June the first foundation stone was laid. The building was completed in November 1569.

On 19 June, Mary Queen of Scots gave birth to a son, who was to be baptized in December according to Catholic rites. The child was named James, and Elizabeth was his godmother. Darnley, now Duke of Albany and the king-consort, did not attend the service or celebrations, as his relationship with Mary had by then almost entirely broken down. The previous March, Mary's Italian secretary, David Rizzio, had been brutally assassinated in front of her at the palace of Holyroodhouse, the result of a conspiracy involving Darnley.

During the summer, Pius V sent a Catholic exile, Lawrence Vaux, to England with a mission to inform Elizabeth's subjects that attendance at Protestant church services was a mortal sin. His mission was successful in Lancashire, where church absenteeism – recusancy – increased; but elsewhere Vaux's authority was questioned and most Catholics continued to attend their parish churches.

The Royal Exchange

The exchange is a great square place like the one in Antwerp, a little smaller though, and with only two entrances and only one passage running through it, where all kinds of fine goods are on show; and since the city is very large and extensive merchants having to deal with one another agree to meet together in this palace, where several hundred may be found assembled twice daily, before lunch at eleven, and again after their meal at six o'clock, buying, selling, bearing news, and doing business generally.

[THOMAS PLATTER, *Thomas Platter's Travels in England, 1599*, TRANSLATED BY C. WILLIAMS, P. 157]

PREVIOUS PAGE: **The earliest printed map of London** *shows a densely populated city (about 100,000 people inhabiting little more than one square mile). Especially to be noted are the city walls in the north and east, the bull- and bear-baiting rings in Southwark, the Tower of London, and St Paul's complete with its spire (which was actually destroyed by lightning in 1561). Wealthy Londoners stand in the foreground. The print appeared in the German atlas of European cities* Civitates Orbis Terrarum *by Georg Braun and Franz Hogenberg, published in 1572.*

RIGHT: **Westminster** *was a separate community from the City of London. It was the centre of the government and home of the court. The 'Preuy bridge' (private landing stage) led to the Palace of Westminster. To the left of the 'Courte gate' is the tilting ground used for tournaments (an elongated 'S' shape behind a wall). Westminster Hall can be seen backing on to the Star Chamber by the river, and beyond that in the bottom left corner is Westminster Abbey. The map, from the later 16th century, is a woodblock print by Ralph Agas.*

In the Low Countries, severe rioting and Calvinist iconoclasm took place during August, forcing the regent, Margaret of Parma, to make concessions and moderate the laws against heresy. Philip II, however, decided on a military solution to restore order.

While on her summer progress in Oxfordshire, Elizabeth visited the University of Oxford. The students entertained her with disputations, comedies and tragedies. Unfortunately, at the performance of a play at Christ Church, 'by the fall of a wall and a pair of stairs, and great press of the multitude, three men were slain'.[20] On 5 September, Elizabeth delivered a 'wise and pithy' oration to the university.

In Ireland during the autumn, Lord Deputy Sidney marched against Shane O'Neill, who had been declared a traitor on 3 August after he had burned Armagh Cathedral. By December, O'Neill had lost almost all power in Ulster.

Parliament opened in September. In November, it urged Elizabeth to marry or to name a successor. The House of Commons also introduced six bills reforming religion, which had the support of the bishops in the House of Lords; but Elizabeth made sure that they were lost.

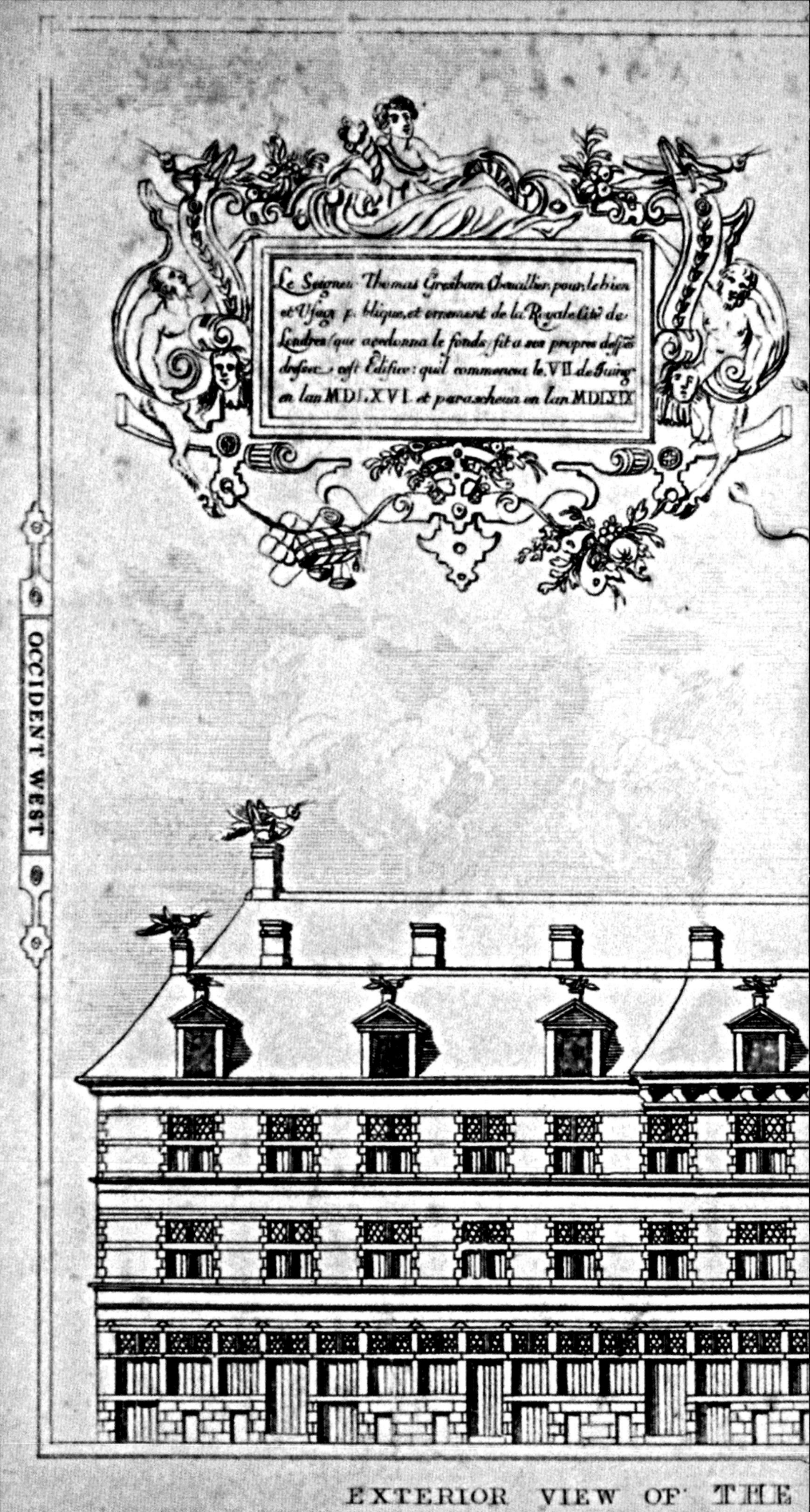

The text in the cartouche (in old French script):

Le Seigneur Thomas Gresham Chevallier, pour le bien
et Usage publique, et ornement de la Royale Cité de
Londres (que accordonna le fonds) fit a ses propres despens
dresser cest Edifice: quil commença le VII de Juing
en lan MDLXVI. et parascheua en lan MDLXIX

The Royal Exchange in London
(based on the bourse in Antwerp)
was the brainchild of the merchant
Sir Thomas Gresham.
Construction began under a
Flemish architect, after a site had
290 been cleared in Cornhill, in May
1566. The building was finished in
November 1569 and opened by
Elizabeth in January 1571. This
print by Frans Hogenberg shows
an exterior view from the south;
the royal arms appear above those
of Gresham surmounted by a
grasshopper (Gresham's personal
emblem). The building was
destroyed in the 1666 Great Fire.

EXTERIOR VIEW OF THE

HONI SOIT QVI MAL Y PENSE

DIEV ET MON DROYT

FORTVNA MY

Heer Thomas Gresham, Ridder heeft dees Edeficie ofte
del plaetse, tot ghemeine nutte di cieragie der Coningh-
lyke Stadt van London (die den grondt hiertoe schonke)
tsynen coste doen maken, beginde den VII dach Junij
A°. MDLXVI. ende is Volendt Anno MDLXIX.

ORIENT OOST

ROYAL EXCHANGE, 1569, FROM A SCARCE ENGRAVING.

1567

On 10 February the Scottish king-consort, Darnley, was staying at a house at Kirk o'Field, outside Edinburgh, when it was blown up: he had probably escaped before the explosion but was strangled outside the damaged building. The prime suspect for the assassination was James Hepburn, the Earl of Bothwell. Over the next few months, rumours circulated that Mary was also implicated – that she had committed adultery with Bothwell and helped plan the murder. Mary agreed to put Bothwell on trial, but he was acquitted because prosecution witnesses were intimidated and did not attend the hearing. Afterwards, on 15 May, Bothwell divorced his wife and married Mary – by Protestant rites. Consequently, the suspicions about them hardened and came to be exploited by Bothwell's many enemies among the Scottish lords. Furthermore, Mary's marriage to a Protestant alienated the Catholic nobility. On 15 June, Mary and Bothwell's army met a force raised by the opposition lords outside Edinburgh at Carberry Hill. No fighting took place; Mary simply surrendered and was taken prisoner, though Bothwell escaped.

In Ireland too, there was a political assassination. On 2 June, Ulster chieftain Shane O'Neill was murdered by Scottish settlers in Antrim.

At the end of June, Thomas Radcliffe, 3rd Earl of Sussex, departed for Vienna to push forward the negotiations for a marriage between Elizabeth and the Archduke Charles of Austria. However, Elizabeth refused to agree to the archduke's demand to hear mass in his own household in England, and she recalled Sussex, who returned home the following January.

Admonishing the Queen of Scots

Madam [Mary Queen of Scots], *it hath been always held for a special principle in friendship that prosperity provides but adversity proves friends, whereof at this time finding occasion to verify the same with our actions, we [Elizabeth] have thought meet both for our profession and your comfort in these few word[s] to testify [text not clear here] our friendship not only by admonishing you of the worst but to comfort you for the best ... Madam, to be plain with you our grief hath not been small that in this your marriage [to Bothwell] so slender consideration hath been had that as we perceive manifestly no good friend you have in the whole world can like thereof, and if we should otherwise write or say we should abuse you. For how could a worse choice be made, for your honour that in such haste to marry such a subject who besides other notorious lacks public fame [widespread rumour] hath charged with the murder of your late husband [Darnley] ... And with what peril have you married him that hath an other lawful wife alive ...*

[ELIZABETH'S LETTER TO MARY QUEEN OF SCOTS, 23 JUNE 1567, FROM THE NATIONAL ARCHIVES DOCUMENT SP/52/13/71, FF. 137]

In Scotland, on 29 July, the 13-month-old heir to the throne was crowned James VI. His mother Mary had abdicated five days earlier under duress, while imprisoned in Lochleven Castle. Mary's half-brother James Stewart, Earl of Moray, now ruled as regent. Elizabeth was outraged at Mary's deposition and wanted to send her aid. However, Sir William Cecil and other councillors – who were hostile to Mary and in fact supported the Scottish lords' action – persuaded Elizabeth to do nothing.

In the Low Countries, the regent had already suppressed the uprisings of the previous year, but on 22 August the Duke of Alva arrived in Brussels with a large military force and orders to restore strong Spanish rule throughout the Low Countries. While Elizabeth, as a monarch, recognized Philip II's right to punish rioters and rebels, she disliked his harsh treatment of her co-religionists and was alarmed at the presence of a sizeable Spanish army so near her realm.

ABOVE: **The memorial of Lord Darnley** *indicts Mary Queen of Scots for complicity in his murder in February 1567. The painting, by Livinus de Vogelaare, was commissioned by Darnley's parents, the Earl and Countess of Lennox, who are depicted kneeling beside their son's tomb. In front of them is their grandson, James VI of Scotland, and behind them is Darnley's younger brother, Charles (later to be the father of Arbella Stuart). On the tomb are two reliefs, one showing Darnley's murder and the other his body and that of his servant in the garden of Kirk o' Field, where the murder took place. In the corner is an inset picture of Mary's surrender at Carberry Hill, on 15 June 1567; in the background her third husband, the Earl of Bothwell, can be seen riding away from the field. Some of the inscriptions – those that maintain Mary's guilt – are nearly illegible and may have been erased later by James.*

The Duke of Alva's severe repression *in the Low Countries became legendary among Protestants in the 16th century. Alva arrived in Brussels in August 1567 at the head of a huge army to suppress the disorder of the previous year. He established a tribunal known as the 'Council of Blood', which resulted in over 1000 executions, including those of the prominent counts Egmont and Horn. Fear of prosecution led many – perhaps one per cent of the entire population (mainly Protestants) – to flee the country, and many of the refugees came to England. In this allegory, attributed to Frans Pourbus II (1569–1622), Alva is about to be crowned by the Devil. The kneeling figures, whom he holds in chains, represent the 17 provinces of the Low Countries. Scenes of torture are depicted behind him, while the executions of Egmont and Horn are visible through the arch. The Devil is also depicted placing a papal tiara on a cardinal. He is Cardinal Granvelle, Philip II's unpopular minister, thought to be responsible for the policy of religious intolerance that provoked the unrest of 1566.*

ABOVE: **The family of Lord William Brooke (1527–1597)**, 10th Baron Cobham, and Lady Frances (after 1530–92) is depicted in this group painting of 1567, by Hans Eworth. The three sons sit before their father (with a woman who is probably Frances's sister Joanna) and the three daughters before their mother. All six children were born within the first seven years of the marriage (two of the daughters were twins), and another son was born in 1568. The four oldest children are dressed as adults and the younger two are not yet breeched. The diamond and ruby ship worn by Frances symbolizes her happiness (because the ship represented on a Roman coin under Hadrian is inscribed Felicitas). The family is shown eating dessert, an elaborate part of the meal that was often taken in a separate room or building. Indeed, for taking dessert Cobham had a house erected from a lime tree specially trained by gardeners: it was three-storeys high and reached by wooden stairs. Here, however, the space is artificial, for the figures are flanked by the base of a classical column on the right and a plinth on the left. Lord Cobham became Lord Warden of the Cinque Ports in 1558, and in the last year of his life served as lord chamberlain.

1568

On 2 May, Mary Queen of Scots escaped from Lochleven Castle and quickly mustered support from loyalists. However, her army was defeated at Langside on 13 May, and three days later she fled over the border to England. Greeted courteously by Elizabeth's representatives, she was nonetheless kept a virtual prisoner for six weeks in Carlisle Castle, before being removed to the more secure Bolton Castle. Over the next months, Elizabeth deliberated about what to do with her unwelcome guest.

In the Low Countries, William of Nassau, Prince of Orange, and his brother, the Calvinist Count Louis of Nassau, refused to submit to the Duke of Alva. Louis won a victory against Spanish forces at Heiligerlee on 23 May, but in July he lost the Battle of Jemmingen and was forced to retreat to France, where soon afterwards William joined him.

In June, Elizabeth recalled the English ambassador, John Man, from Spain. His position there had become untenable once he had called the pope 'a canting little monk'.[21] Because Philip II had rejected Man's demand for Protestant services in his household, Elizabeth appointed no replacement.

On 23 September, a fleet of Spanish ships attacked six English ships commanded by John Hawkins, which were moored in the harbour of San Juan de Ulúa, on the Mexican coast. Hawkins was engaged in his third slave-trading venture (in which Elizabeth was an investor), transporting some 550 African slaves to the Spanish Main. Only two of the English ships survived the encounter, and about ninety of Hawkins's men were lost. News of this event, which was brought to London by Sir Francis Drake, one of the survivors, aroused strong anti-Spanish feeling at the English court.

At Michaelmas, the exiled Oxford academic William Allen opened a Catholic college at Douai, in the Low Countries, for English students of theology. Initially four students attended, but the numbers quickly grew, and in 1570 the college attracted financial support from Philip II.

During October and November a tribunal, headed by the Duke of Norfolk, sat at York to inquire into whether or not the Scottish lords had been justified in taking up arms against their queen. Mary herself was not permitted to attend, but her representatives gave evidence along with the Earl of Moray and the rebel lords. In December, the proceedings were transferred to London, where Moray produced the 'Casket Letters' that implicated Mary in adultery and her husband's murder. Confronted with this evidence, Elizabeth could not insist on Mary's restoration and return to Scotland.

On 11 October, an unusual fishing tale was recorded, for '17 monstrous fishes, some of them 27 foot in length, were caught at Downham bridge in Suffolk.[22] A more valuable catch, though, occurred in November, when five Spanish ships laden with bullion landed on the south coast of England, taking refuge from storms and privateers. Learning that the treasure was a loan from Genoese bankers and destined for the Duke of Alva (to pay his Spanish soldiers), Cecil and Elizabeth decided to impound the money and take over the loan. Getting wind of their plan, the Spanish ambassador advised Alva to seize English shipping and goods in the Low Countries as a form of reprisal.

A fête at Bermondsey *shows the intermingling of all social groups – gentry, citizens, servants and country folk – at a London celebration, possibly a marriage feast, on the south bank of the Thames. On the north side of the river, in the distance, can be seen the Tower of London. This painting by Joris Hoefnagel, who was in England from about 1568 until 1570, is unique: there exists no other 16th-century painting depicting England's outdoor social life in the manner of Pieter Brueghel the Elder in the Low Countries. It hangs in Hatfield House, Hertfordshire.*

298

ESPERANCE. EN. DIEV,
MA . COMPHORT : ∞

THOMAS. PERCY.
7 EARL. OF. NORTHVMBERLAND.
Æ TATIS. SVÆ. 38.
AN . DÑI: 1566. ¶ET. DIE. DEC. IVN.

1569

On 3 January, Alva seized the property of English merchants and imposed a trade embargo on England. Elizabeth immediately followed suit, and so began a five-year suspension of trade. During this period Anglo-Spanish political relations deteriorated badly.

In June, rebellion broke out in Munster, Ireland. It was suppressed over the summer, but one of its leaders, James FitzMaurice Fitzgerald, began a guerrilla war that would continue for several years. He presented his cause as a holy war, although the rebels were also resisting government schemes for introducing English settlers to Munster.

While on her summer progress, Elizabeth learned that the Duke of Norfolk – the realm's most senior nobleman – had proposed marriage to Mary Queen of Scots without her knowledge. In fact, Norfolk was not planning sedition but believed the marriage would neutralize the danger from Mary while securing a stable succession. His mistake lay in keeping his negotiations secret. Now anticipating disgrace or punishment, Norfolk left court on 15 September, and a week later he ignored Elizabeth's order to

ABOVE: **Thomas Percy (1528–72), 7th Earl of Northumberland**, *remained a committed Catholic after the accession of Elizabeth and was consequently sidelined in the government of the North of England. Disaffected, he made overtures to Mary Queen of Scots after her arrival in England in 1568. Summoned by Elizabeth to court for questioning in late October 1569, he and his friend Charles Neville, 6th Earl of Westmorland, wrote to Pope Pius V on 8 November calling for Elizabeth's excommunication. The next day, they raised the North in rebellion. This portrait of 1566 displays Northumberland's Catholic faith. He kneels on a cushion before a low table, upon which is a missal. Written on the canvas are the words, in French, 'hope in God – my comfort'.*

RIGHT: **The Bishops' Bible** *was the work of at least 11 bishops as well as various other scholars. Archbishop Parker commissioned it because the widely used Great Bible contained many errors in translation, while the 1560 Geneva Bible (published in English) contained marginal notes that he considered dangerously radical. On the title-page, Elizabeth sits enthroned between the cardinal virtues of Justice and Mercy, with Fortitude and Prudence below. The folio edition for churches appeared in 1568; this quarto edition for private use was printed in 1569.*

IVSTICE

MERCIE

FORTITVDE

PRVDEN CE

The holi bible

GOD SAVE THE QVEENE

301

return. Instead he fled to his estates, but, unwilling to rebel, he returned to London and was immediately incarcerated in the Tower. Elizabeth, however, feared that a wider conspiracy was in existence and ordered that security around Mary be strengthened.

Hearing rumours of unrest in the North, Elizabeth summoned Thomas Percy, 7th Earl of Northumberland, and Charles Neville, 6th Earl of Westmorland, to court on 24 October. The earls, who were supporters of Norfolk, immediately panicked, and towards midnight on 9 November they launched a rebellion. Displaying a banner of the 'Five Wounds of Christ', they rode into Durham on 14 November and tore up bibles and prayer books in the cathedral, pulled down the communion table and restored the mass. Within days, some 6000 armed men joined their rebellion and began to march through the North into Yorkshire, where they held mass in a number of towns. Their initial plan, to liberate Mary, was foiled when the government quickly moved her to the Midlands. Some of the leaders appealed to the pope for help.

The rebels may then have intended to take York, 'but their minds being suddenly altered'[23] they simply rode aimlessly through the North until one group captured Barnard's Castle in December and another took the port of Hartlepool, from where they hoped to receive Spanish troops from the Low Countries. However, once Elizabeth and Cecil had mobilized a large army in the South, the earls knew their cause was lost. On 16 December, they disbanded their infantry and soon afterwards fled over the border into Scotland. This rebellion was a serious crisis for Elizabeth, but the loyalty of other northern lords prevented its escalation.

1570

Reprisals against the northern rebels began on 4 January. Over the month, some 600 of them were executed by martial law. Northumberland was captured and imprisoned by the Earl of Moray, but the other leaders escaped to the Low Countries. On 23 January, though, Moray was assassinated. As a consequence, civil war broke out between Scottish lords loyal to Mary and those who opposed her.

On 20 February, the Catholic Lord Leonard Dacres attempted a new rebellion in the North. However, his army of 3000 men was routed by the smaller force of Henry Carey, Baron Hunsdon, who had been sent to arrest him. The rebels fled to Scotland, where the pro-Marian lords harboured them.

Pope Pius V issued a bull of excommunication – *Regnans in Excelsis* – against Queen Elizabeth on 25 February. A copy was nailed to the door of the Bishop of London's palace on 25 May. The man responsible, John Felton, was arrested, tortured on the rack in the Tower, and on 8 August executed at St Paul's churchyard.

RIGHT: **A watercolour of four ladies,** *painted by Lucas de Heere c.1570, records the dress appropriate to each woman's station in life. The lady on the right, a countrywoman, wears a high crowned felt hat, a chin-clout across her mouth, and a kerchief as a shawl over her shoulders. Her bodice is fastened at the front, and her skirt is covered by a long apron. The other ladies are well-to-do Londoners and they all wear high-collared chemises and close-bodied gowns. The richest lady (second from the left) wears a brocade petticoat under her gown. All of the women hold or wear gloves.*

Een burghers wijf

Een burghers rijck wijf

Een ionghe dochter

Een boerinne.
zoo die nu gaen.

Henry Carey
Lord Hunsdon
BY MARK GERARDS.

ÆTATIS SVÆ 66
AN° 1591

ABOVE: **Henry Carey (1526–96), Baron Hunsdon**, *was the son of Mary Boleyn and thus Elizabeth's first cousin. He was appointed to the military post of Governor of Berwick on 25 August 1568. In 1570 he gave Elizabeth good service by defeating the rebellious Lord Leonard Dacres. On 16 November 1577, he began a new career as a privy councillor and courtier. In 1583, he was appointed captain of the gentlemen pensioners and in July 1585 lord chamberlain of the household. Hunsdon was an important patron of the theatre, and his company played at 'The Theatre' in Shoreditch (the earliest purpose-built London playhouse).*

In April, the Earl of Sussex, the lord lieutenant in the North, began a series of raids into Scotland to punish the pro-Marian lords and to flush out the English rebels. His military action also helped bolster the position of the Scottish lords opposed to Mary.

In the spring, Thomas Cartwright, Lady Margaret Professor of Divinity at Cambridge University, delivered a series of lectures on the first two chapters of the Acts of the Apostles. In them, he suggested that a broadly presbyterian form of church government was the model authorized by Scripture and the primitive church. This lecture opened up a debate about the role of bishops, deans and archdeacons in the English Church. John Whitgift, the recently elected vice-chancellor of the University of Cambridge, led the opposition to Cartwright, who refused to recant his views and, at the end of the year, lost his professorship and went into exile in Geneva.

Owing to an outbreak of plague, the Duke of Norfolk was released from the Tower on 3 August and kept under house arrest in London. In late August, three men were hanged, drawn and quartered in Norwich for conspiring to raise the county of Norfolk in a rebellion, planned for Midsummer's Day.

In France, the third war of religion came to a close. By the Treaty of St Germain-en-Laye, the Huguenots made political gains, and they also increased their influence at the French court. In the autumn, their leaders proposed that the

37-year-old Queen Elizabeth should marry the French king's brother Henry, Duke of Anjou, who was then aged 19. It was hoped that the marriage would result in a close alliance between England and France that would safeguard the Protestants of both realms. In the event, Anjou, a strong Catholic, halted the project by demanding a full public mass in England.

On 6 October, there was 'a terrible tempest' at sea and on land.[24] Severe flooding occurred in Norfolk, causing serious damage to houses and bridges.

1571

On 23 January, Elizabeth visited the new London bourse, which was henceforth called the Royal Exchange.

The queen's secretary, William Cecil, was raised to the peerage as Baron Burghley on 25 February. He would still attend to government business in Parliament, but from his seat in the House of Lords instead of the Commons.

Also in February, the 'sea dog' Francis Drake began to plunder Spanish shipping in the West Indies and Panama. During this year, Spanish losses through piracy amounted to about £100,000.

Parliament opened on 2 April. During the session William Strickland and Thomas Norton introduced parliamentary bills designed to modify the 1559 Prayer Book and to enact Archbishop Cranmer's 1553 reform of church law. Because of Elizabeth's opposition, these attempts at further Protestant reform were lost. In addition, Elizabeth vetoed an anti-Catholic bill that required everyone to receive communion. Parliament, nonetheless, did pass legislation that made it treasonable to call Elizabeth a heretic or to bring papal bulls into England.

RIGHT: **An embroidered smock** *was worn under outer items of dress of the period by girls and women from wealthy families, but it was never intended to be concealed completely. Decorated smocks could also be worn in bed for receiving visitors. Floral motifs, as in this example from the Victoria and Albert Museum, were popular, reflecting the Elizabethan interest in gardens and flowers. The embroidery was probably carried out by the original owner of the garment, for girls learned the skill from an early age.*

305

During the first three days of May, a tournament was held before the queen at Westminster. The challengers were Christopher Hatton (a favoured gentleman-pensioner), Edward de Vere (17th Earl of Oxford), Charles Howard and Sir Henry Lee.

On 1 June, the Catholic exile John Story – at one time, chancellor to Bishop Bonner and active against heretics during Mary's reign – was hanged, drawn and quartered at Tyburn after being abducted from his exile in Antwerp. He had escaped there after refusing to swear the oath of supremacy, a capital offence.

In the Low Countries, on 14 July, Philip II ordered the Duke of Alva to prepare arms and money for an enterprise against England in support of a Catholic rebellion. The intermediary between Spain, the English Catholics and Mary Queen of Scots was a Florentine banker, Roberto di Ridolfi, who was possibly a double agent. In August, servants of the Duke of Norfolk were arrested and found to be passing money on to Mary's supporters in Scotland. In early September, Norfolk was interrogated about his role in the larger conspiracy.

In the wider world of Christendom, on 7 October a fleet of the Holy League – Venice, the Papal States and Spain – defeated the Turks at the Battle of Lepanto, off the coast of the Mediterranean island of Corfu. A month later a sermon was preached in London to offer thanksgiving for the victory of the 'Christian in the Levant seas against the common enemies of our faith'.[25] In the evening, there were bonfires, rejoicing and banqueting.

306

ABOVE: **Sir Christopher Hatton (c.1540–91)** *grew in importance as a courtier during the early 1570s. The queen particularly appreciated his skill at the tilts and his grace in dancing. In July 1572, she made him a gentleman of the privy chamber and captain of the yeomen of the guard. In 1577, he was knighted, created vice chamberlain of the queen's household, and he entered the privy council. Ten years later he was appointed lord chancellor. He was painted as such in this miniature by Nicholas Hilliard. Elizabeth gave him the pet name of 'lids' or 'sheep', and he used a symbol of three parallel triangles in writing to her.*

RIGHT: **Edward de Vere (1550–1604)** *was the 17th Earl of Oxford. He became Lord Burghley's son-in-law on 19 December 1571, when he married Anne Cecil. The marriage was disastrous for much of its duration. Oxford was an attractive man, but violent, extravagant and arrogant. After Oxford's mistress, Anne Vavasour, bore him a son in 1581, he (and she) spent time in the Tower. The earl, depicted here in an anonymous portrait from the 1570s, wrote at least 16 poems and served as the patron of a theatrical company. It has been suggested, without much foundation, that he wrote the plays and poetry attributed to William Shakespeare.*

English plans to establish plantations in Ireland were given the go-ahead in November when Sir Thomas Smith and his illegitimate son (Thomas) were granted land in the Ards Peninsula, with a view to establishing a colony in the province of Ulster.

On 19 December, Lord Burghley's 15-year-old daughter, Anne, married the Earl of Oxford at Westminster Abbey, with Elizabeth in attendance. There followed a celebratory dinner at Cecil House, on the Strand. Anne, however, gained little joy from a husband who was wild and undisciplined. Furthermore, he unfairly accused his wife of infidelity and refused to acknowledge their daughter, born in 1575, as his own child. The couple lived apart for many years, and only in December 1580 did they become reconciled.

The English Prayer Book

... we [Elizabeth] think it expedient, *that if he [Henry, Duke of Anjou] should be our husband, he should accompany us to the church, and why should he not, or may not use our manners of prayers and divine service ... for in ours, there is no part that has not been, yea that is not at this day used in the Church of Rome, as of late the same has been allowed by the last Council of Trent; and if anything be more in ours, the same is part of Holy Scripture ... ours is in the English tongue ... the same is also in the Latin tongue as the service of the Church of Rome, and so ordered to be used in our universities ... Neither does the usage of the divine service of England properly compel any man to alter his opinion in the great matters now in controversy in the church; only the usage thereof doth direct men daily to hear and read the scriptures, to pray to Almighty God by daily use of the Psalter of David, and of the ancient prayers, anthems and collects of the Church, even the same which the universal church has used, and doth yet use.*

[ELIZABETH WRITING TO FRANCIS WALSINGHAM, 11 MAY 1571, FROM SIR DUDLEY DIGGES, *The Compleat Ambassador*, PP. 98–9]

307

Exurgit

Nic. Morton

The rebellion of the Earles of Northumber. and

Nous diffipantur — Inimici

Northumbert.

Vestmoreland ✳ FridHuls19. inv. et sculp.

1572

On 16 January, the Duke of Norfolk was found guilty of treason, but Elizabeth deferred the execution. She was either unconvinced by the evidence against him or reluctant to execute the premier peer of the realm.

On 1 March, Elizabeth expelled Dutch Protestant refugees who were operating as privateers from England. On 1 April, these 'Sea Beggars' unexpectedly occupied Brill in the province of Zeeland in the Low Countries and opened up a second phase in the Dutch Revolt. Although Elizabeth did not openly help the rebels, she allowed Sir Humphrey Gilbert to serve in Zeeland with 1100 English volunteers from June until November.

On 19 April, an Anglo-French defensive treaty was signed at Blois. The French royal family was seeking a rapprochement with Protestants at home and abroad.

On May Day, a trained band of London pikemen mustered before the queen at Greenwich. There 'they showed many warlike feats, but were much hindered by the weather'.[26] Parliament assembled later that month, on the 8th. It quickly introduced bills against Mary Queen of Scots, but Elizabeth stopped them: one excluded Mary from the succession; another demanded her execution as well as that of Norfolk. Parliament did pass several important acts, including legislation that

309

LEFT: **The execution of the Earl Northumberland,** *who had launched the failed uprising with the Earl of Westmorland in 1569, took place on 22 August 1572 in the market place at York. The fugitive rebel, who had fled over the border, had been captured by the Scots and ransomed to the English. He is depicted here with his head on the block, in the right of this 17th-century engraving. In the left foreground, the two earls conspire with a friar.*

provided compulsory relief for the 'deserving' poor but enacted that vagrants over the age of 14 should be whipped and a hole be burned through their right ear. The punishment for a second offence was hanging.

In June, *An Admonition to the Parliament* appeared, having been published on a secret press. Calling for a reform of popish abuses and the establishment of a presbyterian church, the *Admonition* aroused royal disapproval. Its authors – John Field and Thomas Wilcox – were imprisoned for a year.

The Duke of Norfolk was at last beheaded for treason on 2 June, on Tower Hill. His son, Philip, was allowed to retain many of the family lands but not his father's title. Elizabeth hoped that his execution would silence calls for the death of Mary.

In July, Elizabeth made several important appointments: on the 13th, the Earl of Sussex became lord chamberlain and Sir Thomas Smith replaced Lord Burghley as principal secretary; on the 15th, Burghley was made lord treasurer. A little later, Elizabeth went on summer progress to the Midlands, visiting various towns and noblemen's houses. At Warwick Castle, the entertainments were marred when a magnificent firework display set fire to the home of an elderly couple. During this progress, Elizabeth also visited Kenilworth, the castle owned by the Earl of Leicester.

On 22 August, the Huguenot leader, Admiral Gaspard de Coligny, was shot in Paris. The attempted assassination, orchestrated by the king's mother Catherine de' Medici, and Henry Duke of Guise, was followed by a massacre of Protestants on St Bartholomew's Eve, 23–4 August. The violence spread through France, leaving tens of thousands – perhaps as many as 75,000 – dead. English Protestants were horrified, and the event intensified hostility towards English Catholics as well as Mary Queen of Scots, who was a first cousin of the Duke of Guise. The Treaty of Blois was now under serious threat.

On 24 November, the Anglophile James Douglas, 4th Earl of Morton, was elected regent of Scotland after the death of his predecessor, the Earl of Mar. The civil war in Scotland was not yet over, but the lords opposed to Mary were in the ascendant.

'Vagrants over the age of 14 should be whipped and a hole be burned through their right ear'

PREVIOUS PAGE: **The Massacre of St Bartholomew's Eve** *(or Day) in France began on 23 August 1572. As seen in this painting, the royal Swiss Guard and civilians alike murdered men, women and children who were thought to be Protestant. Their bodies were mutilated and thrown in the Seine or burned on pyres. The painting also shows Gaspard de Coligny's house in the middle distance and a wounded Coligny being thrown out of a window. The figure in black, in the background towards the left, is meant to represent Catherine de' Medici, who was held responsible for ordering the massacre. This painting was made by the Huguenot artist Francis Dubois between 1572 and 1584. He was probably in Paris at the time of the massacre: he wrote what he claimed was an eye-witness account.*

1573

This year's winter saw 'a great and sharp frost ... with sometimes great and deep snows'.[27] In January, diplomatic relations with France improved after the rupture caused by the St Bartholomew's massacre and the re-opening of the religious wars. William Somerset, 3rd Earl of Worcester, was sent to the christening of Charles IX's daughter as proxy for Queen Elizabeth. *En route*, however, pirates plundered his ships. The Edict of Boulogne, in July, brought a temporary halt to the religious wars in France.

In March, the Anglo-Spanish commercial embargo was finally lifted, and Elizabeth hoped an improvement in political relations would follow. Not all English merchants returned to Antwerp, however, preferring to use instead new markets developed during the dispute.

On 9 July, Elizabeth granted Walter Devereux, Earl of Essex, the right to colonize County Antrim in Ulster. His first task, though, was to subdue the Scottish inhabitants in the region, although Elizabeth warned him against using excessive force.

During her summer progress, Elizabeth travelled through Kent and on 14 July visited Dover. Further to the west, Francis Drake arrived at Plymouth on 9 August after a 14-month raiding expedition in the (West) Indies. Although far less successful than his earlier venture – of his ships, three pinnaces and the

ABOVE: **Sir Francis Walsingham (c.1532–90)** *was appointed principal secretary on 20 December 1573 and a privy councillor on the following day, and he proved especially active (with Lord Burghley) in protecting the security of the Elizabethan regime; hence his popular reputation as a 'spymaster'. Elizabeth nicknamed him her 'Moor'. In 1572, he was ambassador in Paris and sheltered Huguenots fleeing the Massacre of St Bartholemew. His knighthood came in 1577.*

His daughter Frances married first Philip Sidney and afterwards Robert Devereux, the 2nd Earl of Essex. Dressed sombrely in black in this portrait (c.1587) by John de Critz, Walsingham wears a cameo portrait of Elizabeth, which hangs from a long ribbon. She gave out many such cameos to her courtiers and councillors.

The 'Antiquitate Britannicae Ecclesiae' by Archbishop Matthew Parker *contained biographies of 69 previous archbishops. Parker had no more than 20 copies of the book made, by the London printer John Day, in 1572. This copy, in a binding of dark green velvet worked with gold and silver threads and coloured silks, was a gift to Elizabeth: it now resides in the British Library. The subject of its design, a deer park, may be a punning reference to Parker's name. On the upper cover within the paling is a rose-bush, bearing a large Tudor rose and two white roses. Flowers and tufts of grass grow about the rose-tree, including two pansies.*

Swan were lost – he returned home a rich man. His seafaring compatriot, John Hawkins, was less fortunate. On 11 October, an assailant 'cruelly wounded'[28] him with a dagger as he rode near the Strand. The man responsible – who seemed to be insane – claimed he had mistaken Hawkins for Christopher Hatton, who had recently been appointed captain of the queen's bodyguard.

On 20 October, Sir Thomas Smith's son, also called Thomas, was killed in the Ards peninsula 'by the revolting of certain Irishmen of his own household, to whom he overmuch trusted'.[29] So ended this attempt at colonizing Ulster.

Francis Walsingham was appointed as a second principal secretary on 20 December, and on the following day he was made a privy councillor. During this month, the more conciliatory Luis de Requesens replaced the Duke of Alva as Philip's governor-general in the Netherlands. Hopes were raised that a peaceful settlement of the Dutch Revolt could now be found.

1574

Despite offering concessions in the Low Countries, Governor-General Requesens could not end the revolt. Its leaders – notably William, Prince of Orange – demanded religious toleration, an unacceptable condition for Philip II.

During this year, four Catholic priests arrived in England from the seminary at Douai, which had ordained its first clerics the previous year. These men came to England to administer the sacraments to Catholics and keep the faith alive, rather than to stir up rebellion. On Palm Sunday, 4 April, Catholic houses in London were searched, and three ladies hearing mass were committed to the Tower.

Charles IX of France died on 30 May. His brother and successor Henry returned from Poland, where he had been elected king, to take up the French throne as Henry III. However, civil war still raged in the kingdom.

During her summer progress, Elizabeth visited Bristol. While there, she signed a treaty with Spain that formally ended the commercial embargo. A new Spanish ambassador – Bernardino de Mendoza – took up residence in England. A more unusual visitor to the realm was a monstrous fish or whale, which was beached near Ramsgate on 9 July.

Plague hit London again in October, with an estimated 65 fatal victims. One survivor, though, was Jacob Verzellini, a Venetian glassmaker living in the capital, who this year obtained a patent for making decorative wine glasses. An innovator, Verzellini was responsible for introducing a process that used soda ash instead of crude potash.

'A more unusual visitor to the realm was a monstrous fish or whale, which was beached near Ramsgate'

1575

Elizabeth granted the musicians Thomas Tallis and William Byrd a 25-year monopoly to print music on 22 January. They dedicated the collection of motets entitled *Cantiones sacrae* to the queen.

On 3 April (Easter Day), 27 foreign 'Anabaptists' were arrested in London. Most of them recanted their heretical views, but two were burned at Smithfield on 22 July.

In April, Pope Gregory XIII, elected in 1572, granted an annual pension to the English seminary at Douai. The English Church, though, lost its archbishop about midnight on 17 May, when Matthew Parker died at Lambeth. He bequeathed his vast library to Corpus Christi College, Cambridge. His replacement at Canterbury was Edmund Grindal, the Archbishop of York.

On 12 June, five Englishmen who were members of the religious sect known as the Family of Love recanted at Paul's Cross. This initiated a campaign against the movement, which stressed the spiritualist teachings of the Dutchman Hendrik Niclaes.

During her summer progress this year, Elizabeth visited Kenilworth Castle in July. Her host was the Earl of Leicester, who treated the court to entertainments on a grand scale.

In July, the Earl of Essex planned an expedition against the Scottish inhabitants of County Antrim. An army under Captain

Kenilworth entertainments

... a little of the Coventry play her highness also saw ... whereat Her Majesty laughed well ... They prayed for Her Majesty, long, happily to reign and oft to come thither ...

Thus though the day took an end, yet slipped not the night sleeping away ... So, after supper was there a play presented of a very good theme, but so set forth by the actors' well handling, that pleasure and mirth made it seem very short, though it lasted two good hours and more ...

After the play out of hand, followed a most delicious and (if I may so term it) an ambrosial banquet: whereof, whither I might more muse at the daintiness, shapes and the cost; or else at the variety and number of the dishes (that were a three hundred), for my part I could little tell them, and now less, I assure you ...

Unto this banquet there was appointed a masque; for richness of array, of an incredible cost; but the time so far spent, and very late in the night now, was cause that it came not forth to the show.

[MODERNIZED FROM ROBERT LANEHAM, *Robert Laneham's Letter ...* , ENTRY FOR SUNDAY 17 JULY 1575, pp. 32–3]

RIGHT: **This portrait of Elizabeth** *is thought to have been commissioned by the Earl of Leicester for display at Kenilworth Castle during the royal visit of 1575. The castle was granted to Dudley in 1563, and he spent an estimated £40,000 on its rebuilding and refurbishment. The entertainments provided during that royal visit were unusually spectacular – allegorical masques, dancing, tilting, bear-baiting, banquets and fireworks – and some thought they were the prelude to marriage proposals. In this portrait, Elizabeth is wearing a white satin doublet decorated with gold thread, button and braid, almost certainly a gift from the earl. The gold chain hanging over her shoulders is decorated with armillary spheres, daisies and Tudor roses. It was hung near a matching portrait of Leicester.*

John Norris went over to Rathlin Island, in ships provided by Francis Drake, and stormed the castle there. On 26 July, the castle's commander surrendered, but the English soldiers massacred 200 or more of the Scots as they filed out. They then slaughtered another 200 people, including women and children, who had taken refuge in caves.

In December, a delegation from Holland and Zeeland arrived in London

ABOVE: **The 'Cantiones quae ab argumento sacrae vocantur ...' (1575)** *was the first publication by Thomas Tallis (c.1505–85) and William Byrd (1543?–1623), appearing shortly after they had received a royal monopoly for the printing of music. It was a collection of 16 compositions by Tallis and 15 by Byrd, but the works were produced as 17 motets apiece so that the number corresponded to the length of Elizabeth's reign. The printing project, whose title-page is shown here, was a financial failure. Tallis was probably a Catholic; Byrd was cited for recusancy, for the first time in 1585. Despite their religious sympathies, Tallis was employed in the Chapel Royal from the beginning of the reign and Byrd from February 1572.*

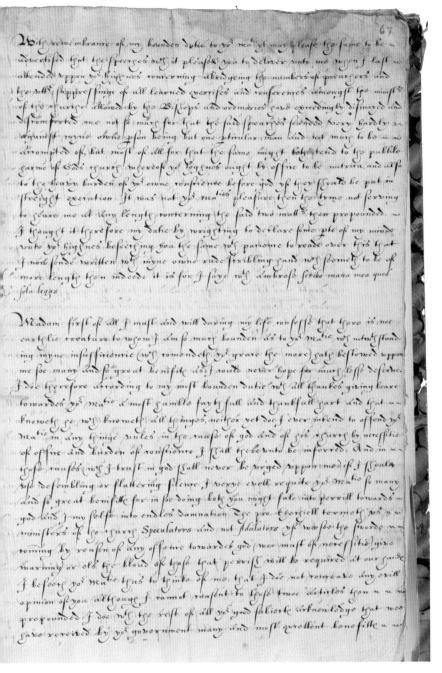

to offer Elizabeth the sovereignty of the Dutch provinces that were in rebellion against Philip II. She rejected the offer. However, by now Governor-General Requesens was unable to pay his troops, on account of the financial difficulties of the Spanish government.

1576

On 8 February, the first day of the new Parliament, Peter Wentworth claimed the right of freedom of speech for MPs so that the House of Commons could discuss subjects (such as religion and the succession) that Elizabeth treated as out of bounds. On 15 March, he was imprisoned in the Tower for a month.

In June, Martin Frobisher left on his first voyage to seek a northwest sea passage to Cathay (China). He travelled 'north-west beyond any man that hath heretofore discovered',[30] before returning home in October. He brought with him an Inuit man, who died within days of his arrival, and a piece of black stone that Frobisher's financial backers believed contained gold. The queen's rather less adventurous travels, on her summer progress, took her this year to Northamptonshire, Leicestershire and Surrey.

On 22 September, the Earl of Essex died in Dublin as a result of dysentery. Consequently,

ABOVE: **This page is from a letter** by the recently appointed Archbishop Edmund Grindal (1516?–83), written to the queen on 20 December 1576. In it, he justified his refusal to obey her command that he suppress 'prophesyings', those local meetings where members of the clergy gave sermons that were afterwards criticized and discussed. Grindal was determined to encourage preaching, and he bravely – but unwisely – told Elizabeth that he put his duty to God before his obedience to his monarch. Deeply affronted, Elizabeth contemplated his immediate dismissal, but her councillors persuaded her to suspend the archbishop until he submitted. In fact, Grindal remained in office until his death in 1583, although he neither apologized nor obeyed the royal order.

the second attempt to colonize Ulster also resulted in failure. He was succeeded in the earldom by his son Robert.

On 4 November, unpaid Spanish troops entered Antwerp in Brabant and went on the rampage. The 'Spanish Fury' that followed over the next few days resulted in some 8000 deaths and the destruction of about 1000 houses. On 8 November, all the provinces of the Low Countries signed the Pacification of Ghent, which demanded the withdrawal of Spanish troops and agreed to liberty of conscience. Elizabeth came under pressure to send an army to assist the rebels, but she preferred to send just financial aid.

In December, England's Archbishop Grindal challenged Elizabeth's order that he suppress preaching at gatherings of the clergy and laity, known as 'prophesyings'. Grindal strongly believed that these meetings were invaluable for training ministers to teach the Word to the laity.

1577

On 24 March, John Aylmer, an opponent of prophesyings and nonconformity, was consecrated Bishop of London. In May, Elizabeth ordered a crackdown on all unlicensed preaching, and in June she placed Archbishop Grindal under house arrest and suspended him from the exercise of his office.

Elizabeth was entertained at Lord Burghley's house at Theobalds, in Hertfordshire, in May.

ABOVE: **Sir Martin Frobisher (1535?–94)** *made three voyages to the Arctic between 1576 and 1578 in search of a northwest passage to China. He was, however, distracted from making major discoveries by the prospect of finding gold. After his backers lost money on the ventures, his influence at court waned. His good service during the Spanish war, however, restored him to favour, but he died of gangrene poisoning after incurring a wound during the 1594 Breton campaign. In this portrait from 1577, by Cornelius Ketel, Frobisher is wearing voluminous breeches called 'venetians' and holding a gun. He is shown as a man of action rather than a courtier.*

During her previous stay in 1571, she had been critical of its small size. After that, Burghley started upon a programme of substantial rebuilding to make the house more suitable for a royal visit.

On 31 May, Martin Frobisher sailed out from Harwich on a mission to bring back further quantities of the black ore that was thought to contain gold. Elizabeth was one of his financial backers. He returned to Wales on 20 September with a few Inuits and some 160 tons of the stone, 'but neither the man, woman nor child lived long in this country, nor his ore proved gold but dross'.[31]

In July, a strange illness afflicted all those attending a court case in Oxford: 300 died in the town and another 200 sickened there but died elsewhere.

There were new appointments in church and state this year. In the summer, John Whitgift took on the role of Bishop of Worcester. On 12 November, Thomas Wilson entered the privy council and was appointed principal

---

ABOVE: **The great comet of 1577** had a tail that spread in a great arc across the sky. An unusual number of comets appeared during the 16th century, but the 1577 one attracted the most interest. The Danish astronomer Tycho Brahe used the evidence of the comet, and of the supernova he had seen in 1572, to overturn Aristotle's notions that the heavens are unchanging and that the planets move in a system of fixed 'crystal spheres'. This engraving is a German one, made by Georg Mack the Elder in 1577.

The 'Great Conjurer'

And, so, hath the fiend Infernal, *most craftily and unduly, gotten the honest name and fame of one extraordinary studious gentleman of this land [John Dee] within his claws: that diverse his mere malicious and willful enemies do verily hope, that it is impossible that this gentleman shall with this English or British state either (during his life) be counted a good subject, or a commendable (nay scarce a tolerable) Christian ... From henceforth to repress, abolish, and utterly extinguish this very injurious report (for these 20 years last past, and somewhat longer) spread and credited, all this realm over: it is to wit, that the foresaid gentleman, is or was, not only a 'conjurer', or caller of devils: but 'a great doer therein: yea the Great Conjurer' and so (as some would say) the Arch Conjurer of this whole kingdom ... Oh Lord, with how tickle [enticing] and strong snares, and with how wily labyrinths, hath the most envious traitor to the honour of our God and Christ, bewrapped and daunted many a thousand of simple and honest men's fantasies: inducing them, to credit this infamous report?*

['AN ADVERTISEMENT TO THE READER BY AN UNKNOWN FRIEND', PREFACING JOHN DEE's *The Perfect Art of Navigation*, 1577]

An Inuit encounter

I [Dr Doddling] showed the body [of the Inuit man Kalicho] to the woman [his Inuit widow, Arnaq] ... and at my persuasion she was led with me, albeit unwillingly, to the burial, which I purposely wanted to be carried through without ceremony, lest there be implanted in her any fears about human sacrifice among us. She was kept there all the time until the body had been completely covered over with earth; I showed her human bones which had been dug up, and made her understand that we were all to be buried in the same way. This I did to remove her anxiety about human flesh being eaten (a practice which had become deeply rooted among them), and that she might learn to put aside the fear henceforward. But that woman either excelled all our people in decorum and stoicism or else was far outstripped in human sensitivity by the wild animals themselves. For she was not in any way disturbed by his death ... So much so that, by this recent behaviour of hers, she has expressed quite clearly ... that she had regarded him with an astonishing degree of contempt, and that although they used to sleep in one and the same bed, yet nothing had occurred between them apart from conversation, his embrace having been abhorrent to her.

[Translated from the Latin postmortem report of Dr Edward Doddling, Bristol, 8 November 1577, in George Best (d.1584?), *The Three Voyages of Martin Frobisher*, edited by R. Collinson, p. 191]

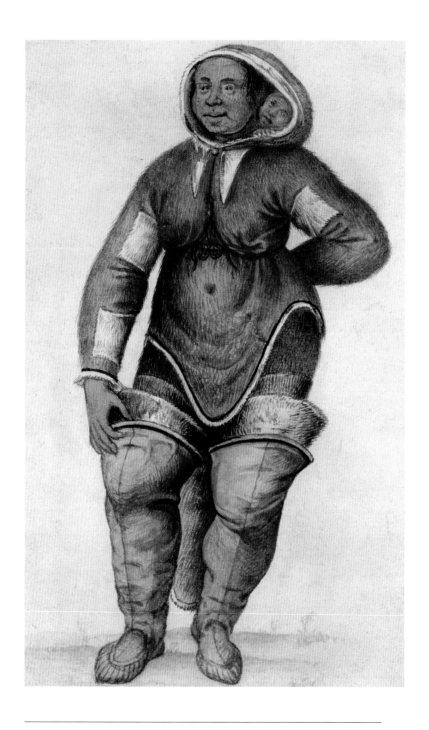

ABOVE: **The Inuit woman 'Egnock' and child 'Nutiock',** *and an unrelated man 'Collichang', were captured during Frobisher's second voyage to Arctic Canada in 1577. They were brought back to England as curiosities, but soon afterwards died. This watercolour drawing was executed by John White (fl.1570–93), who was probably on the voyage.*

secretary alongside Sir Francis Walsingham.

There 'was seen a blazing star with a long stream' On the night of 11 November.[32] On the last day of this month, Cuthbert Mayne became the first seminary priest to be executed in England. He was found guilty of treason for having in his possession an *Agnus Dei* and papal bull, both of which were now prohibited by law.

The end of the year witnessed the beginnings of a major privateering expedition, when, on 13 December, 5 ships and 164 men under Francis Drake's command left Plymouth to seize Spanish bullion and explore the southern coasts of South America. Investors in the voyage included the Earl of Leicester, Christopher Hatton and Sir Francis Walsingham. Drake's flagship was named the *Pelican* after Queen Elizabeth, who had adopted the bird as one of her emblems.

During this year, the 'Curtain Theatre' opened in Shoreditch. It was the second public playhouse in London; the first was 'The Theatre' built by James Burbage the previous year.

Also during this year, Christopher Hatton, a favourite of the queen, was knighted and entered the privy council.

1578

In March, William Allen's seminary closed at Douai, but it was reopened in April at Rheims.

Martin Frobisher, 'with fifteen sail of good ships',[33] left on his third voyage on 31 May. He arrived at some islands, which were named by the queen *Meta incognita*, and loaded his ships with some 1370 tons of the black stone, before returning to England. The ore was found to be worthless.

In May also, Elizabeth visited the Earl of Leicester's house at Wanstead, where she was entertained with a performance of a masque called

Her Majesty's sea captain

The said Captain Francis Drake having in a former voyage, in the years [15]72 and [15]73, (the description whereof is already imparted to the view of the world) had a sight of, and only a sight of the South Atlantic [the Pacific Ocean], and thereupon either conceiving a new, or renewing a former desire, of sailing on the same, in an English bottom; he so cherished thenceforward this his noble desire and resolution in himself, that notwithstanding he was hindered for some years partly by secret envy at home, and partly by public service for his prince and country abroad ... yet against the year 1577, by gracious commission from his sovereign, and with the help of diverse friends adventurers, he had fitted himself with five ships.

> The Pelican ...
>
> The Elizabeth ...
>
> The Marigold ...
>
> The Swan ...
>
> The Christopher ...

These ships he manned with 164 able and sufficient men, and furnished them also with such plentiful provision of all things necessary, as so long and dangerous a voyage did seem to require ... Neither had he omitted, to make provision also for ornament and delight, carrying to this purpose with him, expert musicians, rich furniture (all the vessels for his table, yea many belonging even to the cook-room being of pure silver), and diverse shows of all sorts of curious workmanship, whereby the civility and magnificence of his native country, might, amongst all nations whithersoever he should come, be the more admired.

[FRANCIS FLETCHER *et al.*, *The World Encompassed*, 1652 EDITION, PP. 2–3]

The Lady of May, a literary work by Philip Sidney. During the summer, she went on a long progress to East Anglia. In Suffolk, the local gentry provided the court with 'such sumptuous feasting and banquets, as seldom in any part of the world have been seen before'.[34] The gentlemen and nobility of Norfolk then followed suit, and in mid-August the citizens of Norwich took their turn. They presented the queen with six days of pageants, which 'gained their city more fame and credit than they wot of'.[35] On her return, Elizabeth passed through Cambridge and ended up again at Leicester's house at Wanstead. While on her progress, Elizabeth opened up discussions with French ambassadors about a marriage between herself and the king of France's 23-year-old brother Francis, the Duke of Anjou (previously the Duke of Alençon), who was 21 years her junior. Although he was a Catholic, he was prepared to assist the Calvinist rebels in the Low Countries in their struggle against Spain. On 21 September, the Earl of Leicester himself secretly married. His bride was Lettice, the widowed Countess of Essex.

In October, Alexander Farnese, Prince of Parma and a nephew of Philip II, was appointed the Spanish king's new governor-general in the Low Countries, following the death of the previous incumbent, Don John of Austria.

ABOVE: **Sir Philip Sidney (1554–86)** *was the eldest son of Sir Henry Sidney and Lady Mary Dudley, the sister of the Earl of Leicester. He attended court after 1575, leaving it occasionally on diplomatic missions for the queen. Sidney was also a poet, and his first composition,* The Lady of May, *was probably performed before Elizabeth when she visited Leicester's house at Wanstead in 1578. During his lifetime, Sidney's poetry was widely circulated in manuscript. After his death in 1586, his most important works – the pastoral prose romance* Arcadia *and his sonnet sequence* Astrophel and Stella *– were printed. The portrait is dated 1576.*

RIGHT: **Lettice Knollys (1543?–1634)** *was the grand-daughter of Mary Boleyn and the widow of Walter Devereux, 1st Earl of Essex, who died in September 1576. Two years after his death, Lettice married the Earl of Leicester in a ceremony at Wanstead House that was initially kept secret from the queen. Once she knew of the marriage, Elizabeth barred Lettice from court. Eventually, in March 1598, a decade after Leicester's death, Elizabeth received her at court as a mark of favour to her son, Robert Devereux, 2nd Earl of Essex. Lettice was by then married to Sir Christopher Blount, who was later executed for his role in Essex's rising.*

1579

Jean de Simier arrived from France on 6 January to negotiate a marriage between his master, Francis, Duke of Anjou, and Elizabeth. Members of the council considered the ramifications of a match but were divided, Burghley and the Earl of Sussex approving it while Leicester and Walsingham led the opposition.

In January, divisions among the rebel provinces in the Low Countries hardened. On the 6th, the predominantly Catholic provinces in the south signed an accord at Arras in which they expressed their loyalty to Philip II and support for the Catholic Church. On 23 January, the northern provinces concluded an act of alliance and union at Utrecht, in which they committed themselves to fighting for independence against Spain and agreed to freedom of worship.

Heavy snows fell that February in England, followed by severe flooding.

On 23 April, a college was founded at Rome to educate priests for the English mission. At home, on 13 May, a wheelwright, Matthew Hamont, who was charged with heresy and blasphemy for 'denying Christ to be our Saviour',[36] had his ears cut off in the market place at Norwich. His punishment did not end there, for a week later he was burned.

RIGHT: **Francis (1554–84), Duke of Anjou,** *the brother of Henry III of France, courted Elizabeth between 1578 and 1581. Although she was over 20 years older than him, Elizabeth appeared ready to marry 'her little frog'. However, most of her councillors and subjects opposed the match, and so Elizabeth remained single. The duke is depicted here at the bottom right of this jousting scene. It is a detail from one of the eight 'Valois Tapestries' representing French courtly spectacles and festivities, which were made by Flemish weavers in the late 1570s.*

Aprill.

Ægloga Quarta.

ARGVMENT.

THis Æglogue is purpofely intended to the honor and prayfe of our moft gracious foueregine, Queene Elizabeth. The fpeakers herein be Hobbinoll and Thenott, two fhepheardes: the which Hobbinoll being before mentioned, greatly to haue loued Colin, is here fet forth more largely, complayning him of that boyes great mifaduenture in Loue, whereby his mynd was alienate and withdrawen not onely from him, who mofte loued him, but alfo from all former delightes and ftudies, af well in pleafaunt pyping, as conning ryming and finging, and other his laudable exercifes. Whereby he taketh occafion, for proofe of his more excellencie and fkill in poetrie, to recorde a fonge, which the fayd Colin fometime made in honor of her Maieftie, whom abruptely he termeth Elyfa.

Thenot.   Hobbinoll.

TEll me good Hobbinoll, what garres thee greete?
  What? hath fome Wolfe thy tender Lambes ytorne?
  Or is thy Bagpype broke, that foundes fo fweete?
  Or art thou of thy loued laffe forlorne?

  Or bene thine eyes attempred to the yeare,
  Quenching the gafping furrowes thirft with rayne?

Like

Across the Irish Sea, on 17 July a group of several dozen Spanish and Italian soldiers, under the command of James FitzMaurice Fitzgerald, landed in Kerry to raise rebellion. During the summer, members of the house of Desmond came out in revolt too. Fitzgerald was killed in Limerick on 18 August, but the violence continued.

Danger confronted Elizabeth from an unexpected quarter in the summer. At about 9 p.m. on 17 July, a young servant-boy, Thomas Appletree, who was shooting at random from a boat on the Thames, hit a waterman not six feet away from the queen, who was travelling in her private barge accompanied by the French envoy Simier. Appletree was condemned to death, but 'when the hangman had put the rope about his neck, he was by the queen's pardon delivered from execution'.[37]

The Anglo-French marital negotiations continued, and on 17 August Duke Francis arrived incognito at Greenwich and remained there for 11 days in a romantic pursuit of the 45-year-old queen. After his departure, Elizabeth went on a short progress into Essex, and on her return, 12 privy

ABOVE: **'The Shepherd's Calendar' by Edmund Spenser (1552?–99)** *was printed in 1579 and became something of a bestseller, with four Elizabethan editions. Its 12 poems – one for each month – covered subjects that ranged from a satire of the church to a love lament. When it was written, Spenser was in Leicester's household, but in 1580 he went to Ireland as the secretary of the lord deputy. On his return to England in 1590, Elizabeth granted him a small annuity, but Spenser left again in 1591 after he had offended Burghley by lampooning him. Spenser's masterpiece was his epic poem, The Faerie Queene. The first three books appeared in 1590. The poet died penniless in 1599 and was buried near Chaucer in Westminster Abbey, at the expense of the Earl of Essex.*

RIGHT: **Elizabeth adorned the cover of Christopher Saxton's 'Atlas',** *published in 1579. The work contained a general map of England and 34 coloured maps of the counties of England and Wales, and it provided a new standard of cartographic representation in Britain. The enthroned queen is shown as the patron of geometry and astronomy. In the medallion over her head 'Peace' embraces 'Justice' in an allusion to Psalm 85.*

Clemens et Regni moderatrix iusta Britāni
Hac forma insigni conspicienda nitet.

Tristia dum gentes circùm omnes bella fatigant,
Cæciq; errores toto grassantur in orbe.
An Dñi pace beas longa, Vera et pietate Britannos: 1579
Iusticia moderans miti sapienter habenas.
Chara domi, celebrisq; foris, longævaq; regni
Hic teneas, regno tandem fruitura perenni.

councillors discussed Anjou's marriage proposal. Despite her known desire for the marriage, eight of the councillors rejected it outright, mainly on the grounds that Francis was a Catholic.

At about this time, the match was vigorously attacked in a pamphlet entitled *The Discoverie of a Gaping Gulf*, written by a lawyer, John Stubbs. On 13 October, Stubbs, his printer Hugh Singleton and William Page 'were condemned to lose their right hands for writing, printing and dispersing a libel'.[38] Singleton was pardoned, but the other two underwent the punishment at the market place in Westminster on 3 November, with surgeons present to prevent them from bleeding to death. After his hand was chopped off (it took three blows), Stubbs managed to cry out 'God save the queen' before he fainted. The crowd watched in silence 'either out of an horror at this new and unwanted kind of punishment; or else out of commiseration towards the man'.[39] Stubbs was confined in the Tower until 1581. However, other activists continued to speak out or write against Elizabeth's marriage to the duke, whom she had affectionately termed her 'frog'. The queen, nevertheless, exercised her right to have a marriage treaty drawn up, which Simier took to France, where it was signed.

Massacre at Smerwick

About this time [in 1580] there arrived on the west coast of Ireland a certain company of Italians and Spaniards, sent by the pope to the aid the Earl of Desmond in his rebellion, which fortified themselves strongly near unto Smerwick, in a fort which they called 'Castell del Ore', there erecting the pope's banner against Her Majesty. Which when the Lord Grey of Wilton, Deputy of Ireland, understood, he marched thitherward, and on the sixth of November, hearing of the arrival of the Swift, the Tiger, the Aid, the Merlion, and other of the Queen's Majesty's ships, and also of three barks freighted from Cork and Limerick with victuals, on the morrow after marched towards the fort, unto the which he gave so hot an assault, that on the ninth of November the same was yielded, all the Irishmen and women hanged, and more than four hundred Spaniards, Italians and Biscays put to the sword: the coronel [colonel], captains, secretary, and others to the number of twenty saved for ransom. In which fortress was found good store of money, biscuit, bacon, oil, wine, and diverse other provisions of victuals sufficient for their company for half a year, besides armour, powder, shot, and other furniture for two thousand men upwards.

[RAPHAEL HOLINSHED, *Holinshed's Chronicles of England, Scotland and Ireland*, 1807 EDITION, VOL. IV, P. 433]

1580

On 6 April, an earthquake 'caused such an amazedness among the people' that they made 'their earnest prayers to almighty God'.[40] Some property was damaged, part of Dover cliff fell into the sea, and two servants were killed in London. In May, another earthquake tremor was felt in Kent.

The first Jesuit mission arrived in England in June, with the aim of bolstering the Catholic cause. Robert Persons crossed first, and then came Edmund Campion (disguised as a travelling salesman from Dublin) and a lay brother, Ralph Emerson. On 29 June, Campion preached at Smithfield, and in early August he administered the sacraments to Catholics in Berkshire, Oxfordshire and Northamptonshire. Before they left, Pope Gregory XIII had absolved Catholics from obeying the 1570 bull of deposition, *Regnans in Excelsis*, until its enforcement became practicable. The Jesuits, therefore, were not engaged in acts of subversion; but they did intend to encourage the practice of recusancy and thereby disobedience to the law.

In September, 'a certain company of Italians and Spaniards, sent by the pope to the aid of the Earl of Desmond in his rebellion', occupied Smerwick on the southwest coast of Ireland.[41] Lord Arthur Grey of Wilton – dispatched to Ireland in July to suppress the rebellion as it spread to Munster, Leinster, Ulster and Connaught – bombarded the Spanish garrison for two days, until it at last surrendered in the expectation of mercy. However, all the soldiers were massacred on 10 November.

On 19 October, Elizabeth issued a proclamation against the followers of the Family of Love sect. Nonetheless, she allowed some 'Familists' to continue as members of her yeomen of the guard.

Francis Drake returned to England on 3 November, after his three-year privateering voyage circumnavigating the globe, having sailed perhaps 50,000 miles.

On the Continent, Philip II entered Lisbon and was crowned King of Portugal in December, thereby acquiring another vast empire. He had claimed the throne after the death of the previous Portuguese king, Henry II, and his army under the Duke of Alva had defeated the opposition at the Battle of Alcántara on 25 August.

In Scotland on 31 December, the 4th Earl of Morton, who had acted as Scottish regent between 1572 and 1578, was arrested in Edinburgh on a charge of involvement in the murder of the king's father, Lord Darnley. Found guilty, he was executed the following June by the 'maiden', a precursor of the guillotine.

331

ABOVE: **Edmund Campion (1540–81)**, *the Jesuit, arrived in England in June 1580. He travelled around Berkshire, Oxfordshire and Northamptonshire, staying with Catholic families, administering the sacraments, preaching sermons and publishing polemical works on a secret press. In 1581, his activites were stopped, when he was captured, tortured and executed in London. He is depicted here in an engraving from an edited collection of his writings produced in Antwerp in 1631.*

FINLANDIA

Islandia

TARTA

RVS

SILA

ASIA

GERMANIA

EVRO · PA ·

Armenia

HISPA
NIA

ANATOLIA

PERSIA

Turchestan

BARBA
RIA

Ægyptus

ARA

INDIA

CHINA

AFRICA

Æthiopia

NVBIA

GVINEA

MA
NI

A

IS

CON
GO

CAPRICORNI

100 200 300 400 500 600 700 800 900 1000

Scala Leucarum ·

10   20   30   40   50   60   70   80   90   100   110   120   130   140   150   160   170   180

Quam misere super recente scopulis nabis
illisa latera quassarentur 20 horaru spatio, at
tandem/ac filio divino servata/ipsa descriptio
indicat·

1581

Fearing an influx of missionary priests, Elizabeth's government ordered the arrest of all Jesuits on 10 January. A little later, Parliament, which opened on 16 January, passed a statute making it treasonable to convert anyone to Catholicism. It also called for the execution of Mary Queen of Scots.

At jousts held on 22 January, it was not only the participants who risked injury: many of the spectators 'were sore hurt, some maimed, and some killed, by falling of the scaffolds overcharged'.[42]

To the fury of Spain, on 4 April Queen Elizabeth knighted Francis Drake on board the *Golden Hind*, near Deptford upon Thames. Much of the Spanish treasure that Drake had plundered on his voyage was put in the Tower.

During April, French commissioners spent time in England with instructions to conclude both a military alliance against Spain and the marriage between Elizabeth and Duke Francis of Anjou. A banqueting house – said to have cost £1744 – was erected at Westminster as a place of entertainment for them. Its canvas walls were painted on the outside 'most artificially with a work called rustic, much like to stone';[43] its roof was decorated with flowers, 'strange fruits' (spangled with gold), clouds, stars, a sun and sunbeams. In addition, Elizabeth's courtiers performed 'a triumph' (called 'the Fortress of Beauty') before the commissioners in the tiltyard at Whitehall. Soon afterwards, Elizabeth explained to the envoys that her marriage to the duke could not go ahead because of her subjects' hostility towards it. The French, however, rejected a military alliance without marriage.

On the night of 21 June, 'certain young men' broke and defaced religious images on Cheapside cross in London. When caught, they 'were whipped from Newgate to west Smithfield' and put on the pillory.[44]

Unknown hands, on 27 June, secreted printed copies of Edmund Campion's *Rationes Decem* (giving ten arguments against Protestantism) into the Church of St Mary's in Oxford, for members of the university to read. This bold act resulted in an intensification of the search for the Jesuit, and on 17 July a Catholic informer alerted the authorities to his whereabouts. He was arrested in Berkshire, together with two other priests and a layman. Initially, Campion was questioned by the Earl of Leicester, Sir Christopher Hatton and Lord Chancellor Thomas Bromley, but later he was interrogated under torture. After this ordeal, Campion was made to defend his theological position at a public disputation held in the Tower on 31 August and for three days in September. The plan was to discredit him, but Campion held his own despite all the disadvantages he faced. The debate had to be abandoned when he seemed to be attracting sympathizers.

Meanwhile, in the Low Countries, the rebels offered Duke Francis of Anjou the sovereignty of the 'United Provinces' (the provinces that had entered the Union of Utrecht), and on 26 July an 'Act of

PREVIOUS PAGE: **Francis Drake's circumnavigation of the globe** *took place between 1577 and 1580. This manuscript map tracing his route also marks his 1586 voyage to the West Indies. In the insets are illustrations of events on the first voyage: Drake's arrival on the island of Ternate in the Moluccas (Spice Islands) and the Golden Hind stuck on a reef at Celebes. Four flags of St George are drawn on the Americas, indicating England's imperial possession of certain places: one is on the Virginia colony established in 1585 and another on Meta Incognita, discovered by Martin Frobisher in 1576.*

RIGHT: **The pillory and the stocks** *were used as punishments for a range of minor offences. A pillory was a wooden frame on posts, with holes through which the head and hands of a criminal were pushed. Sometimes, the criminal's ears were nailed to the pillory and then cut off and left as warning to others. The stocks, also made of wood, had holes for the ankles. The types of offences that warranted such punishments included selling underweight bread, exposing unwholesome meat (which was then usually burned under the culprit's nose), forging and vandalism. Criminals punished in this way also included dice coggers (cheaters), cutpurses, liars and libellers.*

Abjuration' was published deposing Philip II. Before going to the rebels' assistance, Anjou returned to England on 1 November to attempt to revive the marriage negotiations with Elizabeth. She seemed to respond favourably, kissing him in public, bestowing a ring upon him, and on the 22nd declaring her intention to marry him after all.

On 20 November, Campion and seven other priests were put on trial for treason. On 1 December, alongside two seminary priests, Ralph Sherwin and Alexander Briant, he was drawn on hurdles from the Tower to Tyburn and hanged, drawn and quartered.

'On Monsieur's Departure'

I grieve and dare not show my discontent;
I love, and yet am forced to seem to hate;
I do, yet dare not say I ever meant;
I seem stark mute but inwardly do prate.
    I am, and not; I freeze and yet am burned,
    Since from myself another self I turned.

My care is like my shadow in the sun –
Follows me flying, flies when I pursue it,
Stands, and lies by me, doth what I have done;
His too familiar care doth make me rue it.
    No means I find to rid him from my breast,
    Till by the end of things it be suppressed.

Some gentler passion slide into my mind,
For I am soft, and made of melting snow;
Or be more cruel, Love, and so be kind.
Let me or [sic] float or sink, be high or low;
    Or let me live with some more sweet content,
    Or die, and so forget what love e'er meant.

[ELIZABETH'S OWN POEM ON THE DEPARTURE OF HER SUITOR FRANCIS, DUKE OF ANJOU, WRITTEN IN 1582 (BODLEIAN MS TANNER 76, FOL. 94R.), IN *Collected Works*, EDITED BY L.S. MARCUS, PP. 302–3]

1582

During January, Duke Francis of Anjou, who was still in England, was entertained with 'banqueting and diverse pleasant shows and pastimes'.[45] However, opposition to the marriage ran high in the court and council, and Elizabeth informed the duke that she was withdrawing from the match, closing the matter for good. Instead, she lent him a large sum of money for his campaign to help the Dutch rebels in the Low Countries. On 1 February he left for Antwerp, accompanied by some English noblemen and courtiers.

On 25 February, Pope Gregory XIII introduced a new calendar to bring dates into line with the seasons. It was to be introduced in stages over the next two years. As a result of the reformed Gregorian calendar, England's dates, retaining the Julian calendar, lagged ten days behind the New Style (ns) of Catholic Europe.

By March, the Rheims New Testament, the first instalment of the English Catholic translation of the Vulgate Bible (authorized at the Council of Trent), had been printed. In England, Elizabeth declared on 1 April that all Jesuits and seminary priests who came to the country would be 'taken for traitors',[46] a policy that would result, over the next six years, in the execution of over 60 priests (as well as 18 laymen and 2 laywomen for harbouring priests).

In June, Elizabeth sent an ambassador to the Lutheran King of Denmark to invest him with the Order of the Garter. It was hoped, wrongly, that Frederick II would be interested in joining a Protestant league against Spain. At Europe's southeastern edge, William Harborne became England's first resident ambassador in Constantinople, on 20 November. His function was to represent the commercial interests of the Turkey Company (formed the previous year) and his expenses were to be met by the company's merchants.

In London, on Christmas Eve, water from the Thames flowed for the first time via pipes of lead into various houses of the city, 'no doubt a great commodity to that part of the city, and would be far greater, if the said water were maintained to run continually, or at the least, at every tide some reasonable quantity, as at the first it did'.[47]

Improvements were put in place for the practice of medicine when in this year 'was first founded a public lecture in surgery' in the London college of physicians.[48]

RIGHT: **La volta** *was originally a peasant dance, which became popular at the French court in the second half of the 16th century. The dancers turned constantly and the man threw his partner into the air. Here, Elizabeth is shown dancing the volta with (it is thought) the Earl of Leicester, while courtiers look on. The musicians are playing a bass viol, treble viols and a 'sabeca', better known as a sackbut.*

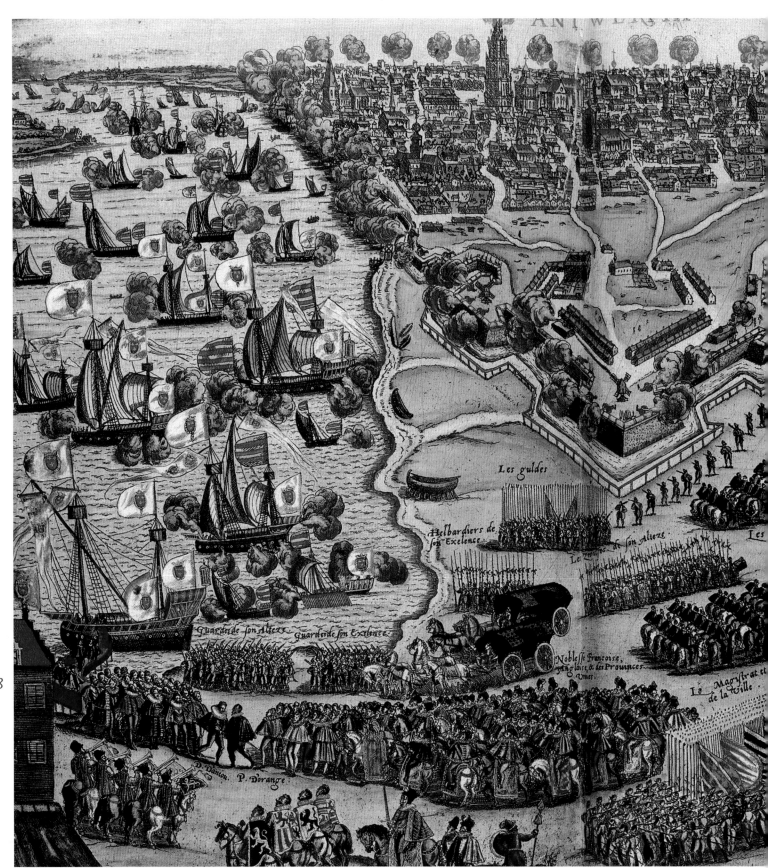

ANTWERPEN

Les guldes

Helbardiers de
son Exelence

Guarde de son Altezε   Guarde de son Exelence

Noblesse Francoise,
Angloise, & des Prouinces
Vnies.

Le Magistrat et
de la Ville

D. Daniou.   P. Dorange

338

1583

On Sunday 13 January, an accident occurred at one of the capital's entertainment venues, the bear-garden at Southwark. Some eight people were killed 'and many others sore hurt and bruised to the shortening of their lives'. For at least one commentator, the event was 'a friendly warning to such as more delight themselves in the cruelty of beasts than in the works of mercy' that were the proper activities for the Sabbath.[49]

In the Low Countries, Duke Francis of Anjou had enjoyed little success. On the contrary, he was soon quarrelling with his Dutch allies about his lack of authority and their reluctance to pay out the sums they had promised to maintain his army. Intending to seize the political initiative, he led his troops into Antwerp on 17 June (ns) to mount a coup. However, he met such effective resistance that well over a thousand of his men were killed and he was forced to flee the city. Five months later, he returned to France.

In April, Elizabeth tried to reach a settlement with Mary Queen of Scots that would allow Mary to return to Scotland. Discussions continued over the next two years – they would, though, end in failure, mainly because James VI objected to sharing power with his mother.

On 11 June, Sir Humphrey Gilbert set out with a fleet of five ships for Newfoundland. On 5 August, he landed in the harbour of St John's, which he claimed in the queen's name; but on his

LEFT: **Francis of Anjou left England** *in February 1582, after the marriage negotiations with Elizabeth came to nought, to assist in the Dutch fight against Spain. Elizabeth escorted him to Canterbury, and other members of her court (including the Earl of Leicester and Lord Hunsdon) accompanied him to Antwerp, where he was invested as Duke of Brabant, the title held by Philip II. This celebratory illustration is from the French account of his arrival,* La Joyeuse & Magnifique Entrée ... en sa très-renommée ville d'Anvers, *printed in Antwerp, 1582.*

way home, at about midnight on 9 September, he drowned in a storm.

A tailor and shoemaker were hanged at Bury St Edmunds, in July, for disseminating books written by Robert Browne, a 'separatist' preacher who did not recognize the authority of the established church. These works argued that local conventicles run by lay elders should supplant the national episcopalian church. The established church's primate, Archbishop Grindal, died at Croydon on 6 July, and 'was there honourably buried under a fair monument for him raised'.[50] His successor, John Whitgift, was moved to Canterbury and enthroned on 23 September.

In September, a mob deliberately set on fire the house of the astrologer John Dee at Mortlake. Dee had for many years advised the queen and England's seamen on scientific, navigational and astrological matters, though his interests had increasingly turned to 'angelic magic'. Fortunately, his great library survived the arson attack.

In the autumn, two Catholic attempts on the life of Elizabeth were thwarted. On 25 October, a certain John Somerville set out from Warwickshire to London, intending (as he later said) to shoot the queen, because he 'hoped to see her head on a pole, for that she was a serpent and a viper'.[51] At an inn on the way, he confessed his purpose to fellow guests and was arrested. Under interrogation, he implicated his Catholic parents-in-law, Edward and Mary Arden. Somerville was saved from the usual agonizing execution by committing suicide on 19 December in his cell at Newgate.[52] The next day, Edward Arden was hanged, drawn and quartered, but his widow was released.

ABOVE: **John Dee (1527–1609)** *was the most famous scholar, astrologer, mathematician and alchemist in Elizabethan England, and he is thought by some to be the model for Shakespeare's Prospero in* The Tempest. *At the beginning of the reign he was asked to draw up an astrological chart to determine the most propitious day for Elizabeth's coronation, and afterwards the queen and courtiers consulted him on a range of matters. He owned one of the greatest private libraries in England. During the 1570s, he became an advocate of empire and is credited with coining the term 'British empire'. The oil painting, from Oxford's Ashmolean Museum, is unattributed.*

'Somerville ... hoped to see her head on a pole, for that she was a serpent and a viper'

ABOVE: **Archbishop John Whitgift (1530/31?–1604)** was Elizabeth's last archbishop, from 1583, having formerly held the see of Worcester. Although he was a Calvinist and a church reformer, his priority was to impose discipline on the clergy, ensuring that they conformed to the Elizabethan Prayer Book. This triggered a new drive against puritans, which produced bitterness and division within the church. Yet, thanks to his sustained efforts, presbyterianism was driven underground and moderate puritanism was contained. The portrait is a contemporary one, but the artist is unknown.

New World 'savages'

A ship had arrived [in 1584] having discovered a country or island larger than England and never before visited by Christian people. The master or captain of the ship, named Ral [Sir Walter Ralegh], had brought with him two men of the island [Wanchese and Manteo, from Virginia] whom we asked permission to see. Their faces as well as their whole bodies were very similar to those of the white Moors at home, they wear no shirts, only a piece of fur to cover the pudenda and the skins of wild animals to cover their shoulders. Here they are clad in brown taffeta. Nobody could understand their language, and they had a very childish and wild appearance.

[LUPOLD VAN WEDEL, 'JOURNEY THROUGH ENGLAND AND SCOTLAND', IN *Transactions of the Royal Historical Society*, 1895, P. 251]

The second attempt on Elizabeth's life was far more dangerous. In November, Francis Throgmorton confessed under torture to an international plot to put Mary Queen of Scots on Elizabeth's throne, a plan which also involved Bernardino de Mendoza (the Spanish ambassador), French Catholics, English Catholic exiles and Spanish troops from the Low Countries. Throgmorton was executed the following July, and De Mendoza was ordered home in January. He was the last ambassador from Spain to reside in England during the reign.

On 11 November, the rebel 14th Earl of Desmond was killed by an Irishman, while 'secretly wandering without any succour as a miserable beggar'. [53] His head was sent to England and set upon London Bridge on 13 December.

1584

In April, Walter Ralegh kitted out two ships for a voyage of exploration to the New World. His captains returned in August, bringing with them 'two savage men'[54] and some products from the lands they had discovered.

Catholic–Protestant tensions again threatened the fragile stability of France, when Duke Francis of Anjou, brother to the king and heir presumptive, died in June. This left the Huguenot leader, Henry of Navarre, as the new heir presumptive, and French Catholics together with Philip II of Spain started making plans to resist his future accession.

A more immediate crisis concerned Elizabeth that summer: the Dutch Revolt seemed near to collapse. The rebel leader, William of Orange, was shot dead by a Catholic zealot on 10 July (ns); the Duke of Parma's troops took several towns in Flanders and Brabant; and Antwerp came under siege.

RIGHT: **John Foxe's 'Acts and Monuments'**, *also known as the Book of Martyrs, narrated the sufferings of the martyrs of the 'true church', including those burned under Queen Mary. The title-page of the 1583 edition depicts the Last Judgement, with Christ welcoming the saved (below him on his right) into heaven, and consigning the damned (including those celebrating the mass) on his left to hell. At the bottom are depictions of the true and false church: on the side of the damned is Roman Catholicism, with its idolatry and superstitions (rosary-praying and processions); on the other side is the Protestant Church, with godly men and women reading Bibles or listening to a sermon. Different editions were printed in 1563, 1570, 1576 and 1583, and in 1570 Convocation ordered copies to be placed in cathedrals. The book was also purchased for, or donated to, parish churches.*

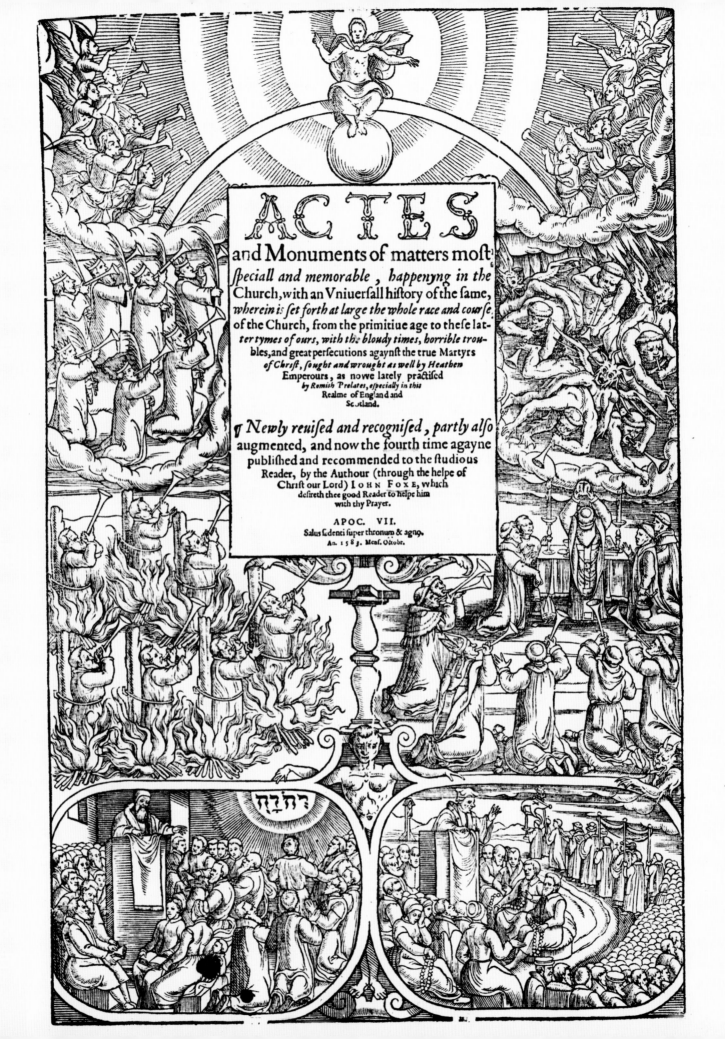

ACTES

and Monuments of matters most
speciall and memorable, happenyng in the
Church, with an Vniuersall history of the same,
wherein is set forth at large the whole race and course
of the Church, from the primitiue age to these latter tymes of ours, with the bloudy times, horrible troubles, and great persecutions agaynst the true Martyrs
of Christ, sought and wrought as well by Heathen
Emperours, as nowe lately practised
by Romish Prelates, especially in this
Realme of England and
Scotland.

¶ Newly reuised and recognised, partly also
augmented, and now the fourth time agayne
published and recommended to the studious
Reader, by the Authour (through the helpe of
Christ our Lord) IOHN FOXE, which
desireth thee good Reader to helpe him
with thy Prayer.

APOC. VII.
Salus sedenti super thronum & agno.
An. 1583. Mens. Octobr.

343

The opening of Parliament

... I believe the opening of Parliament took place on November 25 [1584]. All the streets and lanes in Westminster were well cleaned and strewn with sand when the queen made her entrance into the house, for it is a custom that on the first and last day of the session the king or queen shall be present in the assembly. At the head of the procession rode, two by two, eighteen lords and gentlemen of the court, after them fifteen trumpets, two gentlemen, each with 100 soldiers uniformly clad; now came fifteen members of Parliament in long red cloth coats, lined with white rabbit ... Now followed the queen in a half-covered sedan chair, which looked like a half-covered bed ... (she) had a long red velvet parliamentary mantle, down to the waist, lined with ermine, white with little black dots, and a crown on her head ... the queen dismounted [at Westminster Church], knelt down at the entrance and said her prayers ... Then the queen ... went to the house of Parliament close by ... [there] was a splendid canopy of golden stuff and velvet, embroidered with gold, silver and pearls, and below it a throne, arranged with all royal splendours, on which the queen seated herself.

[LUPOLD VAN WEDEL, 'JOURNEY THROUGH ENGLAND AND SCOTLAND', IN *Transactions of the Royal Historical Society*, 1895, PP. 260–1]

ABOVE: **The white potato** *was probably brought to England by Sir Francis Drake in 1586 from South America, possibly from the Spanish city of Columbia. This, the earliest painting of the potato, appeared in 1588, while the botanist John Gerard described a similar variety in his* Herbal, or General History of Plants *(1597). However, Gerard confused his plant with the red potato that was native to North America and mistakenly called it the 'Virginian potato'.*

As a result, Elizabeth contemplated giving military aid to the rebels, provided that they covered her expenses.

On 12 October, Elizabeth issued a proclamation against seditious books in reaction to the publication of a work defaming the Earl of Leicester. Popularly known as *Leicester's Commonwealth*, this pamphlet – written by English Catholic exiles – accused the earl of murdering his first wife and poisoning the husband of his second.

Alarmed by Catholic plots and militancy in England, the privy council drew up and distributed a Bond of Association in October 1584, which was intended to deter the supporters of Mary Queen of Scots from making another attempt on Elizabeth's life. The signatories of the bond pledged to hunt down and kill anyone who tried to murder Elizabeth or benefit from her murder.

A new parliamentary session began in November. On 14 December, some MPs introduced religious bills into the House of Commons, despite Elizabeth's prohibition of any debate about religion. One petitioned for the adoption of the Geneva Prayer Book and the establishment of a presbyterian system of discipline. Elizabeth had again to prohibit Parliament from discussing religion.

1585

On 6 January, Walter Ralegh received a knighthood, the first of several honours that year. During the first months of the year, he equipped seven ships for a voyage to plant an English colony – to be called Virginia – on the mainland of North America. Sir Richard Grenville was put in overall command of the ships, and Ralph Lane was chosen as the leader of the 300 or so colonists. They departed on 9 April, and among the company were the mathematician Thomas Harriot and the artist-cartographer John White. In August, Grenville left the colonists on Roanoke Island, where Lane laid out a fort and oversaw the construction of housing.

On 2 March, William Parry, an MP, was hanged, drawn and quartered for high treason after a co-conspirator denounced him for planning to assassinate the queen. At one time a client of Lord Burghley, Parry was possibly a double

Aspersions against Leicester

... his Lordship [Earl of Leicester] *hath a special fortune, that when he desires any woman's favour, then what person so ever stands in his way, hath the luck to die quickly for the finishing of his desire. As for example: when his Lordship was in full hope to marry Her Majesty and his own wife stood in his light ... she had the chance to fall from a pair of stairs, and so to break her neck but yet without hurting of her hood ... he fell in love with the Lady Sheffield ... and then also had he the same fortune to have her husband die quickly ... The like good chance had he in the death of my Lord of Essex [the 1st Earl] ... for when he was coming home from Ireland, with intent to revenge himself upon my Lord Leicester, for begetting his wife with child in his absence ... he died in the way of an extreme flux caused by an Italian recipe ...*

Neither must you marvel though all these died in diverse manners of outward diseases, for this is the excellency of the Italian art ... who can make a man die, in what manner or show of sickness you will ...

if it were known how many he hath dispatched or assaulted that way, it would be marvelous to the posterity.

['The copy of a letter, written by a Master of Art of Cambridge, to his friend in London ...' (1584), Early English Books Online edition, pp. 26–33]

Elizabeth receiving Dutch emissaries *in her privy chamber is an imagined scene, relating to the embassy from the Low Countries that negotiated the treaties of Nonsuch in August 1585. Mary Queen of Scots (who never met Elizabeth or visited the English court) is shown on the left, signifying her importance in international relations. The men standing include the Earl of Leicester, Lord Admiral Howard and Sir Francis Walsingham. The painting is from the Dutch school.*

346

Perceptions of a new found land

Since the first undertaking by Sir Walter Ralegh to deal in the action of discovering of that country which is now called and known by the name of Virginia; many voyages having been thither made at sundry times to his great charge ... There have been diverse and variable reports with some slanderous and shameful speeches bruited [publicized] abroad by many that returned from thence ...

Some also were of a nice bringing up, only in cities or towns, or such as never (as I may say) had seen the world before. Because there were not to be found any English cities, nor such fair houses, nor at their own wish any of their old accustomed dainty food, nor any soft beds of down or feathers: the country was to them miserable, and their reports thereof according ...

Seeing therefore the air there is so temperate and wholesome, the soil so fertile and yielding such commodities as I have before mentioned, the voyage also thither to and fro being sufficiently experimented ... And the dealing of Sir Water Ralegh so liberal in large giving and granting land there, as is already known, with many helps and furtherances else ... I hope there remain no cause whereby the action should be misliked.

[THOMAS HARIOT, *A Brief and True Report of the New Found Land of Virginia*, 1588, EDITED ONLINE BY MELISSA F. KENNEDY, PP. 5, 6, 32]

agent and *agent provocateur* rather than a traitor.

In the spring, Elizabeth learned that Philip II had signed a treaty of alliance with the French Catholic leaders, intending to help them resist the succession of Henry of Navarre. When Elizabeth and her councillors heard about this treaty, they wrongly assumed that its objective was to extinguish Protestantism from all of Europe, including England. Their fears of a Catholic crusade were intensified in May, when Philip seized English ships in Spanish ports.

The late Duke of Norfolk's son, the Catholic Philip Howard, 13th Earl of Arundel, was imprisoned in the Tower in April, having been charged with attempting to leave the country without licence. Another prisoner there, Henry Percy, 8th Earl of Northumberland, was found dead in his room on 21 June; he had been incarcerated since January 1584 on suspicion of involvement in Catholic plots. Northumberland had, it seemed, shot himself.

On 26 June, a delegation arrived from the (Dutch) rebels of the United Provinces seeking an alliance with Elizabeth and offering her sovereignty. Elizabeth declined the offer of sovereignty, but on 2 and 10 August, she signed treaties at Nonsuch Palace, promising the provinces open military aid. Elizabeth feared that the rebellion would be suppressed if reinforcements did not arrive from England, but she still hoped a political solution could be reached without recourse to an all-out Anglo-Spanish war. Meanwhile, on 15 August (ns), Antwerp fell to the Duke of Parma.

RIGHT: **Roanoke colony** *was first established in 1585, but the settlers quickly became demoralized and returned home. In 1587, a second group of colonists – 115 men, women and children – went out, but after a few months they too ran into difficulties. Consequently their governor, John White, departed for England to bring back supplies. However, because of the war with Spain, he was unable to return to Roanoke until 1590, when no trace of the English colony could be found. White made some 70 watercolours of the animals and Algonquians who lived in the area; here he has painted an Algonquian man and a woman eating what looks like hulled corn. White's images circulated widely as engravings in the first volume of Theodor de Bry's* America, *published in 1590.*

During the summer, the Catholic League in France led by Henry Duke of Guise pressured King Henry III into signing the Treaty of Nemours, which revoked toleration of Huguenots. The result was renewed violence, in the 'War of the Three Henries'.

On 14 September, Sir Francis Drake set out with about two dozen ships and eight pinnaces for Spain. His instructions were to free the English ships sequestered there, to attack Spanish shipping and to raid the towns of the West Indies.

During the late autumn Elizabeth agreed that the Earl of Leicester could take command of a 7000-strong English army to be sent to the United Provinces. He arrived, in December, at Flushing in Zeeland, where his nephew, the poet Sir Philip Sidney, was already based as the town's governor.

1586

In January, the Earl of Leicester ignored Elizabeth's instructions and accepted the title and office of governor-general, which granted him supreme political and military authority in the United Provinces. Elizabeth was furious, not least because the title implied she accepted sovereignty over the United Provinces. In a tough letter, she rebuked the earl for treating her wishes with such contempt.

In early February, Archbishop Whitgift and the lords Buckhurst and Cobham were admitted to the privy council. Whitgift was the only cleric to be appointed as a councillor during Elizabeth's reign.

An Anglo-Scottish defensive alliance was signed at Berwick on 6 July. Elizabeth secretly agreed to give the Protestant James VI an annual pension of £4000, and in return she expected his friendship.

On 28 July, Sir Francis Drake returned from his raids in the West Indies. On his way home, he had picked up demoralized colonists based at Roanoke.

Between May and July, Mary Queen of Scots entered into correspondence with the Catholic conspirator Anthony Babington. Her letters – intercepted and deciphered by Sir Francis Walsingham's code-breaker Thomas Phelippes – approved an invasion plan and assassination plot against Elizabeth. In August, Babington was arrested, and Mary's quarters were searched.

On the morning of 22 September, English forces supporting the Dutch rebels attacked a Spanish army that was trying to relieve Zutphen in

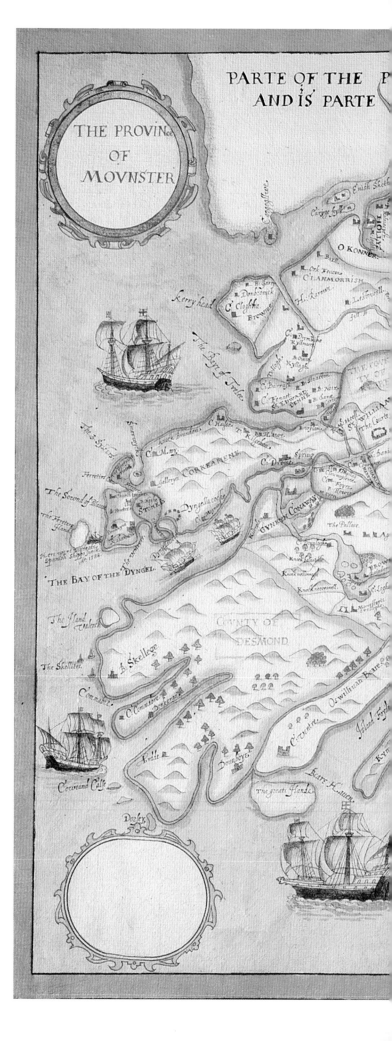

RIGHT: **The Munster Plantation** took place after the Desmond Rebellion (1579–83) had been suppressed. To prevent a repetition, the Earl of Desmond's lands were confiscated and parcelled out for plantation by English people, who were expected to keep order and 'civilize' the Irish. The territory was divided into 'seignories' that were granted to an 'undertaker' who would bring over 91 families to settle on their land. The names of the undertakers are on this map. Most of the new settlers came from the west of England. Although the plantation was swept away in the 1598 rebellion, it was subsequently re-established.

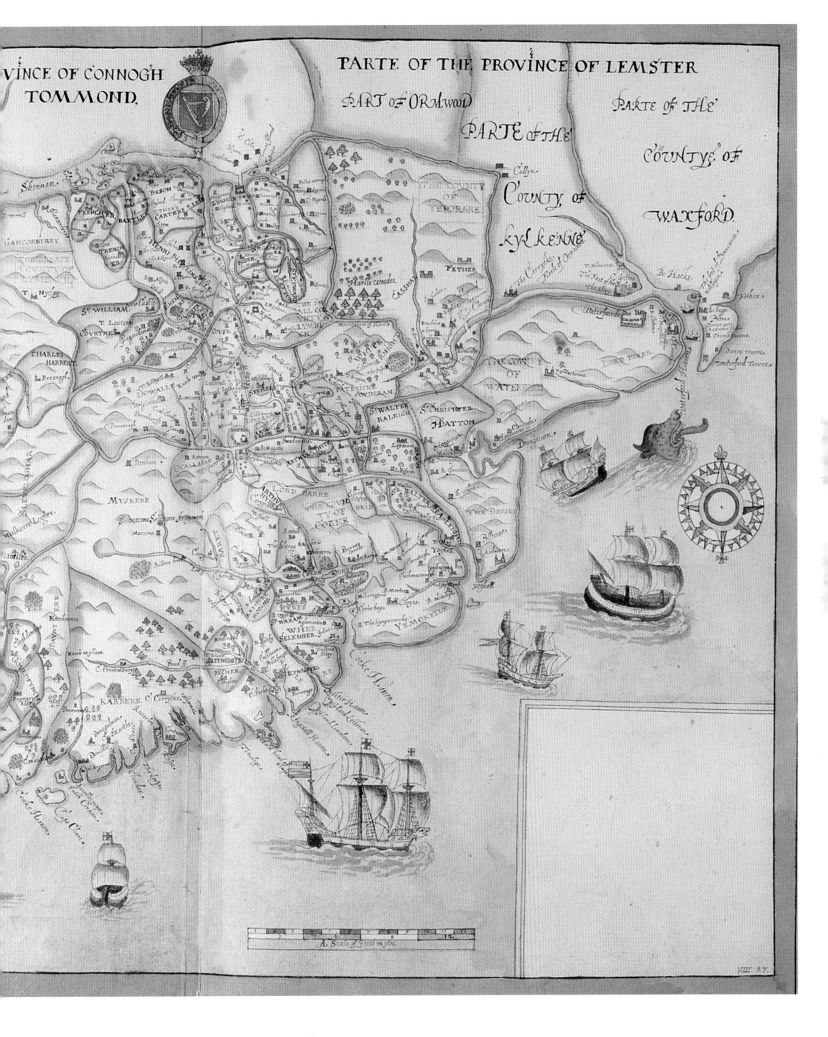

CIVITAS CARTHAGENA in India occidentalis continente sita, portu commodissimo, ad mercaturam inter Hispaniam et Peru exercendam

CARTAGENA

Drake's West Indies raid *of January 1586 was depicted in five engravings by Baptista Boazio, an Italian cartographer (fl. 1588–1606), which accompanied* A Summarie and True Discourse of Sir Francis Drake's West Indian Voyage, *published in London in 1588–9. They show Drake's reception by the California Indians and his capture of Santiago, Santo Domingo, Cartagena and St Augustine. Each of Boazio's plans gives a bird's-eye view of the city and the surrounding country (and coast), showing Drake's attacks in progressive stages. In January 1586, Drake occupied Santo Domingo on Hispaniola (present-day Haiti and Dominican Republic), and in February he attacked Cartagena on the northern coast of South America, taking it within an hour. Here, Drake's ship can be seen approaching Cartagena. A flying fish is shown in the sea just ahead of the English ship, while the creature in the box is probably an iguana.*

the province of Gelderland. Sir Philip Sidney had his horse killed under him and afterwards was hit by a musket shot. Because he was not wearing thigh armour, he was seriously wounded and on 17 October he died from gangrene poisoning.

On 30 September, William Davison entered the privy council as a principal secretary to aid Walsingham. Soon afterwards, Walsingham retired from court, suffering from physical and mental exhaustion partly arising from the death of his son-in-law, Sidney.

Under pressure from her privy council, Elizabeth reluctantly agreed to put Mary on trial at Fotheringhay Castle for plotting her assassination. The judges arrived on 11 October and the judicial proceedings began on the 14th. Although Mary did not recognize the legality of the court, she appeared before the commissioners to declare her innocence. After two days, Elizabeth prorogued the hearing. It reconvened ten days later, on the 25th, in the Star Chamber at Westminster, where Mary was found guilty and sentenced to death in her absence. On 12 and 24 November, Parliament, which had opened on 29 October, petitioned for Mary's execution, but Elizabeth avoided giving her assent. Nonetheless, on 4 December Elizabeth issued a proclamation publicizing the verdict, and two days later Lord Burghley drafted the death warrant.

This year Elizabeth 'took order for the peopling and inhabiting of the countries lately belonging to the Earl of Desmond and his rebellious companions'.[55] Hence began the Munster Plantation.

354

1587

A further setback to the English campaign in the Low Countries occurred in mid-January, when Sir William Stanley, the Governor of Deventer, handed the garrison town over to the Spaniards, and Rowland York did the same with the fort of Zutphen.

After weeks of indecision, Elizabeth finally signed Mary's death warrant on 1 February, and handed it over to her secretary, William Davison, to hold in reserve. She subsequently told him to leave it unsealed. However, he immediately handed the document over to Burghley, who had it sealed and dispatched to Fotheringhay. A week later, on the 8th, Mary was executed. Dressed in crimson (the colour of martyrdom), wearing an *Agnus Dei* around her neck and a rosary attached to her girdle, holding a crucifix, and repeating prayers in Latin, Mary presented herself to the 300 or so spectators as a Catholic martyr. When Elizabeth learned of the execution, she attempted to distance herself from the act. She demonstrated her displeasure by sending Davison to the Tower and by banishing Burghley from her presence for several months.

On 16 February, Sir Philip Sidney's funeral took place in London. Some 700 mourners processed from the Minories, a location near the Tower, to St Paul's Cathedral, where he was buried.

LEFT: **This glass goblet** *was one of those manufactured in the glasshouse of the Venetian Jacob Verzellini at Crutched Friars in London. It is dated to 1586. Verzellini, an innovator, had obtained his patent for decorative glassware over ten years earlier.*

The end of the Scottish queen

Her [Mary Queen of Scots'] prayers being ended, the executioners, kneeling, desired Her Grace to forgive them her death: who answered, 'I forgive you with all my heart, for now, I hope, you shall make an end of all my troubles.' ... Then she, being stripped of all her apparel saving her petticoat and kirtle, her two women beholding her made great lamentation ... Then lying upon the block most quietly, and stretching out her arms cried, 'In manus tuas, Domine', etc., three or four times ... she endured two strokes of the other executioner with an axe, she making very small noise or none at all ... and so the executioner cut off her head, saving one little gristle, which being cut asunder, he lifted up her head to the view of all the assembly and bade 'God save the Queen.' Then, her dress of lawn falling from off her head, it appeared as grey as one of threescore and ten years old ... her face in a moment being so much altered from the form she had when she was alive, as few could remember her by her dead face. Her lips stirred up and down a quarter of an hour after her head was cut off.

['ROBERT WYNKEFIELD' (SIR ROBERT WINGFIELD OF UPTON) WRITING TO LORD BURGHLEY, 11 FEBRUARY 1587, REPRINTED IN *The Execution of Mary Queen of Scots; An Eye-witness Account*, EDITED BY A. MCLEAN]

Elizabeth R.

Elizabeth by the grace of god Quene of England, Fraunce and Ireland &c. To
our right trustie and welbeloved Cousins George Erle of Shrewsbury Erle
marshall Erle of Kent ... Erle of ... George
Erle of Cumberland, Henrie Erle of Pembrooke, greeting: Whereas by the
the statute made by the w[hol]e assent of o[u]r Counsell, Nobilitie, and Judges, against the
Quene of Scottes by the name of Marie the daughter and heire of James the
fifte late kinge of Scotte comonlie called the Quene of Scotte and Dowager
of Fraunce, as to yo[u] is well knowen: All the States in o[u]r late parliament assembled
did not onelie deliberatelie w[i]th great advise allowe and approve the same
statute as iust and honorable, but did also note all ... and circumstes
possible, as sondrie times requisite, solicited, and pressed to procede to the
publishinge of the same, and thereupon to direct further execution against
the person as they did adiudge her to have duelie deserved addinge ther[e] that
the forbearinge thereof was and would be dailie a ... and undoubtedlie danger
not onelie to o[u]r owne life, but to their selves, their posteritie, and the publike
state of this realme, a perill for the ... of the ... and the true religion
of Christ, as to the person of the no[ble] realme: We therupon nevertheless
the same was not ... delay not time publish the same sentence by our
proclamation, and yet ... have forborne to give direction, for the further sa-
tisfaction of the ... most earnest request made by the said Estate of o[u]r
parliament, whereby ... publishinge by all sortes of o[u]r loyinge subiectes
both of o[u]r Nobilitie and Com[m]ons and also of the ... the ... and both
devoted of all other o[u]r subiectes of inferior degree, ... consider[ed]
from the bottome of their hartes they were greived and afflicted w[i]th dailie ...
and greivous feares of o[u]r life and therby constituted w[i]th a dreadfull doubt and
... of the ... of the ... and happie estate of this realme,
if we shall forbeare the further finall execution as it is desired, and ...
their ... and ... requestes, prayers, councells and advises. And
therupon, returne to o[u]r owne naturall disposition, in suche a ca[se] ...
to ... the ... ... of their Com[m]ons and their ... ...
... ... importune suit ... necessitie, as appeareth directlie tendinge to
the ... not onelie of o[u]r self, but also of the no[ble] of o[u]r realme: Now
have considered to suffer iustice to take place: And for the ... thereof
... the speciall trust experience and confidence we ... have in yo[u]r loyalties
faithfullnes and love ... towardes o[u]r person and the safetie thereof, and also
to o[u]r nation Commons thereof y[ou] are most noble and principall members:
We doe will and by warrant hereof doe direct and authorize y[ou] o[u]r said ...
as y[ou] shall have time ... to repaire to o[u]r castle of ... wherin our
... the said Quene of Scotte is in custodie of o[u]r right trustie servaunt and
Councellor S[i]r Amyas Poulet knight, and there takinge her into yo[u]r charge
to cause by yo[u]r com[m]andment execution to be don upon her person in the presence
of yo[u]r selves and the said S[i]r Amyas Poulet and of suche other officers of

356

On 27 February, Anthony Cope presented a 'bill and book' to the House of Commons. The bill was for the reformation of religion, and the book was a book of discipline produced by the presbyterian Walter Travers. Elizabeth had both bill and book seized, and on 2 March Cope and other MPs of a puritan disposition were imprisoned in the Tower.

Sir Francis Drake left Plymouth on 2 April, for another attack on Spanish shipping. On this voyage, he plundered and burned more than two dozen vessels anchored at Cadiz before sailing on to the Azores, where he captured Philip II's carrack the *San Felipe*, with its rich cargo of china, silks, velvet, a small quantity of jewels and some black slaves. Drake returned home in June and later described the raid on Cadiz as the 'singeing of the king of Spain's beard'.[56] This action was a setback for Philip's plans to invade England.

On 24 April, Sir Christopher Hatton was appointed the new lord chancellor, replacing Sir Thomas Bromley who had died earlier that month. Although he had no formal legal training, Hatton had acquired ten years of legal experience sitting in Star Chamber. He was also a trusted councillor, an able administrator and a loyal defender of the Elizabethan Church.

On 18 June, the Earl of Leicester surrendered his position of master of the horse to his stepson, Robert Devereux, the 2nd Earl of Essex, who was his political protégé now that his nephew, Sidney, was dead. A week later, Leicester returned to the Low Countries, but ill health forced his resignation in December. As a reward for his service, the queen appointed him lord steward of the household.

'The queen's majesty, having diverse ways understood the great and diligent preparation of the King of Spain'[57] to build an armada, commissioned Lord Admiral Charles Howard of Effingham on 21 December to organize and command the English naval forces. Drake was to be his second-in-command.

> '*Sir Francis Drake left Plymouth on 2 April, for another attack on Spanish shipping*'

LEFT: **The execution warrant for Mary Queen of Scots** *was destroyed, and this copy is the only contemporary one known to survive. (In 2007 it joined other documents relating to Mary at Lambeth Palace.) Elizabeth gave the original to the principal secretary, William Davison, on 1 February 1587, but the next day she told him – too late – not to have it sealed. At a council meeting held in Lord Burghley's house on 3 February, the privy councillors agreed to send the sealed warrant to Fotheringhay without telling the queen. After she learned of this deception, Elizabeth banished Burghley from her presence for four months. As for Davison, he was suspended from office and tried in Star Chamber, but he was released from the Tower in 1588, probably never paid his fine, and kept his office.*

The execution of Mary Queen of Scots *took place on 8 February 1587. Mary is shown in this Dutch watercolour (c.1613), from the Scottish National Portrait Gallery, holding a crucifix on the block. Her two attendants are Jane Kennedy and Elizabeth Curle; the two seated men are the earls of Kent and Shrewsbury, and the man standing pointing to Mary is the Dean of Peterborough. Outside, Mary's garments are burned to prevent their use as relics.*

coninginne van schotlant

'Let tyrants fear'

My loving people, *I [Elizabeth] have been persuaded by some that are careful of my safety to take heed how I committed myself to armed multitudes, for fear of treachery. But I tell you that I would not desire to live to distrust my faithful and loving people. Let tyrants fear: I have so behaved myself that under God I have placed my chiefest strength and safeguard in the loyal hearts and goodwill of my subjects. Wherefore I am come among you at this time but for my recreation and pleasure, being resolved in the midst and heat of the battle to live and die amongst you all, to lay down for my God and for my kingdom and for my people mine honour and my blood even in the dust. I know I have the body but of a weak and feeble woman, but I have the heart and stomach of a king, and of a king of England too, and take foul scorn that Parma or any prince of Europe should dare to invade the borders of my realm ... I myself will be your general, judge and rewarder of your virtue in the field.*

[ELIZABETH, ADDRESSING HER SOLDIERS GATHERED AT TILBURY, 1588 (BL MS HARLEY 6798, ART. 18, FOL. 87), IN *Collected Works*, EDITED BY L.S. MARCUS, PP. 325–6]

1588

During the first months of this year, great preparations were made by land and sea to withstand the expected Spanish invasion attempt. On 19 July, the Spanish Armada, under the command of the Duke of Medina Sidonia, was first sighted off the Lizard, in Cornwall, heading towards Plymouth, where the English fleet, commanded by Howard and Drake, was assembled. Strong winds and currents prevented Howard from immediately sailing out and intercepting the enemy. The Armada therefore continued on its way towards the English Channel, where Medina Sidonia was supposed to rendezvous with the Duke of Parma. The plan was for the Armada to protect Parma's invasion army travelling in barges from Dunkirk to the English coast.

The English commanders were able to leave the ports by hauling their ships by ropes from the land out to sea against the heavy wind and currents. They then tracked the Armada towards the Channel. Small-scale encounters took place off Portland Bill on 23 July and the Isle of Wight on 25 July, but the Armada continued its voyage in a defensive crescent formation, until it anchored off Calais on 27 July to await the arrival of Parma's barges. The next day, Howard sent some eight fire-ships in among the Armada, forcing the Spanish captains to cut their cables and sail away in disorder, unable to meet up with Parma.

On 29 July, the Spanish and English fleets met in 'a vehement conflict' off Gravelines.[58] During the eight-hour battle, the English navy sank about three ships and drove others ashore. The remainder of the Armada was dispersed northwards and, propelled by the winds, was forced to sail home via Scotland and the west of Ireland. Howard initially gave chase but turned back because of a lack of ammunition for the cannons.

RIGHT: **Charles Howard (1536–1624), 2nd Baron Howard of Effingham,** *was Elizabeth's cousin and married to one of her intimates (another cousin), Katherine Carey. Because of this close relationship, Howard was appointed lord high admiral in January 1585 despite his lack of experience at sea. With Drake as his second-in-command, he led the navy that defeated the 1588 Armada. After the victory he showed an unusual compassion towards the sailors and used his own resources to pay for their welfare. He was created Earl of Nottingham in 1597.*

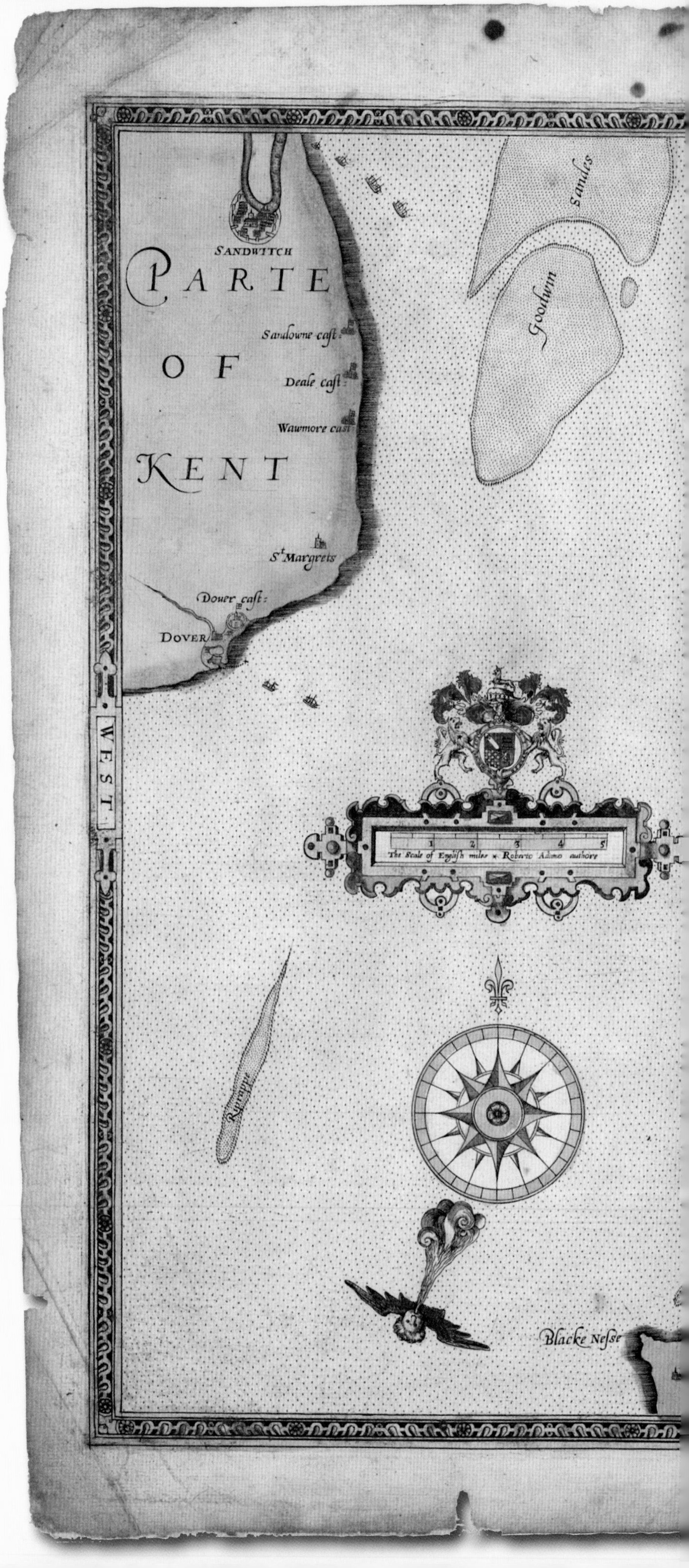

The Spanish Armada – *a fleet of 130 ships*
362 *carrying over 18,000 men – was dispersed in the*
Channel by English fire-ships. In the Battle of
Gravelines on 29 July 1588, a small number of
Spanish ships was lost, and the winds forced the
remainder to sail north around Scotland and the
west of Ireland on their way home. Storms
wrecked or damaged about 35 of the vessels, and
perhaps as many as 15,000 men from the original
Armada died. This chart is Number 10 of 11 made
by Robert Adams about the Armada. They were
engraved by Augustine Ryther and published in
1590, dedicated to Lord Admiral Howard.

NORTH

The Spanishe fleete

SEMPER EADEM

The Englishe fleete

EAST

PARTE

GRAVELING

OF

FLANDERS

Oye

CALAIS

Herring hilles

Scales cleeues

PARTE

OF PICARDIE

SOVTH

10

223.2/50

On 8 August, Elizabeth visited her soldiers encamped at Tilbury under the command of the Earl of Leicester: 'she passed through every rank of them to their great comfort and rejoicing'.[59] The next morning, she returned to the camp before leaving for St James's and delivered a stirring oration before her assembled troops.

Less than a month later, on 4 September, the Earl of Leicester died in Oxfordshire and was buried in Warwick. The queen was grief-stricken at the death of her long-time friend and she kept the last letter he wrote to her in a special place.

On 8 September, eight Spanish ensigns captured by the English were displayed at St Paul's. 'The same banners were on the next morrow hanged on London bridge ... for all beholders to their great rejoicing.'[60] On Sunday 24 November, Elizabeth and her court attended a service of thanksgiving at St Paul's. The queen arrived 'in a chariot throne made with four pillars behind to have a canopy on the top whereof was made a crown imperial and two lower pillars before whereon stood a lion and a dragon' holding the arms of England.[61]

An Armada battle report

... God hath given us so good a day in forcing the enemy so far to leeward, as I hope in God the Prince of Parma and the Duke of Sidonia shall not shake hands this few days. And upon so ever they shall meet I believe neither of them will greatly rejoice of this day's service. The town of Calais has some supplies thereof whose mayor Her Majesty is beholding unto ... God bless Her Majesty our gracious sovereign and give us all grace and love in his favour. I assure Your Honour this day's service ... no doubt has encouraged our army.

From aboard Her Majesty's good ship The Rob ... 29 July 1588

Your lordship most solely to be commanded, Francis Drake

[SIR FRANCIS DRAKE WRITING TO SIR FRANCIS WALSINGHAM, 29 JULY 1588, FROM THE NATIONAL ARCHIVES DOCUMENT SP 12/213 NO. 65]

In October and November, a small group of puritans began the publication of a series of seven scurrilous pamphlets against the bishops, under the pseudonym of Martin Marprelate. The so-called 'Marprelate Tracts', written in a colloquial style, brought the case for a presbyterian church – one that rejected the hierarchy of bishops – to a popular audience.

Throughout the year, a power struggle took place in France between King Henry III and the Catholic League, led by Henry Duke of Guise and his brother Cardinal Louis of Guise. In May, the king had been driven out of Paris, and in July he had been coerced into signing an edict asserting his commitment to the eradication of Protestantism and redirecting the succession to Charles Cardinal of Bourbon. Fearing that the Guises were plotting his murder, King Henry arranged for his elite guard to assassinate the duke on 12 December (23 December, ns) and then his brother on the following day.

LEFT: **Elizabeth's Tilbury speech** delivered on 9 August 1588 was not published until the mid-17th century, nor is there any contemporary record of it. A lengthy paraphrase of the speech, however, appears at the bottom of this painted panel, which was produced after the 1605 Gunpowder Plot. The oil panel – from St Faith's Church in Gaywood, Norfolk – shows Elizabeth addressing her troops at Tilbury, while the Armada burns in the background.

1589

In January, the bishops produced a collaborative work answering the charges made against them in the Marprelate Tracts. On 9 February, Richard Bancroft, a canon of Westminster, delivered a sermon at Paul's Cross denouncing the presbyterian message of the tracts. Later in the year, he spearheaded a successful drive to discover and destroy the secret presses that had produced them.

During the parliamentary session of February, MPs launched an attack on purveyance, the crown's right to compulsorily purchase provisions for its household. Tempers cooled only when Elizabeth promised reform.

Also during February, a number of soldiers were punished 'for abusing their captains' in the Low Countries: 'some were set on the pillory with their ears nailed, some their ears pierced with an hole, some hanged on trees'.[62]

On 23 February, Elizabeth ordered Sir Francis Drake and Sir John Norris to destroy Spanish warships at Santander, on the Spanish Atlantic coast, and then to capture the Azores treasure fleet. The two men, however, preferred to make for Lisbon and raise Portugal in rebellion against Philip II. On 18 April, they set out with over 20,000 men towards the Iberian Peninsula. Landing at La Coruña on 24 April, they took and looted the deserted harbour, but then wasted nearly a fortnight failing to take the well-fortified upper town. On 9 May, they sailed on to Peniche, a town 45 miles north of Lisbon, where they forced the Spanish garrison to withdraw. Encouraged by this success, Norris decided to march his depleted army to Lisbon, while Drake headed there by sea. The march in the summer heat took six days. On 26 May, Norris's army – now small and exhausted – arrived at the strongly fortified city, but it lacked the artillery to breach its walls. On 8 June, he and Drake finally left Portugal to carry out the queen's instructions in the Azores, but the winds proved unfavourable. Unable to embark on a privateering raid, they returned home empty-handed. Between 4000 and 11,000 men died on this fruitless mission, most of them from disease.

In France, King Henry III was murdered in revenge for the assassinations of the Guise brothers the previous December. On 1 August (ns), the Dominican friar Jacques Clément stabbed him to death. This action left the Protestant Henry of Navarre as the legitimate King of France, and he would need to fight the French Catholic forces, and possibly their Spanish allies, to make that title a reality. He therefore requested military aid from Elizabeth. She agreed to send 4000 men to fight alongside him for a limited period, and on 29 September Peregrine Bertie, 13th Baron Willoughby, arrived at Dieppe to join Henry in a short but successful campaign.

366

RIGHT: **Sir Francis Drake (1540–96)** *was the hero of the naval war against Spain until the disastrous Portuguese expedition of 1589. After this fiasco, he spent most of his time at his home at Buckland in Devon, until he devised the equally unsuccessful 1595 Panama expedition, on which he met his death. Despite these later failures, he remains in most people's minds one of the iconic figures of the Elizabethan era.*

OVERLEAF: **The assassination of Henry III of France** *was carried out by the Dominican monk Jacques Clément in 1589. Though a Catholic himself, Henry had ordered the murders of the leaders of the Catholic League in the previous year. This engraving, made shortly after the regicide, portrays Clément receiving the pope's blessing for his plan, carrying it out and suffering the consequences.*

SIC PARVIS MAGNA

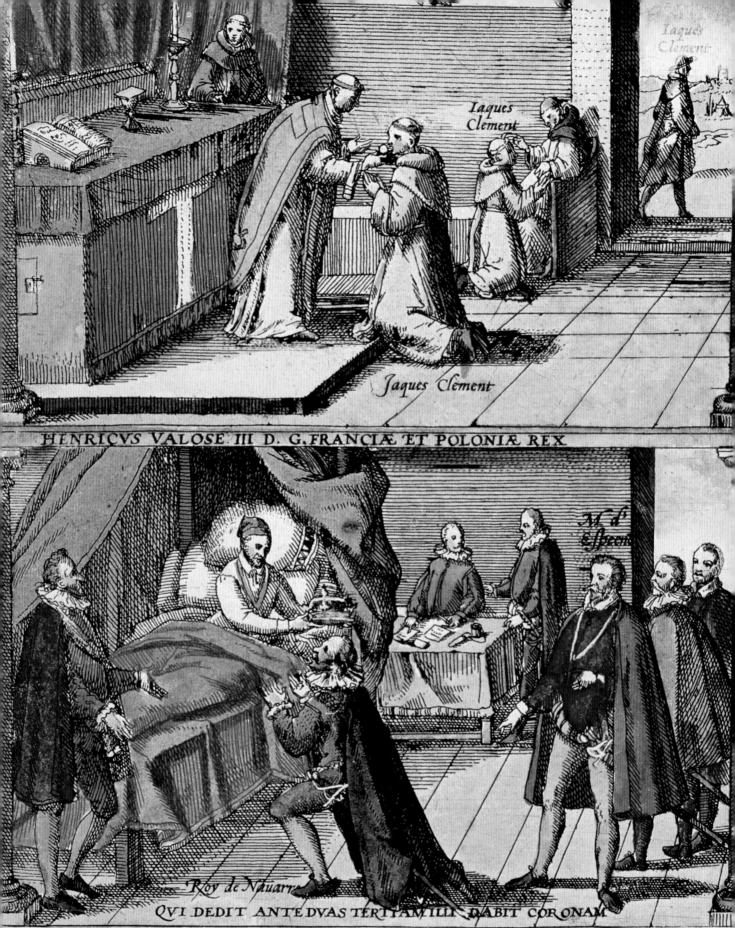

Jaques Clement

Iaques Clement

Iaques Clement

HENRICVS VALOSE III D. G. FRANCIÆ ET POLONIÆ REX

M d'
Espern

Roy de Nauarre

QVI DEDIT ANTE DVAS TERTIAM ILLI DABIT CORONAM

König Heinrich der dritt des namen
Zu S. Clou sein leben endt on stämen
Ein Jacobiner mönch in sticht
Mit vergistem meßer zugericht

Iacob Clement von Sens geboren
Den ersten Augst im 89 Jare
Die Gwardi in erschlug zuhandt
Ward nacher gevierttheilt vnd verbrant

Jaques
Clement

Roy de Fran.
ce

Jaques Clemet

Des andern tags der König starb
Heinrich Bourbon die Kron erwarb
Als nechster Erb dem Gott verleyh
Sein gnad gluck heil vnd frid darbey

Au tems que selon le vieil droiet
de L'Eglise, lon celebroit
Le jour de S. Pierre aux liens
Vn moine natif de sens
qui le noir caperon portoit
vn gentil homme à mort mettoit
qui Couronne et sceptre portoit.

1590

In January, Lord Willoughby left France. Henry IV was now doing well against the French Catholics. On 14 March (ns), he won a great victory at Ivry, in Normandy, and advanced to besiege Paris. Philip II could not allow the city to fall, however, and ordered the Duke of Parma to leave the Low Countries and lift the siege, which he did.

At home Archbishop Whitgift and Richard Bancroft rounded up scores of presbyterians and brought them before the Court of High Commission during the year. Among them was Thomas Cartwright, who was arrested in October. This activity against fellow Protestants greatly displeased Lord Burghley and some other councillors, not least because of the High Commission's use of the 'ex officio oath'. They argued that this oath contravened principles of England's common law, because it required the accused to answer all questions on oath even if the answers were incriminating. Nonconforming puritans and presbyterians usually refused to take the oath; as a result they were imprisoned for that offence.

This year saw the deaths of the Earl of Warwick and Sir Francis Walsingham, who had both sought to protect puritans.

ABOVE: **The victory of Henry IV** *over his Catholic rivals at Ivry in March 1590 was viewed with great interest and enthusiasm in London. It was celebrated in ballads, ditties and newsletters as 'the most notable victory that of late was heard of'. This etching of the fighting is by Giuliano Giralda, and dated to 1610.*

1591

Now that the Duke of Parma was assisting the French Catholic cause, Elizabeth agreed to augment her aid to Henry IV. In April, Sir John Norris was sent to Brittany, and in July the Earl of Essex took several thousand men into Normandy.

Fearing that archery, 'whereby our nation in times past hath gotten so great honour', was falling into disuse, Elizabeth issued instructions on 6 June that games – such as dicing, bowls and cards – should 'be forthwith forbidden' and that instead 'archery may be revived and practised'.[63]

In May, Thomas Cartwright's case was transferred from the Court of High Commission to the Star Chamber, where the presbyterian was charged with sedition. The trial incensed William Hacket, a self-styled prophet, and his two followers Edmund Coppinger and Henry Arthington. They planned a political coup that would result in Cartwright's release and the establishment of a presbyterian church. Early in the morning of 19 July, Coppinger and Arthington mounted a cart in Cheapside and announced to bystanders that Hacket was the Messiah. All three were arrested. Hacket was executed for uttering treasonous words and defacing a picture of the queen; Coppinger died in prison after a week's hunger strike; Arthington recanted and was freed.

On 2 August, Lord Burghley's younger son – the recently knighted Sir Robert Cecil – was sworn a privy councillor. Over the next few years, he helped his father carry out the secretarial duties.

During her summer progress in Sussex, Elizabeth spent a week in August at Cowdray, the home of the Catholic Anthony Browne, 2nd Viscount Montague, and stayed several days in September at Elvetham, the residence of the formerly disgraced Earl of Hertford. Both noblemen put on a great show for the queen.

A Protestant victory

Triumph good Christians and rejoice,
This wondrous news now hear:
Wherein the power of mighty Jove,
So greatly doth appear.
God is the stay and strength of those
That in him puts his trust:
And what he ever promised them,
He keepeth firm and just.

> *Let canons roar and muskets shoot,*
> *Let fife and ensigns play:*
> *Let trumpets shrill and dubbing drums,*
> *Sound forth this joyful day …*

The Duke de Maine [Mayenne] for all his power,
Was forced from field to flee:
His heels were better than his hands,
He fought so valiantly.
His power was stricken with such fear,
That they did fly in haste:
Whereby the king did win the field,
His enemies were disgraced.

> *Let canons roar and muskets shoot [etc.]*

[FROM THE ENGLISH PROTESTANT BROADSIDE 'An excellent ditty made upon the great victory [Battle of Ivry], which the French king obtained against the Duke de Maine, and the Romish rebels in his kingdom, upon Ash Wednesday being the fourth day of March last past, 1590, to the tune of the new Tantara']

At sea, the queen's ship the *Revenge* was lost to the enemy on 31 August, in an encounter with Spanish galleons off the Azores. Lord Thomas Howard, the admiral of a fleet of about 16 ships, had retreated to avoid an engagement with a far superior force; but Sir Richard Grenville in the *Revenge* refused to give way and attempted to pass through the Spanish line. When the Spaniards made to board his ship, Grenville and his men resisted heroically but to no purpose: the ship was captured, and Grenville died at sea on 2 September, as did most of the 250-strong English crew.

There was also military disappointment in France. In November, English troops under the Earl of Essex joined Henry IV in the siege of Rouen. The campaign, though, was a costly failure, as the Duke of Parma relieved the city the following April. However, there was better news in the Low Countries, where, during this year, English troops performed well under their commander, Sir Francis Vere, helping the Dutch rebels recapture Zutphen, Deventer and Nijmegen.

On 20 November, Lord Chancellor Hatton died. During his last illness, Elizabeth had visited him at his home in Ely Place, Holborn. More than 300 people attended his funeral at St Paul's on 16 December.

ABOVE: **Elizabeth's visit to Elvetham** *took place between 20 and 23 September. Her host, the Earl of Hertford, had converted his small estate into a backdrop for elaborate entertainments by creating a crescent-shaped pond in a natural setting. In this engraving, Elizabeth, seated under a canopy of state on the left, is watching an elaborate sea battle, featuring Nereus, the Virgin Neaerea, Triton and five satyrs, all meant to evoke the* successful Armada campaign. The picture is *from* The Honourable Entertainement Given to the Queen's Majesty in Progress at Elvetham in Hampshire, by the Right Honourable the Earl of Hertford, *published in 1591.*

ABOVE: **'Orlando Furioso in English Heroical Verse'** *by Ludovico Ariosto (1474–1533) was translated from the Italian by Elizabeth's godson John Harington (1561–1612) and printed in 1591. The engraved frontispeice contains a portrait of Harington and his dog. It is thought that Shakespeare borrowed from the work for parts of* Much Ado about Nothing *and* The Tempest. *Harington is also known for producing the earliest designs for a water-closet, which appeared in his* Metamorphosis of Ajax *(1596).*

1592

Early in the year, on 7 January, Elizabeth granted a 12-year monopoly of trade with the Venetian and the Ottoman dominions to the newly formed Levant Company, an amalgamation of the Venice and Turkey companies. Also in January, Elizabeth founded a college in Dublin, later named Trinity College.

On 14 January, the Earl of Essex returned to court after leading the English expeditionary force in Normandy. Elizabeth had been critical of his service in France as he had disobeyed her instructions and failed to win military success. He had to wait another year before his admission into the privy council.

In March, Thomas Cartwright and the other puritan prisoners were released from prison under strict conditions. By this time Cartwright, effectively now under house arrest, was a broken man.

On 12 June, apprentices and 'masterless men' caused a riot in Southwark. Fearing that further disturbances would occur around Midsummer, the council imposed a curfew on apprentices and closed the London playhouses 'that draw together the baser sort of people' until 29 September.[64]

In June also, Sir Walter Ralegh was cast into the Tower, after it was revealed that Elizabeth Throckmorton, the queen's lady-in-waiting, had given birth to his child. After his release on 7 September, he was debarred from court and lost most of his offices.

Plague spread throughout London in September and October, so that orders were issued to 'keep the sick from the sound' and for fires to be lit in the streets 'to purge and cleanse the air'.[65] It was so rampant that the law courts were transferred to Hertford. It was estimated that over 11,000 died in the city as a result of the pestilence.

Elizabeth visited the University of Oxford in September, while on her summer progress. She heard a number of academic disputations but found some of the orations rather long and tedious: she twice told an orator to cut short his words, as she meant herself to make a speech that night. She was much displeased when he did not do so.

On 3 November, Sir John Perrot died in the Tower. The privy councillor – and one-time Lord Deputy of Ireland – had been found guilty of treason at his trial the previous April and sentenced to death in June. An unreliable Irish priest had alleged that he had written a letter of support to Philip II. Perrot was also found to have spoken ill of the queen, among other insults calling her a 'base bastard'.

On 3 December (ns), the Duke of Parma, Governor-General of the Spanish Low Countries, died in Flanders. The next month, a plot between Parma's master, Philip II, and Scottish Catholics was revealed. Plans were evidently afoot to invade England from the north.

1593

In January, plague returned to London, and Elizabeth criticized the mayor and aldermen for failing to contain the infection. Sermons, plays, bear-baiting, bowling and other entertainments were prohibited until the disease abated.

On 19 February, Parliament met at Westminster, and on the 24th of the month Peter Wentworth and Sir Henry Bromley delivered a petition on the succession: Elizabeth was so offended that the next day Wentworth was sent to the Tower and Bromley to the Fleet Prison. MPs also presented a bill in this session that criticized the bishops for enforcing adherence to the prayer book. In response, Elizabeth told MPs, through her parliamentary speaker, not to meddle in matters of state or religion. Parliament passed a statute against Catholic recusants, but it was so worded that it could also be used against Protestant separatists – those nonconformists who denied the royal supremacy and worshipped in independent conventicles.

On the basis of this statute, two separatists, Henry Barrow and John Greenwood, were hanged at Tyburn on

374

ABOVE: **Sir Walter Ralegh (1552–1618)**, *the soldier and explorer, was also an accomplished courtier until he lost Elizabeth's favour in 1592 after lying about his secret marriage to the queen's lady-in-waiting. In many of the depictions of Ralegh, such as that by Nicholas Hilliard in 1585 and this French miniature of the period, Ralegh's good looks and love of finery are evident.*

6 April, after having endured five years in the Fleet Prison. On 29 May, the separatist John Penry was hanged for publishing scandalous writings against the church: it was believed he was responsible for the Marprelate Tracts.

For different crimes, three executions took place on 7 April. Alice and John Samuel and their daughter Agnes were hanged for bewitching several children at Warboys in Huntingdonshire.

On 18 April, Richard Field was assigned the right to print *Venus and Adonis*, the first published poem of the actor and playwright William Shakespeare. The dedication was to Henry Wriothesley, 2nd Earl of Southampton. Shakespeare may have turned his mind to poetry when the playhouses were closed because of plague.

In Ireland, rebellion brewed, as the English-educated Hugh O'Neill, 2nd Earl of Tyrone, directed his brother Cormac to revolt in Ulster, although he himself continued to profess loyalty to the queen and serve, albeit half-heartedly, with her lord deputy.

On 20 May, the playwright Christopher Marlowe was examined by the privy council and charged with blasphemy. His ex-roommate, the writer Thomas Kyd, claimed that Marlowe had written papers that denied the existence of God. Ten days later, Marlowe was murdered at the Bull Inn at Deptford.

In July, Henry IV of France publicly abjured his Protestant faith and was received into the Catholic Church. Although he went to great lengths to demonstrate his sincerity, many believed that his conversion was simply political opportunism, an act designed to win the allegiance of his Catholic subjects. Perhaps for this reason, some leaders of the Catholic League continued to oppose his accession and they received military aid from Philip II of Spain. As for Elizabeth, she was disgusted

The witches of Warboys

The examination of Alice Samuel of Warboys, in the county of Huntingdon, taken at Buckden before the right reverend Father in God, Willam by God's permission Bishop of Lincoln, the 26th December 1592.

Being asked whether a dun chicken did ever suck on her chin, and how often, the said examinate said, that it sucked twice and no more since Christmas Evens even last. Being asked whether it was a natural chicken, she said it was not, she knew it was no natural chicken, because when it came to her chin she did scarce feel it, but when she wiped it off with her hand, her chin did bleed. She said further, that the said dun chicken did first come unto her and suck on her chin before it came to Master Throckmorton's house, and that the ill and the trouble that hath come to Master Throckmorton's children, hath come by means of the said dun chicken; the which chicken she knows is now gone both from them and from her.

[FROM THE ANONYMOUS *Most Strange and Admirable Discovery of the Three Witches of Warboys* (1593), EARLY ENGLISH BOOKS ONLINE EDITION, H1v]

375

OVERLEAF: **The 'Ditchley Portrait' of Elizabeth** *commemorates the queen's visit to Sir Henry Lee's manor of Ditchley in Oxfordshire, during her summer progress of 1592. It was painted by Marcus Gheerhaerts the Younger. Lee (1533–1611) supervised Elizabeth's Accession Day tilts after 1580, though he resigned as the queen's champion in 1590. In the portrait, Elizabeth is shown standing in the heavens on a map of England, with her feet on Oxfordshire, and turning away from the stormy sky towards the sun. In the sonnet (within the cartouche) she is referred to as 'The prince of light'. From her left ear hangs a jewelled armillary sphere, and in her hand she holds a folding fan. Her dress is a fashionable French 'farthingale', richly embroidered and bejewelled.*

at Henry's abjuration and immediately withdrew her soldiers from Normandy. However, she retained a small army in Brittany under Sir John Norris, because of fears that Spain might use one of its ports as a naval base.

Elizabeth spent most of the summer and autumn at Windsor. The summer fairs usually held in London were now prohibited because of the plague. During August and September, more than 1000 people were dying each week, and in November there was a new scare when one of the pages died at court. The plague abated only in December, having claimed 10,675 lives over the year.

On 29 November, Richard Hesketh was executed for attempting to persuade Ferdinando Stanley, 5th Earl of Derby, to rebel against the queen. Hesketh was working on behalf of English Catholic exiles in Flanders.

1594

In January, Elizabeth's Portuguese physician, Dr Roderigo Lopez, was implicated in a plot to poison the queen. Although he denied the charge at his trial on 28 February, he was found guilty on the basis of the evidence of witnesses, intercepted letters and his own earlier confession (extracted under torture). In early June, he was hanged, drawn and quartered. On the scaffold he affirmed 'that he had loved the queen as he loved Jesus Christ, which from a man of the Jewish profession was heard not without laughter'.[66] Elizabeth allowed his widow to keep her late husband's estate except for a jewelled ring given to Lopez by the Spanish king.

In February, Henry IV was finally crowned King of France in Chartres Cathedral. The following month he entered Paris, a staunchly Catholic stronghold which had held out against him for four years.

On 16 April, the 5th Earl of Derby died, 'not without suspicion of poison, being tormented with cruel pains by frequent vomitings of a dark colour like rusty iron'.[67]

Great rainstorms caused severe flooding in Sussex and Surrey during April and May. The bad weather continued throughout the summer, causing widespread scarcity of

377

ABOVE: **Witchcraft** *was a felony in England and therefore its punishment was hanging. Sixty-four people – 90 per cent of them women – were hanged in the Home Counties for witchcraft between 1570 and 1609. Belief in witchcraft was widespread in Elizabethan England, and few people seemed to share the scepticism of Reginald Scot, who maintained in his* The Discovery of Witchcraft (1584) *that the accused were innocent and that witch trials were unjust. The picture here comes from a pamphlet narrating the 1589 story of* The Apprehension of Three Notorious Witches at Chelmsford.

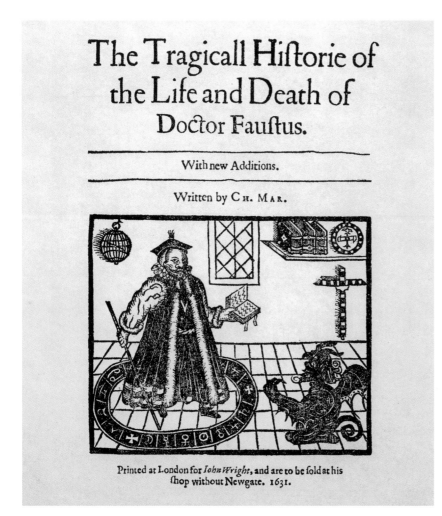

The Tragicall Hiſtorie of
the Life and Death of
Doctor Fauſtus.

With new Additions.

Written by C H. M A R.

Printed at London for *Iohn Wright*, and are to be ſold at his
ſhop without Newgate. 1631.

food. This marked the beginning of a series of dreadful harvests.

In August, Edmund Yorke and Richard Williams confessed to their involvement in a Spanish plot to murder the queen. The assassination scare prompted an order at court that no man should come into the queen's presence wearing a long cloak, which might hide a weapon. Later in the year, Lord Burghley summarized the government's version of events in the *True Report of Sundry Horrible Conspiracies of Late Time Detected*. This account – published in French as well as English – implicated Philip II in the recent plots on Elizabeth's life.

That autumn, England enjoyed military success in Brittany. On 12 September, Norris helped Henry IV's army to capture the Castle of Morlaix. In October and November, Norris and Frobisher participated in the successful assault on El León, a Spanish fortress near Crozon.

However, the latter battle resulted in 60 English casualties, including Frobisher himself, who died on 22 November from gangrene poisoning. On the queen's accession day, three flags captured from the Spaniards were displayed at a great banquet.

In December, copies of *A Conference of the Next Succession* were circulated at court. This Catholic tract, published under a pseudonym, was the work of the Jesuit Robert Persons. It argued that the English Parliament should elect a Catholic as Elizabeth's successor, and it promoted the candidacy of the Infanta Isabella, Philip II's daughter.

ABOVE: '**Dr Faustus**' *was a stage success for the Cambridge-educated Christopher Marlowe, the first great dramatist England produced. The play exists in two versions, published early in the 17th century, and may have been a collaboration. It was first produced around 1588, and is recorded as being played at the Rose Theatre in 1594. However, by then its (principal) author was already dead, murdered at Eleanor Bull's tavern at Deptford on 30 May 1593. According to the inquest, Ingram Frizer stabbed him after a dispute over the bill, but a political motive could explain his murder. Ten days earlier he had been investigated for holding atheist opinions.*

RIGHT: **Robert Devereux (1565–1601), 2nd Earl of Essex,** *was promoted at court by his stepfather, the Earl of Leicester; but he soon gained the favour of Elizabeth, becoming one of the most important figures of the later reign until his disgrace and ill-advised rebellion. In this miniature by Nicholas Hilliard, he is presented as the queen's champion, with her glove on his arm. It may have been commissioned to celebrate his role in the Accession Day tournament of 1595. As he is shown beardless, it was certainly painted before the 1596 Cadiz expedition.*

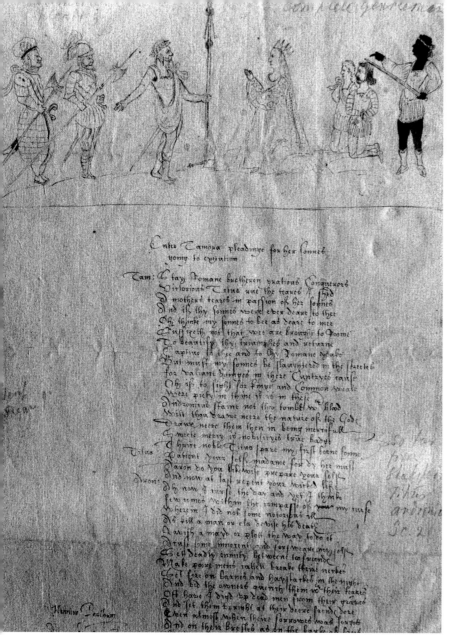

1595

In February, the Earl of Tyrone openly joined the Ulster rebellion and moved against the English garrison at Blackwater Fort. He proclaimed himself the champion of native Irish Catholics against English Protestant settlers.

On 20 February, the Jesuit and poet Robert Southwell was tried and condemned to death after three years' incarceration in the Tower. At his execution at Tyburn, the next day, he prayed for the queen. Because the crowd took pity on him, he was allowed to hang until he was dead, before being disembowelled.

Civil commotion hit London when a number of riots broke out in June over the high price of fish and butter. The council punished leading trouble-makers, but apprentices tore down the pillories in Cheapside. On Sunday 29 June, some 1000 apprentices and former soldiers assembled on Tower Hill, where 'unruly youths' threw stones, but in the evening the lord mayor 'cleared the hill of all trouble'.[68] On 4 July, Elizabeth went so far as to impose martial law; the council imposed a curfew; and five young men were accused of treason. On 24 July, these unfortunate youths were hanged, drawn and quartered on Tower Hill.

In late July, four Spanish galleys landed some 400 Spanish soldiers in Cornwall, where they looted and burned the fishing port of Mousehole and the towns of Newlyn and Penzance. The government planned a retaliatory strike on the Spanish mainland, and on 28 August Sir Francis Drake and Sir John Hawkins sailed

ABOVE: **'Titus Andronicus'** *was performed and printed (in a quarto edition) in 1594. The play is generally thought to have been an early work of William Shakespeare. This pen and ink drawing depicts what seem to be two or more moments in the play, and records some lines, not all of which appear in the printed edition. The endorsement, identifying the owner or illustrator as Henry Peacham and the date as 1595, is in a modern hand, and it may not be accurate.*

RIGHT: **The Swan Theatre** *was built about 1595, by Francis Langley. It was situated south of the Thames close to the Rose Theatre, in Surrey. Shakespeare's company, the Chamberlain's Men, may have played there while they were looking for a permanent home. The Swan is represented in this, the only, contemporary drawing of the inside of an Elizabethan playhouse. The drawing was created in 1596 by Johannes de Witt, a Dutch traveller who made the sketch while on a trip to London.*

from Plymouth as commanders of a fleet of 27 ships. Their instructions were to cross the Atlantic and seize Spanish treasure at Porto (Puerto) Rico and at Panama. Hawkins, however, fell ill and died at Porto Rico, on 12 November. In a separate expedition, Sir Walter Ralegh returned from a voyage to Guinea in September. However, as he brought back no riches, his enemies claimed that he had not left Cornwall at all.

Philip Howard, the Catholic Earl of Arundel, died in the Tower on 19 October, having been imprisoned there since 1585. Some believed he had been poisoned by his cook; others that he 'pined himself with an austere kind of life'.[69] The previous August, he had written to Elizabeth to ask to see his wife and children before he died, as she had once promised him. She replied that if he would only attend church services, he would be freed and restored to his family.

To defend the realm, on 12 November the council ordered the country's lords lieutenants to raise men to fight against a rumoured Spanish invasion. Rejecting the advice of the Earl of Essex, Elizabeth refused to send an army to Picardy to provide reinforcements for Henry IV, who was under pressure from the Spanish army.

The queen's accession day this year was marked as 'a day of great triumph for the long and prosperous reign of her majesty', with sermons, bonfires, bell-ringing and anthems.[70] At court, the Earl of Essex devised lavish and elaborate entertainments before the queen. The next month, the queen went 'much abroad', visiting Lord Keeper Puckering at Kew, as well as the Dowager Countess of Huntingdon on 17 December, to comfort her on her husband's death a few days earlier.

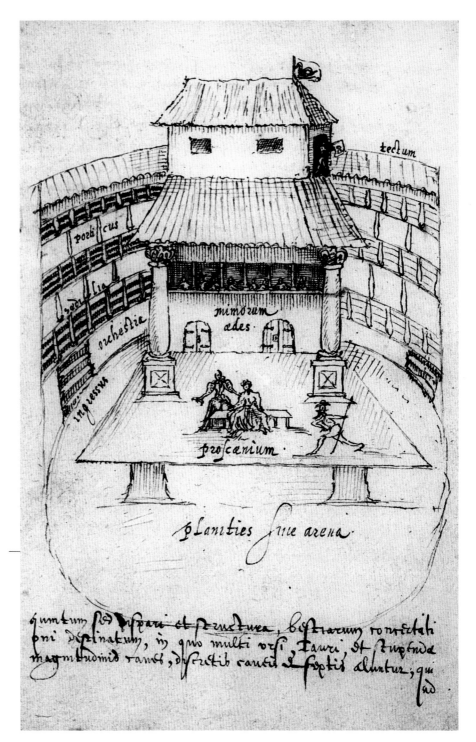

381

1596

After failing to capture Panama in his Caribbean expedition, Sir Francis Drake set fire to the Spanish settlement on Nombre de Dios and sailed towards Honduras. On 27 or 28 January, however, the 55-year-old sailor and explorer died of dysentery and was buried at sea.

In Ireland, the Ulster rebels and English government tried to reach a peaceful settlement. In February, English commissioners concluded a truce with the Earl of Tyrone and delivered the grievances of the Ulster rebels to Elizabeth. Although she contemptuously dismissed their petitions, she allowed 'some of their private demands' and agreed to pardon the chieftains, 'rather than the purpose of pacification should fail'.[71]

Across the English Channel, in April, a Spanish army under Archduke Albert of Austria, the new governor-general in the Low Countries, captured Calais from the French – before Elizabeth could send 6000 men under Essex to relieve the town. She had delayed while awaiting Henry IV's agreement that she could hold the town as surety for the money he owed her.

Elizabeth also hesitated before sending out a naval expedition against Spain. An attack on the Spanish fleet harboured at Cadiz had long been planned, but in mid-May Elizabeth cancelled the operation, only to change her mind an hour later. On 3 June, 100 English ships and 18 Dutch vessels set out for Spain under the command of the Earl of Essex and Lord Admiral Howard. On the 20th, it entered the bay of Cadiz, and the next day took 18 galleys, sunk 4 more, and burned a great ship of war. A landing on the mainland followed, and the English troops quickly took the citadel and plundered the town. However, the Spaniards torched their merchant ships rather than allow the rich cargoes on board to fall into enemy hands. Not long afterwards, the English commanders quarrelled when Essex tried – and failed – to persuade Howard to leave him behind to hold onto Cadiz as an English garrison. They all left Spain on 4 July and arrived in England in early August.

During their absence, on 5 July, Sir Robert Cecil was formally appointed principal secretary, a role he and his father had been unofficially discharging since the death of Walsingham in 1590. His promotion encouraged accusations by political rivals that England was a *regnum Cecilianum* (a 'kingdom of the Cecils').

On 11 July, Elizabeth ordered that 'blackamoors' who had recently been brought to England should be transported out of the realm. Her reason was that 'there are already here too many, considering how God hath blessed this land with great increase of people of our own nation', many of whom were unemployed.[72] Arrangements were made to take them to Spain and Portugal instead.

'The harsh economic climate continued and encouraged discontent among ordinary people in the realm'

Also during July, the Irish situation deteriorated, when Ulster rebels led by Hugh Roe O'Donnell overran Connaught.

On 7 and 8 August, Lord Admiral Howard and the Earl of Essex arrived home from the Cadiz expedition, and on Sunday 8 August a 'great triumph was made at London' to celebrate their victory.[73] The festivities provided some much-needed good cheer, since England experienced a third summer of harvest failure. Grain was imported from eastern Europe without payment of customs dues, but prices still rose sky high.

On 29 August, Elizabeth concluded a league with France against Spain, and 2000 men were raised for fighting on the Continent. On 10 October, Henry IV was invested with the Order of the Garter. However, Philip II sent a fleet towards England in October 'to recover his honour' lost at Cadiz and 'heal himself of his losses'.[74] This armada was dispersed by a storm, but an invasion scare gripped England throughout November.

The harsh economic climate continued and encouraged discontent among ordinary people in the realm. In November, a carpenter, Bartholomew Steer, and a few friends tried to organize a rising in protest at the scarcities, enclosures and high prices. But no one came to join them at the appointed assembly point. Steer was arrested and probably died in prison. As the dearth continued, new orders were issued on Christmas Day to prohibit 'suppers on fasting days and on Wednesdays and Fridays at night'.[75]

This year saw the deaths of Lord Keeper Puckering, the Bishop of London, Lord Hunsdon and Sir Francis Knollys.

ABOVE: **The Roman poet Ovid's 'Metamorphoses'** *was widely read in Elizabethan England, and it became a source for many Elizabethan plays and sonnets, including Shakespeare's* Titus Andronicus. *This plaque (possibly part of a locket cover) illustrates a mythological episode described by Ovid, when the huntsman Actaean is turned into a deer by the goddess Diana and is about to be torn apart by his hounds. Below is the figure of Cupid. The artifact is from Burghley House, Stamford, Lincolnshire.*

384

1597

In the Low Countries on 24 January (ns), Sir Francis Vere participated in the Battle of Turnhout, in which Dutch forces routed the Spanish army.

Sir Walter Ralegh finally returned to court in June, after several years of disgrace caused by his secret marriage. The Earl of Essex and Sir Robert Cecil had both persuaded Elizabeth of his usefulness in the war effort, and all three men now planned a new naval expedition against Spain.

In July, an envoy from King Sigismond of Poland arrived in London. During his audience with the queen, he unexpectedly delivered a Latin oration criticizing her treatment of Polish merchants. Elizabeth reprimanded him 'learnedly and eloquently' in Latin to the admiration of all.[76]

On 17 August, Essex, Ralegh and Vere sailed out in three squadrons to attack the Spanish fleet at Ferrol. Because of rough weather in Biscay, Essex decided it would be better to sail to the Azores and intercept the Spanish silver fleet. However, he missed the Indies treasure convoy by just three hours. Meanwhile in early October, the Spanish fleet at Ferrol set off 'with great provision against England'.[77]

The baptism of a 'black more'

Mary Filis of Morisco being a black more [blackamoor], she was of late servant with one Mrs Barker in Mark Lane, a widow, she said her father's name was Filis of Morisco, a black more being both a basket maker and also a shovel maker. This Mary Filis being about the age of 20 years and having been in England for the space of 13 or 14 years and as yet was not christened. Now being become servant with one Millicent Porter, a seamstress dwelling in the liberty of East Smithfield, and now taking some hold of faith in Jesus Christ was desirous to become a Christian. Wherefore she made suit by her said mistress to have some conference with the curate of this the parish of St Botolph's Aldgate ... [he] demand[ed] of her certain questions concerning her faith whereunto she answered very Christian like ... willed [her] to say the Lord's Prayer and also to rehearse the articles of her belief which she did both say and rehearse very decently and well ... then the said curate did go with her unto the font and desiring the congregation with him to call upon God the father ... that he would grant unto her that thing which by nature she could not have, that she might be baptized with water and the Holy Ghost ...

[PARISH CLERK'S MEMORANDUM BOOK FOR 1597, CHURCH OF ST BOTOLPH'S ALDGATE, LONDON (GUILDHALL MS 9234/6)]

LEFT: **Elizabeth Vernon (1573?–1655), Countess of Southampton,** is shown here at her toilet. She is wearing a pink silk corset – with rows of stitching to hold whalebones – that is laced at the front. Her petticoat and jacket are richly embroidered. In her hand is a double-sided comb, and on the table to her right a pincushion, a small coffer and jewels. The daughter of John Vernon and a cousin of the Earl of Essex, Elizabeth was maid of honour to the queen until her secret marriage to the 3rd Earl of Southampton (p. 388) in August 1598. After a short spell in prison for this offence, she left court and became the mother of three daughters and two sons.

Its objective was to seize Falmouth in Cornwall and use the port as a base from which to attack Essex's ships on their return from the 'Islands Voyage'. The operation caused another invasion scare in London, but it came to nothing. Essex managed to arrive safely at Plymouth and a violent storm scattered the Spanish fleet before it could land. Nonetheless, the episode did expose England's vulnerability to attack when its fleet was absent on privateering expeditions.

On 23 October, a few days before Essex's return, Lord Admiral Howard was created Earl of Nottingham, as a reward for his service the previous year at Cadiz. He was now the second peer of the realm, giving precedence only to the Earl of Oxford. The next day, Parliament opened. Numerous people 'were smothered and crushed to death, pressing betwixt Whitehall and the college church, to have seen her majesty and nobility riding to the said Parliament'.[78] Elizabeth prorogued the session until November. Among the pieces of legislation then passed were an anti-enclosure statute, an Act for the Relief of the Poor and one for the Repressing of Rogues, Vagabonds and Sturdy Beggars. In addition, the MPs introduced a bill to remedy the abuses arising from patents and monopolies (royal grants of the sole right to manufacture or sell a certain article). Although not passed, the bill was referred to a committee for investigation.

In early November, Essex left court, affronted by Howard's promotion. Elizabeth persuaded him to return by awarding him on 28 December the vacant office of earl marshal, a prestigious position that gave him precedence over the new Earl of Nottingham.

LEFT: **Gardens were a new passion** *in Elizabethan England, and there soon developed a market for books on gardening. Thomas Hill's* The Gardener's Labyrinth, *first published in 1577, was a cheap bestseller that gave advice on growing flowers, fruit and vegetables. This page illustrates irrigation by an overhead pump; it also shows the symmetrical layout of an idealized garden, hives in the top-right corner to attract bees, and the gardeners' tools.*

IN VINCVLIS
INVICTVS·

FEBRVA:8:1600
602:603:APF

1598

In January, Queen Elizabeth closed the Steelyard and expelled the Hanseatic merchants living there. Their presence and privileges had long been resented by English merchants, but the royal ban on their activities was an act of retaliation for the expulsion of the Company of Merchant Adventurers from the Holy Roman Empire in August the previous year,

On 23 February, Thomas Bodley announced his intention of refurbishing the public library at the University of Oxford. He also endowed it with an annual income for the purchase of books.

Also in February, Sir Robert Cecil sailed to France, in an effort to preserve the Anglo-French alliance. He was undoubtedly pleased when, in early April, Henry IV issued the Edict of Nantes that guaranteed freedom of worship and political rights for the Huguenots. However, he was dismayed a few weeks later on learning that Henry had signed the Treaty of Vervins with the dying Philip II of Spain. By its terms, Spain withdrew from Calais and recognized Henry's title as King of France. Elizabeth protested at the separate peace but looked for ways that she, too, could end the war without betraying the United Provinces.

In the spring, quarrels that had been fermenting within the community of English Catholic priests for several years became more intense when Rome appointed George Blackwell as archpriest with authority over the clergy working in England. The secular (or seminary) priests believed Blackwell was a Jesuit stooge and that the scheme was a sinister plot by the Jesuits to take control of the English mission. In late summer they appealed to the pope against the appointment.

On 30 June or 1 July, the Earl of Essex quarrelled with Elizabeth. During their argument he turned his back on her 'as it were in contempt, with a scornful look'. She 'waxing impatient gave him a cuff on the ear' and Essex impetuously laid his hand on his sword. The Earl of Nottingham stepped in between the two, but Essex 'swore a great oath that he neither could nor would swallow so great an indignity' and 'in great discontentment hastened from the court'.[79] He did not return until 10 September.

On 4 August, William Cecil, Lord Burghley, died, after being sick for most of the year. Queen Elizabeth took the news very grievously. A state funeral with above 500 mourners took place at Westminster Abbey, and his burial followed at Stamford in Lincolnshire, the family seat. The title passed to his eldest son, Thomas, while Lord Buckhurst became the new lord treasurer.

'All this year was the Irish rebellion very hot.'[80] It also went badly for England. On 14 August, Sir Henry Bagenal, the marshal in Ireland, and his troops fell into an ambush at Yellow Ford. Bagenal was shot dead, his soldiers routed, and an estimated 2000 footmen and 15 captains were slain or wounded. The remaining English soldiers surrendered Blackwater Fort and evacuated Armagh. 'This was a glorious victory to the rebels'.[81]

LEFT: **Henry Wriothesley (1573–1624), 3rd Earl of Southampton**, *never recovered Elizabeth's favour after his secret marriage to Elizabeth Vernon (p. 384), who had been maid of honour to the queen. A close friend – and relation by marriage – of the Earl of Essex, he accompanied the earl to Ireland in 1599 and participated in his attempted coup of 1601. Condemned to death for treason, his sentence was commuted thanks to the intervention of Sir Robert Cecil, but he was imprisoned in the Tower for the remainder of Elizabeth's reign. On the top right of this portrait (c.1603), possibly by John de Critz the Elder, can be seen a view of the Tower, the dates of his imprisonment, and a defiant motto 'Undefeated in chains'. Shakespeare dedicated his poems* Venus and Adonis *and* The Rape of Lucrece *to Southampton.*

On 16 August, the Treaty of London was signed, in which it was agreed that the United Provinces would now pay for and command most of the remaining English soldiers in the Low Countries.

In late September and October, soldiers who had been pressed into service mutinied or deserted on their way to Ireland. Of the new soldiers who actually arrived there, many were found to be 'so poor and simple as utterly unserviceable'.[82] In October, the Ulster rebellion spread to Munster and then throughout the whole of the island, and during the autumn and winter news spread of massacres of English settlers and their families.

In England during the autumn, there occurred severe flooding that reduced many counties 'to great distress'.[83] On a more positive note, the prospect of peace with Spain improved after September, when Elizabeth's arch-enemy, Philip II, died. His son and successor, Philip III, was for a time interested in ending the war with England.

Parliament met in October, and MPs again attacked royal monopolies. Towards the end of the month, a new Catholic plot was uncovered. Edward Squire, 'one of the ordinary sort of men',[84] allegedly made separate attempts to kill both Elizabeth and the Earl of Essex by smearing poison on her saddle and his chair. A special prayer of thanksgiving was issued to celebrate the queen's escape from death.

During the autumn and winter, Elizabeth made plans to crush the rebellion in Ireland, no matter how much it cost her in money and men. In the hope of winning martial glory, the Earl of Essex offered to lead the English army into Ulster. On 30 December, he was appointed lord lieutenant – rather than lord deputy – to signify his military role.

A 'very majestic' monarch

Next came the queen [Elizabeth], in the sixty-fifth year of her age [1598], as we were told, very majestic. Her face oblong, fair but wrinkled, her eyes small, yet black and pleasant, her nose a little hooked, her lips narrow and her teeth black (a defect the English seem subject to, from their too great use of sugar); she had in her ears two pearls, with very rich drops; she wore false hair, and that red. Upon her head, she had a small crown, reported to be made of some of the gold of the celebrated Luneburg table. Her bosom was uncovered, as all the English ladies have it till they marry; and she had on a necklace of exceeding fine jewels. Her hands were small, her fingers long, and her stature neither tall nor low. Her air was stately, her manner of speaking mild and obliging. That day, she was dressed in white silk, bordered with pearls of the size of beans, and over it a mantle of black silk, shot with silver threads; her train was very long, the end of it borne by a marchioness. Instead of a chain, she had an oblong collar of gold and jewels.

[PAUL HENTZNER, *Journey into England in the Year 1598,* 1757 EDITION, PP. 47–51]

1599

During January, about 16,000 infantrymen (including 2000 veterans from the Low Countries) and 1400 cavalry were levied for service in Ulster. On 27 March, the Earl of Essex left London for Ireland. He was accompanied by the earls of Southampton and Rutland, lords Grey, Audley and Cromwell and his stepfather Sir Christopher Blount. Essex was ordered to fight against the Earl of Tyrone and obtain his total submission. However, the lord lieutenant did not immediately make for Ulster but instead marched south through Leinster and Munster, where he captured

LEFT: **Ballad singers** were much in evidence in late Elizabethan London. Singing the ballad was one way of selling a printed copy, and stationers often recruited unemployed young men for the task. Ballads were sung to familiar, often country, tunes; they were cheap to purchase and had a wide appeal, not least because they were decorated with woodcuts. The ballad singer here is dressed in far fancier clothes than could have been the case in reality.

A day at the playhouse

On September 21st [1599] after lunch, *about two o'clock, I and my party crossed the water, and there in the house with the thatched roof witnessed an excellent performance of the tragedy [by Shakespeare] of the first emperor Julius Caesar with a cast of some fifteen people; when the play was over, they danced very marvellously and gracefully together as is their wont, two dressed as men and two as women ...*

Thus daily at two in the afternoon, London has two, sometimes three plays, running in different places, competing with each other, and those which play best obtain most spectators. The playhouses are so constructed that they play on a raised platform, so that everyone has a good view ... during the performance food and drink are carried round the audience ... The actors are most expensively and elaborately costumed; for it is the English usage for eminent lords or knights at their decease to bequeath and leave almost the best of their clothes to their serving men, which it is unseemly for the latter to wear, so that they offer them then for sale for a small sum to the actors.

How much time then they may merrily spend daily at the play everyone knows who has ever seen them play or act.

[THOMAS PLATTER, *Thomas Platter's Travels in England*, 1599, TRANSLATED BY C. WILLIAMS, PP. 166–7]

391

Essex's untimely appearance

Within a month [in 1599], the Earl of Essex posted into England before any man thought of it, accompanied with certain of his choice friends ... He went forward to Nonsuch (where the queen then lay) ... and so made such haste, that he presented himself on his knees betimes in the morning before the queen in her privy chamber, when she little dreamed of it. She entertained him with a short conference somewhat graciously, but not with that countenance as she was wont, and willed him to depart to his chamber, and there continue. For whereas she was displeased with him before, he now incurred her displeasure anew, in that, contrary to her command, he had left Ireland without her leave ... his unexpected return into England with such a company gave great cause of suspicion, which his adversaries at court increased with divers fictions and inventions of their own; the queen thought fit he should be committed to custody, yet not in any prison, lest she might seem to cut off from him all hope of her former favour.

[WILLIAM CAMDEN (1551–1623), *The History of the Most Renowned and Victorious Princess Elizabeth ... [the Annales]*,
1688 EDITION, BOOK IV, PP. 573–4]

Cahir Castle on 30 May. Two setbacks now occurred, which weakened his campaign. On 28 May, the rebels ambushed and defeated 500 men under Sir Henry Harrington near Wicklow. On 5 August, Sir Conyers Clifford, Governor of Connaught, was killed and his 2000-strong army routed in the Curlew mountains.

An angry Elizabeth insisted in August that Essex fight in the north. Essex therefore marched into Ulster, although he believed he lacked the military strength to defeat the rebels. Against instructions, he concluded a truce with Tyrone on 7 September and then left Ireland 'in secret manner'[85] with the idea of reaching Elizabeth before his enemies at court could discredit him further in her eyes. He arrived early on 28 September at Nonsuch Palace, and entered Elizabeth's bedchamber while she was still dishevelled and undressed. Flustered but gracious, she commanded him to go to his own chamber. The following day, her councillors summoned Essex before them and charged him with disobedience to the queen. He was taken into the charge of Lord Keeper Thomas Egerton.

In November, Tyrone sent his conditions for peace. These included the demand that Catholicism 'be openly preached and taught throughout all Ireland'.[86] Sir Robert Cecil endorsed his own copy of the articles with the word 'Utopia'. Plans were formed to send Charles Blount, 8th Baron Mountjoy, to Ireland as lord deputy to suppress the rebellion and appoint Sir George Carew as Lord President of Munster to bring order to that province.

On 29 November, the Star Chamber publicized details of Essex's misgovernment in Ireland. Learning of the earl's illness in early December, Elizabeth sent him her doctor with some broth, but she did not permit his release from custody.

Sir Francis Vere (1560–1609) *was probably the most successful and celebrated soldier of the Elizabethan war against Spain. He won renown in England for his part in the Dutch victories at Turnhout (24 January 1597, ns) and Nieuwpoort (2 July 1600, ns) as well as the heroic defence of Ostend in 1601 and January 1602. He was a very good military all-rounder and an even better self-publicist. The portrait, by an unknown artist, is dated to the 1590s.*

1600

In February, Lord Mountjoy left for Ireland 'without any noise; the state of Ireland he found much languishing'.[87] In England, his predecessor, the Earl of Essex, returned to his own house on 20 March, but remained under surveillance. On 5 June, he was brought before a special commission of privy councillors and others to answer the various charges of insubordination levelled against him. Although he appeared very contrite, he denied his guilt. Nonetheless, he was suspended from his offices and kept under house arrest.

In mid-May, negotiations began at Boulogne for a peace with Spain. However, disputes over precedence bogged down the talks, as did mutual recriminations and suspicions: the Spaniards complained of continuing English help to the Dutch rebels, while the English suspected 'double dealing, succours being lately sent into Ireland' for Tyrone and his allies.[88] In late July, the negotiations were suspended for 60 days, and they were not renewed.

Queen Elizabeth attended the wedding of one of her maids of honour, Anne Russell, and the son of Edward Somerset, 4th Earl of Worcester, on 16 June. Elizabeth also danced during the masque after supper.

RIGHT: **A map of Ulster**, *drawn at the time of the Earl of Tyrone's rebellion, shows the families that were dominant in each region. Also marked on the map are rivers, hills, woods, churches and forts. Top right are the arms of Elizabeth and Lord Charles Mountjoy, the lord deputy.*

The civil lawyer John Hayward was remanded in the Tower in July. The previous year he had published a history of England's Henry IV, which dealt primarily with the downfall of Richard II. Elizabeth suspected sedition, as the book described royal misgovernment, a corrupt council, hated favourites and burdensome taxation, all of which resulted in the deposition of a monarch. Just as worrying, the work was dedicated to the Earl of Essex.

ABOVE: **William Kemp** *developed a reputation as a clown and dancer of jigs while a member of the Chamberlain's Men (c.1594–9). On 7 March 1600, Kemp won a wager that he could morris-dance, or jig, from London to Norwich (about 100 miles). After this success, he set out to dance across Germany and Italy. The woodcut frontispiece is from his book* Nine Days Wonder, *published in 1600, celebrating his London–Norwich feat.*

On 26 August, Essex was released from house arrest but restrained from coming to court. On 30 October, he was ruined financially, when Elizabeth refused to renew his lease of the customs on sweet wines: without this lucrative source of income he could not pay his creditors. The queen was said to have remarked that 'an unruly horse must be abated of his provender that he may be the better brought to managing'.[89]

During the summer, 'there was a grievous complaining throughout England of dearth of corn, which grew partly through a rainy constitution of the heaven about the end of the last year, partly through a cold spring this year, and partly through the private avarice of some which, having obtained a licence, transported great store into foreign countries to their exceeding great gain'.[90]

In Ireland, Lord Mountjoy and Sir George Carew had a successful year. Carew brought Munster under control and drove the rebels out of Kerry. Mountjoy employed tactics that allowed fortresses to be established in Derry and near Newry. He also undermined Tyrone's economic base by devastating the Irish countryside in a deliberate scorched-earth policy.

On 31 December, Elizabeth established the East India Company. The 218 subscribers to the new enterprise raised £68,373 and early the next year three ships set off to trade in the Far East.

A law for the poor

Be it enacted by the authority of this present Parliament, that the churchwardens of every parish, and four, three or two substantial householders there ... shall be called overseers of the poor of the same parish, and they ... shall take order from time to time ... for setting to work of the children whose parents shall not by the said churchwardens, and overseers, or the greater part of them, be thought able to keep and maintain their children. And also for setting to work all such persons married or unmarried, having no means to maintain them, or no ordinary and daily trade of life to get their living by, and also to raise weekly or otherwise (by taxation of every inhabitant, parson, vicar, and other, and of every occupier of lands, houses, tithes impropriate, or propriations of tithes, coalmines, or saleable underwoods in the said parish, in such competent sum and sums of money as they think fit) a convenient stock of flax, hemp, wool, thread, iron, and other necessary ware and stuff to set the poor on work, and also competent sums of money, for, and towards the necessary relief of the lame, impotent, old, blind, and such other among them being poor, and not able to work.

[FROM THE 1601 ACT FOR THE RELIEF OF THE POOR, *Statutes of the Realm*, VOL. IV, PP. 973–4]

1601

In late January, armed men started to gather in Essex House in London, to which the earl had returned from the country the previous October. On Saturday 7 February, the council summoned Essex before them, but he refused to attend on the grounds that his enemies – who in his eyes seemed to include most of the council – sought to murder him, and he made specific allegations against Sir Walter Ralegh. That afternoon, his friends paid players to perform William Shakespeare's *Richard II* (including the scene where the king is deposed) at the Globe Theatre, presumably with a view to preparing Londoners for an attempted coup. The next day, the Earl of Worcester and three senior councillors went to Essex House to ask why soldiers were assembling there. The four were kept under guard while Essex left with about 300 men to raise the city of London against his enemies. Riding through the streets, they cried out 'for the queen, for the queen'[91] but could attract no support. Eventually soldiers arrived and barred their way. 'Now did the earl first draw his sword.'[92] In the subsequent skirmish, one of Essex's supporters, Sir Christopher Blount, was severely wounded and taken prisoner. Essex retreated home, but found his hostages had escaped. Deciding to fight to the end, he burned his papers, fortified his residence, and allowed the women – including his wife and sister – to leave. However, at the last minute he surrendered.

On 12 February, Captain Thomas Lee, one of Essex's Irish captains, attempted to seize Elizabeth and force her to sign a warrant releasing Essex from the Tower. Lee was executed at Tyburn on 14 February.

HER MAIESTIES

most Princely answere, deliuered by her selfe at the Court at *Whitehall*, on the last day of Nouember 1601. When the Speaker of the Lower House of Parliament (assisted with the greatest part of the Knights, and Burgesses) had presented their humble thanks for her free and gracious fauour, in preuenting and reforming of sundry grieuances, by abuse of many grants, commonly called MONOPOLIES: The same being taken *Verbatim* in writing by A.B. as neere as he could possibly set it downe.

M. Speaker,

E perceiue by you, whome we did constitute the mouth of our Lower House, home with euen consent they are fallen into the due consideration of the

A 3 precious

/5/

ABOVE: **Elizabeth's 'Golden Speech'** *was delivered at Whitehall on 30 November 1601 before a delegation of MPs who had been complaining in the House of Commons about monopolies. The speech appears to have been a rhetorical triumph, and an official version was immediately printed. However, over the following centuries another version – based on a parliamentary diary – was reprinted many times. This version downplayed Elizabeth's rights as a monarch (emphasized in the 1601 'Princely answere') and focused instead on her expressions of love for her subjects. The label 'Golden' was first coined in a mid-17th century pamphlet.*

Five days later, on 19 February, Essex and his principal ally in the abortive rebellion, the Earl of Southampton, were arraigned in Westminster Hall before a court of peers. Essex attempted to justify his actions by claiming he was protecting the realm from machinations to place the Spanish *infanta*, Isabella, on the throne, even accusing Sir Robert Cecil of supporting the Spanish claim; however, Cecil appeared as a witness to deny the implausible allegation. Both defendants were found guilty of treason, but Southampton's sentence was commuted to imprisonment for life. On Ash Wednesday (25 February) Essex was beheaded. The executioner was attacked as he left the Tower and had to be rescued by the sheriffs of London. On 5 March, five of Essex's followers were condemned to death, including Sir Christopher Blount. Four other adherents were released from the Tower in August.

Around April, highly discreet communications began between Sir Robert Cecil and the Earl of Mar, representative of James VI of Scotland, to discuss the sensitive issue of the succession. Although James was undeniably the leading candidate and the rightful heir in terms of heredity, there were some legal obstacles to his accession as the Scottish line

400

ABOVE: **Embroidered gloves** *were made in professional workshops (often in France or Spain) and sold in London shops. These ones, made from a fine and supple leather (doeskin or kid), are decorated with rich tapestry made at the Sheldon workshops in Warwickshire. Worn as accessories in the hat or belt, as well as carried in the hand, gloves were a signifier of wealth and status.*

RIGHT: **These embroidered mittens,** *made of crimson velvet and white satin, are thought to have been a gift from Elizabeth I to Margaret Denny, the wife of Sir Edward, a groom of the privy chamber. The design of the silk embroidery includes familiar flowers such as borage, pinks and lilies, as well as insects and fruits, scattered among the foliage. In the centre of each is a pillar entwined with a sprouting vine, an emblem that may have been inspired by similar motifs in the popular book* A Choice of Emblems *by Geffrey Whitney.*

'Elizabeth delivered one of her most memorable speeches – her 'Golden Speech' – to a delegation of MPs'

had been excluded from Henry VIII's will. To ease James's route to the English throne, Cecil began a secret correspondence with the Scottish king, advising him to bide his time and await patiently Elizabeth's death.

On 29 June, Elizabeth added three members to her privy council, including the Earl of Worcester, but it remained small at thirteen. While on her summer progress this year, the queen received a large embassy from France's Henry IV in one of her subjects' houses in Hampshire.

In Ireland, Spanish intervention threatened, when in September some 3400 Spanish troops landed at Kinsale in County Cork. In October, Lord Mountjoy besieged the town, but the Spaniards resisted tenaciously.

Parliament assembled on 27 October, and MPs soon resumed their attack on monopolies. On 25 November, Elizabeth promised to repeal or suspend the most harmful patents. Five days later she delivered one of her most memorable speeches – her 'Golden Speech' – to a delegation of MPs, telling them of her sense of responsibility as monarch and care for her subjects. Otherwise, the main achievement of this Parliament was a Poor Law that consolidated previous legislation.

In December, Lord Mountjoy was ready to offer a winter truce to the Spaniards in Kinsale, as his army was suffering from disease and shortages of food. However, on 21 December the Earl of Tyrone arrived from the north, and on the 24th made ready for battle. The Spaniards failed to join him in the attack, however, and Mountjoy quickly won the day.

1602

On 2 January, the Spaniards in Ireland surrendered their forts and returned home. Of the Irish rebels, Hugh O'Donnell left with them, but Tyrone drifted back to Ulster.

In March, Elizabeth sent out a fleet to prevent the Spanish navy from putting to sea and to intercept the silver convoy. However, her navy was not strong enough to attack the warships escorting the treasure, although it did capture a heavily laden Portuguese carrack, the *São Valentim*, in June.

During June, Lord Mountjoy moved into Ulster. Over the next months, his army captured Irish strongholds and laid waste to the land. Abandoned by his allies and unable to feed an army, the Earl of Tyrone tried to negotiate peace terms, but Mountjoy was constrained to follow Elizabeth's orders and so demanded total submission.

Further afield, in Rome, the pope adjudicated in the dispute between the Jesuits and the 'Appellants' (the secular priests who had appealed to Rome against the appointment of George Blackwell as archpriest in 1598). The Appellants won some concessions, but Blackwell continued as archpriest. Exploiting the disputes among the Catholics, Queen Elizabeth issued a proclamation on 5 November. There she declared that the toleration of 'two religions' in the country was 'far from the imagination of Her Majesty', but she nonetheless offered those secular priests who opposed the Jesuits and submitted to her authority the right to remain in the country. Only 13 priests in fact accepted the offer. Those who refused were told they had to depart the realm by 31 December.

1603

Queen Elizabeth spent the new year at Whitehall in festive spirits, but she moved to Richmond on 31 January 'to enjoy quiet'. For a time, she continued to hold audiences and carry out state business. Indeed, on 17 February, she agreed that Lord Mountjoy could take a more lenient stance towards the Earl of Tyrone and offer him life, liberty and a pardon in return for his submission.

A new dynasty

Forasmuch as it has pleased Almighty God *to call to his mercy out of this transitory life our sovereign lady, the high and mighty prince, Elizabeth late Queen of England, France, and Ireland, by whose death and dissolution, the imperial crown of these realms aforesaid are now absolutely, wholly, and solely come to the high and mighty prince, James the Sixth King of Scotland, who is lineally and lawfully descended from the body of Margaret, daughter to the high and renowned prince, Henry the Seventh King of England, France, and Ireland, his great-grandfather, the said Lady Margaret being lawfully begotten of the body of Elizabeth, daughter to King Edward the Fourth (by which happy conjunction both the houses of York and Lancaster were united, to the joy unspeakeable of this kingdom, formerly rent and torn by the long dissention of bloody and civil war) the same Lady Margaret being also the eldest sister of Henry the Eighth, of famous memory King of England as aforesaid ...*

['A PROCLAMATION, DECLARING THE UNDOUBTED RIGHT OF OUR SOVEREIGN LORD KING JAMES, TO THE CROWN OF THE REALMS OF ENGLAND, FRANCE AND IRELAND', LONDON 24 MARCH 1603, MODERNIZED FROM *Royal Stuart Proclamations*, VOL. I P. 1]

However, the death of her intimate and cousin Katherine, Countess of Nottingham, on 24 February, greatly distressed Elizabeth. She 'began to be assailed with some weakness both of health and old age, which the foulness of the weather had increased'. In March, her health steadily deteriorated, and she was refusing to eat or to go to bed. On 24 March, Queen Elizabeth died, bringing to an end a reign that lasted almost 45 years.

On the same day, Sir Robert Cecil read out a proclamation at Whitehall, announcing the accession of James VI of Scotland, and copies were sent throughout the realm. When news of Elizabeth's death reached James, by 27 March, he in turn confirmed the authority of the council to act in his name. It was a peaceful transition from England's last Tudor queen to its first Stuart king.

Sir Robert Cecil (1563–1612)
slowly moved into his father Lord Burghley's shoes during the 1590s, and by 1597 the Earl of Essex had marked him out as an enemy. After the earl's fall in 1601, Cecil entered into a secret correspondence with James VI of Scotland in order to arrange his peaceful accession on Elizabeth's death. During Elizabeth's last illness, Cecil drafted the proclamation that would announce the king's accession, delivering it aloud on 24 March 1603 first at Whitehall and then at the gates to the City of London. He would continue to serve James until his relatively early death in 1612, rising to the peerage as Earl of Salisbury and spending lavishly on building projects, notably the redesigning of Hatfield House. In this portrait, by John de Critz the Elder or his studio, there is no sign of Cecil's hump-back or the other deformities that afflicted him.

SERO. SED SERIO.

James VI of Scotland (1566–1625) *enhanced his wealth and dominions on becoming James I of England in March 1603. The son of Mary Queen of Scots and Lord Henry Darnley, and the great-grandson of Henry VIII's sister Margaret, he had the best claim to the English throne by heredity, even though Henry VIII's will had ignored the Scottish line. Elizabeth favoured his succession and made it difficult for potential rivals to build up a political following, though she refused point-blank to recognize his title publicly. To safeguard his position, James built up contacts with the Earl of Essex during the 1590s, and then with Robert Cecil on Essex's fall. Once Elizabeth died, Cecil took the lead in arranging James's peaceful accession onto the English throne.*

Elizabeth I: Conclusion

Elizabeth is generally considered the most likeable of the Tudor monarchs. Apart from her sharp wit, she has been admired for her personal charm, fidelity to royal servants, lack of brutality, and relative toleration of religious dissent. Her reign has also been seen as the most successful in English history, encompassing the establishment of the Anglican Church, the restoration of the currency, the introduction of a Poor Law that provided systematic outdoor relief, the defeat of the Spanish Armada, the circumnavigation of the globe, experiments with colonization and the flourishing of the arts: all had a huge and beneficial impact on her realm and its future history.

However, while Elizabeth did display many admirable qualities at times, they represented only one side of her character. The truth is more complex. While she could be charming, sensitive and kind, she could also be irascible and quickly roused to anger, as Leicester, Burghley, Ralegh and Davison – not to mention numerous ladies of her privy chamber – found to their cost. Although there was usually good cause for Elizabeth's rages, the effects could be somewhat unpredictable and excessive. At the same time it is equally true to say that Elizabeth did not display the same mistrust and suspicious nature as either her father or grandfather did, with the result that the number of judicial murders and imprisonments during her reign was low compared to theirs. Elizabeth, moreover, showed a marked reluctance to execute Mary Queen of Scots and the Duke of Norfolk, despite their involvement in treason, and even reprieved some of the men implicated in Essex's rebellion. Nonetheless, she showed little mercy to rebels or plotters lower down the social scale: thanks to her personal intervention, the number of executions after the 1569 rising was extremely high, far higher than it had been after the Pilgrimage of Grace in her father's reign. A woman very much of her time, Elizabeth did not object to the use of torture; nor did she flinch from issuing instructions that the Babington plotters should be disembowelled while they were still fully conscious so that they would die in agony.

Elizabeth's religious toleration also had serious limitations. It is certainly the case that (unlike her sister) she allowed freedom of conscience and avoided opening windows into her subjects' souls. Furthermore, she softened or vetoed some early anti-Catholic parliamentary bills and protected from prosecution or punishment a number of recusants or members of the Family of Love sect, whom she knew to be loyal. However, under no circumstances would she permit freedom of worship or speech. She demanded attendance at Protestant church services, insisted upon conformity to the 1559 Prayer Book, and denied Catholics the sacraments that were the life-blood of their faith. As time went on and the activities of Catholic and Protestant nonconformists appeared more dangerous, she agreed to harsh laws against unacceptable religious activities. Together with her ministers, she consistently maintained that the men and women executed or imprisoned were guilty of political crimes and not punished for their faith. Like most of her contemporaries, she believed that confessional uniformity – all her subjects worshipping in the same way – was essential for political unity and that disobedience to the law on matters concerning religion was a sign of disloyalty to the crown.

Elizabeth ruled effectively, commanding respect and exercising authority well. Despite her many difficulties and her moments of miscalculation, she was ultimately successful in imposing her religious settlement on the majority of her subjects in England (though not Ireland), in suppressing rebellions, in overcoming international threats, and in surviving the numerous plots against her life. She has been portrayed as indecisive, but her success in these areas owed much to her sensible decisions, particularly as regards when to act and when to hold back. The other many achievements of the reign added to her reputation, although it must be remembered that she was not primarily responsible for them. The patronage of the arts, for example, owed more to her courtiers than to the queen herself.

Yet despite all the achievements of the reign, near its end the long decade of the 1590s was an unhappy time for many – probably the majority – of Elizabeth's subjects. In Ireland, the land was devastated both by the rebels and the queen's representatives' scorched-earth policy. In England, high taxation, inflation, a succession of bad harvests, recurrent plague and military impressment created hardship and disaffection. Although the government introduced some reforms to improve the situation, the heavy hand of repression was more evident. For many Elizabethans the post-Armada years were no golden age and the queen was no 'Gloriana' – the name memorably given to her by Spenser in the *Faerie Queene.*

ABOVE: **The Phoenix Jewel** *is a golden pendant, which has been dated to between 1572 and 1580 and was bequeathed to the British Museum by Sir Hans Sloane in 1753. On its front is a silhouette bust of Queen Elizabeth, enclosed within an enamelled wreath of red and white roses signifying Tudor rule. On the reverse is a phoenix in flames under the royal monogram ('ER'), a crown and heavenly rays. The mythical phoenix was a favourite emblem of the queen: it symbolized uniqueness (as only one lived at any one time) and renewal. Medallions, jewels and miniatures containing representations of Elizabeth were common during her reign.*

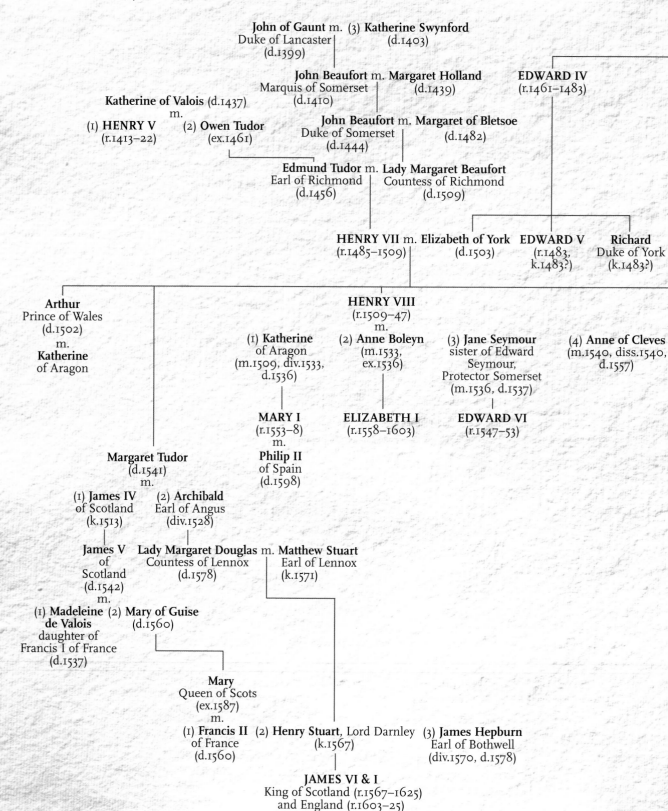

John of Gaunt m. (3) **Katherine Swynford**
Duke of Lancaster (d.1403)
(d.1399)

John Beaufort m. **Margaret Holland**
Marquis of Somerset (d.1439)
(d.1410)

EDWARD IV
(r.1461–1483)

Katherine of Valois (d.1437)
m.

(1) **HENRY V**   (2) **Owen Tudor**
(r.1413–22)   (ex.1461)

John Beaufort m. **Margaret of Bletsoe**
Duke of Somerset (d.1482)
(d.1444)

Edmund Tudor m. **Lady Margaret Beaufort**
Earl of Richmond   Countess of Richmond
(d.1456)   (d.1509)

HENRY VII m. **Elizabeth of York**   **EDWARD V**   **Richard**
(r.1485–1509)   (d.1503)   (r.1483,   Duke of York
                                         k.1483?)   (k.1483?)

Arthur
Prince of Wales
(d.1502)
m.
Katherine
of Aragon

HENRY VIII
(r.1509–47)
m.

(1) **Katherine**   (2) **Anne Boleyn**   (3) **Jane Seymour**   (4) **Anne of Cleves**
of Aragon   (m.1533,   sister of Edward   (m.1540, diss.1540,
(m.1509, div.1533,   ex.1536)   Seymour,   d.1557)
d.1536)   Protector Somerset
                                              (m.1536, d.1537)

MARY I   **ELIZABETH I**   **EDWARD VI**
(r.1553–8)   (r.1558–1603)   (r.1547–53)
m.

Philip II
of Spain
(d.1598)

Margaret Tudor
(d.1541)
m.

(1) **James IV**   (2) **Archibald**
of Scotland   Earl of Angus
(k.1513)   (div.1528)

James V   **Lady Margaret Douglas** m. **Matthew Stuart**
of   Countess of Lennox   Earl of Lennox
Scotland   (d.1578)   (k.1571)
(d.1542)
m.

(1) **Madeleine** (2) **Mary of Guise**
de Valois   (d.1560)
daughter of
Francis I of France
(d.1537)

Mary
Queen of Scots
(ex.1587)
m.

(1) **Francis II**   (2) **Henry Stuart**, Lord Darnley   (3) **James Hepburn**
of France   (k.1567)   Earl of Bothwell
(d.1560)   (div.1570, d.1578)

JAMES VI & I
King of Scotland (r.1567–1625)
and England (r.1603–25)

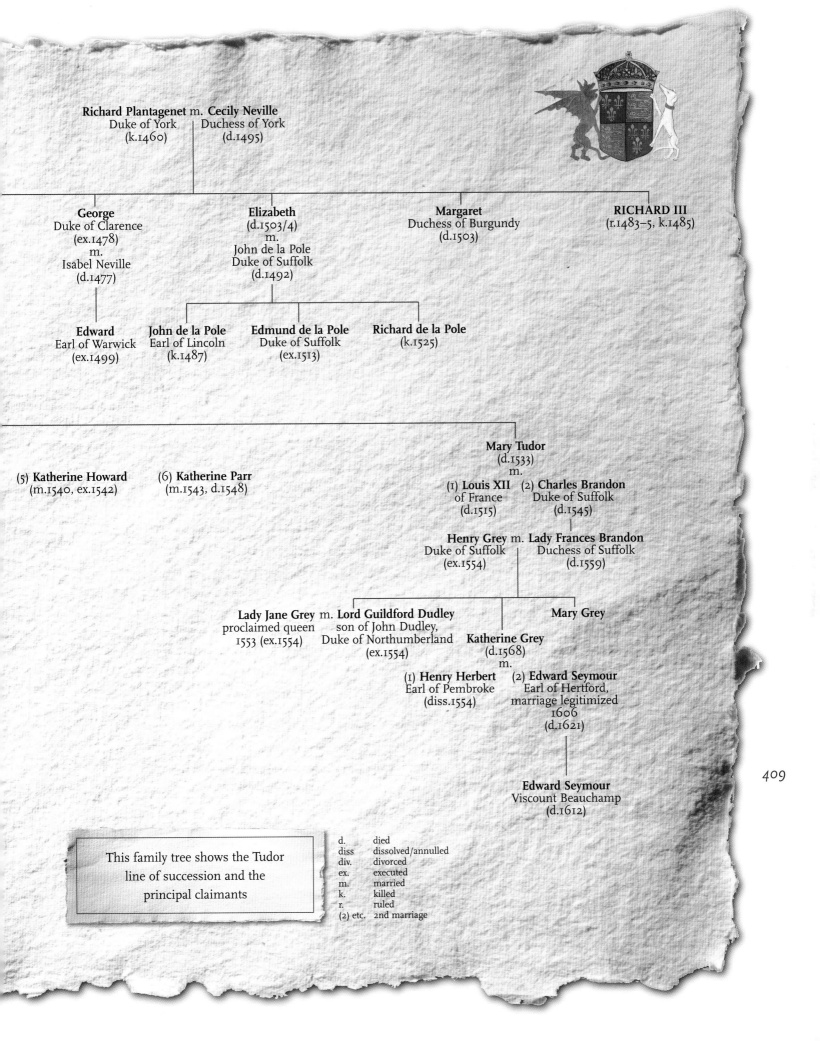

Richard Plantagenet m. **Cecily Neville**
Duke of York | Duchess of York
(k.1460) | (d.1495)

George
Duke of Clarence
(ex.1478)
m.
Isabel Neville
(d.1477)

Elizabeth
(d.1503/4)
m.
John de la Pole
Duke of Suffolk
(d.1492)

Margaret
Duchess of Burgundy
(d.1503)

RICHARD III
(r.1483–5, k.1485)

Edward
Earl of Warwick
(ex.1499)

John de la Pole
Earl of Lincoln
(k.1487)

Edmund de la Pole
Duke of Suffolk
(ex.1513)

Richard de la Pole
(k.1525)

(5) Katherine Howard
(m.1540, ex.1542)

(6) Katherine Parr
(m.1543, d.1548)

Mary Tudor
(d.1533)
m.

(1) Louis XII
of France
(d.1515)

(2) Charles Brandon
Duke of Suffolk
(d.1545)

Henry Grey m. **Lady Frances Brandon**
Duke of Suffolk | Duchess of Suffolk
(ex.1554) | (d.1559)

Lady Jane Grey m. **Lord Guildford Dudley**
proclaimed queen | son of John Dudley,
1553 (ex.1554) | Duke of Northumberland
(ex.1554)

Mary Grey

Katherine Grey
(d.1568)
m.

(1) Henry Herbert
Earl of Pembroke
(diss.1554)

(2) Edward Seymour
Earl of Hertford,
marriage legitimized
1606
(d.1621)

Edward Seymour
Viscount Beauchamp
(d.1612)

409

This family tree shows the Tudor
line of succession and the
principal claimants

d.	died
diss	dissolved/annulled
div.	divorced
ex.	executed
m.	married
k.	killed
r.	ruled
(2) etc.	2nd marriage

Sources for featured quotations

Adams, Simon, *Leicester and the Court: Essays on Elizabethan Politics*, 2002.

Anonymous, *A Relation of the Island of England ... about the year 1500*, edited by Charlotte Augusta Sneyd, Camden Society (Old Series 37), 1847.

Anonymous, *Chronicle of Calais in the Reigns of Henry VII and Henry VIII, to the Year 1540*, edited by John Gough Nichols, Camden Society (Old Series 35), 1846.

Anonymous, *The Chronicle of Queen Jane, and of Two Years of Mary ... written by a Resident in the Tower of London*, edited by John Gough Nichols, Camden Society (Old Series 48), 1850.

Anonymous, *The Most Strange and Admirable Discouerie of the Three Witches of Warboys ...* (1593), Early English Books Online, *see* http://eebo.chadwyck.com.

Archer, Ian *et al.* (eds), *Religion, Politics and Society in Sixteenth-Century England*, Camden Society (5th series 22), 2003 (contains 'A "Journal" of Matters of State Happened from time to time ... until the Yere 1562').

Arthurson, Ian, *The Perkin Warbeck Conspiracy 1491–1499*, 1994.

Best, George (d.1584?), *The Three Voyages of Martin Frobisher*, ed. R. Collinson, 1867.

Brown, Rawdon (ed. and trans.) *Four Years at the Court of Henry VIII: Selection of Dispatches*, by the Venetian ambassador Sebastian Giustinian, 2 vols, 1854.

Camden, William (1551–1623), *The History of the Most Renowned and Victorious Princess Elizabeth, late Queen of England* (i.e. the *Annales*, 1688 edition), Early English Books Online, *see* http://eebo.chadwyck.com.

'Copie of a leter, wryten by a Master of Arte of Cambridge to his friend in London ...' (1584), Early English Books Online, *see* http://eebo.chadwyck.com.

Davey, R., *The Nine Days Queen: Lady Jane Grey and Her Times* (includes 'a letter in the Genovese archives'), 1909.

Dee, John, *The Perfect Art of Navigation*, 1577.

Digges, Sir Dudley, *The Compleat Ambassador*, 1655.

Elizabeth I, *Collected Works*, edited by Leah S. Marcus, Janel Mueller and Mary Beth Rose, 2000.

Fletcher, Francis *et al.*, *The World Encompassed by Sir Francis Drake ... collected out of the notes of Master Fletcher ...* , 1652 edition online, at www.archive.org/details/worldencompassoodrakrich.

Foxe, John *Acts and Monuments ...* (1583 edition), online at www.hrionline.shef.ac.uk/foxe/.

Hakluyt, Richard (compiler), *The Principal Navigations, Voyages, Traffiques, and Discoveries of the English Nation*, 1602.

Hall, Edmund (c.1498–1547), *Hall's Chronicle*, edited by Sir Henry Ellis, 1809.

—, *Henry VIII* (i.e. part of *Hall's Chronicle*), edited by Charles Whibley, 2 vols, 1904.

Holinshed, Raphael (c.1525–80), *Holinshed's Chronicles of England, Scotland and Ireland*, 6 vols, 1807.

Ives, Eric, *Anne Boleyn*, 1986.

Laneham, Robert (c.1535–79/80), *Robert Laneham's Letter: Describing a Part of the Entertainment unto Queen Elizabeth at the Castle of Kenilworth in 1575*, 1907.

Larkin, James (ed.), *Stuart Royal Proclamations I: Royal Proclamations of King James I, 1603–1625*, 1973.

Leland, John (c.1506–52), *De rebus Britannicis collectanea*, facsimile reprint, 6 vols, 1970.

Machyn, Henry, *A London Provisioner's Chronicle, 1550–1563*, edited online by Richard W. Bailey, Marilyn Miller and Colette Moore, at http://quod.lib.umich.edu/m/machyn/.

McLean, Andrew (ed.), *The Execution of Mary Queen of Scots: An Eye-witness Account by Sir Robert Wingfield of Upton*, 2007 (for the Mount Stuart Trust)

Platter, Thomas, *Thomas Platter's Travels in England, 1599*, translated by C. Williams, 1937.

Scot, Reginald, *The Discovery of Witchcraft* (1584), edited by M. Summers, 1972.

Silvester, R.S. and D.P. Harding (eds), *Two Early Tudor Lives: 'The Life and Death of Cardinal Wolsey' by George Cavendish; 'The Life of Sir Thomas More' by William Roper*, 1962.

Thomas, A.H. and I.D. Thornley (eds), *The Great Chronicle of London*, attributed by some to Robert Fabian, 1938.

Van Wedel, Lupold, 'Journey Through England and Scotland', translated by Gottfried von Bülow, in *Transactions of the Royal Historical Society* (New Series, 9), 1895, pp. 223–70.

Vergil, Polydore, *Anglica historia*, 1555 edition (English translation), edited online by Dana F. Sutton, at www.philological.bham.ac.uk/polverg/

Wriothesley, Charles (1508–62), *A Chronicle of England during the Reigns of the Tudors* (i.e. the *Wriothesley Chronicle*), edited by W.D. Hamilton, Camden Society (New Series 11 & 20), 2 vols, 1875–7.

Notes on the text

Abbreviations used in these Notes:

APC	*Acts of Privy Council.*
Camden 1625	William Camden, *Annales, the True and Royall Historie of ... Elizabeth Queene of England*, translated from the Latin by A. Darcie, 1625.
Camden online	William Camden, *Annales ...* [complete text], in Richard Norton's 1630 translation, edited online by Dana F. Sutton, www.philological.bham.ac.uk/camden/.
CSP Sp.	*Calendar of State Papers, Spanish.*
CSP Ven.	*Calendar of State Papers, Venetian.*
GC	A.H. Thomas and I.D. Thornley (eds), *The Great Chronicle of London*, attributed to Robert Fabian, 1938.
GF	J.G. Nichols (ed.), *The Chronicle of Grey Friars of London*, Camden Society (Old Series 53), 1852, online edition at www.britishhistory.ac.uk.
HC	Edmund Hall, *Henry VIII* (part of *Hall's Chronicle*), edited by Charles Whibley, 2 vols, 1904.
Holinshed	Raphael Holinshed, *The Peaceable and Prosperouls Regiment of Blessed Queene Elizabeth: A Facsimile from Holinshed's Chronicles* (1587 edition), edited by Cyndia Susan Clegg, 2005.
LP	*Letters and Papers of the Reign of Henry the Eighth.*
Machyn online	Henry Machyn, *A London Provisioner's Chronicle, 1550–1563*, edited and transcribed by Richard W. Bailey, Marilyn Miller and Colette Moore, online edition at http://quod.lib.umich.edu/m/machyn/.
PV	Polydore Vergil, *The Anglica historia*, edited and translated by D. Hays, 1950.
QJ	*The Chronicle of Queen Jane, and of Two Years of Mary ... written by a Resident in the Tower of London*, edited by John Gough Nichols, Camden Society (Old Series 48), 1850.
Stowe	John Stowe, *Annales, or a Generale Chronicle of England*, various editions from 1580.
WC	Charles Wriothesley, *A Chronicle of England during the Reigns of the Tudors* (the *Wriothesley Chronicle*), edited by W.D. Hamilton, Camden Society (New Series 11 & 20), 2 vols, 1875–7.

Introduction

1. See Clifford L.S. Davies, 'A Rose by Another Name', *Times Literary Supplement*, 13 June 2008, available online at tls.timesonline.co.uk.

Henry VII

1. Polydore Vergil, *Polydore Vergil's English History* (three books of *Anglica historia*), edited by Sir Henry Ellis, Camden Society (Old Series 36), 1846, p. 221.
2. One dissenting voice is Michael K. Jones, *Bosworth 1485: Psychology of a Battle*, 2002.
3. *GC*, p. 240.
4. *Rotuli Parliamentarium*, edited by J. Strachey, vol. VI, p. 278.
5. J. Leland (c.1506–52) *De rebus Britannicis collectanea*, facsimile reprint, 1970, vol. IV, p. 204. *seq.* Sir N.H. Nichols, *Privy Purse Expenses of Elizabeth of York*, 1830.
6. PV, p. 39.
7. *CSP Ven.*, vol. I, p. 181.
8. PV, p. 39.

9. *GC*, p. 242.
10. John Gough Nichols (ed.), *Chronicle of Calais in the reigns of Henry VII and Henry VIII*, 1846, p. 2.
11. *CSP Ven.*, vol I, pp. 207–8.
12. PV, p. 49.
13. PV, p. 51.
14. Cited in Ian Arthurson, *The Perkin Warbeck Conspiracy 1491–1499* (1994), p. 51.
15. *Chronicle of Calais*, op. cit., p. 2.
16. PV, p. 59.
17. PV, p. 67.
18. PV, p. 75.
19. PV, pp. 69–71.
20. *GC*, pp. 251–2.
21. *GC*, p. 260.
22. *GC*, p. 264.
23. *GC*, p. 280.
24. *GC*, p. 281.
25. PV, p. 111.
26. *GC*, p. 287.
27. PV, pp. 115, 117.
28. PV, p. 117.
29. PV, p. 119.
30. Ibid.
31. *Chronicle of Calais*, op. cit., p. 4.
32. *Chronicle of Calais*, op. cit., p. 294.
33. PV, p. 125.

34. *GC*, pp. 301–2.
35. Leland, *Collectanea*, op. cit., vol. V, pp. 373–4.
36. *GC*, pp. 321–2.
37. *GC*, p. 322.
38. *GC*, pp. 323–4.
39. PV, p. 137.
40. *GC*, p. 330.
41. PV, p. 139.

Henry VIII

1. Rawdon Brown (ed. and trans.), *Four Years at the Court of Henry VIII: Selection of Dispatches*, by the Venetian ambassador Sebastian Giustinian, vol. I, pp. 75–6, 86–7, 90–1.
2. *CSP Milan*, vol. I, no. 669, p. 415.
3. *HC*, vol. I, p. 7.
4. *HC*, vol. I, p. 9.
5. The date of the death of miscarriage of Katherine's first child is problematic. The *Wriothesley Chronicle*, p. 7, says the child – a boy – died on 23 February. Exchequer accounts record payments for hanging over the royal cradle on 12 March. The queen's chancellor wrote to Ferdinand that the queen had miscarried on 31 January: *LP*, vol. 1(i), p. 284. Katherine wrote to her father on 27 May that she had some days before been delivered of a daughter.
6. *CSP Sp.*, vol. II, p. 1510.
7. *HC*, vol. I, p. 28.
8. PV, p. 153.
9. *HC*, vol. I, p. 22.
10. *HC*, vol. I, p. 27.
11. *LP*, vol. I, no. 880.
12. *HC*, vol. I, p. 40.
13. PV, p. 175.
14. PV, p.175.
15. *HC*, vol I, p. 51.
16. *LP*, vol. II(i), no. 2166.
17. PV, p. 217.
18. *CSP Ven.*, vol. II, no. 555.
19. *CSP Ven.*, vol. II, no 691.
20. *WC*, vol. I, p. 10.
21. Ibid.
22. *CSP Ven.*, vol. II, no. 887.
23. Ibid.
24. *LP*, vol. II(ii), no. 3259.
25. *HC*, vol. I, p. 165.
26. *WC*, vol. I, p. 12.
27. *LP*, vol. II(ii), no. 4481.
28. Ibid.
29. *CSP Ven.*, vol. II, no. 1103.
30. *CSP Ven.*, vol. III, no. 50, p. 15.
31. *LP*, vol. III(i), no. 869.
32. *CSP Ven.*, vol. III, no. 106.
33. PV, p. 283.
34. *LP*, vol. III(ii), no. 1443.
35. *CSP Ven.*, vol. III, no. 319.
36. *LP*, vol. III(ii), no. 2309.
37. *WC*, vol. I, p. 13.
38. *HC*, vol. I, p. 283.
39. *HC*, vol. I, p. 286.
40. *HC*, vol. I, p. 314.
41. *HC*, vol. II, p. 31.
42. *CSP Ven.*, vol. IV, no. 970.
43. *LP*, vol. IV(ii), nos 1263, 1267.
44. *HC*, vol. II, p. 42.
45. *LP*, vol. IV(i), no. 1319.

46. *HC*, vol. II, p. 56.
47. *LP*, vol. IV(i), no. 1939.
48. *HC*, vol. II, p. 65.
49. *HC*, vol. II, pp. 82–3.
50. *LP*, vol. IV(ii), no. 3340.
51. *LP*, vol. IV(ii), no 4858.
52. *HC*, vol. II, p. 148.
54. *HC*, vol. II, p. 202.
55. *WC*, vol. I, p. 17.
56. WC, vol. I, p. 23.
57. *LP*, vol. VIII, nos 1013, 1193.
58. G.R. Elton, *The Tudor Constitution: Documents and Commentary*, 1972, p. 62.
59. *CSP Sp.*, vol. V(ii), p. 125.
60. *WC*, vol. I, p. 37.
61. *WC*, vol. I, p. 83.
62. A.G. Dickens and Dorothy Carr, *The Reformation in England to the Accession of Elizabeth I*, 1971, p. 84.
63. *HC*, vol. II, p. 299.
64. *HC*, vol. II, p. 341.
65. *HC*, vol. II, p. 350.
66. *WC*, vol. I, p. 156.
67. *WC*, vol. I, p. 160.
68. *HC*, vol. II, p. 356.
69. J.J. Scarisbrick, *Henry VIII*, 1968, p. 28.

Edward VI

1. W.K. Jordan (ed.), *The Chronicle and Political Papers of Edward VI*, 1966, p. 209.
2. *WC*, vol. II, p. 5.
3. *WC*, vol. II, p. 6.
4. *WC*, vol. II, p. 13.
5. *GF* online.
6. *GF* online.
7. *WC*, vol. II, p. 36.
8. *GF* online.
9. *GF* online.
10. *WC*, vol. II, p. 45.
11. *GF* online.
12. *WC*, vol. II, p. 49.
13. *GF* online.
14. *WC*, vol. II, p. 83.

Mary I

1. *CSP Ven.*, vol. IV, p. 533.
2. *GF* online.
3. *QJ*, p. 3.
4. *WC*, vol. II, p. 87.
5. *WC*, vol. II, p. 89.
6. *GF* online.
7. *QJ*, p. 28.
8. *QJ*, p. 34.
9. 'John Elder's letter describing the arrival and marriage of King Philip, his triumphal entry into London, the legation of Cardinal Pole ...', Appendix X to *QJ*, p. 143.
10. Richard Grafton, *Grafton's Chronicle, or, History of England*, 1809 edition, p. 548.
11. *QJ*, p. 79.
12. Machyn online 1555.
13. *GF* online.
14. *GF* online.
15. Machyn online 1555.
16. *WC*, vol. II, p. 130.

17. Machyn online 1556.
18. *CSP Sp.*, vol. XIII, p. 276.
19. Machyn online 1556.
20. Machyn online 1557.
21. *WC*, vol. II, p. 139.
22. Machyn online 1557.
23. Ibid.
24. Machyn online 1558.
25. Ibid.
26. Ibid.
27. 'Count of Feria's Despatch to Philip II of 14 November 1558', *Camden Miscellany XXVIII*, 1984, p. 328.

Elizabeth I

1. Hatfield, Cecil MS 150 fol. 86.
2. John Nichols, *The Progresses ... of Queen Elizabeth*, 1823, vol. I, p. 32.
3. Sir John Hayward, *Annals of the First Four Years of the Reign of Queen Elizabeth*, edited by John Bruce, Camden Society (Old Series 7), 1840, p. 18.
4. *CSP Ven.*, vol. VII, p. 17.
5. Hayward, *Annals*, op. cit., p. 24.
6. Machyn online 1559.
7. *WC*, vol. II, p. 145.
8. 'A "journal" of matters of state ... from and before the death of King Edw. the 6th until the yere 1562 ...', in Ian W. Archer, Simon Adams, Paul E. J. Hammer and Fiona Kisby (eds), *Religion, Politics, and Society in Sixteenth-Century England*, Camden 5th Series, 2003, p. 62.
9. Camden 1625, p. 52.
10. Adams *et al.* 'A "journal" of matters of state', op. cit., pp. 66–7.
11. Adams *et al.* 'A "journal" of matters of state', op. cit., p. 81.
12. Adams *et al.* 'A "journal" of matters of state', op. cit., p. 85.
13. Camden 1625, p. 90.
14. Camden 1625, p. 91.
15. *CSP Sp.*, *1558–67*, p. 263.
16. Stow 1580, p. 1121.
17. Stow 1607, p. 354.
18. Camden 1625, p. 110.
19. Stow 1607, p. 355.
20. Stow 1580, p. 1130.
21. *CSP Sp.*, *1568–79*, p. 29.
22. Stow 1607, p. 365.
23. Holinshed, p. 1212.
24. Stow 1607, p. 375.
25. Holinshed, p. 1226.
26. Holinshed, p. 1228.
27. Stow 1605, p. 1140.
28. Stow 1607, p. 1147.
29. The National Archives SP 63/42, no. 58.
30. Holinshed, p. 1262.
31. Stow 1605, p. 1115.
32. Stow 1607, p. 407.
33. Holinshed, p. 1271.
34. Holinshed, p. 1287.
35. Holinshed, p. 1287.
36. Stow 1605, p. 1161.
37. Stow 1605, p. 1162.
38. Stow 1605, p. 1168.
39. Camden online 1587.
40. Holinshed, p. 1311.
41. Holinshed, p. 1314.

42. Holinshed, p. 1315.
43. Ibid.
44. Stow 1605, pp. 1167–8.
45. Holinshed, p. 1322.
46. *Tudor Royal Proclamations*, vol. II, p. 491.
47. Holinshed, p. 1348.
48. Stow 1605, p. 1170.
49. Stow 1605, p. 1173.
50. Stow 1605, p. 1174.
51. *Calendar of State Papers Domestic, 1581–90*, p. 126.
52. Stow, 1605, p. 1176.
53. Stow 1607, p. 434.
54. Holinshed, p. 1369.
55. Stow 1605, p. 1201.
56. Francis Bacon, *Considerations touching a warre with Spaine*, 1629, p. 40.
57. Stow 1605, p. 1243.
58. Stow 1605, p. 1257.
59. Stow 1605, p. 1259.
60. Stow 1605, pp. 1259–60.
61. Stow 1605, p. 1260.
62. Stow 1605, p. 1261.
63. *APC 1591*, pp. 174–5.
64. *APC 1591–1592*, p. 550.
65. *APC 1592*, p. 221.
66. Camden online 1594.
67. Camden online 1595.
68. Stow 1605, p. 1280.
69. Camden online 1595.
70. Stow 1605, p. 1281.
71. J. S. Brewer and William Bullen (eds), *Calendar of the Carew Manuscripts 1589–1600*, 1867–71, p. 170.
72. *APC 1596–1597*, p. 16.
73. Stow 1605, p. 1283.
74. Camden online 1597.
75. *APC 1596–1597*, pp. 383–4.
76. Stow 1605, p. 1303.
77. Camden online 1597.
78. Stow 1605, p. 1306.
79. Camden online 1598.
80. Ibid.
81. Ibid.
82. *Calendar of State Papers Ireland, 1598–1599*, p. 340.
83. *APC 1598–1599*, p. 264.
84. Camden online 1598.
85. Stow 1605, p. 1400.
86. *Calendar of State Papers Ireland, 1599–1600*, p. 279.
87. Camden online 1600.
88. Ibid.
89. Ibid.
90. Ibid.
91. Stow 1605, p. 1405.
92. Camden online 1601.

Page numbers in **bold** denote an illustration.
Titled individuals are normally listed by their titles (the form in which they usually appear in the main text), with cross-references at their personal names.

413

414

PICTURE CREDITS

Quercus Editions Ltd
55 Baker Street
7th Floor, South Block
London
W1U 8EW

First published in 2008
This edition published in 2011

Copyright © Susan Doran 2008, 2011

UK and associated territories: ISBN 978 1 84724 422 2
Canada: ISBN 978 1 84866 169 1

Printed and bound in China

10 9 8 7 6 5 4

Publishing director: Richard Milbank
Art director: Nick Clark
Managing editor: Mark Hawkins-Dady
Designer: Hugh Adams / ab3 design
Art editor: Paul Oakley
Picture researcher: Elaine Willis
Proofreader: Fintan Power
Indexer: Patricia Hymans
Text researcher: Miranda Kaufmann